★ ★ ★ ★ ★ ★ ★ ★ ★ ★

THE REPUBLICAN PARTY AND

THE SOUTH, 1855–1877

THE FRED W. MORRISON

SERIES IN SOUTHERN STUDIES

THE REPUBLICAN PARTY AND

THE SOUTH, 1855–1877

THE FIRST SOUTHERN STRATEGY

RICHARD H. ABBOTT

The University of North Carolina Press

Chapel Hill and London

Library of Congress Cataloging-in-Publication Data
Abbott, Richard H.
The Republican Party and the South, 1855–1877.
(The Fred W. Morrison series in Southern studies)
Bibliography: p.
Includes index.
1. Southern States—Politics and government—1775–
1865. 2. Southern States—Politics and government—
1865–1950. 3. Republican Party (U.S.: 1854–   ) —
History—19th century. 4. Reconstruction. I. Title.
II. Series.
F213.A16   1986   324.2734'0975   85-16557
ISBN 0-8078-1680-9

For My Aunt
Margaret Ennenga
and My Wife
Marie Richmond-Abbott

CONTENTS

Preface

ix

Acknowledgments

xiii

CHAPTER 1

Republicans Assess the South, 1855–1861

3

CHAPTER 2

Republicans and the Wartime South, 1861–1865

20

CHAPTER 3

A Year of Indecision: 1866

42

CHAPTER 4

Blacks and the Southern Strategy, 1867–1868

75

CHAPTER 5

Whites and the Southern Strategy, 1867–1868

110

CHAPTER 6

Reconstruction Concluded, 1868

150

CHAPTER 7

The Election of 1868

175

CHAPTER 8
Reconstruction Winds Down: The Grant Years, 1869–1877
204

CHAPTER 9
Conclusion
233

Notes
245

Bibliography
281

Index
295

The Republican party has been largely based in the North and West since its inception in the 1850s. Republicans have periodically sought support in the South, however, particularly among the white voters of that section. After Richard Nixon was elected president in 1968, political commentators coined the phrase "Southern strategy" to refer to his courtship of Southern white support.[1] By 1980, enough whites voted Republican to elect five governors, ten senators, and thirty congressmen in the eleven former Confederate states. In the presidential election that fall, Republican Ronald Reagan, running against a Southern Democrat, Jimmy Carter, carried every Southern state except Carter's home state of Georgia.[2]

Historians have pointed out that Richard Nixon was not the first Republican president to seek white votes in the South; rather, they have documented such attempts dating back to the term of Rutherford B. Hayes, who was elected to the presidency in the disputed election of 1876.[3] Ironically, Hayes presided over the termination of the last Republican state governments that were established in the South during the Reconstruction period following the Civil War. For it was during the Reconstruction years that the Republicans first established a foothold in some Southern states and elected governors, legislators, and congressmen in numbers that would not be approximated again until late in the twentieth century. The Reconstruction Republican regimes, however, were based primarily on black rather than white votes. Despite the interest of some Northern Republicans in cultivating white support in the South, it failed to materialize significantly.

Although Republican political approaches toward the South from Hayes onward have received attention from historians, there has been little examination of Northern Republican attitudes toward the

South during the critical period of Reconstruction. One recent study has carefully analyzed the Southern policies of Ulysses S. Grant, but no one has looked back before his inauguration in 1869 to determine how the Republicans then assessed the political potential of the South.[4] This book is an effort to fill that void by extending our historical perspective on the Republican party and the South back to the crucial years between the end of the Civil War and the beginning of Grant's administration, when Congress and the Republicans were formulating Reconstruction policies. I have chosen to stress the Northern Republican approach to the South as a field for political expansion. I have not undertaken a close study of the Southern Republicans, except as their activities affected Northern strategy for the South. For reasons that I note in this study, the chances for Republican survival in the former Confederate states were slim to begin with and depended heavily on Northern encouragement and support. Hence it seemed logical to study Northern Republican attitudes and actions that contributed to the success or failure of Southern Republicanism.

The first two chapters discuss the emergence of the Republican party in the North and survey the earliest indications of Southern support for it, first in the border states and later in some of the Confederate states during the Civil War. The closing chapter is on the Grant years, 1869–77. The emphasis of this book, however, is on the years from the end of the Civil War to Grant's inauguration in 1869. During this time the Republicans undertook the political reorganization of the South, particularly after the enactment of the First Reconstruction Act in 1867. The party developed several methods for seeking to influence political developments in the South and especially sought to bring about a moderate, biracial party there. I have concluded, however, that despite the interest of some Northern Republicans in defining a Southern strategy, most of them did not believe that either Southern whites or blacks provided a secure basis for their party. Rather, throughout the period I studied, Northern Republicans continued to protect their Northern base and repeatedly sacrificed Southern interests. They furnished very little concrete assistance, either in the way of organizational aid or federal legislation, that would appeal to Southern interest groups. Most Republicans regarded their Southern allies as liabilities rather than assets. I believe that by the time of Grant's inauguration, the demise of the

Republican party in the South was predictable, based on the party's policies in the years preceding that event.

I have reached these conclusions about the tentative and ineffective nature of the Republicans' Southern strategy in part because the Northern Republicans engaged in so little discussion of it. Rarely, in personal correspondence, congressional debates, or newspaper editorials, did Republicans openly reveal their hopes and plans for building a party in the South. In the absence of any overt evidence of plan or intent, I have evaluated the actions taken by the Republicans toward the South to assess their political impact on the Southern Republican party. Time and again I found that the evidence proved that the Republicans lacked faith in the prospects for their party there. Hence they consistently and deliberately subordinated the interests of their Southern allies to the demands of their Northern constituency.

If the Republicans never intended to put a major emphasis on party-building in the South, I believe we need to reconsider our interpretation of the motivation of Reconstruction legislation. Historians have long argued over the goals of Congress in reconstructing the South. A number of historians have emphasized Republican hopes that they could build their party in the South after the Civil War.[5] Some have asserted that building the Southern Republican party was one of the primary purposes of Reconstruction.[6] It is my conclusion that both these judgments are questionable; during the time that Republicans were formulating Reconstruction policy, they neither believed wholeheartedly in the prospect of building their party in the South nor made such a goal a primary purpose of Reconstruction. At the end of the nineteenth century, one student of Reconstruction, William A. Dunning, concluded that the leading motive of Congress at the outset was to ensure equal rights for blacks; by the time the Reconstruction process was complete, he argued, the desire to secure the Republican party's control of the South had become the main motive.[7] I believe Dunning's suggestion has some merit. Certainly Grant's Southern policies sought to protect the Republican party there whenever possible. Yet political motives that sustained federal intervention in the South did not necessarily instigate that intervention. Furthermore, both before and after Grant's election, Republicans remained more concerned about maintaining control of the North than about gaining control of the South.

If, then, as I believe, the Republicans never counted on or worked for a permanent political party in the South, the motives for congressional Reconstruction will have to be sought elsewhere. I believe that my findings buttress the argument of historians who like Dunning claim that Congress was primarily concerned with identifying, expanding, and protecting black rights. Yet, ironically, the failure to develop a Republican party in the South meant that blacks lacked a major institutional force for protecting their rights. Further, the efforts that the Northern Republicans did make to build a party in the South in the Reconstruction years were directed at muting or controlling black aims and aspirations so they might gain white voting support in the South or avoid alienating white voting support in the North. The Republican party's "benign neglect" of black interests and courting of white support in the South did not originate with Richard Nixon, as historians have already pointed out; nor did it begin with Rutherford B. Hayes or even with U. S. Grant. Republican political approaches toward the South, and toward both races in the South, had become quite clear by 1868. The party was not ready to dedicate itself to building a permanent organization in the South, and although it accepted black support, it remained primarily concerned with attracting whites. Unfortunately for Southerners black and white, it proved impossible then, and is seemingly impossible today, to develop a Republican party there that is based on biracial support.

ACKNOWLEDGMENTS

I owe a considerable debt to Eastern Michigan University for the various forms of assistance rendered to me in writing this book. The generous sabbatical leave policy of the Board of Regents provided me with time from teaching to undertake research and writing. The library staff was very cooperative, and I would particularly like to thank Joanne Hansen, Rita Bullard, and Mary Clare Beck for their help. Several of my colleagues in the history department offered helpful comments, and Richard Goff read and criticized parts of the manuscript. My department head, Ira Wheatley, and the Dean of the College of Arts and Sciences, Donald Drummond, provided aid and encouragement. Three graduate students, Ed Lowe, Jeff Morrison, and Lynn Peterson, assisted me with the research for this book. An Eastern undergraduate, George Sandford, located an important source for me at a critical moment in the preparation of the manuscript. Our office secretary, Jane Spires, typed several drafts of the manuscript, and another secretary, Nancy Snyder, typed several chapters. My wife, Marie Richmond-Abbott, who also teaches at Eastern, patiently endured my frustrations as I prepared my manuscript and set for me a high standard with her own scholarship.

I would also like to thank the staffs of the various libraries and historical collections whose materials I used and have listed in the bibliography. Without their cordial and helpful assistance this book could not have been written. I am also obligated to James C. Mohr of the University of Maryland, Baltimore County, and to John T. Hubbell, editor of *Civil War History*, for encouraging me to undertake this study. I would like to thank the two readers who criticized my manuscript for the University of North Carolina Press; their comments and suggestions proved to be very helpful. Finally, I would like to thank the editors and staff of the University of North Carolina

Press, particularly Executive Editor Lewis Bateman and Managing Editor Gwen Duffey, for their encouragement and for the expeditious manner with which they prepared the manuscript for publication. I am also obligated to my copy editor, Trudie Calvert, whose practiced eye saved me from many an error and whose corrections certainly improved the book. Any mistakes that remain are, of course, my responsibility.

★ ★ ★ ★ ★ ★ ★ ★ ★

THE REPUBLICAN PARTY AND

THE SOUTH, 1855–1877

During the decade of the 1850s, the nation's two-party political system began to break down, the victim of mounting hostility between North and South. For twenty years both the Whig and Democratic parties had been able to mobilize support in both sections of the Union and as national organizations had worked to contain sectionalism. After 1854, however, the passage of the Kansas-Nebraska Act and the subsequent struggle over the expansion of slavery into the western territories greatly exacerbated tensions between slaveholding and nonslaveholding states. The Whig party was the first to fold under these pressures; the Democratic party was able to compromise differences between its Northern and Southern members until the end of the decade. For some years the Democratic party had favored Southern interests, and after the Whig collapse, many Southern Whigs joined the Democrats, further enhancing the party's sectional orientation. It still maintained enough strength in the North, however, to remain a national organization.[1]

After the passage of the Kansas-Nebraska Act, a large minority of Northern voters, angry at what they believed to be Southern domination of the nation's government, moved quickly to organize a new political party. This organization, which soon became known as the Republican party, championed the interests of the Northern socioeconomic system. According to the Republicans, Northerners recognized and honored the value of free labor, which they identified with farmers, independent craftsmen, and small businessmen. In their aspirations for economic independence, these small entrepreneurs were the agents of economic progress. Their opportunity for self-improvement was enhanced in the North by cheap land, free speech and press, public education, and a democratic political system. The Northerners who organized the Republican party saw economic development, social mobility, and democratic institutions as the hallmarks of the progress of their section.[2]

Republicans argued that in the South slavery had eliminated the progressive features of Northern life. There, they claimed, slavery degraded the status of free labor, drove down the wages of free white workers, and led Southern whites to associate manual labor with bondage. Republicans also contended that forced labor was inefficient and that the Southern economy had failed to diversify and develop because so much capital was invested in slavery. Hence economic opportunities for white workers and nonslaveholding farmers were limited. Republicans further argued that Southern slaveholders would not allow freedom of speech and press for fear the free flow of ideas would threaten the continued existence of slavery. The planters, who controlled the economy and government of the Southern states, showed no interest in spending tax money on public schools, nor were they willing to share political power with the nonslaveholders, who made up a majority of the white population of the South. The common man, according to the Republicans, had no chance to advance within this system.

Worst of all, from the Northern Republican point of view, the Southerners were attempting to expand their unprogressive system into the territories, thereby depriving Northerners of an opportunity to expand their own socioeconomic system westward. The South was also using its influence over the national government to deny Northerners higher tariffs, homestead legislation, and the other economic incentives that the Republicans believed were necessary to maintain an expanding, diversifying economy. Only by wresting control of the government from the Southern oligarchs could the Republicans keep slavery out of the territories and promote their own view of a progressive society.[3]

The Republicans found their posture as a sectional party, advancing Northern interests, to be both an asset and a liability. Party leaders, recognizing that the North had a majority of the nation's population, realized it was possible to win control of the government without Southern support. To do so, they would have to convince Northern voters that they, not the Democrats or any other alternative such as the American or Know-Nothing party that also emerged in the wake of the Whig collapse, could best defend Northern interests. In this case, the absence of a Southern wing of their party facilitated the Republicans' claim to be the most dependable spokesmen for the North.[4] The sectional nature of the party clearly alarmed Southerners, who were concerned about its attacks on their way of life. They were particularly outraged about the Republican free labor criticism of slavery and feared that the new party would never be content until the institution was overthrown throughout the South. As early as 1856 Southern radicals were making it clear that they would consider Republican success in the election a sufficient cause for secession from the Union.[5] Republicans knew that their reputation as a radical, antislavery, sectional party could not only irrevocably alienate the South but could also cost them the support of many in the North who feared disunion.[6]

Although they knew that the base of their party's support lay in the North, some Republican spokesmen hoped that their party would eventually become a truly national organization. No party in the nation's history had succeeded for long with only sectional support. They were not prepared to write off the South, for some believed that their free labor ideology could find support among the masses of Southern nonslaveholding whites. William Henry Seward, a former Whig governor of New York who became a leading spokesman in the U.S. Senate for Republican principles, was convinced that the party could recruit support in the South if it had a chance to present its principles there. Seward believed that slavery was not only a moral wrong but also the major obstacle to the economic development of the South. He attacked the Southern slaveholding aristocracy for opposing public education, internal improvements, and other measures that would promote the welfare of the masses of whites in that section. He believed that if the mass of Southern whites could have a chance to listen to Republican principles fairly presented to them, "you will very soon have in the South as many Republicans as we have Democrats in the North."[7]

Another former New York Whig, Horace Greeley, whose *New York Tribune* had by far the largest circulation of any Northern newspaper, also believed that the Republican party could appeal to Southern nonslaveholding whites. He and Seward both believed that the slaveholders' control over the Southern white masses was shaky, and he shared Seward's conviction that if freedom of expression could be protected in the South, many nonslaveholders could learn about and accept Republican principles. Greeley was especially eager to attract the support of small farmers and urban workers in the South to the Republican party by emphasizing that it could encourage that section's industrial growth. He was most optimistic about Republican prospects in the Upper South and border states.[8] In Maryland, Kentucky, Missouri, and western sections of Virginia and North Carolina, slavery was not as important to the economy as it was in the Lower South. Slavery was not as widely dispersed, there were fewer slaves, and the percentage of slaveholding families was smaller than in the states farther south. There were also more economic and social ties between the border slave states and the North, and there were commercial, industrial, urban, and nonslaveholding agricultural interests that might be attracted to Republicanism. In the 1850s, organized immigration efforts moved several thousand Northerners into the border areas, especially in Virginia, where they championed free labor and later supplied Republican votes. German immigrants who settled in such border cities as Baltimore and St. Louis also proved to be significant sources of support.[9]

Unfortunately for Republican hopes, the vast majority of Southern whites proved hostile to the Republican program. They remained committed to a rural, agrarian society, and they valued tradition and stability more than change and progress. Although some industry did develop in the South, it was not encouraged, nor were other forms of nonagricultural investments. Hence, although the Southern economy grew, it did not diversify, and most Southerners preferred it that way. Although the majority of Southern whites did not own slaves, they willingly supported the continuation of slavery, largely because for them it seemed the only way to maintain white supremacy. In its own defense, the white South sought to insulate itself against Northern ideas, particularly those that threatened the future of slavery. Southern critics of the institution were discouraged and, in some cases, forcibly repressed.[10]

The few Southern white critics of slavery who did emerge in the two decades before the Civil War tended to come from the border states or Upper South, where, as Greeley noted, slavery was not as important an institution as it was further South. In Kentucky, Virginia, North Carolina, and Missouri, a handful of whites charged that slavery retarded economic growth; they attacked the slaveholders for denying the masses of Southern whites an opportunity to advance themselves. Greeley, Seward, and others who watched the South for signs of sympathy for Republican doctrines were particularly encouraged by the appearance of these free labor critics of slavery, who seemed to validate their own analysis of Southern conditions.

One of the foremost Southern opponents of slavery was Cassius M. Clay of Kentucky, who attacked the institution as early as 1841. Clay supported emancipation not in the interest of blacks but to free white workers and farmers from the ruinous competition of slave labor. He argued that slavery retarded the state's economic progress by discouraging the development of a diversified economy. He condemned the slaveholding minority in the state for resisting industrial development and struggled to rally the white working population against its influence. Clay was joined in his crusade by antislavery ministers including John Fee, who had imbibed abolitionist ideas at Lane Seminary in Ohio, and Robert Breckinridge, a Presbyterian church leader from a famous Kentucky family. Breckinridge's antislavery views, which were well known in the state as early as 1830, were similar to Clay's contentions that slavery hampered the development of the state's economy; he also believed that emancipation would give poor whites a chance to improve their economic condition.[11]

In North Carolina, several other critics of slavery emerged who echoed the views of Clay and Breckinridge. In the early 1840s Daniel R. Goodloe of Louisburg, North Carolina, published antislavery tracts concluding that slavery degraded white labor and, by monopolizing capital, prevented the state's economy from diversifying. In the western part of the state, where slavery was not well established and the white farmers were alienated from the political dominance of plantation owners in the east, other spokesmen for the interests of the white laboring class spoke out against slavery.[12] In 1856 Benjamin S. Hedrick, a professor at the University of North Carolina, expressed his intention to vote for John C. Frémont, the Republican candidate for president, arguing that slavery repressed the wages of white workers.[13] The following year a fellow North Carolinian from the same section of the state, Hinton Rowan Helper, published *The Impending Crisis*, which developed at length the arguments of Clay, Goodloe, and others that slavery held back the development of the

South and oppressed white laborers in the interest of a planting aristocracy. In page after page Helper compared the South to the North and noted the North's superiority in literacy rates, public schools, commercial development, manufacturing, urban growth, libraries, newspaper circulation, and general culture; he blamed slavery for the inferiority of the South in all these areas.[14]

In northern Virginia John Underwood, who had moved there in 1846 from New York, also championed the efficiency of free labor over slavery and worked to encourage other Northerners to follow him into the state to redeem it from its forced labor system.[15] Like native Southerners Clay, Breckinridge, and Goodloe, Underwood was a former Whig, and these men were drawn toward a natural alliance with former Whigs in the North such as Seward and Greeley, whose criticisms of the slave labor system in the South were similar to their own. They also shared Whig ideas about an activist government on both the state and federal levels that would champion public aid to education and assistance to business development through internal improvement programs, banks, corporation charters, and protective tariffs. Critics of slavery like Helper and Hedrick, who had no prior Whig affiliations, were also drawn to the idea of an activist government that would promote economic diversification and improve the life of the working classes in the South. All of these men, Underwood, Clay, Breckinridge, Goodloe, Helper, and Hedrick, eventually joined the Republican party. Clay and Underwood were instrumental in organizing the new party in their respective states, and Helper and Hedrick sought with less success to find Republican support in North Carolina.[16]

The Democratic party, which in the 1850s grew increasingly oriented to the rights of slaveholders and a defense of state rights, and which sought to limit the government's role in economic and social development, was less attractive to men who harbored antipathy to slavery and who sought to promote diversified economic development. Nonetheless in the 1850s there were a few Southern Democrats who hoped to wrest control of their party from the slaveholders and use it to champion the rights of free white labor and to uphold the principle of national unity against Southern advocates of nullification or secession. The best representatives of this group were the Blairs of Maryland and Missouri. Frank Blair, Sr., who lived in Maryland with one of his sons, Montgomery, had been an intimate associate of Andrew Jackson and a longtime power in Democratic circles. His other son, Frank Blair, Jr., had moved to St. Louis, where he had rapidly risen in influence in the Democratic party in Missouri. In 1848 the Blairs backed the Free Soil movement, which was a predecessor of the Republican party; its main plank was opposition to the expansion of slavery. The Blairs endorsed free soil because they believed slavery degraded white workers and they wanted to keep the territories free of the institution. They condemned the leaders of the Democratic party for guiding the organization in a proslavery direction, and they especially attacked Southern Democrats for threatening disunion if Southern rights in the territories were denied.[17]

In Missouri the Blairs drew support from those who believed the state's future lay in strengthening its ties with the North and West rather than with the South. They believed Missouri should develop its mineral wealth, industry, and commerce. One of the men whom Frank Blair converted to his views was B. Gratz Brown, a former Whig who was ready to ally with the Blairs on the basis of free soil, internal improvements, and Unionism. Brown also argued for gradual emancipation in Missouri, claiming such a move was necessary to free whites from competition with forced labor. Emancipation, he thought, would also attract capital and help break Missouri's identification with the South. Brown, with his Whiggish views on promoting manufacturing, commerce, railroads, and immigration in the state, would soon find a congenial home in the Republican party.[18]

Frank Blair, however, was not eager to desert the party of Andrew Jackson and preferred to carry on his struggle against the slaveholders from within Democratic ranks. Like Clay in Kentucky, Blair argued that slavery denied prosperity to the white workers, corroded the morals of its citizens, and divided society into slave aristocrats and poor whites. Unlike Clay, however, Blair found a receptive audience for these arguments; he was elected from St. Louis to the state legislature in 1852 and again in 1854. Horace Greeley, who had been following events in Missouri closely, was ecstatic about Blair's success and urged the family to support the new Republican party. When the Republicans held their first organizational meeting in Pittsburgh in 1856, they managed to coax the elder Blair into attending, but his sons failed to come. Frank Blair, Sr., did announce himself a Republican, but his views were more conservative than those of many of the party's Northern members. He sought to deemphasize the issue of slavery, instead urging Republicans to attack the Democrats on the ground that they were nullifiers who threatened to destroy the Union. The fledgling Republican party, which was eager to expand its base, nevertheless made Blair president of the Pittsburgh convention and also gave him a place on the party's national committee.[19]

Although Frank Blair kept free soil forces from organizing the Republican party in Missouri in 1856, Republicans in the border states of Kentucky, Maryland, Delaware, and Virginia sent delegates to the Republican nominating convention that met later in the year in Philadelphia. The convention selected a member of each border state delegation for the party's national committee; Cassius Clay was named from Kentucky. State Republican organizations in these border states, however, were very weak or nonexistent. In Delaware and Maryland, the party hardly existed outside the cities of Wilmington and Baltimore and had only minimal support there. In Kentucky, Clay and John Fee had organized a skeleton party in Madison County, near the antislavery mountainous region of the state; they also drew scattered support from the state's northwestern counties, which had long nursed a variety of grievances against the eastern slaveholding counties that dominated the state. With John Underwood's help the party launched a newspaper in Wheeling, but no other border state had a Republican journal.[20]

Despite the weakness of Southern Republicanism, at the national convention a few Northern party members expressed optimism about prospects of nationalizing the party. Ebenezer R. Hoar of Massachusetts, saying that his state wished to "advance the column to the South," hoped that if the party won in 1856 it would hold its next convention in Kentucky or Virginia. Party chairman Edwin D. Morgan and Horace Greeley also expressed an interest in a future meeting in a more southern location in an effort to establish the Republicans as a truly national party. In 1856, however, everyone agreed that the Republicans had little choice but to concentrate on the North, where free soil feeling was much stronger and anti-Southern attitudes could be exploited.[21]

The Republican nominee for president that year, John C. Frémont, became locked in a three-way contest with the Democrats and the new American party. The Americans, or Know-Nothings as they were sometimes called, appealed to nativist voters in the North who were frightened about the large numbers of immigrants who were flooding into the country in the 1840s and 1850s. In addition, the party appealed to former Whigs who feared the election of either the pro-Northern Republicans or the pro-Southern Democrats and hoped that the American party would elevate national above sectional concerns. Frémont received 33 percent of the popular vote and lost the election to the Democratic candidate; but the returns revealed both the sectional nature of the Republican party and the strategy it needed to follow to win the next election. Frémont had taken 45 percent of the Northern vote and had won every free state except Pennsylvania, California, Illinois, Indiana, and New Jersey. With some quick calculation, Republicans realized that by holding Frémont's states and adding Pennsylvania and either Indiana or Illinois, they could win an electoral college majority in 1860. To do this, however, they would have to convince enough Democratic or American voters to desert their party to carry those additional states.[22]

Another Republican alternative was to cultivate enough border state support to ensure victory in 1860, but Pennsylvania would still be necessary to ensure the requisite total. Election results in the border states were not at all hopeful, however, for Frémont polled only slightly over a thousand votes there. Nonetheless, the election did produce an encouraging development in Missouri. Although there was no Republican organization in that state, Frank Blair, Jr., had won a congressional seat on a Free Soil platform. Blair ran as a Democrat, but his opposition to slavery in the territories and his support for gradual emancipation in Missouri branded him a Republican in all but name, and Northern Republicans were overjoyed at his success. In 1858, Blair was read out of the Democratic party, and in 1860 he would convince his followers to organize a Republican party in the state.[23]

Most Northern Republicans rejected a border state or Southern strategy in favor of courting more Northern votes, but a few party leaders nonetheless continued to support their Southern allies. Cassius Clay kept in touch with Seward and with Salmon P. Chase, who in 1858 was Republican governor of Ohio; and Greeley continued his solicitous coverage of the younger Frank Blair's activities in Missouri. Seward communicated with leaders of the Republican movement in Virginia and took a particular interest in the schemes John Underwood promoted to advance free labor interests in the state. In 1856

Underwood had gone to the Republican nominating convention, campaigned for the party in the North, and sought help for his fellow Republicans organizing around Wheeling in northwestern Virginia. He secured financial aid from Seward for starting the Republican newspaper there. Underwood also hoped to establish a colony of Northern workers in western Virginia to demonstrate the superiority of free labor in the state, and he succeeded in getting some New York capitalists to finance such an experiment at Ceredo, Virginia. Such communities could be centers of Republican influence in the South, if more were begun.[24]

In the fall of 1856, Greeley was overjoyed to receive news of Benjamin Hedrick's public avowal in North Carolina of his support for Frémont. He claimed that Hedrick represented a "strong cohort" of opponents of slavery in the border and Upper South, who would speak out if freedom of speech were allowed in the slave states. The *New York Times* also took notice of Hedrick and agreed with Greeley that there were "thousands of similar men in the Southern states" who lacked only the opportunity to proclaim their antislavery sentiments.[25] One Southerner who did proclaim such sentiments was Hinton Rowan Helper. Publication in 1857 of his *Impending Crisis* brought the wrath of slaveholders upon him, and he moved to New York City. There he established a close association with Horace Greeley and announced that the Republican party best represented the interests of the Southern masses. Eager to distribute Helper's book to nonslaveholding whites in the South, Greeley sought money and endorsements from fellow Republicans. Cassius Clay and Frank Blair, whose views on the inimical effects of slavery were identical to Helper's, were prompt to recommend the volume, but little money was forthcoming. In December 1859, however, the book became the center of a storm of controversy in the House of Representatives in Washington. Earlier that year Helper had gotten sixty-eight of the ninety-two Republicans in the House to endorse the book, and one of them, John Sherman of Ohio, was a candidate for House Speaker. Angry Southerners denounced him for his espousal of Helper's doctrines, and for two months the House was thrown into turmoil. The consequent publicity surrounding Helper's book brought angry condemnations of it throughout the South. In many slave states possessing it was a crime.[26]

Consequently, the book was not distributed in the South; instead the Republicans agreed to print thousands of cheap copies and distribute them through the Northern states. The party hoped that the book would be particularly influential in the lower Midwest, where many of the inhabitants were Southern whites who might respond favorably to its attacks on slavery in the name of free labor. The decision to use a Southern condemnation of slavery to appeal to Northern voters, however, was reflective of the problems the Republican party faced in trying to reach Southern nonslaveholders. In the wake of the publicity surrounding Helper's book, and especially after the abortive attempt of John Brown to free slaves in Harpers Ferry, Virginia, which occurred in October of 1859, no one in the South dared advocate antislavery or Republican ideas. Goodloe, Hedrick, and Helper had already left their homes for the North, and although Cassius Clay remained in Kentucky, he told Helper that Brown's raid had dashed Republican hopes in his state. John Underwood also saw his free labor colony at Ceredo collapse in the wake of Brown's fiasco.[27]

In September 1859, a month before Brown descended on Harpers Ferry, Hinton Helper had written a friend in North Carolina asking him to recruit Republican support in the western part of the state. His friend refused, claiming it was pointless to organize the party there. Rather, he advised Helper to "let the Southern States alone except Delaware, Maryland, and Missouri and let all your energies be directed to securing the doubtful free states." After twenty years of struggle against slaveholding interests in his state, Cassius Clay had reached the same conclusion. In 1858 he declared that the Republicans could not hope to win in the South. "The battle is to be fought," he argued, "by the free states; and their views should be kept always foremost." Even Horace Greeley decided that the goal of cultivating support among the lower classes of whites in the South would have to be "secondary to the consolidation of a strong antislavery party in the North." A leading Illinois Republican, Abraham Lincoln, echoed these views in 1859, concluding that "if the rotten democracy shall be beaten in 1860, it has to be done by the North; no human invention can deprive them of the South."[28]

Republicans had never counted heavily on cultivating enough support in the border states to enable them to win the presidency. From the time the party emerged, its program had been aimed at advancing Northern interests, and party leaders had attacked the South for scheming to expand slavery at Northern expense. Its goal was always to convince the Northern voters that only a Northern party, without a Southern wing, could successfully resist slave power aggression. The Republicans' main challenge in the late 1850s was not to expand their base of support into the Upper South but to consolidate the Northern states behind them by encouraging Northern voters to vote for them rather than for the Democrats or the American party. To do this, they branded their Democratic opponents in the North as surrogates for the Southern planter class and managed to take advantage of sectional divisions within the American party to coax many of its Northern members into their ranks.[29]

By 1860 the only Republicans still working for border state support were the Blairs, but even they realized that the party's greatest chance for success lay in winning the majority of the Northern electorate. They sought to appeal to border voters by playing down the slavery issue, but they also took this course because they feared its continued agitation by the Republicans would cost them votes of conservative Northerners who feared disruption of the Union. Hoping to steer a course between the extremes of abolitionism on the one hand and fire-eating Southernism on the other, they backed Edward Bates of Missouri for the Republican nomination. Bates was a moderately antislavery Whig, who advocated internal improvements and agreed with the Blairs that if slaves were freed they should be colonized. In the early spring of 1860, the Blairs organized Republican party conventions in Missouri and Maryland, and both gatherings endorsed colonization and sent delegations pledged to Bates to the Republican convention. There they hoped to pick up other border state delegates and enough moderate Northern support to nominate the Missourian.[30]

Despite the interest of some Northern Republicans in holding their national convention in a border state, the party leadership had agreed to convene in Chicago, and it was to that Northern city that the delegations from Maryland and Missouri came. They were joined by Southerners from Delaware, Kentucky, Virginia, and Texas. Unlike the Republican convention in 1856, however, some Northern delegates now protested the seating of Southern delegations with full voting rights. David Wilmot of Pennsylvania, arguing that these states lacked viable Republican party organizations, contended that their votes should not be allowed to determine the convention's choice of a candidate. If these delegates were admitted and allowed to cast the full vote of their state, he charged, in future conventions spurious delegations from other Southern states could appear and "control, demoralize, and break up" the Republican party. Other Northern delegates argued with Wilmot, one stating that "we wish to build up the party in those states." An angry Maryland delegate said he had risked much to join the Republican ranks, and if the party was to spread into the South, it had to have the support, not the opposition, of Northern Republicans. A Connecticut Republican agreed, claiming that by admitting the Southerners, the party could refute the charge that it was a sectional organization. He and several other delegates believed that if the Republicans won in the fall, they could give encouragement to prospective Southern sympathizers and in the next convention could expect to see all the slave states represented. The dispute was resolved by giving all Southern delegations but the one from Texas the same proportional vote to which Northern states were entitled.[31]

Republican advocates of a Southern strategy won a symbolic victory through this decision. Kentucky, with twelve votes, and Virginia, with fifteen, had more voting strength in the convention than such Northern states as New Jersey or Illinois. The convention did, however, reject a recommendation from its rules committee that the nominee be required to receive a majority of the total number of votes when all states—including Southern states not represented—were counted. According to the committee chairman, the proposal, if adopted, would refute the charge that the Republicans were a sectional party. He noted that the call to the convention was directed to the nation, not the North, and asked the convention to count all states, even the Southern states, as "here in spirit." Critics of the report quickly pointed out that because most Southern states were not in attendance, the rule would in practice require a two-thirds vote of delegates actually attending. The convention then voted to accept a minority report requiring a majority of votes represented in the convention to nominate.[32]

On the most significant matter before the convention, the selection of a candidate for president, the border state strategists were easily defeated. Although some Northerners, including Schuyler Colfax of Indiana and Greeley of New York, expressed an interest in the conservative candidacy of Bates, when the first ballot was taken he received almost no Northern votes. Not even the border was a bloc for him because Virginia and Kentucky voted for other candidates. As the voting proceeded, the strategy of the Northern Republicans who eventually controlled the selection became clear. They had written off the border states; few believed that Bates could even carry Missouri. More important, Bates, who was not a Republican and had virtually repudiated slavery as a campaign issue, clearly lacked the appeal to carry Northern states, where almost all Republican strength lay. Many Republicans were convinced that the party's front runner, Senator William H. Seward of New York, would also fail to carry the key states of Pennsylvania, Illinois, and Indiana. Consequently, the convention settled on Abraham Lincoln, a Kentucky-born politician who had made his career in Illinois, as the man most likely to carry the requisite number of Northern states.[33]

To make Abraham Lincoln president, the party had to devote its full attention to Northern voters, especially in the doubtful states. During the campaign the party's stable of speakers was kept busy in the North; only an occasional Northern Republican spoke in Baltimore or St. Louis. The best border state crowd pleasers, Cassius Clay and Frank Blair, however, were both called north to campaign. Blair, speaking in Philadelphia, summed up the dependency of border Republicans on the North, when he urged Pennsylvanians to help elect Lincoln; if they did so, he would "guarantee that Maryland would be with them" in four more years.[34]

The election results demonstrated the wisdom of Republican strategy; Lincoln swept the North, and although he got less than 40 percent of the popular vote, he won the presidency. Returns from the border revealed the weakness of the Republican party there; Lincoln received slightly over 26,000 votes, a considerable increase above Frémont's total but a minute percentage of the entire vote cast in these states. The Republican campaign showed some vigor in Missouri, where Frank Blair's organization gained Lincoln 17,028 votes, 10 percent of the state's total. More than half his votes came from St. Louis. In Maryland, Montgomery Blair faced conservative hostility, lacked newspaper support, and had to cope with divisive tactics from his erstwhile friends. Congressman Henry Winter Davis, a Know-Nothing who had cooperated with the Republicans in Congress, refused to become a Republican and condemned Blair for running a Republican ticket in the state. Davis, who knew Lincoln could not carry Maryland, believed that without him in the field the newly formed Constitutional Union party could win the state, thus denying it to the Democrats. Lincoln eventually polled 2,294 votes in Maryland, 2.5 percent of the state's total. Half of his vote came from Baltimore and the rest from the state's nonslaveholding northwestern counties.[35]

In Delaware Republicans ran a slate of Lincoln electors but chose not to make independent nominations for Congress or for state offices. Instead, they agreed to accept the candidates of an anti-Democratic coalition called the People's party, which in turn supported the Republican presidential ticket. The resulting coalition gave Lincoln 3,815 votes, almost 24 percent of the state's total. In Kentucky, Clay's Republican organization was almost dormant; he did not count on any Southern support for the Republicans and campaigned mainly in the North. Kentuckians cast 1,364 votes for Lincoln, less than 1 percent of the state's total. His vote came from the German population and the nonslaveholding mountain counties. In Virginia, results were no more favorable; Lincoln got 1,929 votes, or slightly over 1 percent of the entire vote. Most of his support came from the area in and around Wheeling in the northwest panhandle.[36]

In the Lower South, Lincoln's name did not even appear on the ballots. Southern radicals now carried out the threats they had made in 1856; finding that the Republicans had gained control of the presidency by uniting the North against them, they led seven Deep South states out of the Union. By February 1861, they had formed the Confederate States of America and were operating as an independent government. Faced with serious crisis, Republican leaders in the North claimed that the secession movement had been organized and executed by slaveholders and argued that the nonslaveholding whites, whom they believed loyal to the Union, would soon reassert themselves and bring their states back. In the meantime, the Republicans strove to keep the other slave states from falling victim to the secession fever. They were encouraged by the obvious strength of Unionist sentiment in the Upper South and border slave states. In Arkansas, Missouri, and Virginia, conventions called to consider secession rejected the proposal; in North Carolina, Tennessee, Maryland, Kentucky, and Delaware, conventions were not held.[37]

Across the border old party labels became obsolete; Democrats and Whigs alike who opposed secession joined in new Unionist coalitions. They urged Lincoln not to take any overt actions against the South and to work instead to strengthen the Unionist movement. This he could do by offering the South a compromise on slavery in the territories and by using his patronage to build up political support for the antisecessionist Union coalitions. Some Southern Unionists suggested to Lincoln and the Northern Republicans that if they dropped sectional issues to take up the cause of national unity, they could build political support in the slaveholding states.[38] In December 1860, a North Carolina Unionist, John Gilmer, urged Lincoln to desert the inflexible Republicans and "come as far South as you can . . . by the preservation of the peace of the country you will nationalize yourself and your party."[39]

Lincoln's secretary of state, William Henry Seward, was particularly interested in following such a strategy, which would give the administration a broader base than it presently held. He urged Lincoln to appoint as many as three non-Republican Southern Unionists to his cabinet and to use his patronage liberally to weld other Southerners to the administration. In particular, Seward urged Lincoln to offer a cabinet position to Gilmer, who was in contact with the secretary as well as the president. Gilmer, a Unionist Whig, was exemplary of the Southerners Seward hoped to attract. Although he was a slaveowner, he and his Whig friends in North Carolina accepted the need for economic diversification in the state and looked to Pennsylvania rather than South Carolina as a model to follow. To encourage Gilmer and other Southern Unionists to support the administration, Seward urged Lincoln not to alienate the South. In particular, he hoped Lincoln would consent to give up Fort Sumter in South Carolina, one of the two federal forts still remaining in the Confederacy, to avoid war.[40]

Seward's strategy of extending Republican support into the South during the secession crisis was similar to the strategy the Blairs had advocated for the border states before the 1860 election. In both cases the Southern alternative meant risking the support in the North that the Republicans had built in their five-year history. If Lincoln fulfilled the hope of Seward and the Southern Unionists, he would split his own party. He could not afford to go back on the Republican voters of the North, most of whom expected him to stand fast against compromise and to hold Fort Sumter, to solicit uncertain support from his former opponents in the South.[41] The most Lincoln was willing to do for Seward's plan was to offer cabinet positions to two men from the border, Bates of Missouri and Montgomery Blair of Maryland. The Bates appointment pleased border state strategists, but his selection of Blair, who was an avowed Republican, disturbed them. Lincoln also agreed to offer a position in the cabinet to Gilmer, but the North Carolinian delayed responding while he waited for Lincoln's Southern policy to develop. He then refused the offer when Lincoln opposed a new compromise on slavery in the territories and indicated his determination to hold Fort Sumter. In April 1861, the president sent a naval expedition to reprovision the fort, and his action led the Confederates to bombard its garrison into submission. The president's subsequent call for troops to put down the rebellion in the Lower South led the Upper South states of North Carolina, Virginia, Arkansas, and Tennessee to secede, and with them went Seward's hopes for any significant reorganization of political parties that would have staved off civil war.[42]

Sumter had possibly cost Lincoln and the Republicans political support in the Upper South and border, for many Southerners who had contemplated joining the Republicans in opposition to secession would not support a war to save the Union; rather, they preferred to join the Confederacy.[43] A residue of Unionists was left in the four Upper South states, however, who did oppose the Confederacy even after the war began. And, more significantly for the immediate future, the border states of Kentucky, Missouri, Delaware, and Maryland remained in the Union even after Fort Sumter. With careful handling, the Republicans could possibly turn this Southern Unionism to their partisan advantage.

REPUBLICANS AND THE

WARTIME SOUTH, 1861–1865

The Civil War, which brought sweeping changes that bordered on revolution into the South, greatly altered the political possibilities that faced the Northern Republicans there. As the power of the federal government, spearheaded by the Union armies, penetrated ever more deeply into the South, the institution of slavery collapsed, and with it, at least momentarily, the power of the Southern political leadership it had sustained. The resulting vacuum provided Republicans with an opportunity to organize wartime coalitions in several Southern states that might be led to support not only the Union government but also the Lincoln administration and the Republican party. President Lincoln pioneered in this effort to promote proadministration parties in the South. As commander in chief of the Union army and as chief executive, he was in a position to exercise military influence, federal patronage, and pardons to promote party reorganization. Lincoln based his initial hopes both for organizing loyal governments in the South and for gaining Republican support there on the presumed existence of a mass of Southerners who were basically pro-Union but who had been misled by secessionist leaders into supporting the Confederacy. By controlling the process of reconstructing the Confederate states as they fell under Union military control, Lincoln hoped to encourage these Unionists to support his administration and his party.

Lincoln's first opportunity to experiment with building a political base in the South was offered in the border slave states that remained in the Union. In addition to Delaware, Maryland, Kentucky, and Missouri, a new border state of West Virginia emerged in 1863, formed by Unionist counties in the northwestern section of Virginia, which seceded from the Old Dominion. In all of these border areas, traditional party identifications disappeared, as the population divided between those who supported the Union and war and those who opposed either or both. The fledgling Republican parties in all these states virtually disappeared, as their individual members committed themselves to the Union cause.[1]

In this situation of party flux Lincoln had an opportunity to use his patronage power to draw people toward his administration and his party. For the president, however, party advantage took second place to securing support for the Union and the war against the Confederacy. Hence he used his appointive powers to reward Unionists regardless of party affiliation. He assured Southerners he would not use patronage to force unacceptable officeholders upon them and would not inquire into their past political loyalties. With the exception of Missouri, there were few Republicans in the border states to appoint anyway, but they complained that the president did not give them priority in filling government jobs. Lincoln did attempt to reward the party faithful, but he gave many positions to old Whigs and Constitutional Unionists, even if they were slaveholders, as long as they were loyal to the Union.[2]

Another power Lincoln had at his disposal to encourage border state Unionism was the federal army. Military campaigns in the first year of the war helped to secure Maryland, Kentucky, and Missouri for the Union and provided the protection behind which West Virginians conducted their separate statehood movement. Federal armies also played a direct role in supporting border state Unionist parties. Union commanders arrested and incarcerated pro-Confederate state officials and in some states broke up Democratic party meetings and arrested candidates suspected of treasonable views. Union troops also patrolled the polls in some areas to intimidate prosecessionist voters and protect those who supported the Lincoln administration.[3] In Kentucky, Missouri, Maryland, and Delaware, Union commanders helped administer loyalty oaths that kept many Unionist opponents from voting or holding office. By the end of the war Unionist legislatures in Missouri, West Virginia, and Maryland also had enacted civil measures disfranchising suspected Confederate sympathizers.[4]

With the help of federal patronage, military protection, and loyalty oaths, the governments of all the border states except Delaware remained under Unionist control throughout the war; after 1862 in that state Democrats controlled the legislature. Except for Delaware, organized opposition to the Unionist parties in the border was slow to develop. Unionists could attack partisan opposition as treasonable; and the Democratic party, around which opposition ultimately coalesced, had lost many of its members and leaders to the Confederacy. Not until the last stages of the war did signs of a two-party system begin to reappear across the border, particularly as the Democratic party began to revive.[5] The Unionist governments that controlled Maryland, Missouri, West Virginia, and Kentucky could not, however, be equated with the Republican party. Before 1865 none of the border state governors had Republican connections. At the beginning of the war, only one of the border state congressmen, Frank Blair of Missouri, was an avowed Republican, and even he recommended that his party drop its name and merge with other Missouri Unionists.[6]

Within a year after the beginning of the war, schisms began to appear within the Unionist organizations in each of the border states, and these schisms, as they matured, helped pave the way for a restoration of the two-party system there. One wing of the Unionist camp eventually merged with the Democrats; its rivals became associated with the national Republican party. Lincoln's distribution of federal patronage was one cause of this division. In Maryland, for instance, Republican Unionists led by Montgomery Blair struggled with Henry Winter Davis's Constitutional Unionists for control of federal offices. Lincoln tried mightily to be evenhanded with his disposition of federal posts, but inevitably his appointments displeased some. In addition to patronage, the presence of Union occupation forces in the border created some division in the Unionist camp. Radical Unionists wanted rebel sympathizers punished and treasonable activities discouraged by army action; more conservative Unionists, however, were unhappy with military interference in elections, suspensions of newspapers, and military arrests of civilians. Also, Unionists disagreed over the distribution of patronage positions assigned by military authority.[7]

The main issue dividing the Unionists proved to be the question of slavery, and it became the clearest indicator of factional loyalties in every state. As the war progressed, pressures developed to emancipate slaves in the Confederacy, and because all of the border states possessed slaves, the future of the institution there came into question also. Border state Unionists who came to favor immediate emancipation, without colonization, became known as Unconditional Unionists or Radicals; in Missouri they were called Charcoals. Their Unionist opponents, who either did not want to free the slaves or advocated gradual, compensated emancipation, became known as Conditional Unionists, Conservatives, or, in the case of Missouri, Claybanks.[8]

As early as August 30, 1861, these divisions over slavery appeared in Missouri, precipitated by General John C. Frémont's order emancipating slaves of rebel owners in the state. When Lincoln rescinded the order and ultimately removed Frémont from command, most of the state's Unionists, led by Frank Blair, rejoiced. A significant minority, however, including former state Republican party chairman B. Gratz Brown, applauded Frémont's action. In March 1862, when Lincoln sought to appeal to moderate antislavery views in the border by recommending that the Union slave states consider adopting plans of gradual emancipation with federal compensation for the owners and colonization for the freedmen, Frank Blair embraced the proposal, but Gratz Brown opposed colonization and called for a speedier end to slavery.[9]

Lincoln's border state proposal precipitated debate over slavery in all the Union slave states; this discussion was intensified in September 1862, when Lincoln issued a proclamation indicating his intention to free all slaves in areas of the South still in rebellion. Democrats everywhere in the border opposed Lincoln's proclamation, but so did most border state Unionist congressmen, as well as all the state governors. Opposition to any tampering with slavery was especially strong in Kentucky and Delaware; in the latter state that fall the Democrats won control of the state legislature and defeated the Unionist congressman who had endorsed Lincoln's action.[10] In Missouri, where Blair and Brown were at odds over Lincoln's proposal for gradual, compensated emancipation in the border states, congressional candidates ran on individual platforms endorsing or opposing immediate emancipation. Six of the ten congressmen elected supported some form of emancipation, and both Charcoals and Claybanks claimed victory. The Radicals' greatest achievement, however, was in making Blair's reelection margin so small that he was eventually unseated.[11] Kentucky and Maryland had no congressional elections in 1862, but in the latter state Montgomery Blair joined his brother Frank in endorsing Lincoln's proposals for the border, while Winter Davis, already at odds with Montgomery Blair over patronage, called for more immediate action on slavery. As in Missouri, both Maryland factions were ready to end the institution but differed over how and when to abolish it.[12]

In 1863, Unionist divisions took clearer form throughout the border. By then the Radical Unionists were identified not only with immediate emancipation but with recruitment of black troops in their states. Radicals also favored stern measures, including continued disfranchisement, to punish Confederate sympathizers and ensure Unionist control of their states. Conservative Unionists, on the other hand, were critical of immediate emancipation and the recruitment of black troops and attacked their Radical opponents as champions of racial equality. The Conservatives were also less likely to favor punitive measures against rebel sympathizers.[13]

In three states in 1863 the Unconditional Unionists or Radical factions held separate state conventions to make independent nominations for office. In the fall elections in Maryland, Davis's Radicals defeated their Conservative Unionist rivals, winning four of the state's five congressional seats and control of the state assembly. Radical control of the Maryland legislature meant that the state would hold a constitutional convention the next year to institute immediate emancipation. In Missouri Radicals also held a separate state convention to make independent nominations for state offices and push for a constitutional convention like that to be held in Maryland to abolish slavery. The Radicals narrowly lost the election and with it a chance for holding the convention in 1864; however, they gained enough strength in the state legislature to send B. Gratz Brown to the United States Senate.[14]

In Kentucky, where both congressional and state elections were held in the summer of 1863, the Unionist party was able to defeat a bid by a revived Democratic party to win control of the state, but the divisions in its own ranks over emancipation also precipitated an independent movement by Radical Unionists. When the Unionist convention refused to endorse even Lincoln's moderate proposals for emancipation, the Radicals, including antislavery advocate Robert Breckinridge, seceded to form their own organization, applauded Lincoln's plan, and proclaimed themselves Unconditional Unionists.

Three of the Unionist candidates for Congress affiliated with the splinter movement, were elected to Congress, and proceeded to vote with the Republicans there, rally support for Lincoln, and ultimately lay the foundations for a permanent Republican party in the state. In Delaware, thanks to Democrats who boycotted the polls in protest against military interference in elections, Nathaniel Smithers, one of the founders of the state's Republican party, won Delaware's lone congressional seat. In West Virginia, the Unionists who had led the separate statehood movement accepted the congressional condition for admission to the Union—that the state agree to abolish slavery. A minority of Conservative Unionists opposed that action, but the free state men controlled the elections, and when the state was added to the Union in 1863, they sent a strong Unconditional Unionist delegation to Congress.[15]

The increase in Radical or Unconditional Unionist strength in the border states owed much to the activity of the Union League, a patriotic organization that first appeared in the spring of 1861 in Maryland, Missouri, and Kentucky. Initially the league operated in secret, organizing Unionists into military companies to resist efforts to take their states out of the Union. In 1863, with the border states secure, league members began to hold public meetings and to engage in political activity. By then the Union League also had organized in most of the Northern states, where its support for the war quickly became translated into support for the Republican party. In the border states, although the league was not identifiably Republican, it did support the Lincoln administration, immediate emancipation, and the recruitment of black troops. In Maryland and Missouri, such Radicals as Davis and Brown joined the organization and soon turned it into an effective weapon in their struggle against the Conservative Unionists, dominated in both states by the Blairs.[16]

By the fall of 1863 factional disputes in Missouri and Maryland had become acrimonious. Military commanders in both states had become involved in the political disputes because they controlled large amounts of patronage and could directly influence elections by administering loyalty oaths, stationing troops at the polls, or suspending newspapers. Representatives of both factions put heavy pressure on Lincoln to intervene in their behalf through military appointments and patronage distribution.[17] Lincoln was reluctant to step into the fray, complaining that the disputes were frequently personal in nature and weakened the administration. With a presidential campaign looming in 1864, however, and desirous of renomination and reelection, Lincoln could not remain aloof from the internal politics of these states.

Lincoln faced difficult decisions in both Missouri and Maryland. The more conservative element in both states was well represented in his cabinet by Bates and Blair, and he had leaned in their direction in the first years of the war. The Blairs had helped found the Republican party and had defended his gradual emancipation program in 1862. The Blair family continued to hope during the war that they could orient the Republican party toward the Unionist Democratic vote, and they were reluctant to alienate such support by moving too rapidly on slavery, raising black troops, or punishing supposed rebel sympathizers through disfranchisement or confiscation of property. They bitterly denounced their Radical opponents, accusing them of prolonging the war through their insistence on immediate emancipation and their occasional advocacy of civil rights for the freed slaves. The Blairs emphasized that their party was a white man's party, and they pushed colonization as an answer to the racial fears of potential Republican recruits.[18]

The Radicals in both states, however, were growing impatient with Lincoln's hesitation on the slavery issue. They were ready for immediate emancipation and by 1864 were calling for a constitutional amendment to achieve it in all the states. They were critical of Lincoln for his association with the Blairs and impatient with indications that he would apply a lenient reconstruction policy in the South. By 1864 they were considering alternatives to Lincoln's candidacy and looked with favor upon the Radical secretary of the treasury, Salmon P. Chase, who funneled patronage in their direction, or on General John Frémont, who had issued the emancipation edict in Missouri in 1861.[19]

In considering which group to support, Lincoln realized that the Blairs were having trouble bringing many of their own Conservative Unionist supporters to accept even gradual emancipation. But Radical strength in both states seemed to be growing as more and more voters accepted that slavery was doomed. It was becoming apparent to Lincoln that the Radicals, with their support of immediate emancipation and the use of black troops and their enthusiastic championing of a war to the end against the Confederacy, were closer to his views than the Conservatives, and that they, not the Blairs, were destined to control their states. It was even more important for Lincoln's calculations that Northern Republican opinion had moved rapidly toward the Radical position. The 1864 election was not different from the one in 1860; for Lincoln to win he had to carry the North. The chances of border state support for Lincoln were much greater in 1864, especially in Missouri and Maryland, but he could not gain Northern votes by continuing his conservative border strategy. Border Radicals like Henry Winter Davis were very popular in the North, and Republican leaders such as Chase and Congressman William D. Kelley of Pennsylvania were campaigning in Maryland for the Unconditionals and pressing Lincoln to support them against the Blairs. In addition, the Missouri Charcoals had persuaded the national council of the Union League of America, meeting in Washington in December 1863, to intercede with the president in their behalf.[20]

Consequently, Lincoln began to shift patronage to the Radicals, making military appointments in both states satisfactory to them. In Maryland, the convening of a state constitutional convention to abolish slavery meant that that issue would no longer divide Unionists. Both wings of the party agreed to hold a joint convention in the spring, and despite the work of Davis and his cohorts, Lincoln's general popularity resulted in the convention selecting a delegation to the Republican national convention pledged to his renomination. In Missouri, however, the factional split, exacerbated by the continued uncertainty regarding the future of slavery in the state, could not be healed. The Radicals again held a separate convention and nominated an avowed Republican for governor. They vigorously debated the advisability of sending a delegation to the Republican national convention, for many, including Brown, wanted to attend an independent convention in Cleveland that was organized to nominate John C. Frémont. The majority of the Radicals, however, agreed to send an uncommitted delegation to the Republican convention. Because the Conservative Unionists, meeting separately, also sent a delegation to the national convention, the president had to make a choice. Even though the Conservative delegation, unlike the Radical, was pledged to his support, Lincoln believed that the Radicals best represented his views and had the best chance of winning the state; hence he gave their delegation the nod, and the convention seated them by an overwhelming vote. His judgment of the Missouri factions was verified when most of the rejected Conservatives affiliated with the Democratic party.[21]

Just as the pressures of an election year forced Lincoln's hand in the factional disputes in Missouri and Maryland, they also helped clarify the national political allegiance of the Unionist factions in the other border states. In Kentucky, the Conservative Unionists, or Unionist Democrats, as they now called themselves, were adamantly opposed to Lincoln's policies of emancipation and recruitment of Negro troops in the state and were angry over what they considered to be military dominance of Kentucky's civil affairs. Never having regarded themselves as Republicans, they agreed to send a delegation to the Democratic national convention. Unconditional Unionists held their own meeting and selected a delegation to the Republican convention, pledged to Lincoln. In Delaware and West Virginia, Unionists avoided factional disputes and also sent delegations to the Republican conclave.[22]

Hence by 1864 partisan lines were becoming more clearly visible in the border states. Unconditional or Radical Unionists fell into line behind the Lincoln administration, and Conservative Unionists endorsed the Democratic candidate for president. Lincoln, who had first used patronage to build up Unionist support in the border, now used his appointive powers to encourage friends of his administration and party. Nevertheless, partisan lines in the border remained blurred. Despite their support for Lincoln, Radicals in the border avoided the label "Republican."[23] They were joined in this aversion by the Northern Republicans; just as in the border states, so even more in the North, Republicans were eager to court Democrats who supported the war and Lincoln. In state elections in the North, as in the border, "Union" parties emerged, encouraged and usually organized by the Republicans. In states that were already strongly Republican, the word "Union" was just a new label for the same organization, but in closely contested states like Ohio and Pennsylvania, Democrats shared in the nominations and in state patronage. In 1864 the national Republican committee issued a call for the party's national convention that nowhere mentioned the word "Republican." Instead, delegates were asked to come to a "National Union" convention. To underscore their desire to be a nonpartisan, national organization, the Republicans agreed to meet in the border city of Bal-

timore, Maryland. As another gesture to Unionist and border sentiment, the convention chose Robert Breckinridge of Kentucky as its
temporary president. Despite these efforts, however, it was clear that
the Baltimore convention was Republican in all but name.[24]

Just as the arrival in Baltimore in 1864 of delegates from Missouri,
Kentucky, West Virginia, Maryland, and Delaware signified the
growing strength of the Republicans in the border, so also the delegations from Virginia, South Carolina, Florida, Arkansas, Tennessee,
and Louisiana heralded the emergence of Republicanism even in the
depths of the Confederacy.[25] The appearance of these Southerners at
a Republican national convention was a reflection of the great political and social changes being wrought by the Civil War. By 1864 at
least a portion of each of these six Southern states was under federal
military occupation, and in all but two President Lincoln had tried to
organize Unionist governments. He hoped that these governments
could extend their control as federal armies advanced through their
states and would gain support at the expense of coexisting Confederate state governments. He also hoped that, as in the border
states, Unionist sentiment could be organized in behalf not only of
the Union but also of the Republican party. Unfortunately, the number of Unionists in all of these states was much smaller than in the
border, and Lincoln faced a great deal of difficulty in establishing
and broadening the base of support for loyal governments there.

From the beginning of the war the president had tried various
expedients to encourage the emergence of loyal governments in the
Confederate states. His efforts began in Virginia, where in 1861 he
had extended recognition to the Unionist government of Francis H.
Pierpont, which had organized itself in the strongly Unionist northwestern counties around Wheeling. After the state of West Virginia
had been formed, Pierpont moved his government to Alexandria,
across the Potomac from Washington. Because Union armies had
made only limited penetration of the state, Pierpont's authority extended to only a few counties in the north, on the Eastern Shore,
and around Norfolk. Lincoln initially hoped that Unionists in other
Southern states would form loyal governments modeled on Pierpont's regime, but the weakness of that government, plus the failure
of spontaneous Unionist movements to develop elsewhere, led the
president to experiment with other approaches.[26]

In 1862, as Union military power began to penetrate other Confederate states, Lincoln sought to initiate Unionist governments there by installing a military governor in each state, who was to marshal support for reestablishing loyal civil governments. He appointed such governors for Tennessee, Louisiana, Arkansas, and North Carolina, but in the latter two states little progress was made in establishing Union military control, and by mid-1863 he had recalled both military governors. In two other states, South Carolina and Florida, Union armies established a foothold along the Atlantic coast but failed to extend their authority inland. Hence the number of potential Unionists was small. Lincoln did send federal tax commissioners and other officials to both states, but appointed no military governors there.[27]

By the end of 1863 the failure of a strong Unionist movement to develop in the Southern states led Lincoln to develop yet another approach to Reconstruction. In December, he issued a proclamation offering amnesty to any Southerner who would take a prescribed oath of future allegiance to the Union. Although Lincoln exempted certain groups from taking the oath, most Confederates were eligible. By making the oath a simple one of future allegiance to the Union rather than one of past loyalty, Lincoln hoped to encourage wavering Confederates to abandon their cause. He pledged that he would recognize any state government that was then organized by at least 10 percent of the 1860 electorate who had taken the oath. Lincoln also made it clear that he expected these governments to abolish slavery within their respective jurisdictions. In this way Lincoln hoped to secure governments pledged both to the Union and to freedom.[28]

The president sent instructions to his remaining military governors, in Tennessee and Louisiana, to implement this plan. In Arkansas, where Lincoln had no military governor, the Unionist minority that had existed at the outbreak of the war was encouraged by Union military success in the state late in 1863 and took its own steps to initiate a loyal government. Through various irregular mass meetings and elections, Unionist delegates were chosen to attend a constitutional convention in Little Rock in January 1864. Lincoln, who was not involved in this process, did instruct the Union commander in Arkansas to cooperate with the organizers and work to bring about a free state constitution. The convention established a provisional Union government, abolished slavery in Arkansas, and approved the use of Lincoln's loyalty oath in state elections held that March.

The vote, which polled more than Lincoln's required 10 percent, easily ratified the constitution and elected its friends to state offices.[29]

Lincoln had high hopes for organizing a Union government in Tennessee. Sentiment in that state had been strongly against secession until the firing on Fort Sumter, and Unionism remained particularly strong in the nonslaveholding counties of mountainous East Tennessee. Lincoln's choice for military governor there was Andrew Johnson, a strongly Unionist Democrat who was serving as senator from Tennessee when the war began. Johnson refused to surrender his seat and instead remained in Washington to advocate a vigorous prosecution of the war. Because he came from East Tennessee, he appeared to be a logical selection to lead Unionist sentiment in the state.

In many respects, however, Johnson was not a good choice to head Lincoln's effort in the Volunteer State. Although he was a Democrat, Johnson had angered many in his party by his condemnations of slavery and secession; in addition, his support of the Southern Democratic candidate in 1860 hurt him with East Tennessee Unionists, many of whom were Whigs. His actions upon taking his new position in Tennessee, which included arresting suspected Confederate sympathizers and suppressing newspapers, aroused antagonism. With Lincoln's urging, Johnson attempted to hold elections in the state, but because of disruptions caused by military campaigns, divisions in the ranks of the Unionists, and Johnson's insistence on applying a more rigorous test oath than that required by Lincoln, he proved unable to reestablish civil government.[30]

After Lincoln's Emancipation Proclamation, Unionist sentiment in Tennessee, like that in the border states, had been divided on the slavery issue. These divisions complicated Johnson's efforts to organize a loyalist government in the state, for neither he nor Lincoln desired a Union government that could not be trusted to endorse emancipation. The Union League, which emerged in the eastern part of the state at the same time as the leagues in Maryland and Missouri, played the same role in Tennessee Unionist politics that it did in the border states. Here as well the league supported radical measures, including emancipation and stringent disfranchisement of the Confederates; hence Conservative Unionists dropped out of the organization. Early in September 1864, Unconditional Unionists held a convention in Nashville to call for reorganization of civil government and a revision of the state constitution to abolish slavery and disfranchise Confederate sympathizers; but as the year ended, the state still lacked a Unionist civil government.[31]

By the summer of 1864, of all the Confederate states with Unionist movements, Louisiana seemed to offer the best chance for success. By that time, Union military forces had occupied New Orleans and several surrounding parishes for more than two years, and approximately 25 percent of the state's electorate had participated in elections creating a Unionist government. In addition, under the guidance of federal military authorities, the state witnessed the most serious effort in the Lower South to build the basis for a viable postwar Republican party. For many in the North, Louisiana became a test case, to forecast the future of Republicanism in the slave states.[32]

In the summer of 1862, operating under the protection of Union military forces that had arrived in May under the command of General Benjamin F. Butler, New Orleans Unionists had begun to organize political associations. Its leaders were recipients of patronage available either from Salmon P. Chase's Treasury Department or from the military authorities who filled offices in the city. There were many potential recruits for the associations in the city who had opposed secession. Butler sought to rally support from the urban workers and business classes. By December, he had held congressional elections in the two districts he controlled, and the total vote had reached 60 percent of the prewar totals.[33]

Despite this auspicious beginning, divisions soon appeared in the Louisiana Unionist movement. Early in 1863 General Nathaniel Banks replaced Butler and proceeded to ignore his Unionist associations. Instead, Banks courted the support of the sugar planters in parishes south of New Orleans. Voters in these areas had opposed secession and had voted for the Constitutional Unionist, John Bell, or the Northern Democratic candidate, Stephen Douglas, in 1860. Hoping to organize these planters in a moderate Republican party, Banks had given them control of parish governments. Although Lincoln's Emancipation Proclamation had left the status of slaves in Louisiana in doubt, Banks strove to ease the fears of the sugar planters by drawing up labor regulations that required them to pay their blacks wages but left much of the control of the labor force in the hands of the landowners. By using the army to ensure social stability in the plantation regions and by working for a gradual transformation from slavery to freedom, Banks hoped to limit the scope of social change within the state and win the support of the planter class that had been hesitant to leave the Union. Despite his efforts, however, Banks made little progress with the planters; they maintained a political organization independent of the New Orleans Unionist associations throughout the war.[34]

Within the city of New Orleans, another approach to Republican organizing developed. In the absence of any direct encouragement from Banks, the city's Unionists, led by Thomas J. Durant, began the process of turning their Union associations into a political party. Durant and his followers were eager to restore civil government as soon as possible, but they wanted it done under a new state government that abolished slavery. They proposed registering all whites who were willing to take an oath to support the Union; the military governor of Louisiana, General George Shepley, could then call an election to a convention to draw up a free state constitution. If the constitution were ratified, elections could be held and the state restored to the Union. In the summer of 1863, Lincoln endorsed Durant's plan and urged Banks and Shepley to assist him.[35]

As was true elsewhere in the South, the Union army played a crucial role in Louisiana politics. Union commanders controlled patronage, regulated voters, and timed elections. In Louisiana, General Shepley proved very slow to implement voting registration until he had checked everything carefully with Washington. Although Lincoln pressed Banks to aid Durant, he refused to do so. In the face of the army's caution, the New Orleans Unionists decided to seek financial aid from Northerners sympathetic to their cause. They had little success in obtaining this out-of-state assistance, nor could they raise much money in the state. The free state movement drew its support from small businessmen, artisans, professionals, and government workers, and these classes lacked significant financial resources.[36]

While the Durant organizers strove to prepare for an election, Conservative Unionists in the state, including many of the sugar planters Banks had attempted to recruit, organized their own efforts to restore the state's loyal government while maintaining slavery. To compound the political confusion, leaders of the sizable free black population of New Orleans began to hold rallies to demand that blacks participate in any political reorganization of the state that might take place. The free state men, led by Thomas J. Durant, began to indicate that they might accept at least limited black suffrage. In view of these pressures from both right and left, Banks determined to seize control of the Reconstruction process and shape a Republican constituency at the center that would accept the end of slavery but prevent the consequences of abolition from extending to enfranchisement of the former slaves. By so limiting the nature of change within Louisiana, he hoped a majority of whites in the state would stand with the Republicans.[37]

Banks's opportunity to move came with Lincoln's announcement in December 1863 of his 10 percent plan of Reconstruction. Convincing the president that Durant was to blame for the slow process of voter registration in Louisiana, Banks got Lincoln's approval to take over the process. He called for an election for state offices to be held in February 1864, followed by a constitutional convention. The free state men led by Durant had preferred to reverse this process; they hoped that a constitutional convention could first rewrite the basic laws of the state, particularly those that favored the old planter elite. Only then would it be safe to allow elections to fill state offices. If the offices were filled first, without sufficient organizing and campaigning on behalf of the free state party, they might never be able to institute the changes they wanted in the state. Banks, who feared that these changes would include some degree of Negro suffrage that would forever alienate the majority of whites, wanted the elections first. These differences over strategy resulted in a division in the free state movement. Banks threw his support behind free state moderates who were opposed to Negro suffrage, and, with the entire influence of the military apparatus behind them, the moderates won an easy victory in February, choosing their candidate, Michael Hahn, as governor of the state. In the following elections for delegates to the constitutional convention, Hahn, whose patronage powers had been greatly increased when he was named military governor of the state, was able to secure control for his wing of the party.

The constitutional convention that met in New Orleans in April 1864 was drawn almost entirely from the ranks of the middle class; the delegates were officeholders, businessmen, and professionals. The old political elite of the state, which was almost entirely Confederate in its sympathy, was absent. The convention abolished slavery, reduced the work day for employees on public works, and provided for separate schools for both races. It did not, however, enfranchise blacks, although Lincoln had cautiously recommended to Hahn that the ballot be given to at least some of the state's black population. Nonetheless, Lincoln threw his support behind the Hahn government. The president was most eager for Unionist governments in the Southern states to abolish slavery by amending their constitutions, and Hahn's forces had achieved that goal. Also, almost one-quarter, rather than 10 percent, of the state's 1860 electorate had participated in the 1864 elections, more than fulfilling Lincoln's requirements.[38]

Although Lincoln was more concerned with organizing loyal governments in the South that would abolish slavery than with building Republican parties there, the men he helped install in power under his Reconstruction plan rallied to his political support. The Hahn party in Louisiana chose a solid Lincoln delegation to the Union convention in Baltimore.[39] It was joined in that border city by delegations from Arkansas, which had also established a loyal government committed to emancipation, and from the counties in Virginia controlled by Pierpont's Unionist government. In addition, Unconditional Unionists in Tennessee had agreed at their September convention to send a delegation to Baltimore. Andrew Johnson was eager for the state to be represented there as evidence of his success in organizing Tennessee Unionists, and he may also have hoped the National Union party would consider him for its vice-presidential nomination. The Tennessee Unconditional Unionists endorsed Lincoln's emancipation policy, and the delegation they sent was pledged to a Lincoln-Johnson ticket. Although there were no Unionist governments in Florida and South Carolina, conventions were held behind Union lines in both states to send delegations to Baltimore. On the east coast of Florida, federal officeholders, Union soldiers, and a handful of local inhabitants selected the delegates; in South Carolina, a mixture of Northern migrants and Union soldiers, many of whom were black, held a rally at Beaufort in the Sea Islands to choose representatives to send to Baltimore. Because four of the South Carolina representatives were black, the delegation drew much attention at the convention.[40]

In Baltimore, the delegations from the Confederate states became a source of considerable controversy. Radicals in Congress, suspicious of Lincoln's Reconstruction governments, particularly in Louisiana, complained that they represented only small minorities of the states' populations and were creations of military rule. They feared that Lincoln was urging Congress to accept them into the Union so that they might cast their votes for him in the 1864 election; the more extreme Radicals wanted someone more in accord with their views to be elected president. Many congressmen also feared that these new governments, particularly in Louisiana, would fail to protect black rights and would eventually allow too many former Confederates to vote and hence control the state's politics. Because of the uncertainties surrounding the implementation of Lincoln's plan, these Republican congressmen did not want representatives from states restored under it to be seated.[41] Pennsylvania Congressman Thaddeus Stevens, fearing that recognizing the Southern delegations in Baltimore would appear to be an endorsement of Lincoln's Reconstruction efforts, argued that the names of the states should not even be read in the roll of the convention. Representatives from the Confederate states rejoined that their devotion to the Union should be honored by having their states called by name and their delegations seated. Ultimately the names of all the states in attendance, including the Southern states, were called, and the question of seating the contested delegations was referred to the credentials committee.[42]

The committee recommended that South Carolina not be admitted and that the other states be allowed seats but not votes. Because the South Carolina delegation represented such a small minority of the state, the convention agreed without debate not to seat it and thereby avoided the embarrassment of seating the state's four black delegates. The convention agreed, however, to seat the Virginia and Florida delegations without votes. Senator James H. Lane of Kansas, who represented Lincoln in the convention, then moved to grant Tennessee, Arkansas, and Louisiana voting rights. The convention first voted on Tennessee and by a division of 310–151 accepted Lane's motion. If several states had not changed their votes before the final tally, however, the result would have been much closer. Once having taken this action, the convention could hardly deny the same privilege to Arkansas and Louisiana, particularly inasmuch as both these states, unlike Tennessee, had organized loyal civil governments. Radical dissatisfaction with the seating of these three delegations was somewhat mitigated by the overwhelming vote in favor of the credentials committee's recommendation to seat the Radical Missouri delegation instead of the Claybanks.[43]

Having disposed of the questions surrounding the Southern delegations, the National Union convention balloted for nominees for president and vice-president. Missourians, who cast the only votes against Lincoln, quickly moved to make his nomination unanimous, and the delegates then moved on to choose his running mate. Lincoln had already indicated his willingness to accept Andrew Johnson on the ticket, and Henry J. Raymond, editor of the *New York Times* and the Union Republican party chairman, also urged the Tennesseean's nomination. Raymond argued that such action would prove that the party sought support from loyal elements everywhere, North and South. On the first ballot Johnson demonstrated enough strength to convince a sufficient number of delegations to change their votes, and he received the nomination.[44]

Party lines were drawn more sharply after the Democrats had held their own convention to nominate former Union General George B. McClellan on a platform calling for a negotiated peace and opposing emancipation of slaves. Lincoln had gotten a platform endorsing a Thirteenth Amendment ending slavery throughout the Union. This provision helped to rally Radical support for his campaign, but continued disagreements over Reconstruction policy still threatened to split the party. During the summer Republicans in Congress enacted the Wade-Davis bill, in which they spelled out their own terms for restoring the South. The congressional plan was similar in many respects to Lincoln's but required that a majority of voters in any Southern state would have to take a loyalty oath before elections could be held to reconstitute its civil government and also stipulated that only Southerners who could take an "ironclad" oath of past loyalty to the Union could vote in those elections. Such provisions would clearly postpone the return of any Southern state to the Union, and because their application would invalidate his Unionist government in Louisiana, Lincoln vetoed the bill. Radicals were furious with Lincoln. In the Senate, Republicans voted not to seat representatives from the Unionist government of Arkansas, suggesting that the same treatment awaited Louisiana's senators-elect when they arrived in Washington. In addition, Republican congressmen pushed through a bill providing that the electoral vote of the reconstructed Confederate states would not be counted. Lincoln accepted these actions and also pacified Radicals by obtaining Montgomery Blair's resignation from the cabinet. In the face of the Democratic challenge in the 1864 presidential election, most Republicans agreed to back Lincoln; the president even got the supporters of John C. Frémont to withdraw his independent candidacy.[45]

Once again, as in 1856 and 1860, the Republicans waged their strongest battle in the North, for there the election would be won or lost. Although the border states were not ignored, the Republicans spent their time, money, and effort to carry the same states that had made Lincoln president in 1860, and once again they were successful; although the vote in several states was close, New Jersey was the only Northern state to go Democratic. Lincoln and the Republicans were successful in the border states of Maryland, Missouri, and West Virginia, but in Maryland the results were not encouraging to them. The Radicals had drawn up a constitution emancipating slaves in the state to present to the electorate; traditional Democratic areas voted overwhelmingly against it, and it carried only on the strength of votes cast by Maryland's soldiers in the Union army. In the presidential election, Lincoln got 54 percent of the state's vote. Republicans were able to carry Maryland primarily because the state authorities administered loyalty oaths that kept many Democrats from the polls. Lincoln won an easier victory in West Virginia, carrying the state by twenty-three thousand to ten thousand for McClellan. In Missouri, Lincoln won by a comfortable margin of more than two to one, but the victory was at least in part owing to the disfranchisement of Radical opponents.[46]

Lincoln failed to carry Delaware and Kentucky. In Delaware, the Democrats organized an effective campaign, attacking the Republicans for advocating racial equality and calling themselves the "White Man's Party." They carried the state by a small margin, and they also won its congressional seat and strengthened their control of the state legislature. In Kentucky, Union Democrats joined with the Conservative or Conservative Democratic party, and the coalition easily carried the state for McClellan. Diehard Conservative opposition to emancipation coerced by the national government kept both Delaware and Kentucky from ratifying the Thirteenth Amendment, further establishing their status as irretrievably Democratic states.[47]

Thus the election results in the border presented the Republicans

with a mixed message. Lincoln had increased his proportion of border state votes from less than 1 percent in 1860 to slightly over 50
percent in 1864 and had won the electoral votes of three states. The
Republican party, which existed throughout the border in all but
name, by 1865 controlled twenty-three of the thirty-eight congressional seats from that region. The overall vote in the border, however, had declined by at least one-third over the two presidential
elections, and Republicans realized that much of the absent vote represented either soldiers fighting for the Confederacy or Southern
sympathizers who had been disfranchised during the war. Radicals
in Missouri, West Virginia, and Maryland, who had used loyalty
tests to maintain their grip on their states during the war, hoped to
continue these measures in the postwar period to protect themselves
against the anticipated tide of returning Democrats. By early 1865, a
few Radicals such as B. Gratz Brown in Missouri and Henry Winter
Davis in Maryland were also arguing for Negro suffrage as a way to
enable the Republicans to hold these states.[48]

In either case, whether by disfranchising whites or enfranchising
blacks, border state Republicans were acknowledging that they had
failed to gain the solid support of a white majority. When Missouri
Radicals wrote a state constitution early in 1865 emancipating slaves,
they seized the opportunity to include provisions disfranchising
many of the state's voters. In large part because of its proscriptive
nature, the constitution received only a bare majority of votes cast on
its ratification, revealing that the Radical hold on Missouri, like that
in Maryland, was very tenuous.[49] Through disfranchisement, border
Radicals hoped to hold their states long enough for them to expand
their base, but they risked alienating potential white support
through such proscriptive devices. It was also difficult for border
Republicans to look toward enfranchising blacks. The black population in the border was not as large as it was in the rest of the South,
and every move the Radicals made toward acknowledging black
rights risked loss of white support. The most effective charge the
Democrats developed against them during the war was to associate
Radicals with racial equality. Unless the issue of race could somehow be defused, the future of Republicanism in the border was not
bright.[50]

Republican prospects in the Confederate states looked even less
encouraging as the war ended. Unionist movements, which held

promise of becoming Republican organizations, were weak everywhere in the Confederacy. In Tennessee, Unconditional Unionists met in January 1865 to hold a convention launching a civil government; the delegates initiated a constitutional amendment abolishing slavery, established voting requirements, and called for state elections. The new government that emerged was based on barely more than 10 percent of the voting population of 1860, and it sustained itself in power under the new constitution only by disfranchising large numbers of former Confederates.[51]

Louisiana's Unionist government, which was based on 25 percent of its voting population, offered the Republicans the most hope for success in the Confederate South. After the presidential election most Republican congressmen overcame their misgivings about the Hahn government and prepared to admit its representatives to Congress. Unionist voters in the state had approved the constitution abolishing slavery, and with that issue resolved, Lincoln and his supporters hoped that Hahn would be able to expand his party's support beyond its narrow base around New Orleans. Governor Hahn and his chief supporter in the federal occupation army, General Banks, were now more willing to explore the possibility of enfranchising at least some of the blacks of Louisiana.[52] Hahn, however, soon resigned his governorship to accept election to the U.S. Senate, and his successor, J. Madison Wells, was not an advocate of black enfranchisement. In Washington, a number of Senate Radicals led by Charles Sumner, convinced that the Louisiana government would not protect black rights, managed by filibuster to prevent the seating of the state's senators.[53]

Consequently, when the war ended Louisiana's Unionist government was not represented in Congress, nor was the government of Arkansas. Republican congressmen had earlier agreed to seat some representatives from Virginia and Tennessee, but both these states lacked full congressional delegations. Northern Republicans looked askance at these Unionist parties that were emerging in the Confederacy; they were clearly composed of small minorities in their respective states and, particularly in Louisiana, were ridden by factionalism. Southern Radicals and Unionists who were willing to work with the Northern Republicans in Congress got very little assistance from them. President Lincoln had been the most active Republican in building up political support in the Confederacy, and even he had been more concerned with getting the states back into the Union under antislavery constitutions than with building up Republican parties. When Lincoln was assassinated in April 1865, the man who replaced him in office, Andrew Johnson, proved to be even less likely to promote Southern Republicanism. Yet the future of Southern affairs, and of the Republican party there, now depended in large part upon his actions.

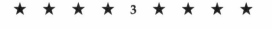

A YEAR OF INDECISION: 1866

As the Civil War came to an end, the Republican party appeared to be at the peak of its power. Within ten years of its birth, the party had won control of the presidency, Congress, and the governorship of every Northern state except New Jersey. In addition, it had established a foothold in several of the border states and had hopes of spreading farther south. Although many Northern Democrats had supported the Lincoln administration during the war, the Republicans claimed most of the credit for Union victory in that conflict and for abolishing the institution of slavery, which had been at the heart of so much of the sectional turmoil. Wartime Congresses had enacted the entire Republican economic program; they had raised the tariff to protective levels, provided free homesteads for farmers, created a new banking and currency system, and subsidized railroad building to the West Coast.

Despite these successes, however, Republicans realized that their hold on national power was tenuous at best. Lincoln's margin over McClellan in 1864 had been very close in several key states, demonstrating that the party's control of the North was not firm. Republicans had even more reason to be concerned about the return of the former Confederate states to the Union. Almost all of these states had become Democratic by 1860, and if they returned to their prewar political allegiance upon being restored to the Union, they could unite with the Northern Democrats and destroy Republican supremacy. Republicans had no wish to see their wartime successes annulled by allowing former Confederates to resume control of both the South and the nation. They feared that unreconstructed Southerners would return the freedmen to some form of slavery, would refuse to modernize their states along Northern lines, and would repeal the Republican economic program. In addition, Republicans feared that returning Southerners would refuse to honor the national debt incurred in conducting the war effort and would demand compensation for the loss of their slave property.

Republicans agreed, therefore, that it was not safe to allow Southerners to return to the Union until they had met certain fundamental conditions prescribed by the North. Not all Republicans, however, were in agreement as to the number and nature of these conditions, and they were further divided as to how to ensure that these terms would be met. The solution to both problems depended in large part on the degree to which Southern whites could be trusted to use the political power that would eventually be returned to them in ways that were not inimical to Northern interests. If the Southern states could be reorganized by whites who were willing to support the Republican party, or at least would not be hostile to its aims, prescribing many conditions for the South would be unnecessary. If the Southern white population proved hostile to Republican interests, however, the federal government would have to intervene more forcibly in Southern affairs and exact certain guarantees before the former Confederate states were readmitted. Here the example of the border states was instructive; during the war Radicals such as B. Gratz Brown and Henry Winter Davis had organized political parties in their states that were Republican in all but name and that in 1865 controlled the governments of Maryland, Missouri, and West Virginia. In each state, these parties had abolished slavery, and in Missouri, Radicals advocated public education, government aid to economic development, and encouragement to the importation of Northern skills and capital. The Republicans could hope that the rest of the Southern states might also be organized by whites friendly to their party and its program.[1]

Hence much of the debate among Republicans concerning Reconstruction reflected different assessments of the possibility of organizing their party in the South. Some Republicans had long regarded the nonslaveholders as potential converts to their free labor ideology. They also thought these Southern whites were fundamentally loyal to the Union. The controversy over slavery, these Republicans believed, had blinded the nonslaveholders to their true interests and had led them to rally behind the planters in support of secession. Zachariah Chandler, Republican senator from Michigan, believed that "a few men [in the South] have done the mischief, and the masses of the people were misled by them." To Carl Schurz, Union general and rapidly rising Republican leader, the war was "a genuine blessing" to the whites of the South, for it had destroyed slavery, whose influence had denied them "even in the slightest degree, a correct realization of their situation." Now that slavery was gone, secession crushed, and the power of the slaveholders obliterated, these Republicans hoped that white Southerners would be brought to endorse the party that had championed the permanence of the Union and the interests of free labor.[2]

Republicans who hoped to gain white voting support in the South at the end of the war were not in agreement, however, over where that support could be found. William Henry Seward and Horace Greeley, for instance, had long hoped to develop support for the Republican party among the nonslaveholding whites, and now that the Civil War was over, they believed their hopes could be realized. Seward argued that with slavery destroyed a new social and political order would emerge in the South that would follow Northern models. Greeley shared these views, arguing that Republican economic doctrines could be used to promote development in the South and help nationalize the party. After the war, both men tended to look to the leadership class, particularly the former Whigs, to lead the South to the Republican party. They argued that the "natural leaders" of the Confederacy could not be ignored because of their influence among the masses. John Andrew, wartime governor of Massachusetts, echoed these views and urged the Republicans to build bridges to the men who were in control of the Southern governments at the end of the war.[3]

Other Republicans who had spent time in the South during or after the war, however, were not sure that the present Southern political leaders, many of whom were planters, could be trusted to lead their states in new directions. Nathaniel Banks, who had courted the support of former Whig sugar planters in Louisiana during the war, found that they would not support the Republican party there. Hence he turned instead to the white workers and mechanics of New Orleans. Benjamin Butler, who preceded Banks in command of occupation troops in New Orleans, had reached the same conclusion; he told an audience in Massachusetts that in Louisiana "I found the aristocracy looked upon us as their enemies; and I found that the working and middle classes looked upon us as friends." Salmon P. Chase, who toured the South at the end of the war, returned convinced that the Republicans could court political support there among "the more active whites of the middle class," who were eager for "peace, business revival, and will take any course the government wants." These views were echoed by Union general William T. Sherman, who told his brother John, a U.S. senator from Ohio, that the Republican party's best chance for recruits in the South was among "the great middle class who want peace and industry."[4]

The Republicans who had the most faith in the possibility of working with the "natural leaders" of the South were the ones who favored the fewest concessions from the former Confederate states. During the war President Abraham Lincoln's restoration plans were based on the hopes of building new governments on a growing base of Southern Unionist support, and his terms for reunion were simple: an abandonment of secession, an oath of future loyalty to the Union, and an acceptance of the end of slavery. Lincoln did hope that lenient terms of reunion would encourage Southerners to profess their Unionism, and he also hoped that he could coax them into the Republican party. In particular, he sought to appeal to old Whigs in the South, many of whom had opposed secession and were antagonistic toward the Democrats. Seward, Greeley, and other Republicans endorsed Lincoln's approach.[5]

Unfortunately for Lincoln and his optimistic associates, loyalist governments and the Republican party in the South showed little strength at the end of the war. The Unionist governments of Virginia, Arkansas, and Tennessee were based on small minorities of the white population. Lincoln had been more successful in Louisiana, where a Union government had emerged based on one-quarter of the state's voting population; its leaders were affiliating with the Republican party. Yet even in this state there was no evidence that the government was likely to expand its base of support. By 1865 it was clear that Democrats had made inroads among the old Whig voters that Lincoln had hoped to attract. Generals Banks and Butler had hoped to gain middle- or working-class support for the Republicans in the South, but their predictions were based on their limited experiences in New Orleans. These classes were stronger in that city than anywhere else in the South, so the Louisiana experience was a poor guide to what would happen in the rest of the Confederacy.[6]

Even before the war ended some Republican congressmen had begun to doubt that Southern white Unionism was strong enough to support new governments. Henry Winter Davis and other Radicals condemned Lincoln's Louisiana government for being based on a small white minority, yet they feared that if the rest of the Louisianans were allowed to vote they would bring in a government unfriendly to the Union and to the Republican party. Congress's initial solution to this dilemma, which it drafted in the form of the Wade-Davis bill, was ambiguous and inconsistent. Congress required that a majority of whites in any state take an oath of future loyalty, much like Lincoln's, before the process of restoring civil government could begin; however, only those who could take the ironclad oath would be allowed to vote. Even Davis admitted that the use of the ironclad oath would exclude all but "a mere handful of the population," who would be "wholly incompetent to form or maintain a state government."[7]

Despite Lincoln's failure to develop a larger core of Unionists on which to base new Southern governments, after the war President Andrew Johnson continued the lenient policies of his predecessor. Johnson, like Lincoln, believed it was possible to organize a Unionist government in the South that would keep former secessionists out of power. Unlike Lincoln, however, who had been a Whig and looked more to Southern Whigs for support, Johnson hoped to organize a party based on the yeoman farmers, many of whom were Democrats. Johnson himself had remained a Democrat, and he had long resented the influence of slaveholders in his party. He hoped to nationalize the Republican party, possibly under a new name, on a basis that would exclude the Southern proslavery and secessionist leaders and would isolate the Northern Democrats who had opposed the war. Johnson also hoped to exclude the Radical Republicans, who favored federal guarantees of black equality in the South. Such a new conservative party would thus be built on the strength of Unionist votes in both sections of the nation and would exclude radical elements both North and South.[8]

Several Republican leaders shared Johnson's thoughts about reorganizing their party on a national basis. Henry J. Raymond, editor of the *New York Times* and the Union Republican party chairman, had urged Johnson's nomination in 1864 on the grounds that it would strengthen the party in the South. The Union Republican movement that had developed during the war reflected such a coalition as Johnson and Raymond sought; it drew votes from Democrats who supported the war and from Unionists in the border, as well as from Republicans. After the war ended Raymond urged the Republican party to support Johnson's efforts to "discard all sectional feeling, and extend its organization into every state" in the South.[9]

Secretary of State Seward also backed Johnson's Reconstruction plans, as he had Lincoln's. But because he hoped that the Republicans would pitch their appeal to former Whigs, he worried lest Johnson's leniency would restore the Democrats to power in the nation. Seward had reason to be concerned, for Johnson was consulting with the Blair family after the war. By late 1865, the Blairs, who had been free soil Democrats before joining the Republicans, had returned to their original loyalties. They were alienated by the policies of the Republicans both in the nation and in the border states; they opposed severe disfranchisement measures and any support for black rights. They shared Johnson's hopes of appealing to Unionist Democratic votes in both sections and were ready to support a party reorganization that would exclude Radical Republicans.[10]

In the summer of 1865, when Congress was not in session, Andrew Johnson announced his terms for restoration of the South. Intent upon pursuing his own hopes of organizing the Union Republican party along more conservative lines, he announced mild requirements for the South. He put each state under a provisional governor, who was to conduct a reorganization of its government. After a majority of Southern whites in a state had taken a simple oath of future allegiance to the Union, they were authorized to hold elections for state officials and congressional representatives. Johnson did exclude from this amnesty, and hence from the vote, a large number of classes of Confederate civil and military leaders, as well as whites who owned more than $20,000 worth of property. These men, however, could apply directly to Johnson for a pardon restoring their political rights, and Johnson issued these pardons rapidly. Finally, as Southern governments reorganized, Johnson expected them to abolish slavery, denounce secession, and repudiate their Confederate debts.

This was the limit of Johnson's program. If the former Confederates accepted his terms, he would welcome them back into the Union. He was unwilling to extend federal power in the South, particularly in the area of protecting black rights. He was prepared to see the Democratic party return to power in the North if it could be reorganized along the lines of the 1864 Union party, with peace Democrat and secessionist elements in the back seat and with Johnson at its head. Although his intentions did not become clear until the spring of 1866, when Johnson did reveal them he lost the support not only of moderate and Radical Republicans, who were concerned about black rights in the South, but also of conservative Republicans such as Raymond and Seward, who did not want to restore Democrats to power, even under a new name.[11]

The breach between Johnson and the Republican party took time to develop. Johnson initially indicated willingness to consider other Reconstruction proposals, and congressional Republicans were willing to wait and see how his plans for the South worked out. Johnson's requirements applied to all former Confederate states except Arkansas, Tennessee, Virginia, and Louisiana, which had already established Unionist governments under Lincoln. Thanks to Johnson's generosity a Confederate majority quickly gained control of all states organized under his plan. In the other four states, a white Unionist minority controlled the governments at the end of the war. Governors Pierpont of Virginia and Wells of Louisiana, eager to broaden the base of their support, extended patronage and the vote to former Confederates and soon lost control of their states to them. By the end of 1865 the only former Confederate states to remain in Unionist hands were Arkansas and Tennessee, where strong test oaths were used to disfranchise Confederates and their sympathizers. In the summer of 1866, after the state supreme court had invalidated Arkansas's loyalty oath, former Confederates seized control of that state as well.[12]

Northern Republicans were greatly shocked by these developments. Those who had hoped to find governments in the South controlled by Unionists sympathetic to the Republican party instead found all but Tennessee in the hands of men who had conducted the rebellion. The Southern leaders in 1865, however, were not original secessionists; indeed, the Democratic party, which had been closely associated with the secessionist movement, was in disarray and disrepute in most of the South. The Southern leaders of 1865 were often former Whigs, who had been opposed to secession. When their states left the Union, however, they supported the Confederate government and by the end of the war had emerged as leaders in their states. These Southern politicians became known as Conservatives, a label that avoided identification with either of the prewar political parties in the South.[13]

The emergence of these Conservative governments in the South presented a challenge both to Johnson and to Northern Republicans. The president, who had hoped to base his government on Unionist yeoman farmers, found instead that Southern voters had elected men who represented the more wealthy and influential classes. Because they were not original secessionists and appeared ready to accept the end of slavery, Johnson was willing to pardon them and contemplated incorporating them into his new, more conservative version of the Republican party. Republicans in Congress, however, were not so eager to embrace the new Southern leadership. Although many identified the Conservatives as the natural leaders of the South and hoped to find them receptive to Northern influences and ideas, they wanted assurances that the new governments would protect the rights of the freedmen and white Unionists. When Congress assembled in December 1865, Republicans decided that Southern representatives would have to be denied seats in Congress until they had clearer evidence of the results of Johnson's program. The president did not immediately object, but he would soon make it clear that he opposed exacting any further conditions of the Southern states.[14]

Evidence was not long in coming that confirmed Republicans in their suspicion of the Johnsonian governments. Northerners in the South wrote their representatives at home that they were threatened and harassed; in the unsettled conditions that existed there, they claimed it was not safe to invest Northern capital. Southern loyalists wrote bitter letters to Republican congressmen, complaining that their devotion to the Union was being rewarded by handing them over to the domination of their former Confederate enemies. Southern legislatures passed Black Codes that severely limited black freedom. Freedmen were denied property rights, freedom of movement, and civil rights such as the opportunity to testify in court against whites. They were rarely given educational opportunities, were refused the right to vote, and faced the physical violence of white vigilante groups and the economic oppression of white landowners.[15]

In response to these conditions in the South, Congress acted first to protect the freedom of the former slaves. During its winter session, legislation was passed strengthening the powers of the Freedmen's Bureau, a federal agency created during the war to protect black interests. The bureau was ordered to supervise labor contracts, provide education for the freedmen, and set up military courts to take cases of blacks denied justice in state courts. Congress in addition passed the Civil Rights Act, declaring blacks to be citizens, defining their citizenship rights, and empowering federal courts to protect those rights. Andrew Johnson, invoking a strict interpretation of the Constitution and arguing that these bills violated state rights, vetoed them both. He also insisted that no legislation affecting the South should be debated until the Southerners took their seats in Congress and criticized Congress for not allowing this to happen. Johnson's determination to limit federal intervention in the South pleased Southern former Confederates and also satisfied Northern Democrats but alienated the vast majority of Republicans, who favored federal protection for blacks in the South. Republican majorities managed to pass both bills over Johnson's veto, but in the process a virtually unbridgeable gap appeared between the Republican party leadership and the president.[16]

The differences between Congress and Johnson over the proper limits of federal power in the South were greatly exacerbated by disagreement over how to restore the former Confederate states. Johnson insisted that Congress should admit the Southern states without further conditions. Many Republicans in Congress, however, were now much more dubious about the strength and quality of Southern Unionism and began to fear that their hopes for the emergence of Radical or Republican parties similar to those in the border states in the former Confederacy would not be fulfilled. Carl Schurz, who had once expressed confidence in the loyalty of the Southern masses, visited the South at the end of the war to gain information on Southern attitudes for President Johnson; he returned convinced that "the Union men of the South are almost all governed by their old prejudices, and no good can be expected of them." General William T. Sherman warned his brother, Senator John Sherman, that "for some time the machinery of state governments must be controlled by the same class of whites as went into the Rebellion against us." Senator Henry Wilson of Massachusetts came back from a trip to Charleston, South Carolina, in May 1865 to declare that he had seen "one loyal union man" in the whole city.[17]

Congress had a great deal of difficulty drafting a plan to restore the former Confederate states that would take into account this apparent weakness in Southern Unionism. Some conservative congressmen, like Jacob D. Cox of Ohio, believed that Congress should not delay the readmittance of the Southern states and that they would have to come in under the leadership of the former Confederates. Radical Republicans disagreed, arguing that there was no need to hurry the Southern states back into the Union. Charles Sumner observed that "thirty years were passed in training for the rebellion. How long it will take to train out of it I know not; *but time is necessary.*" Radicals like Sumner, Stevens, and George Julian believed that the only safe way to restore the Confederate states to the Union was by holding them under military rule and completely reconstructing their social, economic, and political fabric along Northern lines. Only after Southern plantations had been broken up and the land redistributed to blacks and poor whites, leading Confederates deprived of the vote and blacks enfranchised, and systems of public education established would these Radicals allow the South to reenter the Union. By then the power of the old planter class would be completely destroyed and new political organizations created that were led by people more in sympathy with the Republican party.[18]

Most Republicans could not accept this radical program. They had no wish to prolong military control of the South, were too conservative to consider property confiscation, and were hesitant about disfranchising large numbers of Southerners. Many of these moderate Republicans still hoped for the support of Southern whites, and, like Lincoln, did not want to alienate them unnecessarily. But these Republicans were not sure that Johnson's program had gone far enough to protect the freedmen and to ensure the future of the Republican party in the South and in the nation. Most therefore looked to a solution that would return the South reasonably soon, with some minimal guarantees that the results of such a restoration would not be harmful to Northern interests.[19]

Southern Unionists insisted to congressional Republicans that the only way to guarantee loyalty effectively in the South was by disfranchising the former Confederates and reorganizing the new governments with loyal votes. Although Radicals like Stevens and Sumner were ready to make large-scale disfranchisement an element in their program, most Republicans were not. The absence of signifi-

cant loyalist strength in the South was making it clear that such disfranchisement would put governments there in the hands of small
minorities. This most Republicans were unwilling to do, nor did they
think their constituents would accept Reconstruction based on such
unrepresentative governments. Those still eager to court white supporters in the South were also unwilling to risk alienating them by
proscribing large segments of the white population. Disfranchisement in the border states was already proving to be a shaky foundation for the Republican party there; as whites regained the vote
in Kentucky, Delaware, and eventually in Maryland, they used it
against those who had disfranchised them.[20]

Senator Lyman Trumbull of Illinois, who continued to believe that
the masses of Southern whites had been induced to take up arms
against the government "from mistaken views of Northern sentiment, brought about by ambitious and wicked leaders," preferred to
disfranchise only the leading former Confederates. A number of
other Republicans agreed, perhaps hoping to allow Southern Unionists to gain control of the situation by denying former Confederate
leaders access to political power. At the very least, most Republicans
agreed that such men should be denied access to federal office; to
do otherwise would be to reward disloyalty, and Northern voters
wanted to punish, not please, the Confederate leaders.[21]

During the war Congress had enacted a provision to require all
federal officeholders to take an ironclad oath of past loyalty, but even
this form of political proscription threatened to be embarrassing for
the Republican party in the South. Johnson's cabinet members complained that because of the ironclad oath they could not find enough
men eligible to appoint to office, but Southern Unionists complained
when the oath was not enforced. Republican congressmen received
conflicting advice from the South on the subject. An army officer in
Georgia told Senator Richard Yates of Illinois that insisting on the
oath would mean "excluding almost every honorable man in the
South from office"; a Treasury official from the same state, however,
assured Yates that "we do not want the test oath modified. There are
plenty of men in Georgia who can take it." Ultimately, because Congress wanted to control federal patronage in the South and deny
Johnson an opportunity to reward his supporters there, Republicans
decided to keep the oath.[22]

Even though some of the men in the Southern congressional delegations elected in 1865 could take the ironclad oath, Republicans used it to deny all of them the right to take their seats and hence keep the Johnson-organized governments in the South from acquiring congressional representation and recognition. According to many in the South, this action cost the Republicans a significant opportunity to gain white support. W. T. Sherman warned his brother in the Senate that by this step the Republicans had "lost forever the best chance they can ever expect of gaining recruits from the great middle class" in the South. One of Tennessee's congressmen-elect asserted, after he was finally seated, that former Whigs like himself had come to Washington in 1865 expecting to cooperate with the Republicans, "believing them the Union party," but were repelled by their refusal to seat his and other delegations. Such action, he averred, proved the Republicans intended to "be a sectional party." Lewis Hanes, a wartime Unionist from North Carolina, contended in 1866 that if the Republicans had seated that state's delegation the previous year, the party "would have been all powerful in North Carolina today." A. H. H. Stuart, a prominent Whig from Virginia, told Horace Greeley that the Republicans' rejection of the Southern delegation had cost them support by forcing Southern whites to cooperate with the Democrats.[23]

Fearing such political repercussions of proscriptive measures, Republican moderates like Greeley and John Andrew recommended granting amnesty to former Confederates. Both men believed that the Conservatives elected to office in the South represented the natural leaders of their section, with whom the Republicans were somehow going to have to come to terms. In return for this Northern generosity, however, both men hoped that the Southern leaders would agree to treat the black population in their states fairly and give them at least qualified suffrage, based on some literacy or educational test. Some of the moderate Republicans were in touch with Conservative leaders in the South and believed that they would indeed support giving some blacks the vote. The result, according to Greeley, would bring a "mixed-color Republicanism" that would control at least some of the Southern states.[24]

The possibility of enfranchising blacks as a way to support loyal, preferably Republican, governments in the South had emerged with the end of the war. Until then, Northern Republicans who had anticipated building their party in the South had considered only white

voters. The difficulty of locating and developing that Unionist white
vote during the war and immediately afterward, however, and the
unwillingness of many Republicans to endorse amnesty for whites,
led Northern congressmen to eye the potential of a black electorate.
Such enfranchisement would help blacks to protect their newly won
freedom and also build up a party in the South that would cooperate
with the Republicans. A number of Northern Republicans who either
visited the South immediately after the war or who had contacts with
Unionist Southerners became convinced that Southern white Unionists were doomed without black political support. Chief Justice Salmon P. Chase returned from his tour of the South warning that "the
old secession element is rapidly gaining the ascendancy in consequence of the disfranchisement of the colored loyalists"; he urged
that blacks be given the vote. John Covode, congressman from Pennsylvania, visited New Orleans early in the summer of 1865 and returned to Washington convinced that black suffrage "is no longer a
matter of taste but of necessity" if Louisiana were to remain in loyal
hands. His colleague William D. Kelley, also of Pennsylvania, who
had kept in close touch with Louisiana Republicans, agreed with
Covode's assessment. Henry Wilson returned from South Carolina in
1865 convinced that the South "must be kept in subjection by the
bayonet of the white man or the ballot of the black man," and he
favored the ballot.[25]

Some Republican politicians, however, were reluctant to endorse
Negro suffrage during the immediate postwar era. Some of the most
radical, like Stevens and Julian, disagreed with Wilson and preferred
the bayonet to the ballot. They believed that black suffrage should
not be undertaken until the political, social, and economic reorganization of the South they favored had taken place. Otherwise, they
feared the newly enfranchised voters would fall under the control
of their former owners and vote as they were told. Other Republicans, such as Governor Oliver P. Morton of Indiana and Senator
William Pitt Fessenden of Maine, who were not Radicals, were likewise doubtful that the black vote would make a dependable base for
the Republican party in the South. Some Republicans worried that
enfranchising blacks would forever alienate Southern white allies.
Border state Republicans, with some exceptions, felt this way and
refused to call for Negro suffrage in their own states. Most important, Republicans in Congress were acutely aware that Negro suf-

frage was an unpopular issue in many areas of the North. Blacks could not vote in most Northern states, and in 1865 voters from Connecticut, Minnesota, and Wisconsin refused to amend their constitutions to allow black suffrage.[26]

Because of internal disagreement over the advisability of seeking the vote for blacks, when Republicans began to formulate their Reconstruction program in 1866, they chose to subordinate the suffrage issue to the question of how much representation the Southern states would be entitled to upon their return to the Union. With slavery abolished, Republicans were alarmed that the Southern states could now count their entire black population in apportioning representation in Congress. The South would then gain seats at the very time that Republicans had doubts about Southern loyalty. Hence Republicans decided to link the question of Negro suffrage to the issue of representation. They drafted a constitutional amendment stipulating that if the Southern states chose to enfranchise their black population, they would receive the additional seats; if not, they would lose as many seats as the black population represented. Congress thereby refused to require Negro suffrage of the South; Republicans hoped that Southern whites would voluntarily agree to enfranchise blacks rather than lose strength in Congress. If they chose not to enfranchise blacks, the South would return with fewer votes in the House than it had had before the war.[27]

It took Congress months to arrive at this compromise on the issue of black suffrage. Republicans also experienced difficulty in determining whether the political rights of Southern whites should be limited. The House was ready to deprive at least some classes of whites of the vote, but the Senate strongly opposed the idea, and the compromise section that finally went into the amendment instead deprived a number of former Confederates of the right to hold state or federal office. The amendment did provide that this disability could be removed by a two-thirds vote of both houses of Congress. Thus this measure attempted to compromise the views of Radicals, who wanted to destroy forever the power of the Southern aristocracy, and more conservative Republicans, who wanted to conciliate the same aristocracy. It also marked another effort by the Republicans to drive a wedge between the masses of Southern whites and their leaders, hoping to encourage the masses to look to their own ranks for candidates for office.[28]

In addition to the sections on representation and political disqualifications, Congress approved a provision declaring blacks to be citizens of the United States and of the states wherein they resided and identifying the rights of citizens in general terms; other provisions pledged the government to honor the national debt and not to reimburse Southerners for their lost slave property. The final result, which Congress approved in July, was sent out to the states as a proposed Fourteenth Amendment to the Constitution.

From beginning to end, the amendment had been drafted with an eye to the Northern electorate. Congressional elections were coming in the North in the fall of 1866, and the amendment was sure to become an issue in the campaign. The Republicans who drew it up were convinced that their Northern constituents would accept no more and demand no less than what the amendment contained.[29] Reluctant to press forward with extended military control of the South, disfranchisement of whites, or enfranchisement of blacks, the Republicans had consequently failed to build a suitable basis for party expansion in the South. The most they felt able to do was put constitutional limitations on the power of Southerners to disrupt Northern interests once they were back in the Union. The amendment left much in the hands of the majority of Southern whites. They could choose whether or not to enfranchise blacks, and, most important, could decide whether or not to accept the amendment at all. The more optimistic Republicans hoped that the Southerners would take the proposal in good grace as the legitimate terms of the victors offered to the vanquished. They also hoped that white Southerners would agree to honor the citizenship rights of blacks, provide at least qualified suffrage for them, and elect state and federal officials more acceptable to the North than the men holding office under Johnson's program.[30]

Republicans did refuse to promise that the Southern states would be readmitted upon ratification, a point made by many opponents of the amendment in the South. The Northern public was eager to resolve the Reconstruction question, however, and it would have been difficult to deny any Southern state readmission if it had accepted the amendment. The first and, as events were to prove, the only Southern state to test Congress's will in this matter was Tennessee, whose legislature rushed through ratification in July. Tennessee was the only state to remain in loyal hands throughout the postwar period. Under the leadership of Governor William G. Brownlow, the Tennessee legislature had already passed liberal codes for blacks, which gave them more civil rights than they had received anywhere else in the South. Although the Tennessee Unionists turned a deaf ear to black petitions for the right to vote, Governor Brownlow admitted that he would rather let illiterate blacks vote than disloyal whites, and by the summer of 1866 he was endorsing qualified suffrage for the freedmen. The legislature did enact stringent laws barring former Confederates from office and the ballot box, and most of the state's congressional delegation could take the ironclad oath. Brownlow and his followers had not identified themselves as Republicans, but as the struggle between Johnson and the Congress developed in 1866, the governor announced that he sided with the congressional Republicans and not with the president. As a former Whig, Brownlow feared that Johnson's leniency toward the South would bring the Democrats back to power, both in the nation and in Tennessee. Hence he hoped Congress would protect Unionists like himself, and after considerable pressure he got his state legislature to ratify the amendment.[31]

Tennessee's action posed a problem to the Republican leadership in Congress. Moderates who hoped to build a party in the South on white votes were eager to admit the state, arguing that Tennessee had complied fully with Northern expectations. To turn Tennessee away at this point, they argued, would be to discourage white Unionists elsewhere in the South who might wish to follow Tennessee's example. Republican Radicals such as Thaddeus Stevens were reluctant to admit the Volunteer State, fearing the action would set a precedent for admitting the other Southern states before further conditions could be exacted of the South. Many Radicals wanted to require universal suffrage and complained that Tennessee had not provided it.[32]

After the Radicals failed to get Congress to require black suffrage in Tennessee, they gave up their effort to delay restoring the state. The moderates prevailed because of their insistence that Tennesseans had demonstrated their loyalty and there was no reason to keep them out; furthermore, they believed that the state would soon voluntarily enfranchise its black population. These moderates still wanted to obtain Southern acquiescence in Northern terms and did not wish to force further conditions upon the South. Many Northern congressmen were also convinced that despite any legislative provision to that effect, their constituents expected the Southern states to be returned when they had ratified the amendment. To deny Tennessee admittance, then, was to risk losing Northern support at a time when vital congressional elections were about to be held. Radicals were displeased; Theodore Tilton, editor of the *New York Independent*, bemoaned the decision to admit Tennessee without Negro suffrage, contending that the Republicans "abandoned for the sake of party a principle which they ought to have maintained." Once again, with an eye on the forthcoming congressional elections, Northern Republicans let their concerns about Northern attitudes govern their disposition of Southern affairs.[33]

The final action in readmitting Tennessee took place in the Senate, where one of the state's senators-elect, David Patterson, was unable to take the ironclad oath. Patterson's situation provided excellent evidence of the difficulty of identifying and disfranchising supposed Confederate sympathizers; no one questioned his loyalty to the Union, but he had held a minor post under the Confederate state government during the war and hence could not take the oath. The Senate compromised by altering the oath to suit Patterson's situation, but the problem of discriminating against former Confederates without injuring Unionists remained to confound party leaders.[34]

Republican hopes that the rest of the Southern states might accept the Fourteenth Amendment were not to be realized. President Johnson made known his opposition to the proposal and encouraged the Southern Conservative leadership to expect restoration without having to meet any congressional conditions. Everywhere in the South the men who controlled the state governments were prepared to reject the amendment. The only Southern whites to favor it were the Unionists, who saw in the measure some protection against the power of their Conservative opponents. But in every state the sides were mismatched; the amendment's opponents controlled the governments, had the support of the president and Northern Democrats, and represented the bulk of the wealth, education, and political experience of the South. In 1866, the Unionists were everywhere in a minority. They lacked skilled leadership, significant newspaper support, and effective organization.[35]

The Southern loyalists clearly needed outside support, and they looked increasingly to Northern Republicans to provide it. In many cases, they were already identifying themselves with the Republican party and presented the Northerners an opportunity to establish at least a foothold for their organization in most Southern states. In 1866, however, other than drafting the compromise Fourteenth Amendment, Northern Republicans offered their Southern allies little help and encouragement. Most Republicans were poorly informed about the Southern political situation, but it was increasingly clear to them that the Unionists were a beleaguered minority who could never come to power in their own states, at least unless they had black support. They had little acquaintance with, or knowledge of, the Southern loyalists and were sometimes suspicious of them. Even John Forney's *Philadelphia Press*, which was sympathetic to the plight of the Southern Unionists, did not want a bitter and vindictive man like William G. Brownlow of Tennessee as governor of Pennsylvania.[36]

Consequently, no prominent Northern Republican politician offered any private aid or advice to the embattled Southern white minority, nor did the Republican party organization, which was customarily dormant between presidential elections, send any help southward. Most Northern assistance to the struggling Unionists in the South came from private associations, particularly the Union League, and from Northerners who were already present in the South, such as missionaries, teachers, and holders of federal patronage. Such Northern emissaries, particularly officials in the Freedmen's Bureau and representatives of Northern churches and freedmen's aid societies, also encouraged black leaders who were organizing their followers to petition for suffrage. None of this organizing effort was coordinated, however, and when initiatives appeared to organize black and white loyalists on an interstate basis and to encourage Southern loyalist cooperation with Northern Republicans, these initiatives came from the South, not the North.

During the war the Union League had moved through the border states and into areas of the South occupied by Union troops. Promoted in part by army officers and federal officeholders, it had spread most rapidly in areas of the South where opposition to secession had been significant. It was strongest in Tennessee, where its members supported the Brownlow regime. It was less well organized in Arkansas, where it also backed the Unionist government. By the end of the war the league had also appeared in the northern counties of Alabama and Georgia and was just beginning to organize in Texas. By 1866 the national council of the Union League, claiming there were two million potential white recruits for the Republican party in the South, was calling for the organization of the league in every state.[37]

Northern league members watching the South for signs of Unionist organizations similar to that of Brownlow's party in Tennessee were particularly hopeful about North Carolina.[38] The mountainous western regions of that state had exhibited much disaffection from the Confederacy during the war and had supported a Unionist movement led by William W. Holden, a prewar Democratic leader. In 1865 President Johnson named Holden provisional governor of North Carolina. Holden used his new position to build a Union party, which he hoped would deny former Confederate Conservatives control of the state. He appealed to whites who had opposed the Confederacy and to inhabitants of the western counties who were unhappy at the dominance of the state by easterners, many of whom were former slaveholders. Holden had almost no outside help; the Union League had not yet appeared in the state, and Republican politicians in the North, who were mainly ignorant about the state's politics, regarded Holden with suspicion. His Unionist party failed to elect him governor in the fall elections in 1865, and North Carolina fell under the control of the Conservatives.[39]

Events in Texas followed a pattern similar to that in North Carolina. Here, too, Johnson's provisional governor, A. J. Hamilton, sought to organize a coalition of Unionists to control the state. Like Holden, Hamilton played upon regional differences, hoping to form an alliance of various interests who opposed domination of Texas by the planters in the central part of the state. Hamilton tried to keep former Confederates out of office and to delay state elections until he could organize his Unionist party more effectively. When the elections were eventually held in June 1866, however, Conservatives easily gained control of Texas.[40]

Arkansas was the only other Southern state where loyal whites had enough organization to contest for control of the government with the former Confederate Conservatives, but in August 1866, after the state's supreme court had invalidated the loyalists' test oath disfranchising former Confederates, the Conservatives easily defeated Governor Isaac Murphy's Unionist party. Although white loyalists organized Union Leagues in the northern counties of Alabama and Georgia and in at least one county in Mississippi, they did not run candidates for election in any of these states. By the summer of 1866, loyalists in the South were all following the lead of Governor Brownlow of Tennessee, looking to congressional Republicans to protect them against President Johnson and his Southern governments made up of former Confederates.[41]

Despite their plight, most white Unionists in the South initially chose not to ally themselves with blacks in their states who were agitating for the vote. Their petitions to Congress asked for military government and disfranchisement of former Confederates, but not for black enfranchisement. Because white loyalists were a minority in every state, black enfranchisement would greatly boost the anti-Conservative vote, but racial antagonisms inhibited cooperation between the two groups except in isolated cases.[42] Blacks were organizing and holding conventions in every Southern state in 1865 and 1866 and were clearly gaining in political sophistication. In Tennessee, blacks held several mass conventions to petition the Unionist legislature for the franchise, but to no avail. By the summer of 1866, Governor Brownlow, worried about maintaining his regime, was considering at least qualified suffrage for blacks, but he got little support from his white followers for the idea. In North Carolina, as in other Southern states, blacks organized the Equal Rights League to agitate for suffrage. William Holden spoke to a league convention and expressed some sympathy for its efforts but refused to commit his Union party to its support.[43] No other prominent Unionist white in the South endorsed black suffrage until late in 1866, when many of them finally became convinced of its necessity.

Congressional Republicans also failed to provide any encouragement to Southern blacks fighting for the vote, and consequently it was left to a scattered group of Northern Union League organizers, missionaries, and government officials in the South to lend them a hand. By 1866 the national Union League leadership was endorsing the organization of blacks as well as whites into local councils. In October 1865, the league's leadership convinced General O. O. Howard, commissioner of the Freedmen's Bureau, to allow his agents to distribute league pamphlets to blacks in the South. James Edmunds, president of the Union League of America, believed that such organization of blacks would stimulate their political ambition and prepare them for using the vote intelligently when enfranchisement came. Despite his hopes, however, the state and local councils in Tennessee, Arkansas, Texas, North Carolina, Mississippi, Alabama, and Georgia included only whites.[44]

In Georgia, the Union League in 1866 did contribute funds that allowed John Bryant, a white Freedmen's Bureau agent, and Simeon Baird, a Georgia mulatto, to establish the *Loyal Georgian*, a newspaper devoted to encouraging black political aspirations. Early in the year Bryant also had convened a meeting of freedmen in Augusta to form the Georgia Equal Rights Association, which called for limited suffrage for blacks. The group proved to be an important training ground for future black politicians and helped raise the political consciousness of freedmen in the state. Henry M. Turner, a black minister in the African Methodist Episcopal church, joined the organization and in the spring of 1866 journeyed north to gather funds for the *Loyal Georgian*. Turner was dismayed to find that Republicans in Washington had no knowledge of the association, and although they were glad to hear about the newspaper, they proved reluctant to aid it with subscriptions. Turner did get some prominent Republicans to endorse the *Loyal Georgian*, but he got no money.[45]

Bryant's labors in behalf of black political awareness in Georgia were not appreciated by his superior, General David Tillson, who wanted blacks to settle down to work and not waste time agitating for the vote.[46] Although Tillson's attitude was not unusual among Freedmen's Bureau officers in the South, there were many, like Bryant, who supported black political aspirations. In Tennessee the assistant commissioner of the bureau, Clinton B. Fisk, endorsed a petition from blacks asking the state legislature to grant them suffrage based on literacy tests; in Alabama Wager Swayne, head of the bureau in that state, did the same. Swayne and John Keffer, also on the bureau's staff, were helpful in organizing the Union League among whites in the northern counties of Alabama.[47]

In South Carolina, Freedmen's Bureau agents, along with white and black missionaries from the North, encouraged black political organization even during the war. As early as the summer of 1864 a Unionist meeting in the Sea Islands had sent an integrated delegation to the Republican national convention. By the end of the war, Union League organizers, who had not been able to create any white councils in the state, were having success in recruiting blacks. Northerners were quick to aid the league. In the spring of 1865, when blacks in Charleston organized a council, James Redpath, a white missionary teaching in a freedmen's school in the city, was on hand to offer advice. Another Northerner active in organizing the Union League in the state was Francis Cardozo, a black minister from Connecticut who came to the state in 1865 under the auspices of the American Missionary Association. In 1865 and 1866 several Northern officers of the Freedmen's Bureau, including two whites, Assistant Commissioner Rufus Saxton and Superintendent of Education Reuben Tomlinson, and two blacks, Martin Delaney and O. S. B. Wall, also encouraged blacks to organize and demand the vote.[48]

In Florida, Freedmen's Bureau agents, along with Northerners holding federal patronage posts in the state, were active in promoting organizations for both white Unionists and blacks. In 1864 Harrison Reed, a federal tax commissioner, helped organize the Union Republican Club in Jacksonville that sent a delegation to the Republican national convention. He and other tax commissioners also organized white Union Leagues in the area around Jacksonville, and by the end of the war blacks were forming their own councils. When Salmon P. Chase visited Fernandina in May 1865, he found that blacks were organizing leagues everywhere and warned President Johnson that "they form a power which no wise statesman will disregard." In the summer of 1866 Thomas Osborne, the assistant commissioner of the Freedmen's Bureau for Florida, who believed that universal suffrage was a necessity for the South, organized secret Lincoln Brotherhoods among blacks, first in Tallahassee and then across the northern part of the state.[49]

Although black political activity was increasing in both South Carolina and Florida, the white Unionist movement was nonexistent in the former state and weak and divided in the latter. In only two states of the South, Virginia and Louisiana, was there any effort before the end of 1866 to organize both whites and blacks in a coordinated opposition to the state Conservative governments, and in both states the Unionists agreed to call themselves Republicans.

In Virginia, the state's handful of Republicans had lent their support to the Unionist government of Francis H. Pierpont, which Lincoln had recognized early in the war. As peace returned to the Old Dominion, Pierpont, who recognized that his base of support was extremely small, sought to enlarge it by appealing to moderates of both Whig and Democratic antecedents; he hoped to build a party somewhat like that Holden was attempting in North Carolina. Eager for expanded white support, Pierpont favored amnesty for Confederates and opposed enfranchisement of blacks. To his dismay, however, former Confederate Conservatives took advantage of the removal of disfranchisement provisions to dislodge the wartime Unionists from power in Virginia. Although Pierpont remained governor, former Confederates controlled the legislature and the Virginia congressional delegation.

Opponents of Pierpont's cautious course sought to mobilize white loyalists and blacks. The Union League, which had entered the state with federal troops during the war, was actively recruiting blacks by the summer of 1865. One of the league organizers assured Massachusetts Republican Benjamin Butler that if the blacks gained the vote, "a truly Republican party could be organized in the state with the certainty of success." In June of that year, radical Unionists, whose ranks were drawn chiefly from the men who had organized the Republican party in the state, held a convention in Alexandria and passed resolutions endorsing black suffrage. In May of the following year, another group of loyalist whites, chiefly former Whigs led by John Minor Botts, held a meeting in Alexandria to organize resistance to Pierpont's government on a more moderate basis. This convention drafted resolutions condemning the existing state government, called for disfranchisement of Confederates, and, after some debate, endorsed qualified suffrage for blacks. The delegates then declared that they were founding the Union Republican party.[50]

Northern whites did not play an important role in expanding Republican organization in Virginia. A few federal officeholders did become involved, and General Alfred Terry, who in 1865 commanded Union occupation forces in the state, helped the Republicans establish a newspaper in Richmond.[51] Northerners played a more important part in creating the Republican party in Louisiana, but here, too, the main impetus came from whites and blacks who were either natives of the state or had resided there for some years. Louisiana's white Unionists were far ahead of their compatriots in other Southern states in recognizing the claims of blacks for the vote and organizing them politically. New Orleans, which had been the center of wartime Unionist activity, had a large population of free, educated, and prosperous blacks, who had been agitating for the vote since early in 1864. The Durant faction of the Union party had endorsed at least qualified Negro suffrage before the war ended. By the summer of 1865, when with Johnson's aid the state had fallen under the control of Conservatives, moderate Unionists represented by Michael Hahn and Nathaniel Banks also endorsed Negro suffrage. In September, both wings of the Unionist party met in an interracial convention in New Orleans and petitioned Congress to enact universal suffrage. A number of federal officers in the state, led by Assistant Commissioners Absalom Baird and Thomas Conway of the Freedmen's Bureau, encouraged these steps. The convention delegates agreed to adopt the name Republican for their party and put several blacks on their state committee. Knowing that they stood no chance in the state elections that fall, the Republicans held their own mock election, in which large numbers of blacks voted.[52]

Thus, by the summer of 1866, halting efforts were under way in most Southern states to organize white Unionist parties, to encourage blacks to seek the vote, and to mount some protest against the Conservative regimes that governed every state except Tennessee. Although some Unionist leaders visited Washington and consulted with Republican leaders there, most of the anti-Conservative organization took place without guidance from the North. Some Republicans in Washington did try to maintain contacts with their brethren in Louisiana because the party there was avowedly Republican and a more significant factor than in any other Southern state. Even Louisiana Republican leaders, however, were frustrated at not obtaining any more assistance and encouragement from Washington and complained that they were being ignored.[53]

In the absence of any encouragement from Congress, in the summer of 1866 Louisiana Republicans decided to initiate their own movement to reorganize the state. In this effort, they now had the support of Governor Wells, who had begun to realize that former Confederates were bent on controlling the state and driving all Unionists, including Wells, out of power. Hence the governor was drawn in the direction of the Republicans; he too concluded that Negro suffrage would be necessary to protect the interests of both white and black loyalists in the state. Wells and some of his advisers decided to reconvene the 1864 constitutional convention and rewrite the constitution to allow blacks to vote. Uneasy about taking such a provocative step without assurances of support from Washington,

Louisiana Republicans wired Republican congressional leaders but got no response. An emissary was then sent to the capital from New Orleans, and he returned complaining that the congressional Radicals were not supportive enough. Although Republicans expressed sympathy with the plight of their Louisiana compatriots, they claimed Congress had no authority to reorganize the state.[54]

The Louisiana Republicans nonetheless proceeded with their plans and ordered the constitutional convention to meet on July 30, 1866. When the delegates met in New Orleans on that day, they were joined by large numbers of blacks who marched to the convention hall. There they were met by a mob of angry whites, determined to prevent the convention from assembling. Shooting began, and in the resulting carnage at least 37 Unionists were killed and another 136 wounded; most of the victims were blacks.

The New Orleans riot aroused the North and greatly weakened Andrew Johnson's contention that under his policy life and property were safe in the Southern states. Radicals North and South now used the riot as further evidence of the need for Congress to intervene to protect loyal inhabitants of the Southern states by reconstituting their governments.[55] The riot also stimulated efforts of Southern Unionists to organize a conference of representatives of the loyal population of all the Southern states to coordinate policy and bring their plight to the attention of the Northern people before the fall elections. It was clear that the chief issue in the election would be Reconstruction policy; Northern voters would be asked to render a verdict on the president's program by choosing congressmen pledged either to his course or to support of the Fourteenth Amendment.

On June 25, 1866, Andrew Johnson's supporters had already seized the initiative by calling for a convention in Philadelphia of all Northerners of both parties who supported the president. Seeking to demonstrate that their movement, which some of the organizers characterized as an attempt to reconstruct the National Union party of 1864, was truly national in scope and aimed at restoring national harmony, the call requested Southern states to send delegations as well, and many Southern Conservatives agreed to cooperate.[56]

The call to the Philadelphia National Union convention sparked Southern Unionists into recommending a counterconvention of their own to rally support for Congress and to condemn Johnson's Conservative governments. Radical members of the Tennessee congressional delegation, who in July were still waiting to take their seats, were particularly eager to rally Unionists from across the South to demonstrate that they were more numerous than many Northerners had come to believe. They were joined in Washington by other staunch Southern Unionists who had come to the capital to present their case to Republican leaders. The former provisional governor of Texas, Andrew J. Hamilton, was involved, as was Daniel H. Bingham of Alabama, who had been driven out of the state because of his strong Unionist views. A number of Republicans from the neighboring state of Virginia also participated in the Unionists' deliberations. On July 4, 1866, these men issued a call addressed to the "Loyal Unionists of the South," asking them to attend a convention in Philadelphia on September 3. The authors of the statement condemned the state governments established by Johnson for failing to honor the equal rights of all of their citizens and called upon "Congress, and the great Union party" to protect the Southern loyalists. The purpose of the convention, according to its initiators, was to bring these loyalists "into conjunctive action with the true friends of Republican government in the North." After some discussion, the men who issued the call agreed to invite representatives from the border states as well as the unreconstructed states; this decision was to have a great effect on the deliberations of the convention.[57]

The Philadelphia loyalist convention proved to be an important milestone in the formation of a Southern Republican party. Although procedures for selecting delegates varied from state to state and often resulted in the choice of men who represented very small constituencies, the convention call did provide the impetus for holding meetings or conventions in states where Unionists were poorly organized. The largest delegations came from the border states and from Virginia and Tennessee; the rest of the unreconstructed states sent much smaller numbers. In several states Unionists found it difficult to publicize the convention call, for newspapers were generally hostile to the idea. Mississippi and Georgia, for example, which had no organized Unionist party, sent only a few delegates; Holden's Unionist organization in North Carolina decided not to send representatives, but several men came from that state anyway, representing local constituencies. The atmosphere in South Carolina was so hostile to Unionist efforts that no one from that state attempted to travel to Philadelphia, making it the only Southern state to be unrepresented. The lack of substantial delegations from the unreconstructed states reinforced the contention of Henry Raymond's *New York Times* that the Southerners in Philadelphia represented only a small minority of whites in their home states. Even the editor of the *Great Republic*, the newspaper of the Union League, admitted that it was difficult to determine if the Southern representatives "were the fair exponents of popular sentiment" at home.[58]

If the Philadelphia convention provided an opportunity for the minority of Southern Unionists to improve their organization and draw the nation's attention to their plight, it also gave them a chance to mix for the first time with significant numbers of Northern Republican leaders. Although Johnson's opponents in both sections of the Union were working toward the same ends—defeat of the president's program and protection for black and white loyalists in the South—they had not yet effectively merged their efforts. Both Southern organizers of the convention and their leading Northern sympathizers, such as William D. Kelley of Pennsylvania and Benjamin Butler of Massachusetts, saw in the Philadelphia meeting an opportunity to push the organization of the Republican party further into the South. Initially, however, the Northern response to the convention was not enthusiastic. Congress was still engaged in debates over Reconstruction and remained in session until the end of July. With a congressional campaign in the offing, Republicans then rushed home to canvass for votes.[59]

In the middle of August, John W. Forney, editor of the *Washington Chronicle* and a dedicated spokesman for the Southern Unionists, anxiously wrote to Senator Zachariah Chandler of Michigan, urging him to help "call your best men" to Philadelphia. By the end of the month, the party's machinery had begun to move. Wisconsin's governor Lucius Fairchild worked hard to rally state governors to support the convention, and the governors in turn used their state committees to urge leading senators and representatives to attend. Ultimately, almost every Northern Republican leader, from both state and national governments, attended the convention, mingling there with almost four hundred delegates from the Southern states. From the standpoint of public relations, the loyalist gathering was a great success in offsetting the impact of President Johnson's Union convention. Even reporters from papers hostile to the gathering noted that the crowds in Philadelphia were huge, the speakers effective, and the delegates generally confident about defeating Johnson's backers in the fall congressional elections.[60]

Beneath the surface unanimity and enthusiasm, however, tensions appeared between Southern and Northern delegates. Few of the men from either section had had any previous association with those from the other; they were strangers, attempting to define a common ground upon which to organize their party and resist the president. The contrast between the Northern and Southern delegations was striking. The Northern states were represented by men who held positions of power and influence; they included in their ranks governors, senators, representatives, mayors, and newspaper editors. In almost every state they could claim to represent the majority of the voters. The Southern delegates, however, represented a minority of whites in their states; in some cases their constituencies were almost nonexistent. Few were professional politicians; they were often plain, politically inexperienced men who faced hostile majorities at home. Nonetheless, they were determined and earnest, convinced that they were doomed if they could not gain control of their state governments.[61]

By September most delegates from the unreconstructed Southern states had concluded that the only solution to their plight was enfranchisement of the freedmen. With the black vote, the loyal whites hoped to control their states. For these white loyalists, the Fourteenth Amendment, though acceptable, was not enough. They came to Philadelphia earnestly intent upon convincing the Northern Republicans to endorse Negro suffrage. Although some of the Radical members of the party agreed with the Southerners, most were convinced that calling for black enfranchisement would cost them the 1866 elections. Hence most Northern delegates at Philadelphia hoped to discourage any discussion of the issue.[62]

When they arrived in Philadelphia, Southern delegates were fearful that Northern Republicans would force them to accept a program "calculated to subserve the interests of the party north of Mason and Dixon's line to the detriment of their Southern constituents." Hence they insisted that they meet independently to formulate their own resolutions without any appearance of Northern dictation. Consequently, after listening to several speeches attacking Johnson and praising the Southern loyalists for their staunch Unionism, Northern and Southern delegations withdrew to separate meetings. In the Northern conclave, much debate ensued over the advisability of allowing the Southerners to state a radical position on Reconstruction that would embarrass the Republican party in the coming elections. Governor Oliver P. Morton of Indiana insisted that "our southern friends do not want to take any action that we cannot sustain. They are helpless. . . . We have got to fight the battle for them." Although some Radical Republicans in Philadelphia spoke for Negro suffrage, the majority, led by Morton and the other state governors, lobbied with individual members of the Southern delegations, warning them that saddling the Republicans with any program that went beyond the Fourteenth Amendment would bring defeat in the fall.[63]

Northern lobbying efforts increased tensions that already existed within the Southern meeting. Although most delegates from the unreconstructed states favored Negro suffrage, representatives from the border states, particularly Maryland and West Virginia, were strongly opposed to the idea. They were barely able to control their own states through disfranchisement of former Confederates and were convinced that any endorsement of Negro suffrage would forever destroy their thin majorities. When a resolution endorsing black voting was introduced, Governor Arthur Boreman of West Virginia exclaimed that "we did not come here to commit suicide" and argued that if the convention endorsed the resolution, "we are damned to all eternity." Hamilton of Texas led the argument for the men from the unreconstructed states, pointing out that the purpose of the convention was to formulate a policy that would protect Unionists in those states and not to devise a way to elect one more congressman from the border states. Unfortunately for Hamilton and his followers, however, the border delegations, along with some sympathizers from Virginia, had the votes to control the convention.[64]

Ultimately, after some bitter debate, the Southerners worked out a compromise. The convention approved a set of resolutions condemning the president's plan and endorsing congressional intervention in Reconstruction; then the border states withdrew, allowing the delegates from the unreconstructed states to draft a resolution endorsing Negro suffrage. In this way border state Republicans could claim they were not associated with the idea, and Northern Republicans could endorse the more moderate set of resolutions drafted by the entire convention.[65]

The Philadelphia convention dramatically revealed some of the major problems confronting Republicans as they attempted to nationalize their party. Border state Republicans preferred to try to maintain power by disfranchising some of their opponents; Unionists in the unreconstructed states, who were much fewer in number, realized that their salvation lay in black suffrage. Northern Republicans, however, found it difficult to endorse either white disfranchisement or black enfranchisement. Facing a critical election at home, they preferred to stand on the platform created by the Fourteenth Amendment. But, as a correspondent of the *New York Times* noted, the Northern quest for loyal governments in the South led logically to black suffrage; there were simply not enough white Unionists there on which to base new governments. Yet the blacks, who had become clearly necessary to the future of the Republican party in the South, were an embarrassment to the Republicans in the North. Even Thaddeus Stevens of Pennsylvania objected when Frederick Douglass, a leading Northern black spokesman for racial equality, attended the convention as a delegate from New York, appearing arm-in-arm with the white editor of the *New York Independent*, Theodore Tilton. Oliver Morton and some other Northern Republicans attempted to persuade Douglass to return home, but he refused, instead giving a bold speech to the Southern delegations urging them to endorse Negro suffrage. Only one other black, a representative from Louisiana, attended the convention, and his presence was clearly an embarrassment to many of the white delegates.[66]

Men from the Deep South were angry over their treatment at Philadelphia. Hamilton of Texas expressed his disappointment that "a few Northern men . . . thought more of their own election to Congress than they did of alleviating our condition at home." Determined to take their case to the Northern electorate, delegates from the unreconstructed states selected a committee of speakers to travel through the North, promoting congressional candidates who endorsed Negro suffrage. Many Southern Republicans realized, however, that Governor Morton was right; without Northern success at the polls, they were doomed. As one of them observed, the racial prejudices of voters in such key states as Pennsylvania, Indiana, and Ohio would have to be acknowledged. Southern Republicans were ahead of their party; perhaps after the election the Northerners would catch up.[67]

Although congressional elections were held in the border states, as well as the North, again, as in 1860 and 1864, Republicans kept their best speakers north of the Ohio River. The chairman of the Missouri Radical Union state executive committee wrote several prominent northern Republicans asking them to make speaking tours in his state, but only Benjamin Butler appeared. Instead, as in previous elections, Southern speakers were sent North. Republicans never forgot that their base of support still lay in the states that had elected Lincoln in 1860; protecting that base continued to take priority over extending the party southward.[68]

Fortunately for the Southerners, the election returns from the North revealed substantial majorities for congressional candidates who endorsed the Fourteenth Amendment and opposed Johnson's program. Overwhelming Republican dominance in the forthcoming Fortieth Congress was assured. The party's only reverse occurred in Maryland, where the governor undermined the application of the state's loyalty oath through his appointments of registrars and thereby enabled the Democrats to gain control of the state. Radicals in Missouri and West Virginia continued to control elections through disfranchisement acts; Delaware and Kentucky, which lacked such legislation, remained under Democratic control.[69]

Border state returns suggested the inadvisability of continued reliance on disfranchisement to maintain Republican or Radical control there. Although Forney's *Washington Chronicle* dismissed the defeats in Maryland and Delaware as inconsequential, in light of Republican success across the North he hoped that Radicals in those two states, as well as elsewhere in the border, would see the logic of moving toward universal suffrage. Other Northern Republican newspapers also called on the border to enfranchise the blacks before the entire region was lost to the Conservatives. After the fall elections, Radicals in Missouri and Maryland began to agitate for Negro suffrage, encouraged by the example of Governor William G. Brownlow of Tennessee. Despite disfranchisement acts in his state, Conservative strength was increasing, and he recognized the advisability of adding some sixty to seventy thousand black votes to the Radical column. Although Brownlow's followers in eastern Tennessee were opposed to any form of racial equality, they saw the practicality of his advice, and in January 1867 Tennessee became the first Southern state to extend the vote to blacks.[70]

Many Radicals, North and South, saw in Tennessee the realization of their hopes for building a Republican party in the South. The state government and congressional delegation were in the hands of Republicans, and the party had moved to strengthen its base by enfranchising blacks. Voting results in the unreconstructed states proved again the futility of organizing Republican or Unionist tickets on white support alone. In only three states, Arkansas, Texas, and North Carolina, did Unionists contest elections. They put up candidates for state offices and endorsed the Fourteenth Amendment; in each case, they were overwhelmingly defeated.[71] If white loyalists were to gain control of their state governments, Congress would have to achieve it by intervening to reorganize them on the basis of black suffrage. Only then would the Republican party have a chance for success. In December 1866, a group of Radical Unionists in Arkansas organized a state Republican party and sent a delegation to Washington asking Congress to abolish the existing state government and reorganize one based on the votes of all loyal men, black and white. At the same time many of the white Unionists who had organized the Philadelphia convention created the Southern Republican Association and established a lobby in the capital to seek the implementation of the program called for by Arkansas Republicans.[72]

In Washington, momentum was now swinging behind the Radicals. The elections of 1866 had registered a stinging rebuke to President Johnson's program; the only question that remained was whether or not Congress wished to go beyond its own Reconstruction proposal in the form of the Fourteenth Amendment. Although some leading Republicans, including a delegation led by Senator Benjamin Wade of Ohio that toured part of the South in December, urged Southerners to accept the Fourteenth Amendment and be returned to the Union, others, led by Thaddeus Stevens, were not willing to endorse that moderate view.[73] They watched grimly as one Southern state legislature after another refused, by overwhelming votes, to ratify the amendment. Although some party leaders proposed that the Southern states remain out of the Union until they were ready to approve the measure, most Republicans did not want to wait. They argued that the nation was impatient for restoration of the Union, and if the South would not willingly comply with congressional terms, Congress would dictate them. In light of continued Southern intransigence, continued evidence of violence and hostility

directed against loyal whites and blacks, and the continued impor-
tuning of Southern Unionists for support, many Republicans hitherto hesitant about endorsing Negro suffrage were now ready to
make it a condition of restoration of the Southern states.[74]

The year 1866 was indeed critical for the Republican party and for
the nation. By December it was clear that the Republicans were almost unanimously committed to a reorganization of the South based
on Negro suffrage. With the backing of the freedmen and the support of white Unionist minorities, the Republican party for the first
time had an excellent opportunity for expanding into the entire
South. The following year, 1867, would prove to be equally critical,
for at that time Republicans would have to undertake the organizational work in the South that the party's leaders had heretofore failed
to foster. They had to find out if the black vote could be organized
and made into an effective force for the Republican party and if that
work could be done without alienating the white support they hoped
to gain. They had much work to do and not much time to do it.
Hardly had the 1866 congressional elections been held than politicians of all parties began to look ahead to the 1868 presidential election. First, however, the Congress had to define more precisely the
new plans for restoring the South.

★ ★ ★ ★ 4 ★ ★ ★ ★

BLACKS AND THE SOUTHERN

STRATEGY, 1867–1868

After the overwhelming victory Republicans had won in the elections of 1866, many Radicals in the party were emboldened to embark upon more stringent measures to reconstruct the Southern states. Republican moderates who had advocated the Fourteenth Amendment as the means for restoring the South found that they had no ground to stand on when one former Confederate state after another rejected the proposal. Consequently, they, too, were ready to join the Radicals in proposing new Reconstruction measures. And in 1867, unlike the previous year, the plans they discussed offered the decided prospect of building the Republican party in every Southern state.[1]

In December 1866, when the second session of the Thirty-Ninth Congress convened in Washington, large numbers of Southern white Unionists from almost every state in the former Confederacy thronged into the capital. Most of these men were now avowed Republicans and had organized the Southern Republican Association to press for new Reconstruction measures. According to John Forney, editor of the *Washington Chronicle*, the Southern Unionists formed "a complete network, extending . . . to the remotest hamlets, thus constituting the basis of a formidable and resistless combination." As the Republican party began to organize in state after state, Forney rejoiced in its "extraordinary progress."[2]

Forney exaggerated the Southern Republicans' prospects. Tennessee remained the only state in the former Confederacy whose government they controlled. Unless they could gain dominance in the other states, the party might not survive long enough to establish itself in the face of Conservative opposition. Hence Southern Republicans eagerly pressed upon Congress proposals that they believed would establish loyal, and Republican, governments in the Southern states. Although their recommendations varied in detail, Southern Republicans wanted Negro suffrage, disfranchisement of former Confederates, and replacement of the Johnson governments with some form of territorial government staffed by Unconditional Unionists, who would then supervise the reorganization of the civil government of the state.[3]

Of the three goals, the Northern Republicans were most willing to endorse Negro suffrage. Since the end of the war, a number of Northern Republicans had been insisting that enfranchisement was the best way to secure black rights. By 1867 most of the rest of the party, faced with continued evidence of white intransigence in the South, had come to the same conclusion. With the congressional elections of 1866 behind them, they were less fearful of the opposition of white Northerners to black enfranchisement. Faced with the choice of adopting Radical proposals for extended military government of the South or of governing the Southern states with the aid of black votes, the moderate Republicans opted for the latter. Viewed in this light, Negro suffrage proved to be a conservative option, for it avoided significant extensions of federal authority into Southern states.[4]

Most Republicans believed the blacks would vote for their party. Henry Wilson, an ardent champion of universal suffrage by 1867, was sure that the freedmen would "know their friends" and vote Republican. The editors of *Harper's Weekly* agreed, stating that "blacks will vote with their new friends and against the party of the lost cause." The *Boston Commonwealth* was convinced that with the black vote, the party "would sweep the Union from Maine to Florida, and from the Atlantic to the Pacific." According to the *Atlantic Monthly*, the Republicans could "by means of the loyal Negroes and loyal white men of the South build up a national party there." Horace Greeley, who had for some time been agitating for black suffrage, also contended that the former slaves would vote for the Republican party. By 1867 even Thaddeus Stevens, who had opposed Negro suffrage until the South had been thoroughly reconstructed, now endorsed immediate enfranchisement of blacks on the grounds that "it would ensure the ascendancy of the Union party." Fellow Radical George Julian also endorsed black enfranchisement, admitting that although some freedmen might vote on the side of their old masters, he was ready to take that risk.[5]

Other Radicals, however, continued to warn of the dangers of enfranchising an illiterate and politically inexperienced population. Ignatius Donnelly of Minnesota warned his House colleagues that "a people just snatched from barbarism cannot compete with the cunning, skill, knowledge, and influence of the ex-rebels." George Boutwell agreed, stating that the Negroes, "unaccustomed to political struggles, timid, careworn, broken down in spirit to some degree by the institution of slavery," could not be expected to resist the influence of their disloyal former masters, "who possess all the means of information, command in a large degree the intellect of the South, [and] control the institutions of learning."[6]

More conservative Republicans echoed these views. The editors of the *New York Times* and the *Nation* alike feared that the black vote would be controlled by the former rebel leaders and hence used against the Republican party. Thurlow Weed, longtime associate of William Henry Seward and editorial writer for the *New York Commercial Advertiser*, warned that "the ignorant and stolid masses [of blacks] would be controlled, as the 'white trash' of the South has ever been, by superior wills." One of the leading Republicans in the Senate, William Pitt Fessenden, also warned that if blacks were enfranchised their vote would be manipulated by the wealthy and intelligent whites of the South. He bitterly complained about the Radicals' haste to "secure the votes of those [Southern] states through the aid of the Negroes."[7]

Senator Joseph Fowler of Tennessee, whose state had given blacks the vote in January 1867, chided his Northern colleagues for not trusting freedmen to vote wisely. Black spokesmen in the South and in the nation also repeatedly assured congressmen that blacks would not vote for their former masters. But congressional Republicans also received communications from some Unionist whites in the South warning that many blacks, particularly in the interior regions, were susceptible to the influence of their former owners. Hence Republicans watched apprehensively for indications of the freedmen's political proclivities. In the House, one Republican justified enfranchising blacks in the District of Columbia by noting that its inhabitants held four thousand subscriptions to the two Republican newspapers printed locally. In January 1867, Congress did enfranchise blacks in the District of Columbia, passing the measure over Johnson's veto; when municipal elections were held in Georgetown in February and in Washington the following month, Republicans rejoiced to see that the black vote had gone overwhelmingly for their party.[8]

Whatever their doubts about the potential of black suffrage, most Republicans agreed that they had little choice left except to enfranchise the freedmen. As Benjamin Butler, now a congressman from Massachusetts, told a correspondent from Mississippi, "I must either give power to unrepentant, merciless and flagrant enemies of the government, or to untaught, ignorant, but loyal friends." The Republicans hoped that through education and tutelage blacks would be able to free themselves from subservience to their former masters. In any case, as James Harlan, senator from Iowa, argued in 1867, after a return from the South, he would rather trust "ignorant people who are honest and patriotic than educated knaves and confessed traitors." Congressman David Allison agreed, contending that the only hope of restoring loyal governments in the South lay with "the uneducated, the poor, and now powerless masses," rather than with the aristocratic white Southerners. The editor of the *Nation*, E. L. Godkin, reluctantly endorsed black suffrage, arguing that without the vote, freedmen could not protect themselves from white violence or obtain public schools. The *Nation* commented that although the black vote might well go to Southern candidates in local and congressional elections, "we do not doubt that it can, with very little difficulty, be had for the Republican Presidential candidate . . . in the next election." Even Indiana's Oliver P. Morton, who in 1866 had vigorously opposed enfranchising blacks because of their ignorance and dependence on whites, now accepted its necessity. His conversion prompted a Radical to comment on the irony of Morton "advising our Plantation friends" on the importance of voting, "after how he behaved at the Philadelphia [loyalist] convention."[9]

Such Radicals as Stevens, Butler, and Julian, who feared that the political advantages of black suffrage would be jeopardized by the continued influence of white Conservatives, agreed with their Southern white Republican colleagues that former Confederates should be disfranchised. Many Northern congressmen believed that at least some classes of Southern whites should lose the right to vote. By early 1867, however, no one, not even Thaddeus Stevens, was willing to recommend massive or prolonged disfranchisement; as one critic of the idea expressed it, if Congress denied the vote to all men who had voluntarily aided the rebellion, "there will not be a corporal's guard of white men in each state" who could vote. The consequence, according to John Sherman, would be to "place the power of ten states in the hands of ignorant, emancipated freedmen." Many other Republicans shared his unwillingness to give blacks the power to dominate a white population reduced to minority status by disfranchisement. They also believed that such a policy could be enforced, if at all, only by stationing a large army in the South. Critics of large-scale disfranchisement also pointed to the difficulties border state Republicans were having in effectively excluding masses of former rebels from the polls.[10]

The solution to the problem of disfranchisement, according to many Republicans, was to proscribe only the leading ex-Confederates, perhaps those classes already affected by the Fourteenth Amendment. Even this solution, however, met with Republican opposition in Congress. Sherman contended that almost all whites had been involved in the rebellion to some degree, so it was impossible to determine whom to disfranchise and whom to allow to vote. The only solution, he argued, was to allow all whites to vote under whatever Reconstruction program Congress adopted, thus offering them one more opportunity to cooperate with Northern Republicans. In taking this position, Sherman spoke for those Republicans who still hoped to gain significant white support for their party in the South, even from the ranks of former Confederates. Congressmen including Sherman and John Bingham of Ohio insisted that loyal white men were a majority in the South, if Congress included in the definition of loyalty those who had been forced by conscription or other coercive devices to aid the Confederacy. Senator William Stewart of Nevada also was eager for the support of "the great mass of the [Southern] people who went into the rebellion blindly, or even were driven into it."[11]

Stewart agreed with Sherman that the best way to handle voting rights in the South was to allow both whites and blacks unrestricted access to the ballot box. A position of universal amnesty and universal suffrage had already been recommended by Horace Greeley, who believed that such a policy would "build a great national party, which can hopefully contest nearly every state in the Union." Fellow

editor Samuel Bowles of the *Springfield Republican* endorsed the proposal, warning that "there can be no real, no true, no lasting reconstruction in the South that does not include all classes of its people.
Disfranchisement is as great a folly as applied to the whites, as omis-
sion to enfranchise is wickedness toward the Negroes." Henry Wilson of Massachusetts enlarged on these sentiments, stating that
"disfranchisement will create more feeling and bitterness than enfranchisement." In 1867, however, Northern bitterness about the rebellion was still too strong to allow advocates of Greeley's policy to
have their way. Indeed, Greeley's reputation as a party spokesman
suffered from his advocacy of amnesty. Senator Richard Yates of Illinois spoke for a majority of his colleagues when he declared that
"the verdict of the people has been against universal amnesty as well
as for universal suffrage. It has been rather for universal suffering for
rebels who raised their arms against the government, and universal suffrage and every right to the men who have stood by the
Government."[12]

Thus congressional Republicans, though united in favor of one of
the Southern Republicans' requirements for Reconstruction, that of
suffrage for blacks, proved to be divided over the wisdom and practicality of white disfranchisement. They experienced similar difficulty
in resolving the remaining request of the Southern Republicans: that
the Johnson governments be disbanded and Conservative officials
immediately replaced by men loyal to the Union. Southern Republicans argued that only in this way could they gain control of state
patronage, which was necessary to build their party in the South and
control the reconstruction of their states. To leave government in the
hands of the Conservatives, they argued, would allow their enemies
to dominate Reconstruction, maintain their influence over blacks,
and neutralize the benefits of universal suffrage.[13]

The Southern Republicans found support for their views among
the Radicals in Congress. Sumner warned that if the Southern state
governments were not disbanded, the Conservatives, "with their experience, craft, and determined purpose," would be able to control
the Reconstruction process. The congressional Radicals believed that
neither the blacks nor the Unionist whites would be able to resist the
Conservatives, who, as George Boutwell put it, would "manipulate
the timid people, black and white, who adhere to authority, who

naturally place confidence in men of power." Again and again congressional Republicans questioned the ability of Southern Unionists, even with the black vote, to control the Reconstruction process without outside support. Stewart of Nevada said that "the Southern people who are Unionist are not in the front rank of intelligence: many of them are poor, low, and oppressed." Samuel Arnell, Unionist Republican congressman from Tennessee, echoed this view, warning that the Unionists of the South were "a poor, downtrodden, ostracized, maligned, and persecuted class," who needed congressional assistance to control their states.[14]

Radicals were unable to carry the day in Congress. Too many Republicans believed that removing the existing governments and replacing them with territorial or military governments would prolong Reconstruction unduly and discourage potential white support. If Southern whites were not offered a way back to the Union quickly, stated Senator Stewart, the future of the Republican party in the South would be in doubt. A North Carolina Unionist, lobbying in Washington for the return of his state to the Union, agreed, stating that any delays would "greatly weaken the strength of the Radical party [in the South] and eventually cost it its ascendancy." Therefore, moderate Republicans determined to create a Reconstruction process that would maintain the existing governments, put them under military supervision, and encourage them to institute a reorganization of the civil government that could quickly be implemented. The results, they hoped, would maximize Southern white cooperation for Reconstruction and make it appear that the procedure would be implemented by voluntary action rather than through federal coercion.[15]

The Reconstruction Act that Congress ultimately passed over President Johnson's veto on March 2 contained a series of compromises on the issue of the retention of the Johnson governments, the timetable for restoration of the Southern states, and disfranchisement. The former Confederate states were divided by the law into five military districts, and the existing Johnson governments were declared to be provisional and subject to the paramount authority of the military commanders. Military government would be withdrawn from a state after a convention, elected through universal suffrage, had framed a constitution that granted adult black males the right to vote. In addition, the state was expected to ratify the Fourteenth

Amendment. The act declared that all former Confederates affected by the disability section of that amendment were disfranchised and ineligible to be elected to the convention.

Because the Reconstruction Act was a compromise, it failed to satisfy fully either Republican Radicals or moderates. Such Radicals as Stevens and Boutwell, and most Southern Republicans, distrusted the entire existing leadership class of the South and wanted to deprive it of power. Moderates such as John Bingham, on the other hand, did not wish substantially to alter the existing power structure in the South and hoped the present white leadership would take the lead in implementing the restoration process. The moderates got provisions retaining the Johnson governments, although they were declared provisional in nature; Radicals were able, however, to bar at least some classes of Southerners from participating in the elections and constitutional conventions called for in the Reconstruction process. Hence Conservatives were left in control of the Southern governments but were restricted by limitations and disqualifications that weakened but did not eliminate their influence. The chances of securing their cooperation for Republican Reconstruction plans, however, were significantly limited by the effects of the proscriptive provisions of the act. But Republicans faced severe problems in attempting to organize a new leadership from the ranks of Southern white loyalists, who constituted a small minority of the white population, and from the masses of recently emancipated slaves.[16]

The law provided no detailed machinery to implement the restoration process, so it remained to the Johnson governments to set the process in motion. They could set the time and place of elections, supervise the registration of voters, and count the votes. Southern Republicans raised an outcry against this situation, and later in March Congress passed the Second Reconstruction Act, which attempted to correct some of the faults of the initial law. This measure vested in the military commanders the power to register voters and call for elections to a constitutional convention; the registration was to be completed by September 1. The new law also attempted to clarify, and consequently somewhat to expand, the class of former Confederates barred from participating in Reconstruction. The act specified an oath that prospective electors were to take, swearing that they had not held any government office or position before the war and afterward given aid or support to the rebellion. The intent was to stigmatize the Southern leaders, who had supposedly led the masses astray.[17]

The author of the Second Reconstruction Act, Henry Wilson, was eager to hasten the restoration of the Southern states, for he believed the Republican party had a great chance to control their reorganized governments. Wilson was convinced that 99 percent of the blacks in the South would vote for his party. He admitted that they were un-educated and lacked political experience, but he believed they would learn quickly and could be trusted with the ballot. He realized, how-ever, that white voters would constitute a voting majority in most Southern states. Wilson was one of those Northern Republicans who contended that tens of thousands of Southern whites were "earnest, sincere men," who had been forced into support of the rebellion. The senator, who had developed contacts with a number of Southern whites, claimed that these men were now ready to confess their error and "stand on our platform." He was convinced that with this added white support, Republicans could easily carry both Carolinas, Missis-sippi, Alabama, and Louisiana, "and not only for the Union, but for candidates for Congress who will come here and vote as we vote, speak as we speak, think as we think." If the Republicans pressed their political organization in the South, by the time of the next presi-dential election, Wilson predicted, a majority of Southern states would give their electoral votes "for whoever we nominate as a can-didate for President in 1868." Turning to some of his colleagues who were suggesting amendments to his bill that would slow the process of Reconstruction, he asked: "These rebel states are ours if we will accept them. . . . Does any Senator desire to keep these states out till after the next election?"[18]

Senator James Nye of Nevada rose in answer to Wilson's challenge; he was in no hurry to let the South return and complained that "the course of legislation in this body seems to be to accommodate itself in all respects to the necessities of rebels." He charged that Wilson was willing to let the rebels return "if they come sandwiched be-tween two black men." Nye warned that the freedmen could not battle politically on even terms with their old masters. Senator Jacob Howard of Michigan feared that Wilson's bill would allow the return of Southern governments based entirely on black votes and that the white population would remain aloof. Those suspicious of too hasty a restoration and who wanted evidence of white approval were able to modify Wilson's bill to require that a majority of registered voters would have to approve a state's constitution before it could be put into effect. The House also amended Wilson's bill by requiring that voting registrars and superintendents take the ironclad oath; Wilson warned, to no avail, that such action would "weaken our political friends rather than our enemies" by discouraging those whites who had hoped to cooperate with the Republicans but who could not take the oath.[19]

Republicans had moved reluctantly to enfranchise the blacks of the South and were apprehensive about the results of their program. Senator Nye spoke for many of his colleagues when he warned that "for many years their old masters will control the votes of their former slaves; we must not expect too much from these newly enfranchised people." Nye, who noted that in the North workers voted as their employers dictated, feared it would "take a long time to build this [black] race up to the full stature of freedom." Aware of these fears about the reliability of the black vote, Senator Wilson addressed his colleagues shortly before Congress disbanded, urging them to help organize their party in the South and to influence the new voters in the right direction. Noting that the Reconstruction Acts would soon bring the Southern states back into the Union, Wilson told a correspondent that "the only question is—will they be represented by Radical Antislavery men or by Reactionaries?" To him, the answer was clear: "If the organization, the speeches, the work that will be put forward in the state of Connecticut this year were put forth in the ten rebel states we could carry nearly every one of them by a decisive majority."[20]

A number of Northern newspapers echoed Wilson's plea for the Republican party to help its Southern allies control the reorganization of their states. The *Boston Advertiser*, noting that "the race for the Negro vote is on," worried lest the black vote "be controlled as readily by former rebels as by Northern influence." Hence the party had to send its best men into the most promising districts of the South; there was "a great field to be plowed." The Washington correspondent of the *Anti-Slavery Standard* also warned that the success of the Republican party in the South depended on the clarity "with which the new voters see on which side their friends stand." According to the *Indianapolis Daily Journal*, "If we fail to embrace the present opportunity for building up true Republicanism there, we need not be surprised if the old rebel leaders sway the new as they did the old South." Northern concern about organizing Southern voters increased in the spring of 1867, as the Republican party's hold on some Northern states appeared to slip, possibly because of its advocacy of Negro suffrage. In early April state and congressional elections in Connecticut went to the Democrats, who also won a series of municipal elections in Ohio. John Forney hoped that the Republicans could carry most of the Southern states, "hence making up for any temporary losses in the North."[21]

Northern Republicans, however, were slow to respond to the challenge presented by the new political situation in the South. Since the year of its inception the party had concentrated on winning Northern support, which it had managed to gain by appealing to anti-Southern prejudices. Although individuals within the party, particularly President Lincoln, William Henry Seward, Salmon P. Chase, and William D. Kelley, had encouraged the handful of Republicans that had emerged in the border states and in occupied areas of the South during the war, through the elections of 1866 the party leadership continued to focus on winning Northern elections and had given little encouragement to potential Southern support. Until 1867 blacks were not voting in the South, and despite the optimism of Republicans who hoped to gain white votes in the former Confederate states, there was little evidence that such support was forthcoming.

As military authorities in the South began to prepare to register voters pursuant to the terms of the Reconstruction Acts, Southern white Republicans frantically sought assistance from their Northern colleagues in informing blacks about their new political opportunities. They sent representatives into the Northern states seeking funds to finance Southern Republican party organizations and also pleaded for speakers to journey into the former Confederate states to inform the freedmen about their rights. Letters to Northern congressmen from Virginia Republicans were typical. John Minor Botts, a white Unionist from the Old Dominion, warned that the Conservatives might well control the forthcoming elections in the state because "their forces are thoroughly organized, and ours without the least, and not one fifth of the colored vote are yet informed of the fact that suffrage has been extended to them." A direct tax commissioner in Alexandria, pleading with Congressman Benjamin Butler for Republican canvassers and speakers from the North, reminded Butler that "a large proportion of the talent of the state is against us, and without assistance from the Republicans North and West, we shall probably be defeated."[22] Similar admonitions poured into Northern Republican mailboxes from other states in the South. Southern Republicans stressed that the weight of political, social, and economic power in their states would be thrown against them and that the voters, both black and white, that they wanted to reach were poorly informed and easily beguiled by Conservative influences. Without material aid from the North, these correspondents repeatedly warned, the Republicans would lose their opportunity to control the Reconstruction process.[23]

In January 1867, the Republican National Committee, which customarily remained dormant between presidential elections, met to discuss the Southern situation. Its membership included men from the border states, as well as representatives from Tennessee, Virginia, North Carolina, and Arkansas. The group approved a resolution directing its executive committee, chaired by Governor Marcus Ward of New Jersey, to undertake a thorough organization of the Union party, "especially in the so-called seceded states," in anticipation of the presidential election in 1868. Governor William Claflin of Massachusetts, who was a member of the executive committee, argued that "what we do now, will be much more effective than at any future period." The committee members received letters from the South, urging them to commence the work immediately because, as one observed, "the iron is red—yes, white-hot." A Freedmen's Bureau officer in Georgia, writing to Ward, warned him that "the freedman is now the pliant twig, which will be bent, right or wrong." If the blacks, who were "inclined in the right direction," were not to be unduly influenced by their employers, Republicans would have to act promptly.[24]

Despite these pleas, Ward's committee did not begin to operate effectively until May, when it opened offices in New York and prepared an appeal to Northern Republicans for financial aid. In its petition, the committee noted that the party had a great opportunity to expand into the South. "In times past the Republican party has struggled against the unjust reproach of being sectional in its aims and character," the committee stated; now the time had come to prove that the party's concerns embraced the entire nation. It would be necessary to send money and able speakers into the South, to represent the party effectively and to overcome the habit of the new voters of the South of "rendering implicit obedience to able and dextrous politicians who are hostile to our principles." According to Ward, who drew up the appeal, "the necessity is apparent, the duty positive, and our success almost a certainty."[25]

Because the traditional role of the National Committee was to organize and conduct national presidential campaigns, it decided to turn over the day-to-day party organization in the South to the Union Republican Congressional Committee, chaired by Senator Edwin Morgan of New York. This committee had existed since 1860, when it was formed to direct congressional campaigns. It was made up of members of Congress; each Republican state received one representative, appointed by a joint caucus of party members. The committee, which supervised congressional campaigns in both presidential and off-year elections, had assumed greater importance during the election of 1866. The National Committee was then headed by Henry J. Raymond, who supported Andrew Johnson. Hence party funds were funneled to the Congressional Committee, which was in the hands of advocates of congressional Reconstruction. The committee spent $20,000 during the campaign and distributed more than one million speeches and documents. In December 1866, the Republican caucus decided to extend the life of the existing committee into the following year, at least until the Fortieth Congress convened late in March. In the meantime, it continued to raise funds, chiefly through assessing each member of Congress. After the new Congress convened, Republican congressmen caucused again and empowered the committee to disseminate knowledge of Republican principles "to the masses of the South, whites and blacks alike." By early April, the committee had obtained rooms in Washington and had begun its work in earnest.[26]

The executive committee of the Union Congressional Committee undertook the day-to-day responsibilities assigned to the larger group. Under the energetic leadership of its chairman, Robert Schenck of Ohio, and secretary, Thomas L. Tullock, the executive committee tackled the enormous task of raising funds for the Southern work, sending speakers and organizers into the South, mailing documents, and observing the assembling and operation of the various constitutional conventions that were to be called in each state in accordance with the Reconstruction Acts. Tullock opened books in Washington in which he inscribed the names of all the men in the former Confederate states who wished to disseminate Republican propaganda or in other ways aid the organization of the party there. The committee also consulted with the national executive committee, with army and Freedmen's Bureau officers in charge of Reconstruction in the South, with the members of Republican state executive committees as they were organized in the South, and with Union League representatives who were busy expanding their organization through the Southern states. The committee thus functioned for the Republican party as a clearinghouse of information about the progress of Reconstruction in the Southern states, and it also developed the potential for having substantial influence on the course of events there. One visitor to the frantically busy committee rooms in Washington found chairman Schenck "executing doom upon rebels, enfranchising races, deciding between states, manipulating constitutions, and dealing reconstructions to posterity."[27]

The Congressional Committee at first tended to concentrate its efforts on mailing documents; by mid-July Schenck reported that he had a list of twenty thousand loyal Southerners who would distribute reading material to the voters. This was the committee's traditional procedure; in previous congressional elections in the North it had distributed millions of documents to Northern voters, using congressional franking privileges. Now, however, it was confronted with an unsophisticated and largely illiterate voting population, and it soon became clear that the committee would have to change its emphasis from supplying documents to sending speakers into the South.[28]

Although the Southern Republicans were eager to get prestigious members of their party from the North to come South to speak, most ignored or declined their invitations to enter the former Confederate states.[29] Henry Wilson, the most eager of all Northern Republicans to get on with the Southern work, made a trip through several states in the late spring, but he had little company. The Congressional Committee did send William D. Kelley south at the same time that Wilson went, but Kelley returned to declare that "no missionary politicians" were wanted there because "the Negro was capable of taking care of himself . . . without the interference of such people." Benjamin Butler, who was frequently asked to visit the South, declined, stating that the men who went there "have leaped before they got to the ditch." Butler believed that if the party "let the froth run off . . . the stream will be clearer afterwards." The editor of the *Great Republic*, organ of the Union League, complained that of all the men in Congress who had proposed radical changes in the South, only Wilson and Kelley had actually visited the section to help implement these changes. "Members of Congress must respond to these calls for speakers," the editor averred, "or sadly fail in their duty."[30]

Prominent Northern Republicans such as Wilson and Kelley could help and encourage their Southern allies, particularly by appearing as visible evidence of Northern sympathy and support.[31] Certainly their prestige helped to draw crowds; wherever the two men went, they found large audiences made up of voters from both races. Their speeches, however, were delivered in large towns and cities, and most blacks lived outside these urban areas. Southern party organizers particularly stressed the difficulty of reaching blacks in rural areas, where communications were difficult and landowners threatened their field hands with discharge if they attended Republican meetings. The president of the Republican state central committee of South Carolina cautioned Benjamin Butler that "it is with this class that a vast amount of work by way of instruction must be done or the state will be lost." One Northerner living in Mississippi warned Senator Richard Yates that although blacks in town had access to Republican political propaganda, those living in the interior counties did not, and he urged Northerners to send speakers into those areas. A single meeting with black voters, he noted, would not do, "for they are in the midst of enemies, and unless continuously sustained, we will lose them." Another Northerner in Mississippi begged Charles Sumner for "brave white speakers and money to pay the expenses of black ones," observing that "many of the latter can be found here."[32]

Responding to this need, Schenck's committee attempted to recruit speakers who were willing and able to carry the party's message into the interior counties of the South. By early June the committee had the names of fifteen such speakers on its rolls; within a month, the number had been increased to more than seventy. Many of the speakers and organizers assisted by the committee came from the states to which they were assigned. A few were Union war veterans who had remained in the South; some of the native whites had been wartime Unionists. A large majority of the committee agents, however, were black, and they proved most effective in reaching the potential black electorate that was waiting to be informed and organized. A large number of these black agents for the Republican party were ministers, usually of the African Methodist Episcopal church, which was organizing congregations among the freedmen across the South. These men, who came from both the North and the South, did not hesitate to risk life and limb to bring news of the Republican party and its program to the freedmen. Using their influence among the membership of their gathering churches, these ministers carried the brunt of Republican organizing in the South.[33]

The Congressional Committee also leaned heavily on the Union League of America to carry party organization into the more remote areas of the South. Although the league had continued its work in the former Confederate states through 1866, its activity had steadily declined until by the end of the year it had become practically inert. The league lacked funds to carry on its operations, and it admitted in December that large areas of the unreconstructed states had not felt its influence. The passage of the Reconstruction Acts, however, and the interest in Republican recruiting in the South that these laws inspired, rejuvenated the league organization. The *Great Republic* warned that "no legislation will meet the needs of the loyal masses of the South until they shall organize and act in their own behalf." The editor, noting that more than half a million voters in the South had never before exercised political power, urged league members to commence the work of organizing the Republican party in every county of the former Confederacy.[34]

In April, the same month that the Congressional Committee began its work, the Union League reported the establishment of working state councils in Tennessee, Georgia, both Carolinas, and Alabama. Unfortunately, the league lacked money to continue its efforts, and James Edmunds, the president of the organization, appealed to the Congressional Committee for assistance. He noted that the committee was emphasizing the distribution of documents, rather than the creation of party organizations, and suggested the priorities should be reversed: "There are half a million of men or nearly that number who cannot read. These must be talked to and it cannot be done without organization." The league had access to men in the South who were prepared to do the grass-roots work, but it lacked money to pay their traveling expenses. He warned the Republican committeemen that if they did not get organizers to the black population, they would remain "under the eye and to a large extent the influence of their old masters."[35]

Although the Congressional Committee was having difficulty raising funds, it recognized the value of Edmunds's organization and promised to help pay the expenses of league workers. The committee and the league continued their cooperation throughout the year; congressmen turned over the committee's printing to the league's *Great Republic*, which ensured that newspaper additional income.[36]

On April 13, 1867, one of the league's best organizers, Thomas Conway, formerly assistant commissioner of the Freedmen's Bureau in Louisiana, left on a tour that took him through eight Southern states. He was instructed to visit state Union League councils, work to overcome internal quarrels, and help stimulate further organizational efforts. Conway's report on his trip, which he submitted to Edmunds and the Congressional Committee in July, provided a graphic description of the problems of getting political information into the hands of potential Republican voters, particularly blacks. Conway was convinced that only the league, which at that time was a secret, oath-bound order, could offer the freedmen enough sense of security to organize and attend political meetings without fear of white intimidation. The blacks, he found, were eager for information and would walk miles to attend a meeting if they thought it was safe. Conway sought to identify those blacks who had influence among other freedmen on the Southern plantations, initiate them into the league, and urge them to form local councils. Everywhere he found that blacks in the urban areas were "wide awake" and unwilling to vote for their former masters, "but there is deplorable ignorance of matters especially in the country." Conway concluded that "nothing but the League will do in the South. The colored men like it and feel secure by its obligations." Conway claimed that the league was well organized in Alabama and was making rapid progress in North Carolina, South Carolina, Georgia, and Louisiana. Until he arrived in the South, however, neither Virginia, Mississippi, nor Texas had effective state leagues. He was convinced that with sufficient financing from the North, the league could organize five hundred councils in the three states within four months. To date, Conway estimated that the league had organized between two and three thousand councils in the South, with between two and three hundred thousand members. Within six months, he predicted, given adequate financial aid, the league could exist in every county in the South, and "have not less than 700,000 loyal voters."[37]

In addition to authorizing the Congressional Committee to conduct organizational work in the South and aiding the Union League, which was working toward the same end, congressional Republicans sought to develop a party press in the South. In March 1867, the Thirty-Ninth Congress revised the legislation governing the distribution of government printing contracts to newspapers. Previous to the passage of the March law, government contracts for publishing the laws of the United States and for placing government advertisements had been awarded by the secretaries of the executive departments concerned. Republicans were upset because Secretary of State Seward, who supported President Johnson's policies, was giving contracts for publishing the laws, which were the most lucrative jobs, to Conservative newspapers in the South. Hence the new law made the clerk of the House, Edward McPherson, responsible for selecting two newspapers in each of the states affected by the Reconstruction Acts to receive government printing patronage. McPherson, a longtime Republican from Pennsylvania and close friend of Thaddeus Stevens, could be counted on to ensure that these contracts went to papers loyal to the congressional plan of Reconstruction.[38]

At the time the law went into effect, there were only a handful of Republican newspapers in the ten reconstructed states. Some states, such as Mississippi, Florida, and South Carolina, had no Republican press at all. According to the Congressional Committee, only two dailies in the former Confederate states and only fifteen journals in the entire region could be considered Republican. As soon as the new law passed Congress, Charles Whittlesey, editor of the *Virginia State Journal* and president of the newly formed Southern Republican Press Association, submitted a list of newspapers to McPherson which his organization recommended for government printing contracts. During the next several weeks McPherson was deluged with requests from Southern newspaper editors, pleading for assistance. Within a month, he had designated the two papers in each state entitled to print federal laws and advertising; in every case, he had accepted the recommendation of the Southern Republican Press Association. By late June, John Forney could count thirty-six Republican papers in the unreconstructed states, fourteen of which were dailies.

By late October, he claimed there were more than one hundred Republican newspapers in the South, where none had existed before the war.[39]

Even with federal aid, most of these Republican newspapers would not survive. Their editors had exaggerated expectations about the amount of federal money they would receive, and they were forced to ask the Northern Republicans for more aid from either public or private resources, which was not forthcoming. McPherson faced a difficult task in awarding the contracts among various papers competing for them and frequently had to transfer the printing privileges from one paper to another because the original recipient shut down its presses.[40] Nonetheless, the federal contracts remained one of the most evident of the ways in which Northern Republicans undertook to assist their Southern brethren.

Although much Northern aid and encouragement came to the Southern Republicans through the vehicles of the Congressional Committee, the Union League, and federal printing patronage, the most significant outside agency affecting the growth of the Southern Republican party in 1867 proved to be the U.S. War Department. The Reconstruction Acts had given the army great authority over the restoration process. The generals in command of each military district had the power to remove civil officials and fill the vacancies, rescind state legislation, and issue military printing contracts. They were given authority to register voters and call elections in accordance with the processes defined by the Reconstruction Acts. It was also within their power to provide or withhold military protection for the whites and blacks attempting to organize the Republican party in the South.

Events in the border states and occupied areas of the South during the Civil War had already given much evidence of the influence the army could have in furthering the development of Unionist-Republican parties. It was behind a shield of military protection, and with the aid of military supervision of elections, voting lists, and newspapers, that Radical Unionists or Republicans had gained control of the border states. And, as was clearly illustrated in the case of wartime Louisiana, the army could, through the actions of the military governor, determine which faction of Unionists would control the civil government.

By placing the supervision of the Reconstruction process in the hands of military commanders rather than with new provisional governments under white Unionist control, Congress indicated its belief that the generals would be sympathetic to congressional policies. Secretary of War Edwin M. Stanton and Ulysses S. Grant, commanding general of the army, were both supporters of the congressional plan, and Republicans expected that they would counter the influence of President Johnson, who had the power to appoint the district commanders in the South. In March 1867, to restrain Johnson further, Congress passed the Tenure of Office Act, prohibiting the president from removing any of his cabinet members, presumably including Stanton, without the prior approval of the Senate. Congress also enacted legislation providing that Johnson could not remove Grant from his post or order him from Washington against his will without Senate approval. The law also required that all orders from the capital to the commanders in the South had to go through Grant's office.[41]

The five generals Johnson named to command the military districts were recommended by Stanton and Grant, and Republican spokesmen expressed confidence in them. The president appointed John Schofield to head the First Military District, which was restricted to the state of Virginia; Daniel Sickles to the second district, including North and South Carolina; John Pope to the third, composed of Florida, Georgia, and Alabama; E. O. C. Ord to the fourth, including Arkansas and Mississippi; and he assigned the Fifth Military District, composed of Louisiana and Texas, to Philip Sheridan.[42] All of these men proved determined to execute the provisions of the Reconstruction Acts expeditiously and efficiently, but they differed in the reading they gave those laws, which were ambiguous in several critical areas.

Two questions in particular quickly emerged as the generals began to administer the Reconstruction Acts. First, were the commanders properly authorized to remove civil officials from their posts and appoint their replacements? Second, how were the disfranchisement provisions of the first two Reconstruction Acts to be interpreted? The answers to both questions would have great potential for affecting Reconstruction and for aiding or hindering the efforts of Republicans in the South. Native white Republicans had long been demanding that Congress, or now the army, remove from state governments all men whose loyalty was questionable and turn these posts over to them. Such control over state offices, patronage, and power would strengthen the Republican party in the South and weaken its enemies. Conversely, if these offices remained in Conservative hands, they could be used to thwart or frustrate Republican efforts to control Reconstruction. The disfranchisement question was also vitally important; if not enough Conservatives were barred from political activity during the reorganization process, the Southern Republicans feared they might never gain control of their respective states.

Barring any definitive interpretation of the Reconstruction Acts, the generals administered them in their own way. Generally, Schofield, Sickles, and Ord were more conservative, proving reluctant to remove civil officials or to disfranchise large numbers of prospective voters. Pope, and especially Sheridan in the fifth district, used their powers liberally to replace civil officials and to bar many whites from voting. Particularly because of Sheridan's actions, Conservatives in the South appealed to the president to limit the powers of the commanders. In June, Attorney General Henry Stanbery issued a set of opinions interpreting the Reconstruction Acts in such a way as to deny the generals the power to make removals or to purge many whites from the voting lists. Northern congressmen, who were watching intently to see if the executive branch would attempt to obstruct Reconstruction, quickly assembled in Washington to consider legislation nullifying the effect of Stanbery's opinions.[43]

The debates in Congress over further Reconstruction laws renewed earlier disagreements over the advisability of turning over state offices in the South to Unconditional Unionists. Southern white radicals again urged Congress to remove all Southern officials who could not take the test oath. William Holden of North Carolina called the Conservative state governments "nests of treason" and urged Congress to cleanse them "from turret to foundation stone." Senator Henry Wilson, who had written the Second Reconstruction Act, agreed with Holden, telling his colleagues that if Congress had agreed in March to vacate the civil offices in the South, hence destroying "the official and political influence of the men who held them," the Republicans in the former Confederate states would be "from fifty to a hundred thousand [votes] stronger." The Republican majority in Congress, however, had refused to sanction such use of the ironclad oath before, fearing that there were not enough loyal Southerners to fill the vacancies and that such an action would only alienate Southern white leaders whose support they continued to seek. Secretary of War Stanton, who agreed with this moderate view, lobbied successfully against the mass removal of civil officials. The law passed by Congress in July did, however, clearly state that military officials had the authority to remove any officials who obstructed the Reconstruction process.[44]

When Congress turned to consider the portion of Stanbery's opinion restricting the power of registration boards to disfranchise white voters, Republican disagreements over the extent of such disfranchisement again emerged. Here too Stanton argued for the moderate position, claiming that only a limited number of Southerners should be excluded from participating in Reconstruction. He gained support from Senators Wilson and Oliver P. Morton of Indiana, who argued that large-scale disfranchisement cost the Republicans potential white support and made it appear that the party wished to put blacks in control of the Southern states. Other Republicans continued to argue that disfranchisement, though easy to legislate, was difficult to enforce and that denying the vote to "the ruling class" of the South would create a "state of war." A North Carolinian in Washington lobbying for the elimination of all disfranchising sections of the Reconstruction Acts believed that the "leading men" in Congress favored his proposal but complained that "no one will move it." Instead, the new act gave the registration boards even wider authority to disfranchise any whites whose loyalty they questioned.[45]

No one could determine how many whites actually lost their votes under the terms of the Reconstruction Acts. Morton and Wilson, who were eager to prove that the Republican party did not wish to turn over the South to black voters, put the number of disfranchised whites at around fifty thousand; James G. Blaine had a much lower estimate of eighteen thousand.[46] Whatever the actual number might have been, white disfranchisement clearly had unfortunate political repercussions for the Republican party. Congressmen in Washington and commanders in the field were deluged with complaints that the laws failed to discriminate between those who ardently advocated secession and those who stood with the Union until circumstances forced them into aiding the Confederacy. Because anyone who had taken an oath before the Civil War to uphold the U.S. Constitution and then had aided the Confederacy was denied the vote, an outspoken secessionist who had not taken such an oath could register. A number of Southerners who had been reluctant Confederates, and who were disfranchised, were furious that their old secessionist opponents were not similarly penalized, and they blamed the Republican party for their dilemma.[47]

Other Southern Republicans, however, urged Congress to liberalize or do away with disfranchisement on the grounds that it discouraged those who wished to support the Republican party but could not because of the Reconstruction Acts. "It requires but little to build up a very powerful party amongst us," an Alabama Unionist told William Pitt Fessenden, "and that can be done by a little leniency shown to the white population of the State." The head of a local Union League in Georgia wrote to Benjamin Wade to ask him to exempt a list of men from disfranchisement, insisting that it was important for white Georgians to know that "we are not a proscription party." Similar pleas were addressed to Benjamin Butler, who expressed sympathy for the idea of removing disabilities but did not believe it could be done "without enfranchising . . . many rebels who are now held powerless by the same rule." He was convinced that a Southern white who was truly supportive of the Republican party would lend it his influence whether he could vote or not.[48]

Some of the generals in the South who administered the disfranchisement clauses agreed that the result was harmful to the prospects of a satisfactory Reconstruction. General Pope told Grant that "disgruntled leaders" who were disfranchised would do everything they could to "undo reconstruction." General Swayne urged Chief Justice Chase to use his influence with Congress to modify the disfranchisement clauses so as to convert "passive well-wishers to serviceable and efficient helpers" of the Republican party. Daniel Sickles warned Lyman Trumbull that if Congress did not remove political disqualifications from whites, the Republican party would lose the support of white men "of ability and experience in public business," whose influence was needed to guide the newly enfranchised black voters. Not all generals agreed with such assessments; Nelson Miles, head of the Freedmen's Bureau in North Carolina, was furious at Sickles's letter, insisting that a general amnesty "would place the knife again in the hands of government assassins."[49]

The observations of Pope, Sickles, and Swayne indicated that although the military commanders in the South sought to assume a public stance of political impartiality, some of them, consciously or unconsciously, frequently promoted the Republican party. In every district the commanders sought to maximize the number of blacks enrolled; this action inevitably aided the Republicans. Although Ord and Schofield ordered their subordinates to abstain from political activity, frequently military officials on the registration boards advised the new voters on how to cast their ballots. One registration officer in Virginia wrote to Benjamin Butler complaining of Schofield's orders, which restricted his political activity; Butler replied that "being a registrar does not debar you from instructing the ignorant voters on their duties and rights. At any rate do so."[50]

The military's potential for aiding the Republicans was most clearly seen in the fifth district, Louisiana and Texas. General Sheridan used his removal powers freely in both states, including replacing both governors. He also continued his policy of rigidly excluding from registration any whites whose loyalty was suspect. In August President Johnson removed Sheridan from command, eventually replacing him with Winfield Scott Hancock, a Democratic general whose sympathy lay with the president and his Reconstruction views. Despite his efforts, however, Hancock found it difficult to undo Sheridan's work. Preoccupied with affairs in Louisiana, Hancock failed to supervise the actions of his subordinate, General Charles Griffin, who was in command in Texas. Griffin and his successor, General J. J. Reynolds, worked closely with E. M. Pease, the provisional governor previously appointed by Sheridan, and removed several state officeholders, replacing them with Republicans. Although Conservatives continued to hold most of the offices in the state, the patronage made available to Republicans by military action helped sustain their party.[51]

Although no other general's action provided as much partisan support for the Republican party as those of Sheridan and Griffin, General Pope in the fourth district also made removals and appointments that were favorable to the Republican cause. His most clearly partisan action involved an order restricting military and state government printing in his district to newspapers that were favorable to congressional Reconstruction. Pope also kept a close eye on the progress of voting registration and wrote to Schenck's Congressional Committee that he was endeavoring to "get out the full colored vote." To encourage this, he made sure blacks were appointed to the registration boards and paid them according to the number of votes they registered. He assured Schenck that in Alabama "we are secure of success in electing a ticket, Republican in name and principle."[52]

Elsewhere, military commanders were more cautious in aiding the Republican cause. Despite pressure from Mississippi Republicans to do so, General Ord refused to reorient the state's printing in the manner dictated by Pope. He also ordered military officials under his command not to become involved in political activity and urged blacks under his jurisdiction to keep laboring in the fields rather than attend political meetings. Complaints from Mississippi Republicans poured into Washington concerning Ord's course, but when Senator Zachariah Chandler wrote to him inquiring about the charges, Ord insisted that he was sympathetic to Congress's program. He promised Chandler that "there will be a convention in both my states and then you gentlemen will control results." After the passage of the Third Reconstruction Act in July, Ord did order his registration boards to question whites more closely about their loyalty, and he made sure that registrars visited all the large plantations in Mississippi to ensure a large enrollment of black voters. Ord also created election districts for the Mississippi constitutional convention that ensured that the convention would be controlled by delegates from the black counties in the state.[53] Schofield and Pope also defined district boundaries in ways that aided the Republicans, but at least in Schofield's case, the action was probably not done deliberately to aid the party but to secure the fairest method of apportioning delegates.[54]

In executing the requirements of the Reconstruction Acts, the commanding generals in the South used the agents of the Freedmen's Bureau, which was a military agency under the jurisdiction of the War Department. Freedmen's Bureau representatives, who were given direct responsibility for supervising the welfare of blacks in the South, had much more day-to-day contact with them than regular army personnel. They were instructed to explain to the freedmen the nature of their new political rights and to take steps to ensure that blacks were unhampered in the exercise of those rights.[55] Although many agents chose not to go beyond the letter of the law in carrying out their responsibilities, a significant number chose to use their positions as benefactors and guardians of the blacks to influence them to favor the Republican party; some eventually sought political office with the support of the black vote.

The bureau's official position, as defined by Chief Commissioner O. O. Howard, was nonpartisan; agents were not to give political speeches or run for office. Unofficially, however, it was almost impossible to draw the line between informing the freedmen about their new political responsibilities and suggesting how they might vote. Many of the men serving the bureau were sympathetic to congressional Reconstruction; they had witnessed the adverse effects of Conservative rule on the lives and fortunes of the freedmen and believed that only through suffrage could the blacks protect themselves. In 1865 and 1866 some local bureau superintendents had encouraged blacks to seek enfranchisement; now that blacks were able to vote, these agents were ready to urge them to vote Republican.[56]

General Howard was also sympathetic to Republican aims in the South and concerned lest Conservatives maintain control of their states. He made no public pronouncements of his own in favor of the Republican program, but he did not actively discourage bureau officials who did. He removed two bureau agents whom Henry Wilson accused of aiding forces opposed to Reconstruction and asked his subordinates to report the names of any other agents who "denounced Congress and public men." He assured an inquiring Northern Republican that all of his assistant commissioners were "politically right with one or two exceptions." He allowed his representatives in the South to distribute publications of the Union League and helped keep the Congressional Committee informed about the progress of voter registration in the South. In the summer of 1867 he sent John Mercer Langston, a black man from Ohio, through the South, ostensibly as a bureau representative to inspect its schools; actually Langston's chief mission was to aid in the organization of blacks into the Republican party. When Thomas Conway toured the South for the national Union League, he carried with him a letter from Howard, introducing him to Freedmen's Bureau officers and agents and asking them to help him in his work.[57]

Conway kept Howard informed of the role that Freedmen's Bureau agents were playing in forming local league chapters. He was most enthusiastic about the situation in Alabama, where the state's assistant commissioner, Wager Swayne, had openly and actively promoted Republican party fortunes. Swayne spoke at Union League meetings and directed the organization of a freedmen's state convention in Mobile in May, which passed resolutions endorsing the Republican party. Other bureau agents in the state encouraged blacks to register, endorsed the Republican party, and distributed Republican campaign literature. Thanks in large part to Swayne's efforts, Alabama was the first Confederate state to complete its registration and call for a constitutional convention.[58]

Bureau assistant commissioners in Florida and Virginia also actively aided the Republican party in its efforts to organize blacks. In Tennessee, Assistant Commissioner Clinton B. Fisk sought to maintain political impartiality, but some of his agents distributed Republican literature, made speeches, and encouraged blacks to vote. When Tennessee plantation owners threatened to fire their black workers if they registered, bureau agents pledged to feed them until they found new jobs. Bureau officials in Washington upheld this policy, ordering their representatives in the field to "see that nobody starves in consequence of having done his duty."[59] There was less evidence of bureau political activity in the Carolinas, although Unionist leader William Holden of North Carolina told General Howard that the bureau was "exerting good influence," particularly by helping ensure that loyal registrars were appointed to enroll voters. In South Carolina, Assistant Superintendent Robert K. Scott claimed that none of his agents were members of Union Leagues, and he advised blacks not to neglect their farm work in favor of politics. Some two dozen Republican political figures who emerged in the state after the new Reconstruction governments were established, however, had had prior affiliation with the Freedmen's Bureau. In Georgia, at least twenty men who had served the bureau later became officials in the new Republican regime.[60]

In May 1867, General Joseph Mower, head of the Freedmen's Bureau in Louisiana, forbade his men to take part in political meetings or use their official position to influence the freedmen. General Howard immediately wrote Mower, asking for an explanation of his action. Mower replied that his order had been aimed at agents advocating that blacks vote Democratic. He assured Howard that "where the agents are all right . . . where I find they are not a willing tool in the hands of the planter or rebel . . . they are instructed to teach the Negro in political matters." According to Mower, the agents were to encourage the new voters to support "the Great Union Party, the

Party now in power." When Conway visited Louisiana later that month, he reported to Howard that Mower was giving effective assistance to the league and the party.[61]

In Texas, bureau activity was under the direction of General Griffin and later General J. J. Reynolds, both of whom were also acting as military commanders in the state. These men were already actively using their removal powers to benefit the Republicans in the state, and Conway was pleased with progress there. When he turned to Mississippi, however, he found the state "in a condition of Egyptian darkness." He reported in May that General Ord, district commander, and General Alvan Gillem of the Freedmen's Bureau both "need reconstructing themselves." He claimed that neither man was interested in the welfare of blacks "or even in the cause of loyal reconstruction." The process of organizing Union Leagues and informing black voters of their new rights was lagging far behind in the state, and Conway blamed most of the delay on the military authorities. When Howard got a copy of Conway's report on Mississippi, he sent it to Gillem asking for an explanation. In reply, Gillem contended that he did not want to turn the bureau into a "political machine." Howard agreed but warned Gillem that "however your sympathies may be politically, of course, they must be on the side of the government, against all who want to destroy it." Gillem had a responsibility, his superior said, to make sure the "humbler classes" were able to make "intelligent political decisions." Although Gillem refused to work for the advancement of the Republicans, one of his subordinates, Captain Henry R. Pease, actively organized Union Leagues "on the sly." When Pease wrote to bureau headquarters in Washington, questioning Gillem's order prohibiting agents from taking an active part in politics, he was encouraged to continue his efforts. General John W. Alvord, who wrote to Pease in behalf of Howard, added that "we know the man you have to deal with . . . his plan undoubtedly is, to stop the mouths of radicals, and thus give conservatism (falsely so called) a chance."[62]

Despite Gillem's fears, the Freedmen's Bureau never became a political machine. Its chief purpose remained the supervision of the welfare of blacks, not the organization of the Republican party in the South. The bureau was woefully understaffed in all the Southern states, its agents were overburdened with their regular responsibilities, and there was a great turnover in their ranks.[63] Yet whenever numbers of its agents supported the Republicans, party organization went forward rapidly, and the Reconstruction process moved more smoothly toward completion. In states where the bureau or the army was less sympathetic to Reconstruction, the Republican organizers were hampered and discouraged. All in all, despite the complaints from Republicans about individual officers, the army and the bureau, by attempting to maintain order in the South, removing at least some irreconcilable civil officials, and ensuring a large voter registration and turnout among blacks, gave great assistance to the party.

Andrew Johnson was certainly aware that the activities of the district generals and Freedmen's Bureau officers were undermining the Conservative governments he had established in the South, and after Congress adjourned in July he decided to remove some of them. His first target was Secretary of War Edwin M. Stanton, who had resisted any efforts of the executive branch to limit the authority of the commanders. In August he suspended Stanton, replacing him temporarily with General U. S. Grant. This action did not alter the War Department's posture regarding Reconstruction because Grant was supportive of congressional goals there. Johnson, however, removed Phil Sheridan at the same time, and Sheridan was one of the most active generals in aiding the Republicans of the South. General Mower of the Freedmen's Bureau replaced Sheridan until November, when Hancock assumed command. Mower continued Sheridan's policy of removing recalcitrant civil officials in Louisiana, but when Hancock arrived, he declared that he would allow the state's civil administration "to resume its natural dominion." Hancock attempted to replace some of the men removed by Mower and also sought to revise the election lists to allow more whites to vote. Radicals immediately protested to Congress, which could do nothing about the appointment. Fortunately for the Republicans, the Louisiana election to call a constitutional convention was held before Hancock arrived; after his arrival, he was so busy with Louisiana affairs that he did little to alter the political situation in Texas before the election in that state, which was held in February of the following year.[64]

Northern Republicans watched with growing apprehension as Johnson continued to relieve district commanders. In September the president removed Daniel Sickles and replaced him with E. R. S. Canby, who was known as a moderate Republican but was unsympathetic to disfranchisement and revised registration lists in the second district liberally, probably enfranchising many. He made only a few removals and tried to remain nonpolitical in his policies. In December, Johnson replaced Pope in the third district with General George G. Meade. Georgia Republicans were apprehensive about the new appointment, noting that Pope had been helpful to them. Upon news of the change, Senator Henry Wilson wrote to Meade, asking him how he intended to execute the Reconstruction Acts. Meade responded that he intended to be impartial and fair and proceeded to order his subordinates not to make political speeches. One registration clerk told Meade he was surprised at the order, stating that he had previously made such speeches with Pope's knowledge and consent. Meade also softened Pope's order on newspaper eligibility for official announcements. In the fourth district, General Ord resigned, and in December General Gillem, whom Conway had criticized so bitterly as being unfriendly to Republican Reconstruction, assumed command. Gillem undertook no overt partisan actions, but his conservative appointments to civil vacancies angered the state's Republicans.[65]

Early in 1868, Johnson also removed Swayne and Mower from their posts as heads of the Freedmen's Bureau in Alabama and Louisiana. Both men had been among the most active in advancing the interests of the Republican party, and their replacements were determined to stop such partisan activity on the part of the bureau. Mower's successor in Louisiana, General Robert Buchanan, threw his weight on the other side of the political fence, using his office to encourage the Democratic party in the state; Conway complained to Howard that the bureau in Louisiana had become a "copperhead concern." Swayne's successor in Alabama, General Julius Hayden, also sought to stop the bureau's aid to the Republican party.[66]

Fortunately for the Republicans, Johnson's removals came too late to interfere seriously with the party's efforts to control at least the initial stages of Reconstruction in the South. By early October military authorities had completed the process of voter registration, and within a month elections had been held everywhere except Texas on the question of convening state constitutional conventions. Northern Republicans watched closely as the Reconstruction Acts were implemented in the summer and fall of 1867, for they were eager to determine if the combined efforts of the Union Leagues, Congressional

Committee agents, Freedmen's Bureau officials, and newspapers spawned by government contracts had laid a firm basis for Republican control of the South. Some party spokesmen continued to express doubts about the ability of the new black voters to act independently of their former masters. The editor of the *Cincinnati Gazette*, for instance, wondered if "an ignorant mass just released from slavery" could maintain an "artificial domination" over the whites who monopolized most of the economic power and political experience in the South.[67]

The first evidence of the strength of the Republican party, and especially of the reliability of the black vote, came in August in Tennessee. The Volunteer State, which had been restored to the Union in 1866 and hence was not under the jurisdiction of the Reconstruction Acts, had already enfranchised its black males, and in the summer election they were ready to deliver the first votes to be cast by blacks in the South. The state was to choose a governor and state legislature and a full slate of congressmen. The campaign was hotly contested; Conservative candidates actively sought the black vote. Governor William G. Brownlow wrote to Northern Republicans to ask them for aid, reminding them that Tennessee was "the only stronghold Republicanism has in the South." The party's state committee also asked prominent Northern Republicans to speak in the state. No Northerners answered the calls to speak, but they did encourage Brownlow to undertake vigorous measures to control the election. Henry Ward Beecher, a flamboyant abolitionist minister from New York, told the governor that in the campaign "you will carry not only the fate of Tennessee, but of the whole South, and so of the nation." The *Boston Traveller*, in referring to the heated campaign in Tennessee, called the state "the magic mirror in which it is possible to see what time will bring forth for the good or evil of the nation." A great Republican victory there, according to the *Traveller*, would encourage similar results in the unreconstructed states of the South.[68]

Most of the aid that came to the Tennessee Republicans from outside the state was delivered by the Union League. League organizers had been hard at work among the black population of the state since the decision to enfranchise them, and Northerners holding federal posts in the state along with a number of Freedmen's Bureau officials also solicited black votes for the Republicans. The Union Congressional Committee sent thousands of documents into the state, which were read at dozens of Union League meetings, urging the blacks to vote for the Republicans. When Conservative landholders threatened to deprive blacks of jobs if they registered and voted Republican, bureau officials countered by promising assistance to anyone who suffered such reprisals. In Massachusetts, a Reconstruction committee recently formed to aid Southern Republicans also sought to raise funds for the relief of Tennessee blacks punished for voting. To protect blacks from physical intimidation, Governor Brownlow enlarged the state militia, armed it with weapons in part supplied by sympathetic Northern Republican governors, and stationed its units around the state.[69]

The election resulted in a sweeping victory for Tennessee Republicans; they kept Brownlow as governor, won all the congressional seats, and controlled almost all the seats in the state legislature. Although continued proscription of former Confederates helped keep the Republicans in command, most outside observers were more concerned about the black vote, which went overwhelmingly to the party. Northern Republicans rejoiced in the results. John Forney claimed in the *Chronicle* that "the Negro has shown on a large scale that he may be depended upon"; his votes could not be swayed by physical or economic intimidation. The state Republican convention in Massachusetts passed a resolution praising the blacks of Tennessee. The editor of the *Boston Traveller* found the Tennessee election "an excellent beginning" for the work of reconstructing the other Southern states. Marcus Ward believed the elections in Tennessee "would prove to be indicative of our success in nearly all the rebellious states." The *Boston Commonwealth* agreed, stating that after the Tennessee election, there was no longer a question that the black vote would go Republican elsewhere in the South.[70]

Not all Republican journals shared in this optimism. The editor of the *Nation*, who had never been strongly in favor of universal suffrage, feared that despite the evidence from Tennessee, the old Southern aristocracy would ultimately wield "its enormous social influence" in such a way as to gain control of the Southern states. During the rest of the summer of 1867, however, the bulk of information reaching Northern Republicans from the South confirmed the impression that the black voters would be loyal to their party. Agents of the Union Congressional Committee and organizers for the Union Leagues sent dozens of letters to the committee assuring its members that the black vote was safely Republican. Northerners who were living in the South also reported to their home state congressmen that blacks were rapidly gaining political sophistication and could be counted upon at election time. Edwin Morgan, chairman of the Congressional Committee, rejoiced that the blacks of the South were responding so positively to the Republican party's efforts to educate them and praised Northerners for aiding in the organizing process.[71]

The *Great Republic* agreed with Morgan's assessment but warned that the battle in the remaining Southern states would be difficult and that the outcome would depend heavily upon continued support from Northern Republicans. By midsummer the Union League, the Congressional Committee, and the National Union Republican Committee were all short of funds and were having to appeal to Northerners for more aid. In their appeals, all the organizations stressed that if the South were to be controlled by the Republican party and Republican electoral votes for president were to be cast by the South, the work had to be done now, not later. Tullock, Schenck, and Morgan all toured Northern cities in search of money, and they all reported meeting resistance to their appeals. Republican officeholders failed to pay their assessments to the Congressional Committee. James Edmunds and Edwin Morgan reported that Northerners they contacted were reluctant to provide financial aid, either because they were dubious about success in the South or apathetic about the outcome.[72]

Some of the apparent apathy of Northern Republicans toward Southern organizational work was broken in the fall of 1867 when results of Northern state elections became known. The percentage of the vote obtained by Republicans in almost every state was reduced. Particularly ominous were the results in the key states of Ohio, Pennsylvania, and New York. In Ohio Democrats won control of the legislature, enabling them to deny Radical Republican Benjamin Wade his Senate seat the following year; Ohioans also overwhelmingly defeated a Negro suffrage amendment to their state constitution. In Pennsylvania and New York the Republican state ticket was also defeated. One of the consequences of these defeats was to convince at least some Republicans that they would have to redouble their efforts to control the Southern states and get them into the Union before the next presidential election.[73]

At the same time that Northern election results were striking fear into Northern Republicans, Southern prospects grew more encouraging. Voting registration in the unreconstructed states showed that upward of 90 percent of the eligible blacks had been enrolled; and either because of white apathy or refusal to register, blacks had a majority of registered voters in five states. The first elections for constitutional conventions, held in Louisiana late in September and in Alabama and Virginia in October, were easily controlled by the Republicans, who gained approval for the convening of the conventions and elected most of the delegates to them. The voting results were clearly determined by black votes in those states, and the *Washington Chronicle* rejoiced in the further evidence that blacks "cannot be driven by threats nor induced by persuasions to vote away their own liberties or betray their true friends." The *Boston Traveller* also noted the strength of black support for the Republicans, stating that "without their assistance we should not have one chance of getting a solitary vote in the South." By the end of November the results from all other Southern states except Texas, where the election was delayed until early 1868, were in. In every state the Republicans carried the day for the state conventions and controlled most of the seats in these conventions, and in every case their strength was drawn from the huge turnout of black voters. As an Arkansas Republican told Senator Richard Yates of Illinois, "the Ebony Citizens are the truest Republicans in the South—they vote as a unit."[74]

As a result of Northern defeats and Southern successes, the Union Congressional Committee reported more success in its fund-raising efforts. When the committee presented its year-end report to the Republican congressional caucus in December, Schenck reported total collections of $40,673, half of which had been raised since July. The committee had aided 178 speakers in the South and had distributed close to a million documents there. Schenck also reported that his committee had received more than three thousand letters from Southern Republicans. The assembled congressmen then passed resolutions endorsing the committee's efforts and authorized it to continue its work in the South.[75]

The Union Congressional Committee and the Union Leagues, with their associates in the army and the Freedmen's Bureau, had done their work well. Thomas Conway, one of the most prominent Congressional Committee agents and Union League representatives, who had spent several months touring the South in the summer and fall of 1867, was convinced that without the efforts of the committee and the league, the Republicans could not have controlled Reconstruction. Yet the work was not completed; as Schenck reminded his Republican colleagues, their Southern friends were about to prepare state constitutions, and they would need assistance and supervision in the process. The constitutions would then have to be submitted for popular ratification, and Republicans would also have to secure control of state offices to be filled under the new constitutions. And beyond the process of securing the restoration of the Southern states to the Union lay the challenge of gaining their votes for the Republican candidate for president in the 1868 election.[76]

Most Northern Republicans were convinced that if it were to meet the challenge of controlling the South, their party would have to gain more white support. At the end of 1867, firm black majorities, which were clearly Republican, existed only in Mississippi, Louisiana, and South Carolina. In the other states of the South, some white support would be needed to carry the state for the party. Consequently, Northern Republicans were very concerned lest their counterparts in the South adopt party platforms or draft state constitutions that would alienate potential white allies. Hence they bent their efforts not only to building a Republican party in the South but to basing it on a moderate, biracial foundation.

WHITES AND THE SOUTHERN

STRATEGY, 1867–1868

The Northern Republicans who took the most active role in working with their Southern allies were those who were most confident about gaining white support. These Republicans fell into the moderate wing of the party, and they had dominated the writing of the Reconstruction Acts. The moderates had avoided Radical proposals for territorial governments, extended military occupation of the South, large-scale disfranchisement, and confiscation of property. Instead, they had designed a Reconstruction process that they hoped would maximize Southern white cooperation and result in a relatively swift restoration of the former Confederate states. Some of the congressmen most closely involved with drafting the Reconstruction legislation, such as Senators Fessenden, Sherman, and Wilson, were former Whigs, and at least some of them hoped to attract their old party colleagues in the South to the Republican ranks. A number of the key men who staffed the Republican National and Congressional committees, such as Robert Schenck, Edwin Morgan, and William Claflin, and the head of the national Union League, James Edmunds, were also former Whigs, as was William D. Kelley, one of the few Republican congressmen who campaigned extensively in the South and maintained contacts there. These Republicans were all organization men, interested in building their party in the South by attracting whites, particularly former Whigs, to the Republican organization.

Almost all Northern Republicans had been reluctant to enfranchise the freedmen, fearing that their former masters would control their votes. As evidence in the South began to accumulate in 1867 that blacks could be trusted to vote Republican if they were organized properly, many Northern Republicans began to fear that the freedmen might use their new political power against whites. Hence Northern Republicans sought to use what influence they had over Southern party organization in 1867 to advise their new black allies not to take any action that would alienate potential white support. They warned against proposals for property confiscation or large-scale disfranchisement of whites. Also, because Northern Republicans wanted to demonstrate that the party was not dominated by blacks, they advised against equal accommodations laws and the election of large numbers of blacks to office. Instead, they hoped the party would endorse programs in the South that would appeal to both races: public education for all, equal civil and political rights, and encouragement of economic development.

The national leadership of the Union League, upon which the Republicans heavily depended for organizing Southern support, did attempt to keep the organization from falling entirely into the hands of blacks. In almost every state the league was segregated by race, and in South Carolina, Mississippi, Florida, and Texas its membership was overwhelmingly black. In Alabama and Georgia, where the league initially was organized among whites, blacks also came to predominate. To protect its members from white retaliation, league meetings were often held in secret, sometimes at night, and its members were occasionally armed. They were also bound by oath not to reveal its activities. The secrecy and oaths helped reassure anxious blacks, and without the league it would have been difficult to get freedmen actively involved in politics.[1]

Some Northerners, including Henry Wilson and William D. Kelley, applauded the league as being well adapted for organizing blacks.[2] The same secrecy and oaths alarmed Southern whites, even white Republicans, who feared that the league would become an instrument to advance black interests at white expense. This concern existed also in the North. The *Boston Advertiser* worried that if whites stayed away from the league, the organization would "disseminate dangerous doctrines." What the *Advertiser* feared most was that the leagues would be controlled by men who would appeal to the "worst passions of the freedmen" and set race against race. National Union League leaders were aware of this problem and sought to reassure Southern whites who feared the league would inspire blacks to attack them. James Edmunds, president of the league, insisted that his organization stood for temperance, industry, education, and obedi-

ence to the law and to legally constituted authority. He also assured
whites that the league would not advocate confiscation but would
instead seek to develop the industrial resources of the South. When
Thomas Conway undertook his organizing mission through the
Southern states for the league in the spring of 1867, he took with him
similar moderating attitudes.[3]

In the spring and summer of 1867 conventions were held throughout the South to organize state Republican parties. Although local
Union Leaguers played an important role in many of these conventions, the parties they created ultimately replaced the leagues as the
chief instrument for organizing Republican voters. At these conventions, each state party sought to identify its goals and build its constituency; hence they provided important indications of whether or
not the party would be dominated by blacks and black concerns.
Actually, events were to demonstrate that blacks, not whites, had
reason to fear that the party would not represent their interests,
for in almost every state white Unionists dominated the party
conventions.

The first Republican conventions in the South were held in North
Carolina in March and the following month in Arkansas. Northern
Republicans had high hopes of gathering a significant white vote in
each state.[4] During the war Unionist minorities had emerged in both
states, and they were particularly numerous in North Carolina. Although the Union League was active in each state, it was weak, and
native white Unionists took the lead in organizing the Republican
party; Northerners played little role in these first two conventions.
Nonetheless, they watched with interest to see upon what basis their
colleagues would organize their party.[5]

In North Carolina, William Holden and his Unionist following controlled the Republican convention. When Albion Tourgée, a former
Union officer from Ohio who was editor of the *Greensboro Union Register*, warned that Holden would not protect black interests, Union
League president James Edmunds urged him to support Holden "for
the general good of the cause." Tourgée agreed, and Holden showed
his good intentions by making sure that delegates from both races
attended the party convention; several blacks also served as convention officers. In part because of the role of blacks in the North Carolina convention, the platform endorsed the Reconstruction Acts, the
abolition of slavery, civil rights, and biracial voting.[6] The editor of the

Boston Commonwealth, referring to this convention with recent Northern political reversals in mind, exclaimed that "Connecticut, Ohio, and Maryland can take a hint from the fresher Republicanism of North Carolina." Godkin's *Nation*, which was especially concerned lest the Southern Republicans endorse confiscatory schemes, also praised the work of the North Carolina convention and predicted the party would control the state.[7]

Although the white Republican leadership of North Carolina was willing to include both races in its ranks and was committed to civil and political equality, it showed no interest in property confiscation or in securing public accommodations laws for blacks. In Arkansas, white Republicans were even more conservative. Unionists there had been organizing the Union League for several years, but the organization had made little headway among blacks, who were consequently not well represented in the Republican party's councils. The state convention had only three black delegates; although the platform supported the Reconstruction Acts, it was drawn with an eye to the white voters of the state. It said little about black rights and instead attacked the secessionist and Conservative governments for ignoring the economic needs of Arkansas. The party called for internal improvements, equal taxation of property, and the migration into the state of Northern capital. Arkansas Republicans also petitioned Congress for federal aid for levee repair along the Mississippi River.[8]

Northern Republicans had little influence on the conventions in North Carolina and Arkansas. They became more involved in Virginia, which was the next state to hold a party convention. Because Virginia was so close to Washington, Republican party officials had numerous opportunities to consult with the state's white Unionist leaders and were better informed about affairs in Virginia than about matters in other Southern states. Northern Republicans were particularly interested in Virginia because in 1860 the state had the largest electoral vote in the South. If they could encourage the development of a well-organized party in the state that drew support not only from blacks but from a significant number of whites as well, the Virginia party might prove a model for the rest of the South. Hence throughout 1867 and early 1868 Virginia got more attention from Northern Republicans than any other Southern state.

The Republican party that had existed in Virginia since early in the

Civil War was weak and divided in 1867. One wing of the party was led by former Whig Unionists such as John Minor Botts of Richmond and Governor Francis H. Pierpont. Both men hoped to appeal to business and professional men of similar political antecedents by emphasizing that the Republican party would develop the economic potential of the state. They were not primarily concerned about black rights; Botts had opposed universal suffrage at the loyalist convention in 1866. They were prepared, however, to accept the Reconstruction Acts and to include equal rights and free public schools in the party's platform. These moderate Republicans were frightened by the growing strength of the more radical Unionist James W. Hunnicutt, a Baptist minister and newspaper editor from Richmond. Hunnicutt was primarily interested in freedmen's rights and hence drew his strength from the newly enfranchised black voters of the state, many of whom were organizing into Union Leagues. Hunnicutt urged disfranchisement of large numbers of whites, and many of his black followers also wanted property confiscation. Botts, Pierpont, and their followers were convinced that if Hunnicutt won control of the party, it would never gain white support.[9]

Because Hunnicutt's forces had an organizational advantage through their influence in the Union League, the Pierpont-Botts group was more active in seeking Northern support. They found a ready response among Republican former Whigs in the North, who were eager to encourage the program Botts represented. Botts was especially successful in obtaining aid from Republicans in Massachusetts; party leaders in Boston shared his Whiggish mentality and were eager to cultivate support in Virginia among business-minded whites. Senator Henry Wilson had already assisted the white Virginians; at Botts's request, he had provided in the Second Reconstruction Act for voting by ballot rather than by voice, which Botts believed would embolden more whites to vote Republican. Wilson also tried to structure the act to allow Pierpont to administer the elections for the constitutional convention in the state, but Congress refused, vesting this power in the military commander, as was done elsewhere in the South. Had Congress agreed with Wilson's proposal, it would have given Pierpont's group a great advantage in controlling the reorganization of Virginia.[10]

With the Republican state convention due to meet on April 17, white Virginians also appealed to Governor John Andrew of Massachusetts for aid. Andrew, a former Whig, had already announced his support for a reconstruction that would reconcile Southern whites to the Republican party. He sent another former Whig, John Murray Forbes, one of the state's leading businessmen and a close political associate, to visit Richmond. Forbes provided Republicans there with some money and then contacted Wilson in Washington, who agreed to visit the state. On April 3, Wilson arrived in Richmond, consulted with party organizers there, and then went on to Petersburg, where he spoke to an audience of several thousand, most of whom were white.[11]

In his Petersburg speech, Wilson seized the opportunity to appeal for white votes and announced some themes that he would pursue vigorously in the months to come. Although he pronounced himself a radical Republican, he said that the North must share the blame for the war because it had helped establish slavery in the South. He praised the heroism of the Southern soldiers and insisted that with slavery abolished, there was no reason for Southerners not to cooperate with Republicans in Congress in securing the restoration of their states. He warned the whites not to listen to the Democrats, who could not hope to control Congress; the Republican party was destined to rule, and its organization would expand "until it shall reach into Mexico." He assured his audience that the Republicans would be generous in their treatment of former Confederates. The senator had already published a letter avowing that the Reconstruction Acts were not intended to disfranchise the rank-and-file veterans of the Confederate army, and he promised that congressional disqualification laws would "vanish in a few months."[12]

Despite Wilson's efforts to encourage moderate Republicans of the Botts-Pierpont wing, when the state convention met on April 17 Hunnicutt's forces were in control. Some of the black delegates introduced resolutions calling for confiscation, but more conservative members opposed the idea, warning that such a proposal would cost the party white support. Thomas Conway, who was in the city to represent the national Union League, also warned that the Republicans could not hope to carry the state on black votes alone. The convention subsequently agreed to drop the confiscation issue and adopted a moderate platform calling for support of the Reconstruction Acts and the principles of the national Republican party. The convention solicited the support of all classes and races and in a bid for business support called for aid to internal improvements and the importation of Northern capital and skills. The emphasis of the platform, however, was on appeals to the "laboring classes of the state"; it called for free schools, equal civil and political rights for all, and taxes based on ability to pay. The party endorsed the right of both races to hold public office, a prospect that disturbed conservative whites. Finally, when the convention named the party's state central committee, it filled it with Hunnicutt men.[13]

Boston newspapers, which had been watching events in Richmond closely, were satisfied with the convention results. The *Boston Advertiser* concluded that the party would develop along biracial lines in Virginia and might do so in the rest of the South. The *Boston Traveller*, which had been concerned about the debate over confiscation, was pleased that the party did not endorse the proposal. Now that the convention was over, however, the *Traveller* wondered if it would not be wise "for Northern politicians to leave the South alone for the present."[14]

The Botts-Pierpont wing did not share the *Traveller's* views; dismayed by the convention results, the white Virginia Republicans renewed their appeals for support from Northern Republicans. They insisted that Hunnicutt, who now controlled the party machinery, would lead the party in a radical direction, alienating the races and destroying any chance for Republican survival in the state. Botts and Pierpont again found a sympathetic response to their claims, this time from the two leading Republican papers of the North, the *New York Tribune* and the *New York Times*. Both papers were edited by former Whigs who had hoped for some time that the Republican party could develop a Southern wing based on substantial white support. Horace Greeley warned in his *Tribune* that "to organize a campaign on the Hunnicutt plan is to abandon any hope of a permanent Union party in the South." Greeley worried that intemperate men such as Hunnicutt would tempt black voters, who were "mainly ignorant" and had "not been trained to reverence the rights of property," to endorse confiscation. His warning was echoed by Henry J. Raymond's *Times*, which expressed concern that Hunnicutt would appeal to racial hatred to build black support.[15]

Immediately after the Virginia Republican convention adjourned, Governor Pierpont asked Wilson to return to the state to attempt to reconcile the divergent wings of the party, and the senator quickly agreed. Greeley was pleased at news of Wilson's new mission, calling him "a prudent counsellor." Even the *Richmond Enquirer*, a Conservative newspaper, hailed the senator for returning to Virginia "to break down Hunnicuttism." In both private meetings and public speeches, Wilson appealed to Republicans not to divide along racial lines. He asked blacks not to be motivated by hatred against whites and not to ask for confiscation of property. He urged them instead to work hard, save their money, and buy land offered by Congress under an amendment to the Homestead Act. He urged whites to treat blacks fairly and promised those who were disfranchised that they could regain the vote by cooperating with Congress. He continued to appeal to prewar Unionists, especially former Whigs, for support, reminding them that the Republicans could bring public education, industry, and a diversified economy to the state. Wilson's efforts to turn the Virginia Republicans in a moderate direction were seconded by Union Leaguer Thomas Conway. In a speech to several thousand in Petersburg on April 22, he urged blacks to form a biracial party and warned against confiscation schemes. He also assured whites that "we do not propose to have schools where the white and black children shall go together."[16]

Wilson's efforts in Virginia brought limited results. One of the more moderate Conservative papers, the *Richmond Whig*, did endorse his views and edged toward the Republican camp. The *Richmond Enquirer*, however, concluded that despite Wilson's efforts the Virginia Republican party would be dominated by blacks. In the North, Greeley's *Tribune* was pleased by Wilson's efforts, but the *Times* was cautious, noting that his audiences were largely black. Northern support did encourage the Botts-Pierpont wing of the party to press for a new state convention, at which they hoped to be more fully represented.[17]

Apparently convinced that he had succeeded in convincing Virginia Republicans to court biracial support on a moderate platform, Wilson left the Old Dominion to embark on a four-week tour of the South to encourage other state Republican parties that had not yet held conventions to follow a similar course. During his trip Wilson made thirty-two speeches and visited cities in North and South Carolina, Georgia, Alabama, and Louisiana. He undertook the trip on his own, without party or committee backing, and in so doing became one of the few Northern Republicans to visit the former Confederate states. He proclaimed that his intention was to explain the Reconstruction Acts to the South, so that he could get Southern cooperation in implementing them, thus hastening the completion of the restoration process. More specifically, he was intent upon encouraging both blacks and whites, especially the latter, to support the Republican party by encouraging local leaders to repudiate programs that would increase racial tensions.[18]

Wilson brought basically the same message to the blacks in his audiences throughout his Southern tour. He told them he did not believe they would vote as the white secessionist leaders desired. "If any of you hesitate how to vote," he advised the freedmen in Augusta, Georgia, "go and look into the cemeteries where those lie who died that you might be free." He urged blacks everywhere to register and to vote Republican: "I do not expect to hear of a black man who votes against the cause of liberty." He pointed out to his black listeners that the Republican party had championed their freedom, helped grant them equal rights, and provided them with the vote, through which they could gain public schools. He urged blacks to use their new political power responsibly and not to "war against whites." Wilson warned that "we want no black party, or no white party. The man who places a ground of alienation between the races is the worst public enemy."[19]

Wilson also urged his black audiences to avoid the temptations of alcohol and to work hard, save their money, and buy farms. The federal government, he cautioned, would not confiscate property and redistribute it to blacks, but it would provide federal land in the South to blacks at a cost of $1.25 an acre. When he arrived in New Orleans, where black leaders were agitating for equal accommodations laws, Wilson warned that prejudice existed against Negroes in both the North and the South. The way for blacks to overcome this prejudice, suggested the Massachusetts senator, was to be "consistent, steady, and inflexible" in the exercise of their civil rights but "loving, tender, and kind to everybody, and obedient to the laws." Above all, warned Wilson, there could be no law "that can legislate you into any man's parlor." Legislation could guarantee legal equality for the blacks, "but your own brain, heart, conscience, and life must fix your social position."[20]

To whites, Wilson brought a message of forgiveness and conciliation. He entered upon his Southern tour convinced that the South had been punished enough for the war, and although he told his Southern white audiences that their section must bear the main responsibility for starting the war, the North could not escape blame for its tolerance of slavery in the South. Now that the hated institution was gone, he averred, there was no more reason for sectional hostility to be maintained. He was shocked by the wartime devastation that he witnessed in the South and stated that Southern whites "have suffered and have been disappointed more than any body of men in the history of the world." Believing that the bulk of Southern whites had been misled by their leaders and deceived into supporting secession, he praised them for their bravery during the war and then asked them to renounce their past mistakes and commit themselves to the progressive ideas of the Republican party. He appealed especially to original Unionists, to the "Clay Whigs and the Jackson or Douglas Democrats," but he offered a hand even to secessionists who were willing to admit their error. Southern whites turned out in reasonable numbers to listen to him, and he repeatedly told them that the Republicans would exact nothing more from them if they proved willing to cooperate in the restoration of their states upon a platform of equal rights and justice for all. At first, he pledged that Congress would enact no confiscatory measures, but after Thaddeus Stevens complained about this statement, he warned that if Southern whites sought to intimidate black voters, or in other ways interfered with Reconstruction, they could face seizure of their property. Cooperation, however, would result in early restoration of their states and the lifting of political proscriptions against former Confederates.[21]

Wilson made a particular appeal to white economic groups whose support he thought he could gain for the Republican party. In New Orleans, he suggested to merchants that the Republican party might offer federal aid to rebuild the state's levee system. He reminded the white workingmen and mechanics of the city that slavery had dishonored labor and held back public education; now that the Republican party had come to the South, they could get legislation to establish schools and further the industrial interests of the state. Everywhere Wilson portrayed the Republican party as standing for free labor, free speech, a free press, and equal economic opportunity. Through the party, he promised, the South could develop its diversified economic potential and attract Northern capital to make the section prosper.[22]

Wilson considered his speaking tour a great success. Both races turned out to listen to him, and although whites often listened in sullen silence, he experienced almost no overt hostility. In Montgomery, Alabama, he entered into a vigorous debate with Conservative General James H. Clanton, who charged that Wilson's efforts would create a black man's party in the South, controlled by alien Northern carpetbaggers. Wilson denied these charges, arguing that Republicans wanted to avoid a racially oriented party organization. He held similar debates elsewhere and was encouraged because no violence occurred and free speech and open debate were returning to the South. His black audiences were generally enthusiastic, despite his conservative advice to them, and Southern Republicans were pleased with his help in publicizing the party's positions.[23] A few Southern newspapers recognized, as did the *New Orleans Crescent*, that Wilson's speeches were "very conciliatory" and sought to cultivate friendly relations between the races. The editor of the *Charleston Daily News* found Wilson's speech in that city "temperate, and from his point of view, not unfair." Nonetheless, the *News* insisted that "since 40,000 [whites] control the wealth of the state . . . the 60,000 [blacks] must follow, not lead." Benjamin S. Hedrick, the prewar Republican from North Carolina, however, noted that Wilson was roundly abused by most Southern or "rebel" papers. Hedrick added that "if they cannot stand Wilson, I do not know what they will do when they get Sumner, Thad Stevens, Butler and Ashley down on them."[24]

Hedrick's remarks pointed to the differences between Wilson and some of his more radical colleagues on the future of Reconstruction politics. Thaddeus Stevens, who remained dubious about the possibility of gaining Southern white support and adamant in his advocacy of black rights, was angry at Wilson for claiming that no further terms would be expected from Congress if the Southerners cooperated with the Reconstruction Acts. Other Radicals were equally disturbed at Wilson's conciliatory statements; Benjamin Wade of Ohio told Zachariah Chandler that "you and I know that Wilson is a ——— fool . . . I never supposed he would do us any good there or anywhere else." The radical *Boston Commonwealth* warned that Wilson's appeals for former Whig votes reflected a "stupid want of genuine sagacity." The *Cincinnati Gazette* was dubious about the possibility of gaining white votes; Southern Unionists were a feeble few "and of a class accustomed to be domineered." They were not reliable voters, according to the *Gazette*, and unless protected by federal troops, they would be cowed by Conservative pressure.[25]

More moderate Republican papers, such as the *New York Tribune*, continued to praise Wilson's efforts. The editors of the *Boston Evening Journal* were convinced that the senator's trip South had proved that "the harvest is white" and urged the party's "sagacious men" to see that the opportunity to reap the white vote was not neglected. The "sagacious men" who ran the Union Congressional Committee, which supervised Republican organizational work in the South, were ready to do just that. Schenck insisted that his committee was as interested in reaching white voters as it was the blacks. When Benjamin Wade asked Zachariah Chandler, a committee member, to make it clear that Wilson was "speaking on his own hook and not for the party," the committee refused to disavow his remarks. Instead, the members ensured that their speakers followed much the same conciliatory line offered by the Massachusetts senator.[26]

In May the committee sponsored a visit into the South by another leading Northern Republican, William D. Kelley of Pennsylvania. Although Kelley had earned a reputation as a Radical, chiefly by endorsing Negro suffrage immediately after the war, his speeches sounded much like Wilson's. Ten years later, Kelley would complain that the Republicans had lost the South because they failed to reinvigorate "the old Whig or Union party of the South." In seeking Whig votes in the former Confederacy, Kelley echoed Wilson's appeals. Everywhere he urged white Southerners to develop their economic resources and assured them the Republican party could assist them in this endeavor. He reminded his white audiences that the Republicans championed free labor, public schools, fair wages, protection for industry, and aid for internal improvements. He told blacks to assert their rights but also to be "peaceful, industrious, forget the past, overlook the prejudices of your neighbors, and be faithful and gentle." Everywhere he discouraged talk of confiscation and urged blacks to work hard and buy their own homes. In Salisbury, North Carolina, he too stated, as Wilson had before him, that the Reconstruction Acts would be the final step in restoration unless the South refused to cooperate with its terms. A Southern Unionist in North Carolina, listening to the remarks of Wilson, Kelley, and others, urged his friends to "affiliate with all those who take for their watchwords prompt reconstruction under the new laws, no further disfranchisement, no further punishment." He hoped that moderate Republicans would control the party, but he feared lest they "be run over by the car of Revolution."[27]

The Republican Congressional Committee sought to reassure the South that it would not be run over by any "car of Revolution." On May 22 it issued a conciliatory address to the Southern people, in which it stated that the Reconstruction Acts were intended to bring peace and tranquillity to the South, not to punish that section. The committee exhorted blacks to support the Republicans, who had given them freedom and equality, but it also appealed to whites, particularly of the "laboring class," by emphasizing that the party could bring them free public schools and economic aid to develop the resources of the South. Southern whites could expect restoration of their states as soon as they had met the terms of the Reconstruction Acts and Congress was satisfied that the people of the South were "likely to be loyal, by decisive and trustworthy majorities." Presumably, they could demonstrate this loyalty only by voting the Republican party into power, and the Republican committee indicated its expectation that "many former slaveowners and supporters of the rebellion" would see fit to vote with them. Greeley's *Tribune* applauded the moderate tone of the committee's address, and both the *Boston Advertiser* and the *Nation* rejoiced that the committee, by dismissing confiscatory and other Radical schemes, had proved that it was not controlled by Thaddeus Stevens.[28]

If Thaddeus Stevens did not control national Republican policy, it still remained to be seen if James W. Hunnicutt controlled the state Republican party in Virginia. Northern Republicans continued to watch the state closely to see if the moderate, biracially oriented policies favored by the party's national organization would find favor there. Early in May Henry Wilson wrote James Edmunds, asking him to determine whether the Union League and Congressional Committee could send a joint delegation to Richmond to encourage the two wings of the party there to unite in a new convention. A few days later Charles Gibbons, a leader of the Philadelphia Union League, visited Richmond to encourage the Botts-Pierpont wing. He spoke to a black audience in the African church there, urging his listeners to work for a biracial party and not to call for property confiscation. A few weeks later Horace Greeley also visited the city and in a speech to blacks echoed Gibbons's cautions. Radicals in the state, however, continued to call for confiscation, and, in desperation, late in May Governor Pierpont journeyed to New York to ask the city's Union League to intervene in the Virginia party's affairs.[29]

The New York Union League, convinced that the party's divisions in Virginia threatened the Republicans' future not only in that state but across the South, agreed to organize a delegation to send to Richmond. It got the endorsement of the Congressional Committee for the mission and also asked league members in Boston and Philadelphia to send representatives. Republicans in both Northern cities willingly joined in the venture. Bay State Republicans were particularly concerned about the direction of the party in Virginia; not only had politicians such as John Andrew and Henry Wilson sought to influence events there, but Boston businessmen had done so as well. Leaders of the city's business community, such as John Murray Forbes and Edward Atkinson, hoped to work with Southern businessmen in pursuit of common economic policies and thought they could coax them into the Republican party. The *Boston Advertiser*, which believed that former Whigs would be "our best allies in placing the material interests of the country in a healthy condition," had long worried about the likelihood of the Virginia Republican party falling permanently into the hands of Hunnicutt and his black supporters. Atkinson, who had extensive business interests in the South, was particularly eager to "prevent the creation of an exclusive black man's party and also to kill the schemes of confiscation."[30]

Under the leadership of Andrew, Forbes, and Atkinson, Massachusetts businessmen and political leaders formed the Massachusetts Reconstruction Association, which they hoped to use to raise money from Bay Staters to promote the organization of a Southern Republican party on a moderate, biracial basis. One of their first actions was to select a delegation to send to Richmond. Forbes made sure that although the delegation included a "minority of politicians," it was composed chiefly of "active business and professional men, whose report of affairs at Richmond will be valuable here, when we come to raise funds." Henry Wilson, whose moderate views on Reconstruction politics were well known, was one of the politicians selected to go.[31]

The Northern delegations met in Richmond for two days in June with Hunnicutt, Botts, and other representatives of the competing

Virginia Republican factions. Botts argued that the party's base was too narrow racially and geographically because it drew its support mainly from blacks in eastern Virginia. He pointed to a list of three hundred white men of "respectability" who had signed a call for a new party convention; almost all of them were old Union Whigs and landowners. Hunnicutt retorted that such men would be welcome if they endorsed the April platform but stated that blacks could carry the state without the aid of native whites. After arguing all night, the Virginians agreed to call for a new convention in August for the purpose of "perfecting and enlarging" the party's organization. The Northern delegates were particularly pleased because the new call for the August convention included the names submitted by Botts. The Northerners thought the new names would "add to the character and dignity of the party, and convince the country that a large body of the most intelligent and substantial landowners of the South" were ready to avow their support for the Republicans.[32]

E. L. Godkin of the *Nation*, who was worried lest the newly enfranchised fall victim to dangerous advice "from indiscreet and overzealous friends," was greatly pleased by the efforts of the Massachusetts Reconstruction Association in Virginia. He warned that blacks could not be left alone to succumb to the prospect of "enticing programmes which can never be carried out" and thanked the Massachusetts group and the Union Republican Congressional Committee for ensuring that "nothing is done to excite the freedmen to feelings of revenge or delusive hopes of direct benefits from Government." Not all Northern Republicans, however, were pleased by these efforts to moderate black demands and court the support of white former Whigs. John Forney snorted derisively in the *Washington Chronicle* that "the old Whig party is the deadest of all dead things. . . . Why anybody should have thought of it in Virginia, we do not know." According to Forney, the Republicans could not win by seeking the support of men of "respectability." In Southern conservative eyes, he noted, no poor white or black man was respectable; and yet "it is from these classes mainly that our ranks must be recruited." The Washington correspondent of the *Anti-Slavery Standard* warned that "for every white voter who may be influenced by the temporizing and trimming necessary to secure such ante-diluvian Bourbons as the old line Whigs in Virginia must be, a dozen colored voters will be made restless and dissatisfied."[33]

Developments in Virginia revealed that Northern Republicans, although intent on gaining white support for the party, were not in agreement about what group of whites to court. The Northern delegation that visited the state in June was clearly enamored of the Botts-Pierpont alternative, which was to appeal to the "respectable" men of property and standing in the state. Hunnicutt, who was more interested in gaining the support of blacks and laboring-class whites, received almost no encouragement from the North. Some Republican spokesmen, however, agreed with Forney that the Republicans had to appeal to poor whites and blacks rather than to whites of respectability. He claimed that the common whites of the South could be won "by educating and enlightening them." The editors of the *Boston Commonwealth* also hoped that the "masses of uneducated whites, no less than the blacks, will find it for their interest to unite with a party which seeks to elevate all classes in the community." Frederick Douglass, the Northern Republican black spokesman, believed that because of the conflicts between wealthy landowners and poor whites, the latter class would rally with the blacks to the Republican standard.[34]

The Washington correspondent of the *Anti-Slavery Standard*, surveying the political situation in the South, predicted that "the next struggle will be between the Industrial interests of the land on the one hand, and those which may be classified under the general head of Capital." This writer believed that blacks should bolster the forces of industrial labor in its struggle with capital, but noted that the moderate leadership of the Republican party, the men who had controlled the writing of the Reconstruction Acts, were now working through the national party committees to steer the black vote away from a Radical course. He urged other Republicans who agreed with his views to work to wean the blacks away from the party moderates.[35]

Although the Congressional Committee agents in the South attempted to reduce racial animosities, several also played up class differences. They praised the Republican party for "standing up for the poor man" by honoring the status of free labor and supporting free public schools. When the Congressional Committee drew up its address to the South in May, it referred to expected support from the "laboring class," and many of its documents were designed to attract the votes of both black and white workers.[36] But when most Northern Republicans spoke of white support for their party in the South, they apparently believed they could find it among the wealthy landowners and businessmen of the section. John Andrew, Horace Greeley, Henry Wilson, Edward Atkinson, William D. Kelley—almost all the Republicans who were working for a Southern biracial party— hoped to build bridges to the Southern middle- and upper-class whites. In June 1867, when the executive board of the Congressional Committee met with the Republican National Executive Committee in Philadelphia to make final arrangements for a vigorous canvass of the South, its members resolved that "no speaker be sent on this mission who would advocate any more radical idea than those now contained in the Military Reconstruction Bill."[37]

The Northern Republicans' rejection of a more radical political course in the South was most clearly revealed in Virginia. Here the national party leadership made its most serious effort to influence the strategy of a state party, and its influence was clearly thrown on the side of those hoping to gain white upper-class support. The struggles in Virginia continued into August, when state Republicans met to hold a second party convention in accordance with the agreements worked out in June with the Northern delegations. Thomas Tullock, secretary of the Union Congressional Committee, visited Richmond to observe the convention. Although he pronounced himself satisfied with the meeting, calling the convention "a great affair," after it was over Hunnicutt remained in control of the state party. Conservative whites, who had hoped to gain more influence within the organization, were rebuffed by Hunnicutt's forces. Although some ceased their efforts to identify with the Republicans, other whites, led by Botts, continued to attempt to work within the organization to modify its stance. Speakers sent into the state by the Congressional Committee continued to seek white votes. One of its most effective black agents, Reverend John Givens, told Virginia Republicans that "we cannot afford to lose a vote. We intend to keep all good, loyal, Republicans, [including] Botts." The *Richmond Whig*, however, which had sought to encourage the creation of a moderate, biracial party in the state, was disenchanted with the convention and warned Northerners that the Republicans in Virginia represented "social and political revolutionaries" whom respectable Northern Republicans should abhor. Forney's *Chronicle* denied this charge, noting that the Republican platform contained no endorsement of confiscation or extreme proposals for disfranchisement of whites. The *New York Tribune* agreed with Forney's assessment, but the *Times* continued to express dissatisfaction with the party's leadership.[38]

As the rest of the Southern states held their Republican organizing conventions during the summer of 1867, struggles similar to those in Virginia emerged. Whites contested with blacks for control of the party, and again disputes arose over which classes of whites to solicit for support. No Southwide pattern resulted from these internal squabbles; each state convention resolved its problems in its own way. Northern Republican influence in these Republican conclaves remained minimal, as had been the case in the earlier conventions in Arkansas and North Carolina. In the few instances when Northern party influence was exercised, it was always used to moderate black demands and to appeal to white support, usually from the upper classes.

In Alabama, the next state after Virginia to hold a convention, Republicans hoped for substantial white support. Northern Alabama had been disaffected from the Confederacy, and the Union League had penetrated the area during the war. The first Republican organizations to emerge in the state developed in the north, under the leadership of white Unionists. According to the *Philadelphia Press*, "Alabama is as nearly reconstructed as North Carolina, simply because the mountain people never yielded to treason." John Forney, who was closely observing events in Alabama, rejoiced to see that although "the colored population in Alabama is large enough to decide any contest," the initiative in organizing the Republican party in the state "originated entirely among the white men, and has received the support of many of the most distinguished politicians in the state."[39]

By the late spring of 1867, blacks in Alabama were also organizing meetings. Generally their spokesmen were moderate. They pledged their support for equal rights and called for racial cooperation and harmony. Two of the most prominent black leaders, Lawrence Berry of Mobile and Holland Thompson of Montgomery, were agents of the Union Congressional Committee. Berry warned his black listeners against holding conventions only of blacks, and Thompson cautioned against calling for confiscation of land. On June 4, 1867, when the Republican party held its first statewide convention, blacks outnumbered whites two to one, but white Unionists made most of the speeches and controlled the key committees. The party approved a platform endorsing the national Republican party, civil and political equality, free public education, and taxation based on property value. The party's first state chairman was John Keffer, a Freedmen's Bureau official from Pennsylvania, who was also an agent of the Congressional Committee and head of the Alabama Union League.[40]

The Republicans in Louisiana also held a statewide convention in June. The party was already divided in the state, with one wing, led by militant blacks, calling for integrated schools, open accommodations, and perhaps property confiscation. The more moderate Republicans, led by former Union officer Henry Clay Warmoth, hoped to avoid economic and social issues of concern to blacks and looked for support from Washington. One warned Ben Butler that "we have too many empirics in our ranks here misguiding the blacks by venturing on issues alien to the national party." Another described the division in the party in the state as being between "overzealous Negro equality republicanism" and "true, reliable, safe and judicious reconstructionists."[41]

After blacks insisted that at least half the seats at the forthcoming party convention be given to them, Thomas Conway, representing the Union League and the Congressional Committee, spoke in New Orleans, along with Kelley. Conway called on his audience to send "good men, irrespective of color," to the convention; he warned that the racially inspired divisions in the party could wreck it. When the convention met, it drafted a platform containing some planks advocated by the Radicals, including the creation of public schools open to both races, an end to all class discrimination, and a division of political appointments between the races. The party also appealed to white business and labor votes, calling for an eight-hour day for workers and federal aid for levee construction along the Mississippi. The state central committee was controlled by whites.[42]

By the time the convention met, Republicans had gained a major white convert to their party: former Confederate General James Longstreet, one of the South's most well-known military leaders. Longstreet, who had already privately advised Southerners to accept the Reconstruction Acts, had heard Wilson speak when he was in New Orleans. In the middle of June, he published a letter in the *New Orleans Times*, confessing that "he was agreeably surprised to hear such fairness and frankness from a politician whom I had been taught to believe harsh in his feelings toward the people of the South." He then publicly declared his support for Reconstruction and repudiated the Democratic party. Northerners eager for such evidence of Southern white conversion were overjoyed at Longstreet's action.[43]

In Georgia, Republicans won another apparent convert from the ranks of prominent former Confederates: wartime governor Joseph Brown. Brown too had published a letter supportive of the Reconstruction Acts, but he was not ready to declare himself a Republican. He corresponded with W. D. Kelley, however, and urged him to support amnesty and not to exact any more punishment from the South. In return, Kelley recommended to Congress that Brown be relieved of his disabilities under the Fourteenth Amendment. Brown did not attend the Republican state convention that met in Atlanta on July 4, but the platform the party drafted reflected his views. The platform, which pledged "equal rights" for all, was aimed at attracting the votes of whites plagued by debts and poor harvests. It called for free schools, relief measures, and exemption of homesteads from seizure for debts. The party convention also called for the removal of political disabilities on whites and asked Congress to appropriate $30 million for loans to impoverished farmers.[44]

Brown, who joined the Republicans a few months later, wanted the party to appeal to all classes and not build itself around a single issue or race. Although he supported relief measures for poor farmers, he hoped to attract capital to the state and promote its economic development. He believed he could more easily serve his state by working through the Republican party than by returning to the Democrats. A recruit such as Brown was good news for Northern Republicans, who hoped to gain support from "respectable" Southerners. Greeley's *Tribune* welcomed him. So also did the journalist who interviewed Brown for the *Cincinnati Commercial*; he exclaimed that "one Brown is worth to the South and to the nation, more than a million Hunnicutts or Honeypots, or whatever that crazy Virginia devil's name may be."[45]

In Florida, where Republicans met in state convention a week after their counterparts in Georgia, a group of white moderates emerged who wanted to model the party along the lines advocated by Brown. Led by Harrison Reed, a former federal tax commissioner who had helped organize the party in Jacksonville in 1864, and Ossian Hart, a native Unionist and former slaveholder, these Republicans hoped to appeal to native white Conservatives who were interested in developing the state's resources. Most blacks in the state wanted more sweeping social and political changes than those contemplated by the Reed faction, and they flocked to Union League chapters. The leagues were organized by a white Northerner, Daniel Richards, and William Saunders, a black man from Baltimore, both of whom were sent into the state by the Union Congressional Committee. At the party convention, Richards and his followers were able to secure passage of resolutions supportive of black rights, leaving the more conservative white Republicans angry and frustrated at their inability to control the meeting. Harrison Reed accused the convention of "pandering to Negroes." Another white Republican complained to Senator William Fessenden that "the leaders of our party seem to have acted as if the colored vote was in doubt and paid their whole attention to that class" instead of soliciting white support.[46]

Florida proved to be the only state where emissaries of the Union Congressional Committee worked against, rather than for, a more conservative, business-oriented party that would appeal to whites as much as or more than to blacks. In South Carolina, which held its state convention on July 24, Northern Republican spokesmen used their influence to moderate black demands. In this state, more than any other in the South, the blacks far outnumbered the white population, and it proved very difficult for the Republicans to pull in white support. The white Unionist movement had been nonexistent during the war, and the Union Leagues there were almost totally black. The *Boston Advertiser* had South Carolina in mind when it opposed the use of Union Leagues in the South. The paper's editors contended that "the hope that these leagues will unite the white and black loyalists is visionary." The head of the league in South Carolina, however, was a native of Massachusetts, who counseled blacks to be moderate in their demands and avoid the creation of parties along color lines. The Congressional Committee's representatives in South Carolina echoed this advice. Two of its black agents, Beverly Nash and Benjamin F. Randolph, both warned black audiences not to expect property confiscation; Randolph carried this message to the floor of the party convention in July. Also present at the South Carolina convention was William J. Armstrong, a white man sent to the state by the Congressional Committee. Armstrong was also on the

Freedmen's Bureau payroll. He told the delegates he was there "as an agent of the government" and warned them not to set race against race, but to be charitable to native whites. Despite the efforts of such men, however, the convention, which was overwhelmingly black, passed a proposal recommending increasing land taxes to a confiscatory level.[47]

Confiscation was also an issue in Mississippi, where the Republicans met in state convention on September 10. One-third of the delegates were black. Thomas Conway had already visited the state and had warned blacks not to expect Congress to enact confiscation. He also stated that "the idea of some to make a colored party exclusively was not good Republican doctrine, and must be deprecated and laid aside as unworthy of the great platform of the party." At the convention, Radicals called for proscription of whites, strong planks on black rights, and support for property confiscation. Moderates who wanted a broadly based party drawing support from both races were willing to endorse a strong plank on black rights and education but opposed both confiscation and proscription. The moderates were strongly supported by James Lynch, one of the most active and influential organizers the Union Congressional Committee sent into the South. Lynch had already warned blacks not to join the Union Leagues because they created apprehension and resentment from whites. At the convention he opposed both confiscation and proscription of whites. Ultimately, the convention agreed not to recommend confiscation and accepted a compromise on proscription that left the matter up to the forthcoming constitutional convention to decide.[48]

Confiscation also became an issue in North Carolina, which held a second Republican party convention in September before the elections that were to follow voter registration. At this convention some black delegates opposed a new confiscation proposal. They were led by James H. Harris, who had earlier obtained a charter to organize Union Leagues in the state. He was also an agent for the Congressional Committee. Harris warned blacks not to believe "evil-minded men who persuade you that you will get a portion of your master's land." In part because of his influence, the convention defeated the confiscation proposal; it also tabled a disfranchisement motion.[49]

In Texas, which held a convention on July 4, white Unionists had led the way, as in Alabama and North Carolina, in organizing Republican meetings. When the Union League arrived in the state, blacks began to join that organization, prompting some whites to express concern that the league might array the races against one another. More than six hundred delegates attended the convention in Houston; a majority were black. As in the other states, however, whites controlled the key positions. The platform the delegates drew up was moderate; it endorsed the national Republican party, public schools for all, equal rights for blacks, and a homestead law through which landless men from both races could take up unappropriated parts of the public domain. In a bid for the support of whites interested in more rapid economic development of the state, the party also endorsed railroad construction.[50]

For the most part, Northern Republicans could be satisfied with the platforms drafted by their Southern allies. Overt proposals for property confiscation had been headed off in every state, and only a few platforms called for any significant disfranchisement of whites. Most planks emphasized programs that appealed to both races: equal rights, free public schools, and development of the states' economies. Most state conventions had been controlled by whites, and in most states the party machinery was in the hands of whites. Except in Virginia, South Carolina, and Louisiana, there was little likelihood of party support for equal accommodations laws. Most Northern party leaders regarded the black vote as certain to go for their party and apparently saw no risk in bidding for white votes even at the expense of black interests. Only a few voices, from strongly antislavery and equalitarian papers such as the *Boston Commonwealth* and the *National Anti-Slavery Standard*, suggested that the party might lose black votes in its quest for white support.

The military commanders of the South likewise used their influence to discourage black dominance of the Republican party and to solicit white support. The commander in Virginia, John Schofield, was unsympathetic to universal suffrage and feared that uneducated blacks would use their power to oppress the white South. Although Schofield enforced the Reconstruction Acts and registered voters, he favored the Botts wing of the party and sought to weaken the influence of the Hunnicutt men, whom he regarded as "entirely unfit for the offices they aspire to." Whenever vacancies occurred in civil posts, Schofield filled them with men who were "respectable and competent." By this course, he told Grant, he intended to "give strength and influence to the respectable Republicans as against the lower class of men who have acquired control over the mass of colored voters." General Orlando Brown, head of the Freedmen's Bureau in Virginia, also supported efforts to weaken Hunnicutt and broaden the party's base among whites. He and Henry Wilson worked together to steer government patronage to the *Richmond Whig*. During the election campaign for members to the constitutional convention, bureau officials in Virginia sought to encourage blacks to "vote for the ablest and most worthy Republicans."[51]

In Mississippi, General Ord, like Schofield in Virginia, used his appointment powers to develop moderate white support for the Reconstruction Acts. Many of the men he appointed were Whig Unionists of the planter class. In Georgia, General Pope encouraged Republicans to "invite everybody to come in with them." He was impressed by Joseph Brown's support of the Reconstruction Acts and urged state Republicans to make room for him and his many followers within the party. In South Carolina, after he had resigned his post as military commander, General Daniel Sickles spoke to blacks in Charleston, urging them to be patient, maintain respect toward their conservative adversaries, and not expect confiscation. His advice was echoed by Robert K. Scott, head of the Freedmen's Bureau in South Carolina, who warned blacks not to form an all-black party. In Florida, the Freedmen's Bureau also used its influence among the voters to support the moderate wing of the party against the Radicals.[52]

Northern Republicans had another weapon to use in influencing the posture of their party in the South: they could withhold or provide government printing patronage to party newspapers. The act passed by Congress in March 1867, providing government printing contracts to Southern newspapers selected by House clerk McPherson, immediately set up a competition for those awards. In many states, including Mississippi, Arkansas, Texas, and South Carolina, there were only a few Republican papers, and hence McPherson had little choice in granting the contracts. In some states, however, particularly in Georgia, there was heavy competition among Republican or Unionist papers for the printing contracts, and McPherson, who was a former Whig, used his power to encourage more moderate sheets.

Initially McPherson granted printing contracts to the *Savannah Re-*

publican and the *Augusta Loyal Georgian*. The former paper was edited
by John E. Hayes, previously a correspondent for the *New York Tribune*, who had come to the state with General W. T. Sherman's army
in 1864 and had remained to start a Unionist newspaper. John Forney endorsed this selection, claiming that Hayes was one of the
ablest Union editors in the South. The Augusta paper was edited by
John Bryant, the former Freedmen's Bureau officer, who had been
among the first whites in the state to attempt to organize blacks for
the Republican party. Immediately after McPherson announced his
selections, he was besieged by the editors of several other Unionist
newspapers in Georgia, who claimed that they deserved the contracts. The editors complained that Hayes's paper was not truly Republican and that Hayes could not be trusted to adhere to the party's program. As for Bryant's paper, they complained that it was a
weekly, and its readership was almost entirely black. E. M. Pughe,
editor of the *Augusta Daily Press*, argued that "the White people
should have a chance to see the laws."[53]

By the early fall of 1867 evidence had begun to accumulate indicating that the charges against Hayes were true; he was using his paper
to further the Conservative case against the Republicans. Despite
federal aid, Bryant's paper could not sustain itself, and some Unionists bought him out, merged his paper with Pughe's *Daily Press*,
called the new paper the *National Republican*, and applied to McPherson for the government contracts. There were at the time at least two
other Republican papers in the state, the *Union* in Macon and the
Atlanta Opinion; but in light of the recreancy of Hayes's paper and
the failure of Bryant's, a new candidate for government printing appeared in the form of the *Atlanta New Era*, edited by Samuel Bard.[54]

In 1866 Bard had supported Johnson's Reconstruction policy, but
as the president lost control of the situation in the South and Congress enacted the Reconstruction Acts, Bard followed the example of
former Governor Joseph Brown in accepting the situation and urging white Georgians to cooperate with Congress. Like Brown, Bard
hesitated to join the Republican party openly, but he and the former
governor worked closely to encourage the Republicans to formulate
a program that would appeal to a wide cross-section of the state's
voters. McPherson was flooded with endorsements of Bard's paper.
The superintendent of voting registration in the state praised Bard
for "forwarding Conservative Republican principles." General Pope

wrote to Senator Richard Yates of Illinois asking him to intercede with McPherson in favor of the *New Era*, and Yates, who was getting similar letters from Northern carpetbaggers in Georgia, agreed to do so. Bard, in thanking Yates, promised that he would endeavor to see that the entire South went for the Republican party in 1868. Joe Brown wrote to Senator John Sherman, complaining that Bryant's paper "has nothing of the confidence of the people that the *Era* has" and arguing that Bard "was sound and goes as far as prudence will allow." Brown also solicited William D. Kelley's support for the *New Era*. McPherson obliged his petitioners by awarding a printing contract to Bard.[55]

Although the Georgia case illustrated the problem of keeping Republican papers alive long enough to benefit the party, it also revealed that when McPherson had some choice in granting the contracts, he favored a moderate paper like Bard's that had the support of white men whom Northern leaders hoped to attract into the Republican party. In Florida, McPherson followed the same course. He diverted public printing from the *Jacksonville Florida Times*, which supported the Radical wing of the party, to the more moderate *Florida Union*. In North Carolina, despite the efforts of Albion Tourgée, who got Benjamin Wade of Ohio to endorse his Greensboro newspaper, the *Union Register*, McPherson awarded the federal printing to William Holden's *Raleigh Daily Standard*, which supported a more moderate policy for the party. Tourgée's paper, which advocated widespread disfranchisement of whites in North Carolina and ardently espoused the rights of blacks, was not popular in the state, and without federal patronage it expired. In Mississippi, McPherson directed printing contracts to two papers edited by white native Mississippians, both former Confederate officers, who were now working for the Republican party. One of the recipients, John R. Smith of the *Meridian Chronicle*, who was known to both William D. Kelley and Thomas Tullock, worked hard to develop white support for the Republicans and appealed particularly to former Whigs and laboring whites.[56]

In Virginia, McPherson designated both Hunnicutt's *Richmond New Nation* and the *Alexandria Virginia State Journal* as recipients of government printing contracts. Hunnicutt, however, complained bitterly to Charles Sumner that the Alexandria paper got most of the printing, and as a result "they are growing rich, while I am being starved out." By early 1868, as Hunnicutt continued to fall from favor in the national Republican councils, he lost the printing contract, and his paper disappeared. In Louisiana, McPherson at first awarded printing rights to the *New Orleans Tribune*, a black-owned and operated newspaper that initially was the only party daily in the state. The paper was endorsed by such Radicals as Charles Sumner, but white Republicans in the state condemned it for attempting to turn Louisiana into a "Negro state." The paper was the most radical in the South, advocating property confiscation, more black officeholding, and integrated schools. By early 1868, after the *Tribune* had taken a position in opposition to the state Republican ticket, Thomas Conway urged McPherson to deprive it of patronage, and McPherson complied, switching the contracts to a more moderate white-operated paper. The *Tribune*, deprived of federal sustenance, had to suspend operations.[57]

The first indication the Republicans received of the support they could expect from Southern whites came in the fall of 1867, when the unreconstructed states held elections to determine whether to convene constitutional conventions in accordance with the Reconstruction Acts. Northern Republicans waited somewhat apprehensively for the results, and their predictions of the possible outcome varied widely. Few expected to get much white support in states like South Carolina, Louisiana, and Mississippi, where black registrations far outweighed those of whites. They were more confident of white support in states that had significant pockets of wartime Unionism, particularly North Carolina and the hill regions of Alabama and Georgia. The special correspondent in the South for the *New York Tribune* warned Northern Republicans, however, that the elections were coming so closely after the passage of the Reconstruction Acts that there was little time to proselytize "among the non-slaveholding class of whites." Greeley urged Northerners to support the efforts of the Congressional Committee, noting that the people of both races whom the party hoped to reach lacked money and social influence.[58] The Congressional Committee did busy itself preparing for the Southern elections. Committee secretary Tullock kept a close eye on the progress of voting registration in the South and recorded the tabulations by race. He also maintained a timetable for the dates of elections in the Southern states, and as the ballots were cast, whenever he could he calculated the racial composition of the statewide vote.[59]

Although the Republicans controlled every one of the state elections, they were successful in most cases because of a heavy black vote. About 80 percent of the registered black voters cast ballots, and they voted overwhelmingly for the Republicans. Although results varied across the South, in most states the Republicans failed to pick up significant white support. Registered black voters far outnumbered whites in three states, and two others, Florida and Alabama, had black voter majorities because of white apathy, disfranchisement, or refusal to register. Faced with the preponderance of black voters, many whites in those states boycotted the elections. Across the South, as many as 40 percent of the eligible whites failed to register; of those enrolled, less than half voted in the elections, and of that number, only half voted for holding the conventions.[60] Thus the white Republican vote averaged around 15 percent of the white voting population.

In only four states, Georgia, North Carolina, Alabama, and Arkansas, did at least 20 percent of the registered whites support a convention. In Georgia, approximately one-third of the registered whites voted with the Republicans. In North Carolina, Alabama, and Arkansas, the white voters came from areas that had been strongly Unionist during the Civil War. In Georgia, the relative success of the Republicans among the whites was possibly attributable to the party's tailoring its platform to white interests, particularly on the relief issue. Voters in Texas did not go to the polls until early in 1868, but when they did, only 13 percent of the registered whites voted to hold a convention; the size of the white vote was even smaller than that cast for the Unionist party in 1866.[61]

In Virginia, where Republicans had made a great effort to encourage former Whigs and Unionists to join the party, there was no white boycott, but only 12 percent of the registered whites voted with the Republicans. Greeley and some other observers chose to interpret this as a victory, claiming that even a white minority would help save the state for the Republicans. Greeley was even more pleased with the results in North Carolina, claiming that the state provided an "emphatic repudiation of the idea that the Republican party in the South is a Negro party." Considering the South as a whole, Greeley argued that the elections proved that there was a loyal white party in every state, which with the blacks could control most state elections.[62]

Other Northern Republicans were not so optimistic about the meaning of the Southern elections. Even John Forney, who contended that the elections proved that "the Union party of the South is not entirely made up of Negroes," bemoaned the lack of more substantial white support. The *Boston Traveller*, after viewing the initial returns from the South, claimed that without the blacks, "Republicans in the South would be as scarce as roses in New England at the winter solstice." Conservative Republican newspapers feared that the elections would throw the Southern states into the hands of blacks, who would be swayed by "the wildest theories of political revolution . . . proclaimed by those who assume to be their leaders."[63]

Northern Republican anxiety about the radical tendencies of the newly enfranchised Negroes was heightened by Democratic victories in the 1867 state elections in the North. Horace Binney, a New York newspaperman who watched both Northern and Southern elections in 1867 closely, worried that black voting majorities in the South would result in radical men being elected to power there, thus undermining the chances of Republican survival even in the North. Binney also worried that the blacks, emboldened by political success, might resort to civil unrest and even bloodshed to gain revenge against whites. He urged Republican leaders to counsel Southern blacks to cultivate a spirit of peace and brotherly kindness and to "employ legitimate weapons of moral force." He especially asked that Republican agents of the Congressional Committee discourage talk of confiscation of Southern property or massive disfranchisement of Southern whites.[64]

Republicans active in Southern organizing acted quickly to disabuse Northerners of any notions that black political success would increase racial hostility in the South. Thomas W. Conway claimed that after speaking to more than one hundred black audiences in eight states in the summer and fall of 1867, urging them to be kindly toward whites, he had found no signs of "dangerous feelings" among his listeners. In late November Thomas Tullock, secretary of the executive committee of the Union Congressional Committee, hastened into print to assure readers that his agents were not making inflammatory statements in the South. Tullock vigorously took issue with a *New York Tribune* editorial condemning the committee for sending a black speaker, Aaron A. Bradley, into Georgia to advocate confiscation of property. Tullock insisted that Bradley was not an agent of the committee; furthermore, by advocating confiscation, Bradley had indicated that "he is not even personally in accord with [the Republican] party." According to Tullock, the blacks his committee sent South were "earnest and true Republicans," none of whom had ever been guilty of such speeches as those attributed to Bradley. "On the contrary," Tullock averred, "the Southern campaign had been, as a whole, carried on in a spirit of moderation and conciliation."[65]

Now that the Republicans in the South had carried the elections, the actions of the respective state constitutional conventions would provide the best evidence of the "spirit of moderation and conciliation" that Tullock spoke about. The *New York Times*, which had opposed a Reconstruction policy based on universal suffrage for blacks, urged Congress to scrutinize the new state constitutions carefully to make sure that blacks were not abusing their newly won political power. Greeley exhorted the convention delegates "to eschew carefully even the appearance of evil, and especially whatever might seem to savor of revenge or proscription." The editors of *Harper's Weekly* echoed this advice, urging Southern Republicans not to write constitutions that would "embody class and personal hostility." According to *Harper's*, if the states drew up documents establishing equal suffrage and public education, and avoided any property confiscation or proscription of former Confederates, they could expect rapid restoration to the Union.[66]

E. L. Godkin of the *Nation* was also fearful that blacks, under the leadership of men such as Hunnicutt of Virginia, would write constitutions that would alienate white voters. He warned that as the constitutional conventions assembled in the South, "the national leaders of the [Republican party] must find some means of liberalizing the party managers at the South, or the whole plan of reconstruction will fail, dragging the party to ruin with it." Robert Schenck of the Congressional Committee was sensitive to these concerns. In December he told a Republican caucus that as the committee discharged its responsibility of seeing that the new constitutions were adopted in all the Southern states, it also had to ensure that the documents were "just and judicious." He warned the party not to commit itself in advance to a blind support of the conventions' work.[67]

Between the first of November 1867 and the end of January 1868, all Southern states except Texas held constitutional conventions. Alabama's was the first to meet and the first to finish, and hence Northerners watched proceedings there with particular interest. Observers who were fearful that the Reconstruction Acts were paving the way for black domination of the South were relieved to find that most of the convention delegates were white. Visitors to the convention praised its members as a sober and orderly body; the *New York Times*, however, which was skeptical of the entire Reconstruction process, found most of the delegates "untrained in political action" and "well-meaning but horribly naive." The focus of interest both within and outside the convention was on the question of disfranchisement. A number of white Unionist delegates came to Montgomery, where the convention was held, determined to deprive large numbers of former Confederates of the right to vote, and their insistence on such a measure triggered much controversy. Most Northern Republicans were opposed to any further disfranchisement of Southern whites. When Horace Greeley received news of the convention's disfranchisement proposal, he asked Senator Wilson to intercede in behalf of more moderate measures. Wilson immediately wrote to Generals Swayne and Pope in Alabama, asking them to discourage the white Unionists, who by their "ultra speeches" were "doing great injury to reconstruction and bringing odium on the Republican party." Both men hastened to comply, urging the convention delegates to be less proscriptive. Pope personally addressed the convention, warning that severe disfranchisement would hurt the interests of the Republican party in both the state and the nation.[68]

The Republican convention delegates finally decided to send a representative to Washington for instructions on the wording of the disfranchisement clause of their constitution. Party spokesmen in Washington again urged moderation upon the convention; they especially opposed a proposal that would have disfranchised any whites who did not participate in the upcoming referendum on the new document. Ultimately, the convention dropped that idea, but it did draw up a disfranchisement clause that barred anyone from voting who had been disfranchised by the Reconstruction Acts; in addition, it prescribed an oath for all prospective voters, swearing that they accepted the political and legal equality of all citizens of the state.[69]

Some Northern observers who hoped for more lenient treatment of former Confederates in Alabama concluded that the oath would increase white resentment against blacks and the Republican party. Joseph Medill of the *Chicago Tribune* found the test oath "absurd" and warned that it would lead to the defeat of the constitution. Several Republican journals recommended that the convention reconvene and liberalize its voting qualifications; Generals Pope and Meade echoed the advice, but it was not taken. One angry Alabama Unionist wrote to Henry Wilson to complain that by disfranchising whites the new constitution handed the state over to ignorant Negroes and hence set the stage for race war. Wilson replied, insisting that blacks should be given equal rights and the results would not lead to racial conflict. He did admit, however, that mistakes had been made in the South and urged his correspondent and other whites to become involved in Reconstruction instead of standing aside, so that "a better state of things might exist."[70]

Most Northern observers of the Alabama constitution defended its work. Forney's *Chronicle*, which was eager for white support in the South, interpreted the convention action as moderate and indicating that the state's Republicans wished to increase their white support. He argued that the state's constitution "compared favorably" with those of Northern states. Horace Greeley regretted that the Alabamans had not supported universal amnesty but still praised the constitution, as did *Harper's Weekly*. John Murray Forbes, a prominent member of the Massachusetts Reconstruction Association, found the constitution "as solid a document as anybody could get up" and praised the Alabama convention, as well as those meeting in other states, for not calling for property confiscation.[71]

Northern Republicans watching the other state conventions in the South drew encouragement because they were nearly always controlled by whites. Although they were clearly anxious about the actions of the conventions, Northerners could do little beyond offering advice, which delegates frequently requested of them, particularly on the issue of disfranchisement. Northern Republicans almost uniformly recommended liberal treatment of former Confederates. Senator Wilson told the Texas convention that "as for disfranchisement the less the better; the sooner we shall then get out of our present troubles." In North Carolina, when a convention committee considered barring from voting all whites affected by the Fourteenth Amendment, Addison Laflin, a member of Congress from New York who was visiting the state, asked to address the Republican caucus. In his speech, he earnestly advised against proscriptive action, stating that the Republicans wanted "the moral influence of a conciliated loyal South." He cautioned the delegates that Northern Republicans were very eager for the convention to act "wisely and prudently." Two months later, when the convention cast its final vote on disfranchisement, Congressman Jehu Baker of Illinois was there to speak against the idea. Delegates then proceeded to vote against any suffrage restrictions.[72]

South Carolina was of special concern to Northerners because it was the only state where a majority of the constitutional convention was black. John Forney was worried about the fate of the Republican party there, where, unlike North Carolina and Alabama, no significant native white leadership had emerged. When Governor James L. Orr endorsed the Reconstruction Acts and agreed to address the convention, Forney was overjoyed. He hoped the delegates would agree to grant unrestricted suffrage, which would encourage "honest white men" like Orr to come forward to help the party. "Without such aid," Forney contended, "the experiment of governing a state like South Carolina will be difficult indeed." Much to Forney's pleasure, the state convention decided not to disbar whites from voting.[73]

Forney was also worried lest South Carolina, Louisiana, and Mississippi, all states with black voting majorities, might endorse confiscation measures, which Forney derisively termed "agrarian legislation." Other Northerners continued to share this concern; from Washington Henry Wilson warned the North Carolinians to "let confiscation be an unspoken word in your state—it has no meaning here." Ultimately, none of the states, not even South Carolina, endorsed confiscation schemes. One delegate in South Carolina's convention did recommend a petition to Congress asking for an appropriation of $1 million to buy land in the state for freedmen, but Senator Wilson advised by telegram to drop the idea because Congress would never appropriate the money. In Louisiana, where blacks held half the convention seats, confiscation got no serious consideration. Thomas Conway and John Mercer Langston, both agents of the Union Congressional Committee, were in New Orleans to advise the delegates. Conway told General Howard that "the members are below par as to intelligence but that is better than to be so as to loyalty." He assured Howard that he and Langston had "taken them in hand." Although Louisianans did not advocate confiscation, in other respects their constitution was the most radical in the South in that it endorsed desegregated schools, prohibited racial discrimination in public places, and adopted stringent disfranchisement measures.[74] In Mississippi, Commanding General Ord warned that if the constitutional convention adopted extreme measures, it would be defeated. Once again Mississippi Republicans asked their Northern colleagues for advice, and again the Congressional Committee representatives in the state, particularly James Lynch, worked against proposals for confiscation and integrated schools. Ultimately, the convention refused to endorse both those ideas, but it did approve strict disfranchising provisions for former Confederates.[75]

Georgia presented a particular problem to Northern Republicans. In a bid for white support, most Southern conventions considered legislation providing some relief for debtors. Georgia Republicans took this idea farther than any other state; the convention invalidated all contracts made before June 1, 1865. The delegates also exempted $2,000 in real estate and $1,000 in personal property from liability in any court-ordered collection for debts. The Georgia party was not united on either proposal, however, and several members wrote to congressmen complaining that the relief clauses punished large numbers of Unionists who had made loans during the war. These Georgians claimed that the Republican party in the state would suffer serious loss of support by favoring repudiation. When Georgia ratified the constitution and sent it on for approval in Washington, Congress ordered that the relief clause be stricken from it.[76]

The Georgia relief clause was the only example of a specific provision in the Southern state constitutions which Congress refused to accept. In most cases, through advice and some political pressure, Northern Republicans encouraged Southern conventions to draft documents they could approve. In Florida, however, direct intervention by military authorities was necessary to secure a constitution acceptable to Congress. The Republican party in Florida, like that in Virginia, was divided into Radical and moderate wings, and the constitutional convention served as a test of strength between the two. The Radicals, led by Congressional Committee agents Richards and Saunders and joined by Liberty Billings, a former officer in a Negro regiment, became known as the "mule team" because they traveled about the state by wagon. They appealed to blacks for political support and attacked the former slaveholders in Florida. Moderate Republicans were appalled by the Radical tactics, which they believed would set race against race. Harrison Reed, the moderate leader, protested to the Congressional Committee about the behavior of Richards and Saunders. When Thomas Conway came through the state in November, he sent a report back to Tullock supporting Reed and criticizing the "mule team" members. Tullock them struck them from the committee rolls and instead began sending money to the state through Reed. A short time later, Edward McPherson diverted federal printing patronage to the moderate *Florida Union*, favoring it over the newspaper endorsed by the Radicals. Richards also complained that the Freedmen's Bureau officials in the state were using their influence against him.[77]

Despite these adverse developments, the "mule team" controlled most of the seats in the Florida constitutional convention, which met January 20, 1868. The only delegate who was still an agent of the Congressional Committee, George Alden, supported the moderates. Lacking sufficient votes to control the convention, the moderates sought to delay proceedings while they cultivated support, and the meetings became prolonged and disorderly. Ultimately failing to win a majority, they withdrew from the convention halls and allowed the Radicals to draw up a constitution on their own. Richards and his cohorts quickly wrote a document, submitted it to General Meade in Atlanta, and then adjourned to hold a nominating convention. They selected Billings to run for governor and Saunders for lieutenant governor; they named another black, Jonathan Gibbs, to run for the state's only congressional seat.[78]

The moderate press in the state condemned the Radicals' action, as did the *New York Times*. Claiming that the Radicals did not compose a quorum of the convention, the Reed faction seized control of the convention hall, found enough delegates to constitute a majority of the original number chosen, and gained General Meade's support for their action. The reformed convention then proceeded to draft another constitution, which it submitted to Meade. Faced with a choice between the two documents, Meade supported that given to him by the moderate Republicans. The constitutions were alike in most respects. In several crucial ways, however, the moderate version limited the political influence of blacks in Florida. The Radicals had made most state and local offices elective, whereas the moderates had them filled by gubernatorial appointment; this provision would limit the number of black officials. The Radical version also drew up a plan for apportioning representation in the state legislature that gave the largely black counties in the state more seats than the plan drafted by the moderates. Finally, the Radical version incorporated a more stringent disfranchisement provision than that proposed by their opponents.[79]

It was ultimately up to Congress to decide which constitution to submit to the people of Florida for their approval. Both contesting factions sought support for their document, but the moderates had the upper hand. They had many more contacts in Washington than the "mule team." Most Republican leaders in Washington feared being branded advocates of a black man's party and therefore were willing to endorse Reed's constitution. Richards made little headway with his arguments that blacks of the state favored the Radical constitution. Realizing that Washington Republicans were concerned about the racial composition of the party, Richards and his Radical associates even revised their slate of nominations for the forthcoming state elections; he assured Congressman Elihu B. Washburne of Illinois that they were *"all White men."* Richards's efforts came to naught. Even Benjamin Butler of Massachusetts, who had established a reputation as a defender of black rights, endorsed the moderate constitution. Thomas Tullock of the Union Congressional Committee worked for the Reed constitution and perhaps was responsible for converting former Radical Saunders to its support. Liberty Billings campaigned for the Radical constitution and electoral slate but was arrested by military officials in Florida for making "incendiary speeches." The Radical camp's only newspaper, the *Florida Times*, died for lack of funds. By the time the state's election came, the Florida Republican party was firmly in the hands of Reed and the moderate faction.[80]

The state constitutional convention that was of most concern to Northern Republicans was the one held in Virginia. The state's capital of Richmond, where the delegates assembled on December 3,

1867, was less than a hundred miles from Washington, and hence congressmen were able to keep in closer touch with the convention than was true in other states. Northern Republicans had been following events in Virginia closely since their party had been organized there and were particularly apprehensive lest the convention draft a constitution that would alienate white support. E. L. Godkin, who had watched events in Virginia closely, warned in the *Nation* that if Hunnicutt's followers wrote a Radical constitution for that state, "the Republican party [will] put its existence in peril" throughout the South. The *Boston Commonwealth*, which sympathized with Hunnicutt, noted that his supporters had "acted with magnanimity" in giving the bulk of convention seats to whites. Only about one-third of the delegates were black, but the Washington correspondent of the *Boston Advertiser* complained that they were inferior as a group to the members of their race elected to the convention in the neighboring state of North Carolina.[81]

John C. Underwood, who had worked before the Civil War to found the Republican party in the state, was elected president of the convention. Although he had been identified as a Radical, he told his old friend Horace Greeley that "we shall try to make a good Constitution for Virginia" and asked him not to let the *Tribune* "judge us harshly." Several Northern congressmen wrote to Underwood, expressing their apprehensions. Elihu B. Washburne, member of the House Committee on Reconstruction that was to review the constitutions from the South, told him that "it is of the most transcendent importance that you should make a constitution that will commend itself to the enlightened judgment of the country." Schuyler Colfax, Republican Speaker of the House of Representatives, warned Underwood that "our success politically in the coming election depends largely on the wise and judicious action of the Southern Constitutional conventions." Underwood told Washburne that he had read the congressman's letter to the Republican caucus in Richmond and assured him that it would follow his advice and "pursue a course of moderation and magnanimity."[82]

Washburne and Colfax were both concerned lest the convention adopt clauses proscribing masses of Southern whites and urged their fellow Republicans in Virginia to be generous with the former Confederates. If they would do so, said Washburne, "Congress will admit you at once and we shall be relieved from a load of embarrassments." Letting former rebels in Virginia vote would eliminate "ugly questions" in the coming presidential campaign and "secure a triumph of the Union party." Other leading Republicans echoed this opinion when members of the convention solicited their advice. Even Thaddeus Stevens and Charles Sumner advised Virginians not to go beyond the terms of the Reconstruction Acts in disfranchising Southerners. When their recommendations were introduced into the debates in the convention, Hunnicutt objected that Sumner and Stevens had nothing to do with Virginia affairs; he wanted more disfranchisement than that allowed by the Reconstruction Acts.[83]

In December the Republican caucus of convention delegates sent a committee to Washington to consult with Republican congressmen there, and Northern Republicans also visited Richmond to lobby with their allies. In every case the Northerners urged moderation on the Virginia Republicans, particularly in granting suffrage to former Confederates. Henry Wilson was one of those who made yet another journey to Richmond, this time to urge the convention to "deal generously with those who raised their hands against the country." Governor Smythe of New Hampshire visited the state at the same time Wilson did, bearing the same message, and early in January Senator Samuel Pomeroy of Kansas and Benjamin Butler visited Richmond to urge amnesty for former Confederates. Butler also cautioned the delegates not to adopt sweeping confiscation proposals that were then being discussed in the convention and urged them to finish their work without delay.[84]

A North Carolina Republican, observing these Richmond visits by national Republican leaders, claimed that Northern Republicans were more worried about protecting the reputation of their party in the North than about achieving justice in the South. In any case, the Virginia delegates did not take the advice tendered to them. Heated debates over disfranchisement, equal access for both races to public schools, and questions of taxation led to repeated delays. The convention did not finish its work until April 17, 1868. The constitution it presented to the people of Virginia provided civil equality to whites and blacks and guaranteed that all men might vote, hold office, and sit on juries. The constitution established a public school system but said nothing about whether the schools were to be segregated by race. It provided that most state revenue would be raised by taxes on land and gave a $2,000 homestead exemption from collection of debts. The most objectionable clauses, from the point of view of white Conservatives, disfranchised large numbers of former Confederates and required all state and local officials to take an ironclad oath of previous loyalty to the U.S. Constitution. The oath had been included in the constitution despite the urgings of General Schofield to have it deleted; he claimed that not enough eligible men could be found to fill the offices and that the clause would help defeat the constitution.[85]

Of all the state conventions then in operation, only the one in Mississippi finished later than Virginia's; it adjourned on May 15, 1868. Because the Reconstruction process was slower to develop in Texas, that state's convention did not meet until the following December. All in all, the efforts of congressional Republicans, army and Freedmen's Bureau officers, and Congressional Committee agents to encourage constitutions that would attract white support seemed successful. No state, for instance, provided for property confiscation and redistribution. Only two states, Louisiana and South Carolina, expressly provided for integrated schools. Republican moderates were less successful in arguing against disfranchisement of former Confederates; five states, Louisiana, Alabama, Arkansas, Mississippi, and Virginia, did deny varying numbers of whites the right to vote or hold office. On the other hand, most state constitutions contained provisions that were designed to appeal to both races. All of the conventions provided for universal manhood suffrage, equal rights under the law, and public schools for all. Many constitutions provided for other state services, such as institutions for the insane, orphans, and the deaf and dumb. In some cases the constitutions brought more democracy to their states by increasing the number of elective offices and eliminating any remaining property qualifications for holding office. Frequently law codes were codified and liberalized and tax structures revised to bear more heavily on property value. In most states constitutional provisions encouraged economic development, usually by providing for extension of state credit to railroads and other improvement projects.[86]

Northern Republican reaction to the constitutions was generally favorable. Republican House clerk Edward McPherson complained of the "vagaries of the [Southern] constitutions," but other party spokesmen applauded the documents. Greeley pronounced them "thoroughly democratic" and praised them for lacking vindictive or

punitive clauses. *Harper's Weekly* was pleased that the Southern constitutions were modeled along Northern lines and that most did not
disfranchise whites. Godkin's *Nation*, noting that the convention delegates had been chosen by a "largely illiterate, uneducated electorate," praised their moderation and contended that "close examination of them proves the soundness of Congressional reconstruction."
John Murray Forbes agreed and asked journalist Charles Nordhoff
to "give a screed of doctrine on the moderation of the Southern
conventions."[87]

As the states finished their preparation of new constitutions, the
Republican party prepared for the final stages of the Reconstruction
process. Each state would now have to hold an election to ratify the
constitution and to elect a slate of state and federal officeholders to
take positions under the new regime. Republicans, of course, were
eager to gain approval for the constitutions and to elect members of
their own party to administer the governments organized under
them. They hoped these elections would be held expeditiously, in
the spring and summer of 1868, so that the states could be returned
to the Union before the fall presidential election. Hence Congress
turned to remove the last roadblocks standing in the way of restoring
the Southern states.

★ ★ ★ ★ 6 ★ ★ ★ ★

RECONSTRUCTION CONCLUDED,

1868

Despite their success in winning control of the constitutional conventions, Southern Republicans and Congress still faced some problems as they sought to complete Reconstruction. Elections in the Northern states in the fall of 1867 had gone against the Republicans, and Southern Conservatives, emboldened by these results, had begun to organize to defeat the ratification of the new state constitutions. A number of Southern civil officials also used their influence to obstruct Reconstruction. Southern Republicans charged that President Andrew Johnson provided a major obstacle to its successful completion. They complained that the president's struggle with Congress over the Reconstruction process had encouraged Conservatives to resist it. In particular, they charged that many of Johnson's recent appointees to military command in the South used their influence to thwart the implementation of the Reconstruction Acts. Hence they looked to Congress to foil Conservative schemes by cleansing state governments of disloyal officials and by removing the president by impeachment.[1]

Impeachment sentiment among Northern Republicans also had been building throughout 1867. Johnson had resisted almost every congressional program for the South, from his vetoes of the Freedmen's Bureau and Civil Rights bills, through his opposition to the Fourteenth Amendment, to his vetoes of all the Reconstruction Acts. In addition, Johnson had failed to honor congressional requirements that he appoint as federal officers in the South only men who could take the ironclad oath, and he had restricted the implementation of confiscation acts passed by Congress to seize certain rebel properties in the South. After the Reconstruction Acts were passed over his vetoes, he attempted to interpret them to limit the powers of the military commanders, forcing Congress to pass further legislation. His suspension of Stanton from his post as secretary of war and his removal of Sheridan had particularly infuriated Northern Republicans. Hence in December, despite the adverse results of the 1867 elections in the North and increasing public demands that Congress end its interminable debates over Reconstruction and begin to deal with other issues, Republicans brought impeachment resolutions to a vote in the House. Republican moderates, however, arguing that Johnson had failed to commit a specific crime that would warrant impeachment, voted them down by a two-to-one majority.[2]

Southern Republicans were dismayed. Their fears took on increased strength later in December, when the president, apparently emboldened by the defeat of the impeachment motion, removed Ord and Pope from their commands in the South; he also relieved General Swayne, Pope's subordinate, who commanded in Alabama. All of these men, particularly Pope and Swayne, had been helpful to the Republicans. The chairman of the Republican party in Georgia, Foster Blodgett, was discomfited by Pope's removal, which he claimed greatly encouraged Conservative resistance to Reconstruction. He wrote to several Northern congressmen, warning them that "Reconstruction is now on a pivot." If Washington did not act to protect the interests of the Southern Republicans, he insisted, the South would be forever lost to the Democrats. Party leaders in other states also wrote north urging congressional action.[3]

If Congress would not impeach the president, the Southern Republicans hoped their Northern allies would nevertheless reorganize the civil governments Johnson had created in the South. They insisted that disloyal Southern officials were using every means at their disposal to thwart the Reconstruction process. They urged Congress either to allow the Southern constitutional conventions to organize provisional governments to control the states or remove from office all civil officials who could not take the ironclad oath. Such action would both weaken Conservative resistance to Reconstruction and give Republicans control of state patronage. Thomas Conway, who was in New Orleans and witnessing Hancock's action in filling state government vacancies with Conservatives, urged Robert Schenck of the Congressional Committee to get his colleagues to "show a little pluck, and turn out all rebels from office." A delegation of black and white Republicans from Virginia and the Carolinas visited Thaddeus

Stevens to urge him to sponsor a measure cleansing the state offices of disloyal men.[4]

Events in Alabama in February gave even more strength to Southern Republican pleas for congressional assistance. The state's election was the first to be held in the South under the new Reconstruction constitutions. Conservatives had organized a campaign to defeat it, along with the Republican state ticket, by boycotting the election. The Reconstruction Acts required that a majority of registered voters cast ballots in the elections on the constitution, and the entire process would be defeated if the condition was not met. When the election was held early in the month, an overwhelming majority of those voting approved it, but the total vote was below the majority required. Alabama Republicans were quick to identify the cause of their failure. They blamed unsympathetic state officials, especially sheriffs and election judges, for discouraging blacks from voting and for throwing out a number of ballots. In addition, they claimed that the new military authorities in the state, particularly Julius Hayden, who had replaced Wager Swayne as commander in Alabama and head of the Freedmen's Bureau, had removed Radical registrars and replaced them with Conservatives. In some cases, they claimed, polls had not even been opened. Alabama Republicans differed over how to resolve their difficulties. Some urged either General Meade or Congress to remove state officials who could not take the ironclad oath, hence making it easier to control the election if a new one were held; others urged Congress to admit the state despite the low vote.[5]

Republicans in the state could get no redress from General Meade, who told Congress that the constitution had been defeated on its merits and that there was no substance to the charges of fraud. He recommended that the reconstructionists in the state draft a revised constitution that would "allow a larger proportion of what must be the governing class" to vote and hold office. The state could not be governed, he warned, with the support of such a small minority of the white population. He also refused to remove state officials who could not take the ironclad oath, contending that he could not find enough able men to fill the vacancies if this were done. Generals in other portions of the South also warned Congress against turning out Conservative officeholders on a large scale, agreeing with Meade that it would be difficult to find able men to replace them.[6]

Republicans in Congress were no more sympathetic than Meade to the idea of purging Alabama, or any other Southern state, of Conservative or former Confederate officeholders. On several previous occasions Congress had voted down such proposals, using some of the same arguments presented by Meade. Many Republican moderates still wanted to court white Conservative support and were hesitant to alienate them by insisting upon implementation of the ironclad oath. The Unionists who would thus be put into control of the existing governments were not representative of the white population of the Southern states, and many Northern congressmen remained skeptical about their numbers and ability. They were unwilling to entrust white Southern Unionists with control of these governments, at least until they were properly installed by the elective process. The white Republicans in the South were already dividing into factions, as was evidenced most clearly in Virginia and Florida and to a lesser degree in Louisiana and Georgia. At the moment, at least in Virginia, Radicals were in control of the state convention, as they were in Florida, Louisiana, and possibly other states as well. Allowing these conventions to organize provisional governments would permit the Radical factions to control the state government as well as the party. Although some moderate Republicans urged Congress to appoint new state officials in the South, and hence to ensure that Southern moderates got those jobs, Congress decided against reorganizing any state government, including Alabama's.[7]

Congress could have ordered a new election but feared that the turnout would be much the same, and in the meantime Conservatives in other states would be encouraged to follow Alabama's example. Thomas Conway warned the Congressional Committee's executive committee that the tactics that had stopped the Reconstruction process in Alabama could thwart it throughout the South. Hence in March Congress enacted the Fourth Reconstruction Act, requiring that a majority of votes cast would be sufficient to approve the new state constitutions. In the same law Congress responded to Southern Republican concern that blacks who had lost their registration papers or recently changed residence would not be able to vote in the ratification elections. The new law provided that any person duly registered in a state could vote in the election district where he had been residing for the previous ten days, upon presentation of his registration certificate or "other satisfactory evidence" that he was enrolled to vote.[8]

The major effort that Congress undertook in March to expedite Reconstruction, however, was for the Senate to begin an impeachment trial of President Johnson. Republicans throughout the South had continued to call for his removal, but after the failure of impeachment resolutions in December, Congress had given up on the question. On February 21, however, the president reopened the issue by removing Secretary of War Stanton, whom he previously had suspended, in defiance of the Tenure of Office Act. Johnson's bold action led House Republicans to adopt articles of impeachment, and on March 30 the Senate trial began.

Although various considerations prompted Northern Republicans to attempt to remove the president, they were primarily concerned that Reconstruction could not be completed successfully as long as Johnson remained in office. His continued potential for interference in the Reconstruction process and the encouragement he gave to Southern Conservatives to resist it led them to conclude that the Southern states might never be wrested from Conservative control. Congress was also growing more concerned about the pace of the restoration process. The Northern public was increasingly restless about the delay in returning the Southern states. A presidential election was in the offing, and Republicans did not want to face the campaign with their Reconstruction program still incomplete. Some Republicans also wanted the Southern states back in the Union as soon as possible so that they could cast their electoral votes for their party's candidate in November. This could not be achieved, however, if Reconstruction were delayed or if Republicans failed to get control of the Southern states.[9]

In bringing the president to an impeachment trial in the Senate, the Northern Republicans were now committing themselves to a step their Southern colleagues had been urging for over a year. Heretofore, the Northern members of the party, who controlled national policy, had hesitated to acquiesce in the more radical requests from their Southern friends. In particular, they had refused to turn over control of the Southern civil governments to loyal whites and had kept the Johnson-created Conservative governments in place under military supervision. Southern Republicans had warned that this refusal left the president's Conservative supporters in control of state patronage, enabling them to use their influence to undermine or weaken Republican efforts to control state elections. They also warned that Johnson could use his position as commander in chief to weaken the enforcement of the Reconstruction Acts and to encourage Conservatives in their resistance to Reconstruction. All this had proved to be true, and now the Republican Congress was prepared to satisfy the Southern Republicans by removing the president from office. Even here, however, the Northerners undertook the measure not only because it would help their Southern allies but because it would hasten the end of Reconstruction and leave the party in a stronger position in the North to contest the 1868 elections.

Northern Republicans took a risk in impeaching the president. If the effort proved successful, it would greatly encourage the Southern Republicans and expedite Reconstruction, but if it failed, it would dishearten Southern Republicans and greatly encourage their Conservative opponents. Republicans also knew the move was not popular in some quarters of the North, and if the trial dragged on, they feared public opinion might well turn against the party.

The trial did drag on, lasting until mid-May. During this time, however, President Johnson undertook no overt actions to interfere with elections, and outside Louisiana, military officials were generally supportive of Republican efforts. By the time the Senate was beginning to vote on the impeachment articles, six Southern states had ratified their constitutions and were ready to be readmitted to the Union. Although Alabama had failed to meet the requirements of the Reconstruction Acts passed in 1867, it could qualify for restoration under the terms of the Fourth Reconstruction Act if Congress wished to apply it retroactively. Virginia, Mississippi, and Texas had still to comply with the Reconstruction Acts and were thus liable to potential presidential interference; Mississippi had scheduled its elections for June; and Virginia Republicans were hoping for an election later in the summer. Only Texas, which had not yet finished its constitution, appeared certain to be delayed into the following year. Hence, in a way, impeachment had succeeded in its purpose of protecting Reconstruction from presidential interference, and in most states the restoration process was almost complete. Consequently, Republicans had less reason to remove him, and when the balloting began on May 16, it became clear that impeachment would fail by at least one vote. Seven Republicans voted for acquittal, and more might have if their votes had been needed.[10]

Even though Republicans in Congress had been preoccupied with impeachment during the spring, they still watched events in the South with considerable interest. The new Reconstruction law passed in March allowed the Southern states to hold elections for state offices and Congress at the same time that voters cast ballots on the ratification of the new constitutions. Alabama, the first state to complete its constitution, had already established the precedent; when voters went to the polls in February, they voted not only on the constitution but on a slate of officials for state office. Northerners watched closely to see who the party would put forward as candidates for state and national offices. Before his removal, General Pope had cautioned Robert Schenck that when Congress considered readmitting the Southern states, the Republicans had to "look *to the men* and not the constitutions and state legislation" as the best indication of the future political orientation of the South.[11]

Many Northern Republicans were especially worried lest their Southern Republican colleagues nominate blacks for political office. Democrats were constantly warning that Republican rule in the South would bring subjugation of the white race by blacks, and one of the best defenses against the charge was to urge Republicans to run whites for office. John Binney was reassured that in Tennessee, where the Republicans had carried the elections held in August 1867, no black was elected to state office or to Congress and urged Republican leaders in the North to emphasize this fact. John Forney, who kept a close watch on Southern Republican nominations, noted with pleasure that two blacks in North Carolina had refused nominations to state office and contended that "this example of Negro modesty and moderation" went far to disprove Democratic charges that Republican rule in the South would lead to the subjugation of whites.[12]

Even Northern Republicans who achieved radical reputations avoided endorsing the election of blacks. The only prominent Northern politician to do so was Charles Sumner, who hoped South Carolina would send a black to the U.S. Senate. Thaddeus Stevens declared that the question of black officeholding was not an issue; because of racial prejudice, "I should not expect any but white men to be elected to office for long ages to come." Most Republicans, while agreeing that blacks had a right to hold office, argued that it would be impolitic for them to seek such opportunities. Benjamin Butler, reacting to Sumner's suggestion, urged South Carolina freedmen not to send a black to Congress, warning that such an action "would be a weight on the party," a point endorsed by such Northern Republican journals as the *Springfield Republican* and the *Nation*. Southern white Republicans were aware of the concerns in Congress about the racial composition of their state tickets. In Florida, for instance, advocates of the radical constitution drawn up by the "mule team" sought congressional support by emphasizing that their state ticket was composed entirely of whites. On the other hand, the proponents of the more moderate Reed constitution defended it in part on the grounds that it gave the governor wide appointive powers, hence avoiding "the problem of black counties selecting unqualified officeholders."[13]

In Alabama, where the first state election was held in 1868, the entire Republican state ticket was white, as were all the party's candidates for Congress. This pattern was repeated in other states; throughout the South no blacks were selected to run for Congress or for governor. In fact, only two states, South Carolina and Louisiana, put up blacks for any statewide office. In Louisiana, where blacks led by the *New Orleans Tribune* had been vocal in calling for a share of the offices, they received nominations for lieutenant governor and state treasurer. In South Carolina, the Republicans nominated a black, Francis Cardozo, for secretary of state. John Forney, in commenting on this selection, referred to Cardozo as "a light colored man of finished education, great ability, and uncommon acquirements."[14]

Although Northern Republicans expressed pleasure that few blacks were selected to run for office in the South, they were concerned about the nature of white party leadership as well. Forney and Greeley worried that nominations to important posts, particularly to Congress, were being monopolized by Northerners living in the South and urged the party there to recognize the claims of the "loyal citizens" who were natives of the South. Yet in states where native whites were nominated to important positions, complaints continued to be made about them. When Tennessee held its elections in August 1867, some Northerners worried that the new state officials were not able men. Even Forney's *Philadelphia Press*, an ardent advocate of Southern Republicanism, admitted that it would not want to see native Unionist William G. Brownlow elected governor of Pennsylvania. A number of other Republican newspapers and journals were also offended by Brownlow's vehement denunciations of his political opponents and his championing of rigid disfranchisement to sustain his administration in power. John Binney warned William Pitt Fessenden that Tennessee "is not a perfect model of a Reconstruction state." He was especially concerned that so many whites in the state were declared ineligible to hold office and urged Congress to give amnesty to "a few repentant ex-rebels" so that more qualified men might be available to serve the party and the state. The editor of the *Great Republic*, national organ of the Union League, worried that in the rest of the former Confederate states there would be even less talent to draw on for Republican leadership than in Tennessee, which had had a large and vigorous Unionist movement for several years. In the rest of the South, warned the editor, "leaders will be raised from the inexperienced masses."[15]

From Georgia, former Governor Brown wrote to Congressman William D. Kelley to express his concern that Rufus Bullock, the Republican nominee for governor, was a weak candidate and could not carry the state. In North Carolina, longtime Unionist William Holden was the party's gubernatorial nominee, and Thaddeus Stevens worried aloud about his commitment to black rights. Others feared that he had made so many enemies among the white population during the war that he could not carry the state. Rumors circulated that the Union Congressional Committee wanted Holden to withdraw, and finally General Schenck had to write him a public letter to assure him that no one in Washington opposed his candidacy.[16]

The Republican nominations for office in Alabama were particular targets of criticism, perhaps because they were first to be made in the South in 1868. General Meade expressed dismay with the caliber of the men selected by the party. He believed that the nominations were even more objectionable to the mass of voters than the new constitution and contended that many refused to vote in the February election because of the lack of qualified candidates. To save the constitution, he had earlier recommended that it be voted on in a separate election. General Swayne, who was a more ardent advocate of Republican interests in the state than Meade, agreed with his superior's assessment of the Republican slate. When Congress debated the advisability of admitting Alabama despite its failure to comply with the terms of the Reconstruction Acts, some Northerners in the state, perhaps angry because most Alabama offices had gone to native whites, wrote to Washington warning against admitting her on the grounds that "the men coming forward to lead the state are not able, intelligent, or virtuous." John Binney urged Fessenden not to "rush Alabama in if it means they are brought in with inferior office-holders."[17]

Although Northern Republicans watched the Southern elective process with interest in the spring of 1868, they gave little aid to their party allies other than advice. The Union Congressional Committee, noting that between March and mid-May six states had scheduled elections on their constitutions and on state and congressional offices, sent out an appeal for funds to replenish its exhausted treasury. Tullock, pointing out that the committee daily received "importunate appeals from the South for further aid," claimed that an additional $10,000 would help "close up the entire work of reconstruction and secure the ratification of most, if not all, the constitutions." Significant Northern aid was not forthcoming, however, and it fell to the local Union Leagues and Republican organizations to work desperately to carry their state elections.[18]

The results of the voting in the seven Southern states that held elections in the spring of 1868 were not very encouraging to the Republican party. Only in North Carolina did the Republicans attract significant white support; Northern Republicans estimated that around thirty thousand whites, about 25 percent of the state's registered white voters, cast ballots for the Republican ticket. Elsewhere, however, the party attracted little white support and was successful only because of the power of the black vote and white apathy and disorganization or disfranchisement. In Alabama, the first state to vote, the result was particularly disillusioning for those who hoped to get substantial white backing for the party. White support for calling the convention in that state had totaled more than eighteen thousand votes in the fall of 1867, but the 1868 boycott reduced the white vote in favor of the constitution to what *Harper's Weekly* estimated as around six thousand. The *New York Independent* exclaimed in frustration at "what a mere corporal's guard of white loyalists the State was thus proved to contain." The *Nation* concluded that the Alabama election proved the white population of the South would be nearly a unit against Reconstruction.[19]

The Republicans' slimmest victory came in Arkansas, where the constitution carried with only 51 percent of the vote. This was a severe blow to the party, for the election results showed a sharp reduction in Republican support, particularly among whites, since

the election to call the convention the previous fall. John Forney op-
timistically claimed that at least half the Republican vote in Arkansas was furnished by whites, but a close study of the returns conducted by Greeley's *Tribune* reached a more pessimistic conclusion.
Greeley claimed that at least five thousand white votes had been lost
to the Republicans between the two elections and concluded that the
party had been unable to surmount the racial prejudice existing
among uneducated whites. The Washington correspondent of the
Anti-Slavery Standard was also pessimistic about recruiting significant
white support in Arkansas, declaring that the state "will always be
doubtful."[20]

In Georgia, the constitution was ratified by a majority of almost
eighteen thousand, but the Republican state ticket's margin was less
than half of that figure; in addition, the Democrats won three of the
six congressional districts where elections were held, and the state
legislature was almost equally divided between the two parties. In
Arkansas and Georgia the Republicans were able to poll only 36 and
46 percent, respectively, of the state's registered voters. In Florida,
Conservatives and Radical Republicans mounted a halfhearted challenge to Reed and his moderate constitution, which was ratified by
about 60 percent of those voting. In Louisiana and South Carolina,
where whites either boycotted the election or voted against the proposed constitutions, the Republicans won easily; in South Carolina
they polled 72 percent of the total vote. The editors of the *Nation*,
after reviewing the spring elections, concluded that only North and
South Carolina were safely Republican: the former state because of
substantial white support and the latter because of its black voters.[21]

During the elections that were held in the spring, military officials
were generally supportive of Republican efforts. Although General
Meade upset some Radical Republicans by his intervention in the
intraparty dispute in Florida, Forney praised his "wise interposition"
there. Meade also removed the governor and state treasurer in Georgia for obstructing the Reconstruction process. Although General
Gillem was not a Radical favorite, he probably saved the constitution
in Arkansas by declaring it ratified by a narrow margin even though
questions were raised about the legitimacy of the vote in some counties that voted for it.[22]

In Mississippi, however, where the state election occurred about a month after the impeachment vote, Gillem's activities incurred the wrath of local Republicans, who charged him with responsibility for the defeat of their constitution. Gillem, who was in command of the state, did not cooperate with the constitutional convention when it attempted to raise money to pay its expenses. He also used his patronage to favor Unionist Whigs, hence embittering Republicans who wanted to control those offices. Gillem also kept his officers and Freedmen's Bureau agents from making political speeches and appointed Conservative voting officials and registrars. When the Mississippi election was held later in June, the Republicans, who had counted on a potential majority of seventeen thousand, saw their constitution and state ticket defeated by seven thousand votes. There were several reasons for the Republican failure. The proscriptive clauses of the constitution cost them white support and instead unified the Whigs in the state against the Republican party. The black voting majority was undercut by a variety of unscrupulous methods, but Gillem refused to consider complaints about election irregularities. State Republicans blamed their defeat on the continued influence of Johnson and his military officials. They also accused Northern Republicans of failing to support them, either with money for their state campaign or with more effective legislation from Congress. After the vote was taken, Mississippi Republicans appealed to Congress either to reverse the elections or to put loyal whites in control of the state before ordering a new election.[23]

Congress proved unwilling to risk alienating Northern voters by continuing to interfere in Southern state affairs during an election year and decided not to act on Mississippian pleas. Instead, it hastened to complete the Reconstruction process. A few days before the Mississippi election was held, Congress passed a bill admitting Arkansas and also an Omnibus bill restoring the states of Alabama, Florida, Georgia, Louisiana, and North and South Carolina. Congress enacted these measures even though there was increasing evidence that the Republican party's hold on several of these states was weak. In Arkansas, for instance, it was not even clear if the constitution had legitimately been carried. The Republican state ticket had been easily elected, however, and Congress was in no mood to delay the restoration of a state they controlled. Henry Wilson stated that if Congress restored not only Arkansas but the other Southern states that had completed the Reconstruction process, they would "give more than one hundred thousand majority" for the Republican candidate for president in the fall.[24]

The original form of the Omnibus bill had omitted both Alabama and Florida. The Alabama constitution had failed of ratification under the terms of the earlier Reconstruction Acts, and in Florida Congress faced the continued arguments of state Radicals who wanted to defeat the moderate Reed constitution. A number of Republicans in Alabama warned that their hold on the state was weak and that if it were admitted, it might well go Democratic in the fall. Northern Republicans decided to take the risk, rather than leaving the state in limbo under Johnson's control, and agreed to admit the state under the new terms of the Fourth Reconstruction Act. Then, after refusing a last-ditch appeal from Florida's Radical "mule team" proponents, Congress agreed to admit that state to the Union under its moderate constitution. Republicans in Congress acknowledged that their hold over these Southern states was tenuous and that the reconstructed governments might soon be overturned by attaching a "fundamental condition" to the Omnibus bill stipulating that their constitutions could never be amended to deprive any class of its citizens of the right to vote.[25] There was no effective way to enforce these provisions, however, for after the return of the Southern states to the Union, Congress lost any power to supervise their governments. Federal troops were to be withdrawn, and also the Freedmen's Bureau was to expire in June 1868.

Actually, as events were to prove in Virginia, as well as in Mississippi, military influence could be used to deny Republicans control of the state. The Virginia state convention had debated its constitution into April; the chief issue continued to be the advisability of disfranchisement. On April 17 General Schofield addressed the convention, stressing his opposition to any disfranchisement or requiring the ironclad oath for state and local offices. The convention refused to take his advice, however, and adjourned the same day, after approving a constitution that levied political disabilities on former Confederates. Foiled in his efforts to influence the convention, Schofield used his powers as military commander in other ways to defeat the constitution and to promote a moderate Republican party in the state. In April he removed Governor Pierpont, contending publicly that he had taken this action because Pierpont's term of office under the existing constitution had expired. It became clear, however, that Schofield hoped to pass the post on to a man who might have better fortune in solidifying moderate white support behind him. Schofield first offered the job to Alexander Rives, a prominent native white Republican, whom Schofield judged would be "invaluable to the Union cause." Rives refused, and, after consulting with leading white Republicans in the state, Schofield named his friend Henry H. Wells, a Union general from Michigan, to the governorship.[26]

Schofield's action undercut the Radicals in Virginia. Pierpont had been moving toward their position in his quest to solidify his own bid for renomination as governor, and Schofield wanted him out. Putting in Wells, as it proved, made him the most likely Republican candidate to run for governor under the new constitution. The Republican nominating convention was scheduled to meet in May, and Schofield and Freedmen's Bureau head Orlando Brown worked to ensure that the delegates chose nominees acceptable to potential white voters. Brown asked O. O. Howard to allow him to appoint more bureau agents in the state, so he could use them "to head off the influence of a class of incendiaries" seeking to control the convention. Pierpont, furious at his removal from office, protested to Howard that the bureau was being used against him and in support of Wells; but Howard refused to reprove Brown.[27]

When the Republican state convention met in May, moderate and Radical Republicans agreed to unite behind Wells, and he was easily selected over Hunnicutt and other candidates. Schofield again appealed to the party convention to repeal the test-oath qualification for office; and again his advice was rejected. Dismayed that the party was not more inclined to compromise with the whites of the state, Schofield told General Grant he thought the wisest course would be to let the constitution die; he recommended that it not be submitted to the Virginia electorate, for the proscriptive clauses would doom it. Schofield refused to finance the elections with funds at his disposal, and in desperation Republicans turned to Congress to ask it to supply money and to order an election. Congress refused to cooperate, fearing that the constitution would indeed be defeated, and the state ticket with it, as had happened in Mississippi. Republicans in the North also considered the proscriptive clauses to be a potential embarrassment during the campaign in the North. Consequently, no election was called, and the state had to remain unrestored, awaiting the returns of the national elections in 1868 to see what its fate would be.[28]

The last of the Southern states to hold a constitutional convention was Texas; delegates did not assemble in Austin until June. Although Republicans controlled most of the seats, they were divided into factions and argued endlessly over proposals to invalidate or honor debts made during the period of Confederate government, over which part of the state to favor with internal improvements, and over how far to go in disfranchising whites and granting rights to blacks. By mid-August, the convention had not yet drafted a constitution, and sentiment began to build to adjourn until after the forthcoming national election. When General Reynolds, who was in command in Texas, refused to allocate more money for the convention, its members agreed to dissolve and reconvene in December.[29]

In the closing days of the second session of the Fourteenth Congress, Republicans considered renewed pleas from Mississippi, Virginia, and Texas to reorganize their governments to give Unionists control. The Senate passed a bill requiring the ironclad oath of all officials in Virginia and Texas; the House approved a measure giving control of all three states to the constitutional conventions. Neither of these measures received the approval of the other house; hence both failed. As it became clear that none of the three states would be back in the Union before 1869, Congress proved unable or unwilling to take any further steps to aid the Republican party in them. Instead, it approved a bill prohibiting the counting of the electoral votes of any states not restored to the Union. Congress also refused to approve proposals from some of its more radical members to extend the operation of the Freedmen's Bureau until all states were returned to the Union. They were, however, eager to keep the bureau alive in the South, at least through the election of 1868. General Howard, in particular, wanted to make "doubly sure" that the Republicans won in the fall. Bureau agents, Tullock of the Congressional Committee, and Southern Republicans all urged Congress to continue the bureau. Democrats opposed its extension, arguing that the bureau was an election machine for the Republicans, and they were supported by a number of conservative Republicans, who thought that the bureau had become symbolic of continued federal intervention in the South. Just before Congress adjourned, Republicans rushed through a bill to continue the bureau in the South until

January 1, 1869, thus assuring that its agents would be available that fall to assist the Republican campaign.[30]

Republican haste to wind up the Reconstruction process in 1868 was only partly based on the anticipation of obtaining Southern support for the party's candidate for president that fall. The results of the spring elections in the reconstructed states had already indicated that the party would have difficulty maintaining political control of the South. As the presidential election grew nearer, Republicans were more concerned that further delays in Reconstruction would erode their traditional base of support in the North. The Civil War had been over for almost three years; Northern voters were increasingly eager to have the Union restored; and Democrats were accusing the Republicans of continually delaying the process. Hence, even though many Republicans believed the Southern states were not effectively reorganized, they realized that they had to be returned to the Union.

Ever since the state elections in 1867 had gone against the Republicans in the North, John Binney had been warning Republican leaders not to risk losing the North in pursuit of Southern support. To do so, he cautioned, would "set the case on its apex rather than its base." Horace Greeley had also been insisting since the 1867 elections that the party had to restore the Southern states before the 1868 presidential canvass; he estimated that the party would lose two hundred thousand votes in the North if it did not. Early in 1868 the editor of the *Cincinnati Commercial* also warned that Congress was risking the loss of Northern support by giving too much attention to the South. Even party newspapers heartily in favor of building the party in the South, like the *Great Republic*, expressed concern at the delay in Reconstruction. Republicans in Congress were responding to criticisms like these when they decided not to overturn the civil governments in Mississippi, Texas, and Virginia or to extend the Freedmen's Bureau in the South another year, fearing that continued congressional interference in the South could well cost them Northern support. Hence once again Northern Republicans compromised their Southern policy to maintain their Northern base. In continuing to give priority to Northern concerns in 1868, they were acting consistently with the history of their party.[31]

As Congress pushed to finish the Reconstruction process, Republicans encountered another difficulty that embarrassed their party in both the South and the North. In 1868 they had to confront anew the fruits of their policy of leveling political disabilities upon certain classes of former Confederates. Republicans had already experienced some discomfiture over this problem the year before, when it became clear that the Reconstruction Acts had disfranchised many potential white supporters. Now the Republicans in Congress faced the fact that many of these same men were not entitled to hold office, either because of the Fourteenth Amendment or the requirement that federal officeholders take the ironclad oath. Such proscriptive policies discouraged Southern whites who wished to cooperate with the Republicans and angered those Northern voters who wished to grant amnesty to Southern former Confederates as a way of reducing sectional hostilities.

The question of removing the disabilities of the Fourteenth Amendment from individual Southerners first emerged in March of 1867, when Senator John Sherman introduced a resolution asking that Joseph Brown of Georgia and Governor Robert Patton of Alabama be exempted from its provisions. Both men had expressed support for the Reconstruction Acts, and Sherman, who was alert for signs that Southern leaders were willing to cooperate with Congress, wanted to reward them. Although Congress took no action on the resolution at this time, it did point up the dilemma that Republicans faced in the South. The disability clauses, which were intended to punish Confederate leaders and keep them from political influence in the South, were now operating to discourage those who wished to lend their support to Reconstruction and to the Republican party.[32]

In the winter of 1867–68 pressures continued to build on Congress to grant amnesty, as more and more states held their constitutional conventions and prepared for elections. In Alabama, which was the first state to hold its convention, Republicans sent a petition to Congress listing a number of white Alabamians prepared to support the Reconstruction measures and asking that they be relieved of disabilities incurred under the Fourteenth Amendment. Generals Pope and Swayne both endorsed the petition, and in December 1867, Henry Wilson, who also favored amnesty, presented the list to the Senate. No action was taken on it, so in January, to test the will of Congress, Senator Stewart introduced a bill to give relief to one of the most prominent Alabamians named in the petition, Governor Patton. Stewart's bill passed the Senate, but in the House it was referred to the Committee on Reconstruction. Pressure on Congress to act increased after the Alabama state elections in February; approximately two hundred Republican officials who were elected then had to seek relief from political disability. Letters from these men to state and national party leaders emphasized that the Fourteenth Amendment, which Congress had approved before passage of the Reconstruction Acts, was now costing the Republican party dearly by alienating white supporters.[33]

In March, John Bingham, chairman of the House Committee on Reconstruction, reported a bill to extend relief to a number of prominent Southerners who were cooperating with congressional Reconstruction. The list included former governors Brown of Georgia and James Orr of South Carolina, General James Longstreet of Louisiana, and a large number of North Carolinians, led by former provisional governor William Holden. When the names became known, radical Southern Unionists immediately wrote to Congress protesting against relieving some of the individuals listed. A South Carolina Republican, writing in the name of the state's Union League, insisted that James Orr was "one of the worst men we have." Carpetbagger Albion Tourgée warned Congress that many of the whites named from North Carolina had cooperated with the Republicans only because the party was coming to power, and they could not be trusted. William Holden, however, urged Congress to approve the entire list of North Carolinians, claiming that "the relief of these would be of much service to us." Brown of Georgia, claiming that he did not seek amnesty for himself, told William Kelley that if Congress continued to withhold political rights from "the distinguished Southerners whose names appear in this bill," Republicans would forever lose the chance to gain white support.[34]

Such conflicting advice from the South about the advisability of pardoning specific individuals undermined the effort to provide amnesty. The Republicans had no clear process for proposing or approving names for relief and handled the matter in a piecemeal and unsystematic way. Many of the initial applicants for relief were working with the Union Congressional Committee's executive committee and appealed to that organization for support. The members of the committee decided to ask the Republicans in the several state constitutional conventions to scrutinize the applications and to draw up lists of names they could recommend for amnesty. The committee then inspected the lists and submitted them to other "prominent men of the South" for their opinions; Schenck then presented the names to the Congress. At the same time, however, names of other Southerners were reaching Congress through other routes. State central committees and the National Republican Committee submitted their own lists. Schenck complained that some of the names coming from other sources were unacceptable to the men with whom he was in contact in the South; he wanted to delay the amnesty process until more information could be collected on all the names submitted.[35]

Opinion in the Congress on the wisdom of amnesty remained divided. Some Republicans, particularly those from the border states, were reluctant to remove disabilities, and Democrats voted as a group against the proposals, noting that determinations of loyalty were made on an entirely partisan basis. Bingham's bill was finally sent back to committee. Benjamin Hedrick of North Carolina, who was in Washington at the time, observed that Bingham had "stood by the South as long as he could," but that his bill had been ground "between the upper and nether millstones" of Southern Radicals and Northern Democrats. The bill also failed, however, because, although many Northern Republicans were growing more sympathetic to amnesty, they were waiting to see if the men named in the petitions remained loyal to the Republican party in the forthcoming state elections. A Georgia delegation in Washington seeking amnesty for particular whites in the state reported that Congress would not act until it could determine "how those desiring and needing relief have stood in the [state] contest." A North Carolinian desirous of amnesty was warned that he had little chance because he had not "united [his] political fortunes with the Republican party."[36]

Such partisan application of the amnesty process proved an embarrassment in the North. The *New York Herald* objected vigorously to relieving only Republicans, a position echoed by the *New York Times*, which warned that amnesty distributed in such a way would do more harm than good. The Republican party, the *Times* observed, was taking part in a "discreditable bargain and sale." The paper warned that "instead of conciliating opponents, such a policy adds to the existing irritation" among whites in the South. Republican newspapers such as the *New York Tribune* and *Springfield Republican*, which had always favored universal amnesty, increased their pressure for such an act. Greeley continued to argue through the columns of the *Tribune* that the vast majority of whites in the South were loyal and freedom-loving and would support Reconstruction if they had the liberty to do so; he warned that disfranchisement also hurt the party in the North. Samuel Bowles, editor of the *Springfield Republican*, argued that the feelings of Southern whites should not be ignored, warning that "there is always danger so long as the moral sense of the governed is either alienated or aggrieved." The *Boston Advertiser* and *Chicago Tribune* also argued that the time had come to grant amnesty. The consensus among congressional Republicans, however, was that general amnesty could not be provided until Reconstruction was complete and their party established in control of the Southern states.[37]

In June, after seven Southern states had complied with the Reconstruction Acts, elected governments controlled by Republicans, and been admitted to the Union, Congress agreed to reconsider Bingham's bill to grant amnesty to large numbers of individual Southerners. The debates that followed revealed that Republicans were still divided over the advisability of appealing to prominent former Confederates for their political support. Proponents of amnesty argued that because of the social prominence of several of the men on Bingham's list, their influence would bring large numbers of other Southern whites over to the Republican party. Such an accession of white support, amnesty advocates argued, would go far to disprove the charge that the Republicans wanted to establish Negro supremacy in the South. Representative John Farnsworth of Illinois, one of the sponsors of the amnesty bill, repeatedly warned that if amnesty failed, parties in the South would divide along racial lines, with blacks going to the Republicans, and the results would be fatal to the party. He echoed the fears of many who doubted that the black vote could be relied on: "When intelligence is arrayed against ignorance . . . when the politicians are arrayed against those ignorant, inexperienced men who are not politicians, who are naturally timid, and who have been rendered more so by their past experience with slavery," the outcome would not be in doubt; "blacks would go to the wall."[38]

Congressman Henry Bromwell of Illinois said he would rather seek Southern white support among the truly loyal who did not need amnesty; he hoped for a new set of Southern leaders who would not attempt to control the masses to enhance the privileges of a few. John Coburn of Indiana admitted that the true Union men in the South were "poor and unlettered, unused to political management, unskilled in debate, untried in the responsibilities of office, and timid in the exercise of power," but he preferred them to the leaders of the rebellion. "The true representative of the South," Coburn argued, "is the laboring man, the man of vigor, the man of nerve, the man of business, the man of enterprise, the self-reliant, independent, hard-working American." They, not the socially prominent, should be courted, and Coburn argued that based on voting registration figures in the South, there were enough Unionist whites of the laboring class eligible to hold office without resorting to the relief of those who had helped bring on the rebellion.[39]

The arguments of those favoring the Bingham bill prevailed. Many of the men in the proposed legislation had been elected to office under the new Republican governments, and Congress had little choice except to relieve them. Representative James Garfield observed that to defeat the bill, with the names of so many elected officials on it, would defeat Reconstruction, and the states would face either continued rebel control or anarchy. From the pages of his *Washington Chronicle*, John Forney pronounced Bingham's measure "an indispensable supplement to the other legislation looking to the reconstruction of the Southern states" and warned that its defeat would consolidate whites into an anti-Northern party, "against which the Negroes could not be sustained." Only by extending amnesty, argued Forney, could Republicans nurture a biracial party in the South. Bingham's bill passed both houses with the required two-thirds majority and thereby relieved 1,431 Southern whites of disabilities incurred under the Reconstruction Acts and the Fourteenth Amendment. Congress decided to keep the ironclad oath for federal officeholders, but it did amend it in July to allow the Southern whites elected to national offices in 1868 to take it.[40]

The amount of time Congress spent in debating the advisability of relieving individuals in the South from political disabilities provided evidence of the unworkability of the concept of levying penalties against former Confederates. Many Southerners who had been forced into supporting the Confederacy were unable to qualify for voting or holding office, yet ardent secessionists who had not held government positions before the war suffered no loss of political rights. Confederates who were ready to admit their error and support Reconstruction were often discouraged from doing so by political disqualifications. Evidence poured in from every Southern state that the exaction of political disabilities was harmful to the Republican cause. Yet ardent Unionists who had opposed the Confederacy throughout the war were angry at Congress for allowing some of their former opponents to gain exemption from these disabilities. There was no way Congress could adjust this matter to the satisfaction of all parties in the South. Nevertheless, the way Congress dealt with disqualifications, by doling out relief on a piecemeal basis, cast considerable doubt on the efficiency and practicality of the system.[41]

With seven of the Southern states restored to the Union under Republican governments and the former Confederates who were supporting these governments relieved of political disabilities, the party could turn to securing those states in the fall presidential election. The Reconstruction process had been implemented the previous year, and many Republicans were wondering how the South might vote in the national elections. Speculation had also been rife for well over a year about who would receive the Republican nomination. Many Northern Republicans were attracted to Ulysses S. Grant, whose generalship in the Civil War had led the Union to victory. Others, however, who were dubious about Grant's credentials as a Republican and doubtful about his commitment to black rights, looked with favor on the candidacy of Salmon P. Chase, who in 1868 was chief justice of the Supreme Court. Chase had had a long record as a Radical; he had been an abolitionist, an early member of the Republican party, an ardent advocate of emancipation during the war, and an early endorser of Negro suffrage.

Chase's candidacy was especially popular in the South. During the war Chase had made a number of Treasury Department appointments in states undergoing Union occupation, and many of these men still either retained their offices or continued to be loyal to the former secretary. These government officeholders were especially active in Florida and Louisiana. The national Union League organization was also supportive of Chase's candidacy because the league was one of the firmest supporters of Negro suffrage. Many of the league representatives in the South, Thomas Conway being the most important, championed Chase's candidacy. He was popular among Southern blacks because his name was identified with black rights.

He also had money at his disposal to finance his ambitions; his son-in-law was a millionaire senator from Rhode Island. Although the Union Congressional Committee was divided over Chase's candidacy, its secretary, Thomas Tullock, used his considerable influence in Chase's behalf.[42]

By the end of 1867, however, the national Republican leaders were all but unanimous in favor of Grant. The fall elections, which had gone to the Democrats, convinced them that the party had to nominate Grant; his reputation as a war hero promised an outpouring of votes for him in the North, and his lack of strong identification with Negro suffrage meant that he would appeal to conservative Republicans in the Northern states. Chase, on the other hand, appeared to many to be too radical a candidate to carry the Northern states. Consequently, during the winter of 1867–68 the only support Chase could depend on came from the South; no significant Northern leader endorsed him, nor did any Northern state party organization. Instead, they stampeded to embrace Grant.[43]

By January 1868, Grant, who had been Johnson's interim secretary of war, had broken openly with the president, making it easier for Republicans to endorse him. Chase was courting conservatives by attacking continued military occupation of the South and advocating an end to disfranchisement. His behavior as presiding officer in the president's impeachment trial also convinced Republicans of his lack of sympathy for that action. Consequently, it became clear that no matter how the Southern Republicans felt about Grant, he would be nominated by the party. Southern delegations to the Republican national convention did not even know if they would be seated; it was obvious that they would have almost no influence on the convention's action. Northerners were apprehensive, however, that the Southern wing of the party might bolt if Grant were nominated.[44]

By the time the national Republican convention met in May, it was clear that a Southern bolt would not materialize. Grant's candidacy quickly developed strength in the South, as his adherents began to organize against the Chase men and picked up Southern Republican newspaper support. More and more Chase men in the South realized that their cause was lost, particularly after the 1867 Northern elections, and they joined the Grant parade. The only specific endorsements Chase gained came from the Louisiana Union League and from a caucus of delegates to the Georgia constitutional convention. Schuyler Colfax, the Speaker of the House from Indiana who was soon to be nominated as vice-president to run with Grant, was convinced that the Southern party would accept the general. Southern blacks were sympathetic to Chase, he noted, but they realized that the party could not carry the election without Grant at the head of the ticket.[45]

The Republican convention met on May 20 in Chicago. Unlike previous conventions, this time the national committee had not even considered meeting in a city closer to the South. Again, as in all three previous Republican conventions, questions were raised about seating the Southern delegations, but this time everyone agreed, without extended debate, that they should all be admitted with votes, even though at this time the Omnibus bill had not readmitted Southern states to the Union. Several speeches at the convention emphasized the need to finish the work of Reconstruction under Republican guidance and stressed the importance of protecting the Southern blacks and white Unionists who had stood with the nation and the Republican party. Former Confederate Joseph Brown of Georgia, a delegate to the convention, created a sensation by his presence and was well received when he spoke to the gathering. In his address, Brown emphasized that a number of other former Democrats were ready to join the Republican party, but the platform resolutions included no gesture of friendship or forgiveness toward the white South. Neither was the party prepared to endorse Negro suffrage on a national basis, fearing a backlash against the party in the North if it did. Instead, the Republicans required it in the South while leaving it up to state action in the North. Carl Schurz, concerned at the failure of the platform to appeal to Southern whites, did get the convention to add an additional resolution commending former rebels who were now cooperating with the Republicans and recommending that such men be permitted to regain their political privileges.[46]

The main work of the convention was to nominate Grant for president, and this was quickly and unanimously achieved. There was some division in the convention over the vice-presidential selection, and a large number of Southern delegates supported Henry Wilson for the post, but it eventually went to Schuyler Colfax.[47] Thus the Chicago convention followed the same pattern established by the three previous Republican national conclaves; the party went for the standard-bearers who could carry the Northern states. Southern preferences for president and vice-president got little consideration. Grant, who was a war hero in the North, did not appear likely to appeal to former Confederates. Nor did the platform offer anything to the white South until Schurz amended it to propose limited amnesty.

After the convention adjourned, Republican congressmen returned to Washington to take up the final Reconstruction measures of the second session of the Fortieth Congress. The Schurz plank convinced some of them to drop their opposition to the amnesty bill then pending in the House, which Congress then proceeded to pass, along with the measures restoring seven Southern states to the Union. With most of the ex-Confederate states back in the fold, and with the strongest presidential candidate they could nominate, Republicans were now ready for the fall elections. Their nomination of Grant, and their passage of the Omnibus bill, had been motivated more by a concern for protecting their Northern political base than by expectations of winning more Southern support. Republicans continued to hope for gaining white votes as well as black in the South, but with the exception of granting limited amnesty in 1868, they had undertaken no practical measure to encourage such support.

THE ELECTION OF 1868

By the summer of 1868, the Republican party had been able to restore all but three Southern states to the Union, and for the first time since the party had been formed, it could hope for significant Southern support in a national election. The Republicans now found that their most loyal and numerous adherents were among the blacks of the South, a condition the party had not anticipated when it was formed in 1855. At that time, those who hoped to build Southern support for the party expected to find it among nonslaveholding whites, and some in the party continued to hope for significant white support, despite the sectional and racial animosities heightened and sustained by the Civil War and its aftermath. Northern Republicans did little in any positive way, however, to encourage such white accessions to their ranks. Their support of black suffrage alienated many Southern whites, who were further outraged or discouraged by Republican policies that deprived them of political rights. Northern Republicans hoped that by appealing to the economic interests of Southern whites, they could overcome these sectional and racial divisions, but the party failed to give these whites any significant economic incentives for joining their party.

A number of Republicans in the North were aware of the political potential for creating white support in the South by advocating the development of the former Confederacy's resources and promising to revive its commercial and industrial life. At the 1868 Chicago convention, Frederick Hassaurek of Ohio told his fellow delegates that material prosperity for the South was an important element of Reconstruction. "You cannot make an ex-rebel loyal by disfranchising him," he warned, "but wait till he commences to make money under the new regime, and he will soon become reconciled to it." Since the beginning of Reconstruction, a number of Republicans had been urging their party to give tangible signs of economic assistance to revive the war-torn South. John Forney of the *Washington Chronicle* was one of the foremost advocates of the idea of appealing to white voters in the South by economic aid. Since the end of the war he had assured white Southerners that if they cooperated with Congress and the Republicans, the party would enact legislation to develop their section, "as they have always sustained every measure to promote the welfare of the whole country." These arguments were picked up by Congressional Committee agents who traveled south and were also emphasized by Wilson and Kelley in their tours of the section. Both men, as former Whigs, were eager to appeal to others from that party in the South by reminding them that the Republican party had inherited Whiggish ideas about government aid to economic development.[1]

During the Civil War the Republican Congresses had created a new national banking system that had issued a national currency, enacted a protective tariff to protect domestic industry, granted federal lands and loans for transcontinental railroad development, enacted the Homestead Act, appropriated other federal lands to subsidize agricultural schools in the several states, and championed river and harbor improvements. By extending this largesse to the South and by aiding the section in other ways, the Republicans stood to gain more Southern white support. Henry Wilson promised as much; after the war was over he pledged that "whenever I can give a vote that shall improve the value of an acre of land, or . . . develop the resources of [the South], or in any way accommodate that people, I intend to give that vote."[2] Wilson, however, did not speak for many in his party. Despite appeals from the South, the Republicans proved unwilling through the summer of 1868 to grant that section significant economic aid.

Even before the Republican party was organized in the South, whites from Louisiana and Mississippi were petitioning Congress for aid to rebuild levees along the Mississippi River that had been destroyed during the war. When Senator Daniel Clark of New Hampshire introduced these petitions into Congress in the summer of 1866, Forney praised his action as evidence that the Republicans merited white support in the South. Unfortunately for his hopes, however, the levee bills failed, defeated by the New Orleans riots and defiant statements against Congress from Democratic newspapers in Louisiana. In 1867 the recommendations for levee aid were revived, this time by appeals from the Republican state conventions of Louisiana, Mississippi, and Arkansas. General Ord in Mississippi added his support, and several Northern newspapers, including the *New York Tribune*, *New York Times*, and *Boston Commonwealth*, joined Forney in urging Congress to give the memorials serious consideration. Although Congress considered legislation to rebuild levees and improve navigation along the Mississippi, when it adjourned in the summer of 1868 nothing had been enacted, and it appeared nothing would be. Congress also turned a deaf ear to requests to improve harbors along the Gulf Coast.[3]

Forney continued to agitate for Congress to aid the South and thus "impress upon them the beneficent character of Radical rule." Besides continuing to call for levee improvement, he urged Congress to aid Southern railroads with new or renewed land grants.[4] In the 1850s several Southern states had received millions of acres in federal land grants to enable them to build new railroad systems. The Civil War had checked these roadbuilding projects in the South, and in 1867 and again in 1868 Congress considered the advisability of passing legislation punishing the former Confederate states by forcing them to forfeit land grants already made. Congress decided not to do this, but it refused to grant more land to the roads, contending that they had not completed their building within the period prescribed by the prewar laws. Forney urged Congress to release this land. In one case, involving the Little Rock and Fort Smith Railroad, Congress did agree to allow further federal grants to Arkansas to permit completion of the road, but through 1868 this privilege was not extended to any other Southern state. The best Forney could do under the circumstances was to urge Southerners to vote for Grant, offering the hope that after the election some aid for the railroads and levees might be forthcoming.[5]

In June 1868, after the Republican convention, Congress took up a proposal that was aimed at giving the Southern and Western states a fairer share of the nation's new national bank notes. These notes, which were rapidly replacing state bank notes and hence becoming the common currency in the country, had first been issued during the Civil War. The initial legislation authorized the comptroller of the currency to distribute the new money in accordance with population and also "banking capital, resources, and business." Because the Southern states were at that time out of the Union, the bank notes were distributed in the North. In 1866, after the war had been over for more than a year, the average per capita circulation of bank notes in the South was one-thirtieth of what it was in New England and New York. This discrepancy was doubly unjust to the South because its economy needed more currency than did the more developed regions of the nation. The 1868 bill proposed to alleviate the situation by taking the excess circulation from the Northern states for redistribution in the South. Henry Wilson ardently advocated the proposal, but Congress refused to enact it.[6]

If Congress was hesitant to enact general legislation to benefit the South or sections of it, it also proved unwilling to support individual Southerners who had defended the Union during the Civil War. After the war, Congress refused to honor the claims of Southern Unionists against the government for property taken from them by Union armies. Some individual claims did reach the floor of Congress, but in 1867 Congress approved legislation preventing the payment of any funds until it had established some general policy for dealing with claims. Even Henry Wilson supported this action, contending that only in such a way "can we do justice to the really loyal men in that section of the country and prevent the millions of frauds that will be attempted." John Forney also warned against the "monstrous frauds" that could result from Southern claims. Such arguments did little to assuage the anger and frustration of Southern Unionists, however, who grumbled that they would have joined the Confederacy if they could have anticipated how the federal government would reward their loyalty. Not until 1870 did Congress establish a commission to dispose of Unionist claims against the government.[7]

Republican failure to encourage support among whites by offering them economic assistance resulted from a variety of considerations. By 1868 there was a growing concern in Congress about extravagance and waste in the federal budget; many felt, for instance, that the government, already burdened by wartime debts, could not afford to provide aid for levee improvements. By 1868 there was also a growing reaction in the North against further land grants for any railroads. As for national bank note circulation, the 1868 bill would have deprived Northern states of some of the notes to furnish the South, and hence Northern congressmen opposed it. Because as late as 1868 only Tennessee of the former Confederate states was represented in

Congress, there were no other votes from the South to cast in favor of legislation beneficial to that section.[8]

Some Northern congressmen were also motivated by continued hostility toward former rebels when they debated economic policy concerning the South. In March 1867, for instance, some members opposed a bill to grant relief to Southerners suffering from a series of floods and crop failures. General Howard of the Freedmen's Bureau had requested an appropriation of one and a half million dollars to provide aid for those in the former Confederacy who were threatened by starvation. The Senate trimmed the proposal to one million dollars and approved it without debate by a margin of twenty-nine to nine. In the House, however, the relief measure came in for considerable discussion. Ignatius Donnelly of Minnesota led the way for proponents of the bill, arguing that it presented an excellent way to assure the white South that the very Congress that was enacting the Reconstruction Acts was concerned about the welfare of white Southerners. Its passage would help allay sectional hostility; its defeat, he argued, would "diminish Unionism in the South" and allow rebel demagogues to rally white support behind them.[9]

When opponents of the bill objected that the aid could well go to prominent former rebels, its advocates claimed that instead it would benefit the very classes that might respond to Northern overtures. William Kelley insisted the relief would go to mountaineers in Alabama, Georgia, and central South Carolina, "the blind, the dumb, the driven masses of the South," who had been controlled by the slaveholding oligarchy. Donnelly endorsed this view, contending that by extending charity to the great mass of people of the South, their dependence on rebel leadership would be weakened and they would be more receptive to Northern influences. Robert Schenck, the chairman of the Congressional Committee, which was about to encourage the organization of the Southern Republican party, opposed the measure, however, arguing that the former rebels would only construe it as an act of concession and timidity on the part of the North. He was joined by Benjamin Butler, who insisted that if Congress were to appropriate such a sum of money it should be directed to the widows and children of Union prisoners of war who died in the South.[10]

Ultimately most Republicans did vote for the relief bill, which passed the House by a 98–31 vote. The funds appropriated were to be dispensed through the Freedmen's Bureau, a point that brought objections from Democrats arguing that the funds would be distributed on a partisan basis. Because Democrats were suspicious of the bill, John Forney seized the occasion to remind the white Southerners that the Republican party stood ready to aid them in their distress. Although some Republican congressmen were moved by practical political considerations in approving the measure, most who endorsed it viewed it as necessary to relieve suffering in the South and promote sectional harmony. And some Northern Republicans eager for Southern white support were not at all pleased by its passage; Horace Greeley, for one, thought the South should rely on its own labor and resources to recover from natural disasters.[11]

The same mixture of partisan, humanitarian, and vengeful motives characterized congressional discussion of the cotton tax. In 1866, Congress had enacted a law taxing Southern cotton at three cents a pound. Although the measure was part of the country's system of raising internal revenue, it was the only tax on agricultural produce, and that crop was grown only in the South. Hence in part its enactment was designed to force the South to pay some of the costs of the Civil War. The measure, however, did not discriminate between loyal and disloyal planters or between blacks and whites; all farmers had to pay the tax. Because cotton prices fell after the war, the tax worked a severe imposition on the South.[12]

The Reconstruction process begun by the Fortieth Congress in 1867 had hardly begun to function before Southern Republicans began to petition for repeal of the cotton tax. Party conventions across the Lower South passed resolutions against it, and individual party members urged Northern congressmen to oppose it. The petitioners stressed the economic harm the tax was working on the South, and this position was reinforced by Northerners who had invested money in cotton planting in the former Confederacy. In addition, critics of the tax claimed that it created much bitter feeling in the South, on the part of blacks as well as whites, against the North and the Republican party, which had enacted it. Agents traversing the South for the Congressional Committee confirmed this assessment, and its chairman, Robert Schenck, called for repeal of the tax. He was joined by Henry Wilson and William D. Kelley, both of whom had toured the South and noted the harm the tax was doing to Republican fortunes. Willard Warner, a former Union general from

Ohio engaged in cotton farming in Alabama, wrote several letters to Senator John Sherman, asking for repeal. "As a Republican," Warner stated, "repeal . . . is not only wise and just in itself but eminently desirable as a party measure." He and other appellants noted that repeal would prove to the South that the Republicans were interested in the welfare of the war-torn section. Urged in part by such considerations, but also by fears that the tax would stimulate the production of cotton in foreign countries, in February 1868 Congress voted to repeal it.[13]

There was only one economic measure affecting the South that Republican speakers could point to as an indication of federal support for that region's inhabitants. In June 1866, Congress had amended the Homestead Act of 1862 to reserve federal lands in five Southern states to loyal blacks and whites. James Edmunds, national head of the Union League, who in 1866 was commissioner of the public lands, urged this law on Congress as a way to provide lands for poor homesteaders. The alternative, he realized, might be confiscation of Southern estates. George Julian of Indiana sponsored the legislation, but only reluctantly did he allow former Confederate whites to take advantage of it. He was able to delay their use of the federal lands for six months; not until January 1867 were they available to anyone who had aided the Confederacy. The following year Julian introduced another measure to enhance homesteading opportunities in the South. He proposed that Congress revoke the five million acres of federal land it had granted in 1856 to four Southern states for railroad building and turn this acreage over to the Southern homestead program. Julian justified his proposal by claiming that the land had gone to Southerners who had later supported the rebellion, and it was therefore appropriate to deprive them of these lands so that poor Southern whites and blacks could have them.[14]

Julian's new proposal again brought forth divisions among Republicans over the question of what class of Southern whites to appeal to for political support. John Coburn urged Congress to donate the land "to the poor Union soldier, or even to the poor white man of the South who may have been forced to fight in the rebel army" and not to wealthy leaders of the rebellion. Donnelly of Minnesota echoed these thoughts, stating that federal lands should be used "to strengthen the hands of our friends," the poor whites and blacks of the South, rather than "rebel stockholders." Austin Blair of Michigan replied, however, that "there was no worse rebel element in the South than the poor white population," and he saw no need to vote for Julian's bill. James G. Blaine of Maine also opposed it, arguing that the South needed railroads and loyal men would benefit from having them built. Faced with a choice between aiding stockholders or landless whites and blacks, in this case the House went with the latter group, passing Julian's measure by a vote of 86–73, with many Republicans opposed. The Senate, however, buried the bill in committee, and nothing more came of it.[15]

The history of the implementation of the Southern homestead law revealed that only a handful of people were ever able to take advantage of it. Most of the federal land remaining in the South was poorly located, of poor quality, or heavily timbered. The law was to be administered by the Freedmen's Bureau, but the bureau's staff was inadequate to the task, and its commanding officers often were uninterested in using the law. By the end of 1868, when the bureau was terminated, the limited opportunities for Southerners, black or white, for homesteading on public lands in the South disappeared.[16]

Despite the ineffectiveness of the 1866 homestead legislation, Northern Republicans emphasized its value in the South to prospective white voters.[17] Party literature circulated in the South by the Republicans stressed that former Confederate soldiers, particularly poor whites who had been conscripted into the army, could avail themselves of it. Republicans claimed that the law was evidence that their party was not vindictive toward the South. Indeed, according to the Union Republican Congressional Committee, in an address to nonslaveholding whites, "it was in your behalf more than for anyone else that the battle of Republicanism was fought" in the 1860 election. According to the committee, the poor white laboring men of the South had been held in subjection by the planter class and hence deprived of opportunities for personal advancement. Now the Republican party, by offering free land, free schools, aid to internal improvements, and support for a Pacific railroad, would develop the human and material resources of the South and bring prosperity to the masses of whites. The Republican party would protect the rights of all men, whites as well as blacks. The committee hastened to assure whites, however, that the party's commitment to equality of all men before the law "does not mean social but political equality."

The Republican committee buttressed its appeal to the white vote by stressing statistics that demonstrated the North's great advantages over the South in manufacturing product, wages, land under cultivation, land value, and number of schools. According to the party literature, the South could obliterate these differences and approximate the North's economic achievement by "embracing the fundamental principles of national growth and life" represented by the Republican party. The Democrats, on the other hand, were pictured as advocates of the Lost Cause, glorifying the decadence of the Old South and the leadership of the planter class, which had come at the expense of the interests of the white masses. A vote for the Democrats was presented, then, as a vote to maintain the old system of class rule in the South, whereas a vote for the Republicans promised to bring democracy, education, industry, and economic progress.[18]

If in 1868 the national Republican party provided little evidence of its willingness to promote the economic well-being of the South, perhaps the Southern Republican parties, through their control of state governments, could convince white voters that their program was better for them than that offered by their Conservative opponents. Unfortunately, Southern Republicans had little time to make a record to run on before the fall elections. Legislatures were convened in every reconstructed state in the summer of 1868, but most did not sit long and were chiefly occupied with implementing the provisions of their new constitutions. Appointments to new offices had to be made, judicial systems had to be reorganized, an effort had to be made to establish the newly authorized public school systems, and pressing problems of financing state debts and borrowing money had to be met. The Republican governors and legislatures struggled under a variety of handicaps as they attempted to meet the challenges of governing their states. Many of the Republican legislators had had little previous political or legislative experience. They struggled with obstructionist tactics from their Conservative opponents in the legislature and faced a barrage of criticism from Conservative newspapers. In several states they were also beset by divisions in their own ranks. Usually these divisions were along sectional lines, with Northerners, or "carpetbaggers" as they were now known, vying for political office and influence with native white Republicans, known as "scalawags" to their Conservative opponents. An additional source of division within the Republican ranks that was increasingly evident in the Lower South was along racial lines, with

Southern blacks demanding a greater share of offices and civil rights legislation to deal with discrimination against them.

As the new Republican regimes were quickly put to the test in the South, several of them appeared weak and shaky. Nowhere was this more apparent than in Georgia, a state where the Republicans had high hopes. J. H. Caldwell, member of the Republican National Committee from Georgia, claimed the party there had between thirty-five and forty thousand white voters and predicted that when the new governor, Rufus Bullock, assumed control of the state's patronage, white support would be increased. The constitution had been approved by a majority of eighteen thousand, and Republicans in the state professed confidence in the early summer that the state could be carried for Grant that fall by a similar margin. When Bullock assumed control, however, he was beset by problems. His own margin in the gubernatorial race had been much smaller than that approving the constitution. Many Republicans were angry because Bullock's supporters had obtained his nomination from the constitutional convention delegates, rather than through a separate party convention. They were also convinced that Bullock had promised away most of the state's important posts to gain support for his nomination.[19]

The balance in the Georgia legislature between Republicans and Conservatives or Democrats was extremely close, and Bullock and his forces proved unable to control the body. The governor asked General Meade to remove all members who could not take the test oath, but Meade refused to intervene, and consequently the legislative membership remained unaltered. In the first test of strength, election of the state's two United States senators, Republican lawmakers divided, and Bullock was unable to control the choices. One of the men the legislature selected was not even identified as a Republican. The fight over the Senate seats demoralized the Republican party and opened up divisions in its ranks. The demoralization quickly grew worse after September 3, when the Georgia House voted to expel its twenty-five black legislators on the grounds that the new state constitution did not guarantee their right to hold office. The state senate followed suit a few days later, expelling its three black members.[20]

A number of Georgia Republicans, dismayed by the actions of the state legislature, called on Congress to declare the state unreconstructed and return it to military rule. The party was demoralized, they claimed, and the Conservatives were encouraged by the actions of the legislature. Whites were increasing their terrorist attacks on blacks, and some prominent Georgia Republicans contended that unless Congress intervened to protect them, Conservative economic power and physical intimidation of the new voters would carry the state for the Democrats. Grant would win, they averred, only if a fair election could be guaranteed. If it could not, the state's electoral vote should not be counted, and the Congress should refuse to seat the Georgia delegation. One Union League official warned William Claflin that "if Congress suffers these things to go on we Loyal whites and colored freedmen are in a worse condition than the slaves were before the war."[21]

Northern leaders were concerned about the deteriorating state of affairs in Georgia but did little beyond urging party leaders in the state to stop their internal squabbling and unite against the Conservatives. Northern Republicans were also apprehensive about the forthcoming election in Louisiana, where the state party was suffering from internal division. Edwin Morgan, chairman of the Union Congressional Committee, feared the Republicans would lose Louisiana in the fall. Although the party had carried the election for the constitution and for state offices, it had failed to poll the maximum black vote, and it was clear that most whites had voted against the Republicans. The new governor, Henry Clay Warmoth, was a young former Union army officer, whose candidacy had raised divisions within the party.[22]

When Louisiana's legislature convened in July, its activities raised even more consternation among Republicans. Whites were particularly concerned about the efforts of black legislators to push through a bill establishing integrated schools and fining parents who refused to let their children attend them. Thomas Conway, the former Union League organizer, was now state superintendent of education and had drawn up the proposal. Northern Republicans were horrified by the measure; the *Nation* predicted its defeat "if the Republican majority in the Legislature has any sense left." Secretary Tullock of the Republican Congressional Committee was critical of the proposal and warned that "Republicans South should forbear as much as possible." Conway's bill failed for lack of support from Governor Warmoth, but in September the legislature did pass a law requiring equal accommodations in public facilities in the state. To the great pleasure of anxious Northern observers, Warmoth promptly vetoed the bill, thus alienating its advocates, most of whom were blacks. M. A. Southworth, a member of the Republican National Committee from Louisiana, complained that the state legislature "was a very heavy burden to the Republican party." Southworth also noted that the body delayed so long in approving a voting registration law that it was unlikely that the state would obtain a full registration before the election. Congressman Benjamin Butler, upon being informed of developments in the state legislature, declared that "the state of things in Louisiana is horrible."[23]

Factional and racial divisions also continued to plague Florida Republicans. The moderate state constitution had given the governor wide appointive powers, and Reed used this opportunity to appoint whites, many of whom were Conservatives, to most offices. Blacks, who were angry at Reed for not giving them some of the posts, were further dismayed when the governor vetoed a bill similar to that passed in Louisiana, guaranteeing equal treatment of all citizens on railroads in the state. In South Carolina, similar divisions occurred between white and black Republicans over support for a bill prohibiting discrimination in all public accommodations. This proposal, which the *Nation* scornfully referred to as the "Social Equality bill," gained almost unanimous black support, but white Republican legislators resisted it, some claiming its passage would imperil the Republican party's chances in the North in the coming elections. The bill passed the South Carolina House but was tabled in the Senate.[24]

Consequently, no Southern Republican legislature in 1868 enacted public accommodations laws, and Northern whites heaved a sigh of relief. The editors of the *New York Times*, who had never favored universal suffrage in the South and who feared that blacks would abuse their newly won political power, were impressed by the conservatism of the state legislatures. According to the *Times*, blacks had not sought to establish "a negro aristocracy," gain special privileges, or take revenge against whites. Neither had blacks sought to "extend amalgamation," and they had proved to be "scrupulous of property rights."[25] Most Southern whites, however, did not share the *Times*'s assessment of the Republican performance and failed to lend their support to the new governments. Instead, in the summer of 1868 many began to resort to violence in an effort to weaken the new regimes.

Events in the South increasingly indicated that Conservative whites were willing to take almost any means necessary to defeat their opponents in the fall elections, and Southern Republicans grew worried that a fair canvass could not be held in their states. Much of the violence in 1868 was created by the Ku Klux Klan, a white supremacist organization that spread across the South during the spring and summer. The Klan, which was a frankly terroristic organization designed to intimidate blacks, had appeared the year before in Tennessee. White Conservative leaders in the other Southern states quickly realized its potential for intimidating Republican voters, both black and white, and began to organize local Klans in their own areas. Klan leaders particularly sought to disrupt the Union League organizations in the South by killing its leaders and seizing guns belonging to its members. Although the state elections held in the South in the spring of 1868 saw little Klan violence, by the midsummer, after Republicans had won all these elections, the organization had spread across the South and was poised to use its violent methods to drive Republican voters from the polls in the fall presidential elections. A number of other white terroristic organizations emerged along with the Klan, but they all had the same goal: to carry the elections, by force if necessary, for the Democrats.[26]

The Klan and its kindred organizations did not operate openly in every state. In Virginia and Mississippi, where presidential elections were not held, violence was minimal. The Klan also did not operate in areas that were densely populated by blacks or where the population was largely white. It concentrated on counties where the population was divided about equally along racial lines and where its violent tactics could tip the scales to the Democrats. Klan violence was not especially marked in North Carolina, nor was the level of violence unusually high in Florida. In the remaining Southern states, however, whites waged a systematic campaign of terrorism, in which Republican officeholders, Union League officials, and party leaders black and white were murdered. In Louisiana alone, a congressional committee later estimated that 1,081 people were killed between April and November. In South Carolina, two state legislators were slain, one of whom was Benjamin F. Randolph, chairman of the Republican executive committee. Everywhere Republican organizers were threatened with death if they continued their party work. As the summer wore on, Southern party leaders began to grow desperate as they looked for ways to check the tide of violence.[27]

Republicans in the Florida legislature, claiming that their party clearly controlled the state and hence the taxpayers could be saved the expense of a presidential election, passed a law authorizing the legislature to cast the state's electoral vote. Such an idea, which provided a way to circumvent Klan violence that would disrupt an election, found support in several other states in the Deep South. The Georgia legislature considered the idea, but because the parties were evenly balanced there, the proposal got nowhere. In Louisiana, there was much support in the legislature for not holding an election, but Governor Warmoth successfully discouraged the idea. In Alabama, a measure similar to Florida's passed the legislature, but Republican governor William H. Smith vetoed the bill and his veto was upheld. Not until the middle of October, however, did Smith order that a presidential election be held in Alabama.[28]

Some Northern Republicans were not pleased by the actions of the Florida and Alabama legislatures, fearing that such avowedly partisan action to secure those states for Grant would be unpopular in the North. Others argued, however, that despite the apparently undemocratic nature of having state legislatures cast electoral votes, drastic measures were necessary to compensate for Klan violence.[29] The alternative to canceling the popular election was to ensure that the Southern state governments had sufficient means to maintain order during the canvass, and there was little evidence that this was true in the summer and fall of 1868. As the Southern states were admitted to the Union, the military commanders in the South gave way to the newly elected state officials. In the restored states, the new governments were now responsible for maintaining order. Frequently the Republican legislatures, at the governors' request, passed laws creating a state militia to deal with Klan terrorism. In most cases, however, the governors were reluctant to use the instrument they had asked for. In the Deep South, few whites were ready to volunteer for militia service under Republican governments, and hence the militia was largely black. White governors feared that calling forth a black militia would precipitate a worse race war than the one they already faced. Ultimately, only Governor Powell Clayton of

Arkansas proved willing to use his militia, and this was largely because his state had sufficient white Unionists willing to serve. Governors in South Carolina, Georgia, Florida, Alabama, and Louisiana failed to call out their state militias.[30]

One of the impediments standing in the way of Southern Republicans who attempted to protect themselves against Klan violence was a provision in the 1867 Reconstruction Acts that prohibited the organization and arming of the militia in the former Confederate states. At that time, the states were under Conservative control, and Republicans wanted the balance of military power to remain with the occupying federal army. Now, however, the states were under Republican control and clamoring for aid. Most state legislatures, ignoring the congressional legislation, had provided for organizing a state militia in 1868, but they lacked weapons with which to arm their troops and hence called upon Congress to supply them. Late in July Henry Wilson had introduced a bill in the Senate to allow the Southern states to reconstitute their militia and receive arms from the government, but Congress had adjourned without acting on it. Southern Republicans, who had just taken their seats in Congress, had urged their Northern comrades to stay in session and enact the bill, but their pleas went unheard. The Washington correspondent of the *National Anti-Slavery Standard* observed that "it is rather singular that the moment the members from those states were admitted to the floor of the House, [Northern Republicans] should vote with copperheads to leave the city and prevent their being heard."[31]

With congressional and presidential elections approaching, the Northern members were eager to launch their campaigns. They did provide for reconvening both houses in September, if the situation in the South warranted congressional action. As violence in the South mounted, Republicans there urged their Northern colleagues to come to their aid. Many appeals came to Robert Schenck, chairman of the Congressional Committee and one of the men responsible for reconvening Congress. "If we do not get adequate protection," warned a South Carolinian, "the South will be likely to relapse into revolution and a war of races." From Arkansas came word that Republicans, lacking arms, feared they would lose the state in November. Governor Scott of South Carolina told William E. Chandler, secretary of the Republican National Committee, that "we are as thoroughly on the picket-line today as we were at any time during the war—Congress should have given us arms." A representative of the Republican party in Louisiana told Chandler that he and his colleagues faced a "slaughter" because of the failure of Congress to act.[32]

Several Northern newspaper and journal editors added their voices to those calling for congressional action in September;[33] but when Congress did reassemble on September 21, hardly more than a quorum was present. With the results of the national election still in doubt, the party leadership agreed to reconvene Congress on October 16. By that time, the Republicans had won a series of state elections in the North, which seemed to indicate their party would control the outcome in November. Hence once again the Congress failed to enact legislation to maintain law and order in the South. Northern Republicans were ready to use stories of Klan atrocities in the North to convince people to vote for Grant, but they were not eager during an election year to take any steps that would appear to encourage further violence in the South. Congressmen campaigning for reelection were reluctant to consider a special session anyway, and there was some feeling against arming militias in the South that would be primarily black in membership. They also realized that because they had failed to act in July, it was too late to do anything in September or October that would effectively aid their Southern colleagues.[34]

Consequently, Southern governors were left to find arms on their own. Governor Holden of North Carolina sent the state's adjutant-general North in October seeking aid from Republican governors; he eventually obtained a thousand rifles from Vermont. Governor Reed of Florida asked Benjamin Butler if he could arrange for a sale of two thousand arms to Florida, promising payment in Florida state bonds. Reed eventually obtained muskets and ammunition in New York, but the Klan intercepted and destroyed the shipment of arms while it was en route to Tallahassee. In Arkansas, Governor Clayton also purchased weapons in New York, and again the Klan intercepted the shipment.[35]

Southern governors, either lacking a militia, the will to use it, or the means to arm it, had to rely on federal troops to maintain order during the fall campaign. In the face of Congress's failure to act to help the Southern governors, the Congressional Committee urged them to declare martial law and appeal for federal troops to enforce order. Regulations from Washington made it difficult, however, for local civil officials to obtain federal military assistance. Often, by the time the aid was furnished, it was too late. Federal officers in the states were given discretion by Washington as to when or how they would use the military forces available, and often they proved unduly cautious in calling forth their troops. The numbers of troops available had been sharply reduced, also, after the Southern states had been returned to the Union. Although President Johnson was not eager to allow the troops to be used in the South, he did permit it, but some of his commanders, particularly General Lovell H. Rousseau in Louisiana, proved reluctant to undertake any efficient preparations for the election. Johnson also opposed Governor Clayton's request to allow him access to federal arms stored at an armory in Little Rock.[36]

Congress's failure to take steps in the summer of 1868 to help Southern Republicans protect themselves was demoralizing to the party. In Louisiana, Governor Warmoth finally decided he would have to advise blacks not to attempt to vote for fear they would suffer physical harm. Foster Blodgett, former chairman of the Georgia Republican state committee, was so discouraged about election prospects in his state that he told the secretary of the Republican National Committee not to send funds there but to use them elsewhere where the money might be more effective.[37]

Developments in the South during the summer of 1868 led an increasing number of Northern Republicans to question their party's ability to carry that section in the presidential election. The year before, when the Reconstruction Acts had been put into effect and voter registration was proceeding in the South, Republicans had been optimistic. Senator John Sherman, who had been one of the most active lawmakers shaping Reconstruction legislation, assured his brother that "the suffrage and reconstruction questions will be settled before the [1868] election, and in such a way as to secure the Republican party an even chance in every Southern state except Kentucky." Zachariah Chandler, a member of the Union Congressional Committee, was convinced that "we have *certainly* secured ten out of the eleven rebel states and can *rely* upon them." Papers as diverse as the *New York Herald* and *Boston Advertiser* also believed that the Reconstruction Acts had guaranteed the South to the Republican party.[38]

Thaddeus Stevens, on the other hand, was typical of Radical Republicans in the North who did not believe the South could be carried safely for the party largely because the black vote was susceptible to Conservative influence. When a delegation of Republicans from the South visited him in December 1867, Stevens asked if the former masters and neighbors of the freedmen would "seduce them from a proper discharge of their duty." He believed that the South, once restored to the Union, would quickly revert to the Democracy. In this belief he was joined by more conservative Republicans such as Senator William Pitt Fessenden, who contended that because of the unreliability of the black vote, the Southern states should be kept out until after the 1868 election. Even Republicans who were eager to attract support from the South were uncertain about the party's future there. In 1867 Henry Wilson at times claimed that as many as ten Southern states would go Republican, though on other occasions he counted only three or four. Horace Greeley guessed the party would carry half the Southern states. In the fall of 1867, E. L. Godkin of the *Nation* also counted at least half the Southern states for the party, but as violence in the South mounted during the following year, he concluded that only North Carolina, which had a sizable white Republican vote, was secure.[39]

Godkin's growing pessimism about Republican chances in the South was reflected in the attitude of other party spokesmen in 1868. Throughout the year Northern Republicans received letters from the South warning that the black vote would not hold up against white economic pressure and physical intimidation.[40] Congressman George Boutwell feared that the Democrats would carry the South "by force or by fraud." Samuel Bowles, editor of the *Springfield Republican*, warned in August 1868 that "the Republican party cannot long maintain its supremacy at the South by Negro votes alone. The instincts of submission and dependence in them and of domination in the whites, are too strong." The *New York Times* echoed this assessment. Even Salmon P. Chase, long an advocate of black suffrage, believed that the blacks would "vote for whites hitherto prominent in affairs," which would give the South to the Democrats. As the election year began, William P. Robinson, a Radical Republican columnist for the *Boston Commonwealth*, feared that "the entire Southern vote will be likely to go against Grant or any other Republican." The editors of *Harper's Weekly* cautioned that "the Southern states are the weak point of the campaign, for there the probability of a fair expression of the will of the voters is smallest."[41]

The editors of the *Boston Traveller*, though grateful for the support blacks in the South had given the Republican party, had warned as early as June 1867 that "we should not rely on their assistance to get control of the executive branch of the national government." According to this Republican newspaper, "we should not count upon receiving one Southern electoral vote for our candidates in 1868." Instead, stated its editors, the party would have to realize that the same states that elected Lincoln in 1864 "must elect a successor to Mr. Johnson in 1868." Within a year, many prominent Republicans were agreeing with the *Traveller's* opinions. The Republican state committee in Massachusetts declared in 1868 that the coming presidential election could be secured for the party only "by great majorities in the northern, middle, and western states." The political correspondent for the *Philadelphia Press* had for two years been arguing that the Republican party had to be able to carry the presidential election without the aid of the South, stating that "the Republican party will triumph in the next election, but without the Southern vote which will be against us." Even John Forney, who was confident of "sure reinforcements" from the South, believed the Republicans would win the election by taking the same Northern states they had won in 1864. Carl Schurz of Missouri, who by 1868 was a leading Republican campaign speaker, assured party members who worried that the Southern Democrats would control the black vote that "we have votes enough in the North to elect Grant." Horace Greeley agreed with that assessment, arguing that the Republicans could win in 1868 without any black support by carrying the states they had won in the elections of 1860 and 1864.[42]

These remarks from leading Republicans about the continued importance of winning the Northern states were consistent with the history of the party. Ever since it had been organized in 1855, the Republican party had sought to win the Northern and Western states, and with them control of the federal government. Although the Republicans had penetrated the border states during the Civil War and had built up parties in the former Confederate states under the Reconstruction Acts, when another national election arose Republican attention was drawn back to the North. The Southern situation was too unpredictable, the conditions too volatile, to be assured of controlling many electoral votes there. Republicans were increasingly confident, however, that behind Grant, they could win the same states that had twice elected Abraham Lincoln president of the United States.

Decisions made by the national party committees about the conduct of the 1868 campaign provided clear evidence of Republican determination to stake everything on winning the Northern states. When members of the Republican National Committee and Union Congressional Committee gathered in the summer of 1868, they had to make important decisions concerning the allocation of funds and speakers among the various states of the Union. Most state parties still ran their own local campaigns, financing them with money raised locally. Wealthy states, however, were expected to contribute funds to the national committee to be used where the committee thought the money would do the most good. The committee also determined where the leading Republican speakers should spend most of their time campaigning.[43]

At a meeting in July, the members of the national committee made a series of decisions that established regional priorities for the coming campaign. The committee proposed to raise a total of $430,000 by calling on wealthy party supporters, particularly in New York, Pennsylvania, and New England. The Southern states that were holding elections were to be allocated approximately $1,000 per congressional district, a total of $35,000 or slightly over 8 percent of the money the committee pledged itself to raise. These Southern states, of course, were the ones least able to pay for their own campaign expenses, and yet the national committee chose to provide them with only token amounts of money. Instead, the party leaders directed that the bulk of the funds raised be spent in the North, particularly in the several states that held their state elections before the presidential election in November. Maine and Vermont voted for state offices in September, and in October voters in Indiana, Ohio, and Pennsylvania went to the polls for state elections. National party machinery had traditionally concentrated on the so-called "October states" because they were large, and the vote in state elections was considered a reliable prediction of how they would go in November.[44]

Schuyler Colfax, Republican nominee for vice-president, was confident that this strategy would succeed: "If we carry Maine by 20,000 as seems likely, and then follow with Republican victories in Pennsylvania, Ohio, and Indiana in October, the real battlefields, November will be like 1864 all over again." Edwin Morgan, chairman of the Union Congressional Committee, agreed, adding that the committee intended to make a major effort in his own state of New York, and if that state was secured in addition to the October states, Grant's victory would be assured. Carl Schurz, who was waiting to take the stump in the critical states of the North, was sure that if the Republicans carried Indiana and Pennsylvania in October by good majorities, "we shall be quite certain of the result of the presidential election." He told William Claflin, chairman of the national committee, that if the Republicans lost the state elections in October, "our Southern conquests will not be sufficient to save us." He added that "a thousand dollars spent in Indiana or Pennsylvania will do us more real good than five thousand spent in the South." Claflin needed no convincing from Schurz. He had already identified Indiana and Pennsylvania as the states "on which the fate of the campaign hangs." He told Marcus Ward, former chairman of the Union Congressional Committee, that "we are now doing all we can in the states that vote in October, and after that if we are successful, we shall turn our attention to the doubtful states, North and South."[45]

Claflin, Morgan, Ward, Greeley, and other party leaders worked hard to raise funds for the vital Northern elections, and all found difficulty obtaining them. Ultimately only about half the amount that the Republican National Committee targeted was raised, which made it even more important that the money that was available be spent wisely. Party leaders in every Northern state, as well as the South, were clamoring for funds. James Blaine of Maine, who was directing the campaign in that state and was eager to gather an impressive Republican majority, besieged William E. Chandler with pleas for more money; the committee eventually sent him more than $9,000 and was rewarded when the party swept the state election by a majority of twenty thousand votes.[46]

Party leaders then turned their attention to the October states. By the time elections were held in midmonth, the national committee had sent more than $40,000 each to Indiana and Pennsylvania. The Republicans carried Pennsylvania by a majority of 10,000, which was small for such a large state. In Ohio, the Republican majority was 17,000 out of a total vote of over half a million. In Indiana, where the election for state offices was most closely contested of all the three states, the final Republican plurality was 958 out of a total vote of 242,000. Although these were narrow margins, most Republicans regarded them as sufficient evidence of victory in November. They believed that Grant would be a stronger vote-getter than the state candidates the party had selected. William E. Chandler, after heaving a sigh of relief about "what an escape we have had in Indiana," assured Elihu B. Washburne, Grant's close friend and political adviser, that "we have got them, and they know it. People are already beginning to talk about the offices." Blaine assured Washburne that with the October results, "Grant's election is now accepted as a matter of course."[47] Republican journalists, who watched the South closely, also concluded that the October victories for the Republicans in the North had secured the election for Grant, who now seemed certain of taking the states that had voted for Lincoln in 1864. Even Thomas Tullock, secretary of the Union Congressional Committee's executive committee, who was most ardent in his advocacy of the cause of Southern Republicanism, agreed that the October elections in the North "settle all questions."[48]

With the October elections out of the way, the national committee looked to other states. Chandler planned an active campaign in New York, New Jersey, and Connecticut. In addition, the party hoped to send more money to the South, but Chandler found the coffers were almost empty; "we have bankrupted ourselves to aid Pennsylvania and Indiana." He made new efforts to obtain more money for the remaining states, but with Grant's victory apparently assured, few new funds were forthcoming. Henry Wilson, who had given so much of his time and effort to the Southern Republican cause, pleaded with Chandler to send aid to the South, insisting "it would be a great misfortune for us to be beaten in the reconstructed states."[49]

Since 1866, the Republican committee with the most direct involvement with the South was the Union Congressional Committee, whose executive committee was chaired by Robert Schenck. Schenck had been engaged in a battle of his own for election in Ohio, where his opponent was Clement Vallandigham, a Democrat who had obtained notoriety in the North for his opposition to the Union war effort. Day-to-day management of the committee was left to his secretary, Thomas Tullock. Other than supervising the Southern political situation, the Congressional Committee's main responsibility was to distribute campaign documents throughout the Union. Funds for this operation were raised by assessments on Republican federal officeholders, and ultimately Tullock obtained around $46,000 through this means. He did send out appeals for extra funds, one of which he directed to Edward Atkinson, the Boston cotton magnate who had helped form the Massachusetts Reconstruction Association in 1867. Atkinson passed on Tullock's request to John Murray Forbes, who was the most active member of the Reconstruction Association, with the observation that if the group wished to aid in the campaign, "the time and place for your money is in Pennsylvania."[50] Atkinson's remark was indicative of the priority Northern Republicans gave to their own section when it came time to finance elections. After the Massachusetts association was formed in 1867, its members had pledged to raise at least $15,000 for organizing the Republican party in the South. Atkinson, as treasurer, never was able to raise as much as one-third of that amount. In the spring of 1868, however, the association committed itself to raising $7,500 to send to the neighboring state of Connecticut, which was about to choose a United States senator. Later in the year, Atkinson personally pledged to raise another $10,000 to spend in a Massachusetts congressional district.[51]

Southern Republicans were realistic in realizing that their own future continued to be dependent upon their party's success in the North. They were as concerned about the October elections as were their Northern counterparts. They did, however, expect renewed aid in the form of money and speakers once the October campaigns had ended, for they wished to strengthen and enlarge their party base in their own states and relied heavily on Northern aid to do it.[52] Tullock was eager to provide it. He more than any other Northerner had been involved with Southern organization on a day-to-day basis for almost two years. From the beginning of September he had pleaded with William E. Chandler for money from the national committee to send southward. The national Union League was also clamoring for funds to distribute through its network in the South. The national Republican leadership finally decided that all funds distributed in the South should go through Tullock's committee, and he willingly undertook the task. He also assigned his remaining agents in the South to places where their services would be most useful.[53] Tullock's committee also sent millions of campaign documents, tailored to be read to the illiterate black voters, into the South. One of the most effective campaign techniques proved to be the distribution of metallic badges to black voters. These badges, bearing pictures of Grant and Colfax, were popular, and party leaders in the South requested them in large numbers.[54]

Tullock had to battle with great difficulties in his efforts to aid the South. Funds from officeholders were drying up; some complained that both state and national committees were assessing them. Tullock had relied heavily in past years upon aid from clerks in executive departments in mailing documents, but now Johnson's appointees proved uncooperative. When William E. Chandler advised Tullock not to expend any more funds on documents, on the grounds that "the time for argument has passed," Tullock vigorously disagreed. The call for documents, he believed, "was never greater or more urgent than at present, and steadily increasing."[55] After the national committee began to funnel some funds to Tullock for distribution in the South to help pay the expenses of party agents, Tullock had to decide which states to help. Florida was not holding an election, so Tullock decided not to send money there. He also had to wait for Louisiana and Alabama to decide if they would follow Florida's example; hence funds were not distributed in the latter state until late in October.[56]

Because Tullock was besieged by requests from the South for funds, he had difficulty determining to whom the money should be sent. This problem was reflective of the general state of affairs in the Southern state parties. They were already beset by factionalism, and it was often hard for Tullock to determine if the applicant truly represented the state party leadership. He had to rely on advice from the South as to the proper officials to have control of the funds, and sometimes this advice was conflicting. Usually he waited for confirmation from the governor or state party chairman before sending the money to the designated party official. In South Carolina, blacks insisted on naming Benjamin Randolph, one of the Congressional Committee's black agents in the state, as chairman of the state committee, electing him over a white opponent. John W. Morris, who was in the state observing political developments for the Republican National Committee, contended that Randolph was unfit for the job and urged the Republicans to bypass him in sending money to the state. White terrorists in South Carolina soon solved this problem for Morris, however; Randolph was assassinated in October.[57]

Eventually, Tullock distributed about $27,000 to the Southern states for the campaign. Because Virginia, Mississippi, and Texas were not reconstructed and Florida was not holding an election, no money was sent to those states. Alabama, Louisiana, Georgia, and North Carolina each got $5,000, South Carolina $4,000, and Arkansas $3,000. Of these amounts, $11,000 had been obtained from the national committee; the Congressional Committee had supplied the rest from its own resources. Thus the South received only about 5 percent of the total funds raised by the national committee. Tullock was satisfied with the total expenditures in the South, however, declaring that when all the money had been dispensed, "the South will be sufficiently helped." After October, he regarded the presidential election as secure but was eager for the national Republican leadership to stand by its promises to the South for campaign assistance. Overall, his committee had spent $56,000 and had distributed millions of campaign documents and badges across the nation as well as in the South.[58]

The other tangible means of assistance that Northern Republicans could furnish the South was speakers, and after the October elections, pressures from the South increased to have leading Republicans campaign there.[59] From South Carolina Morris sent a plea to Chandler for "white speakers, we have more than enough blacks." General O. O. Howard of the Freedmen's Bureau, who toured the South for two months in the late summer, returned to the North to urge "the bold speakers of the North to go South and discuss the questions of the present day." Howard was convinced that Northerners "could do much to aid the cause of right, and lead the masses of the South." Henry Wilson also urged Chandler to send speakers South and expressed a willingness to go himself. Chandler, who as secretary of the national committee conducted a speaker's bureau for the party, instead assigned Wilson to speak in various Northern states. Subsequently, no important Northerner entered the South during the campaign. Instead, a number of Southern Republicans, former wartime Unionists, went North to speak. Republican leadership, eager to convince the Northern voters that Southern Democrats were perpetuating violence and anarchy in their section, found

Southern speakers to be more useful speaking to Northern audiences than sending Northerners into the South.[60] Again, this decision reflected the party leadership's basic commitment to winning the Northern states for Grant. Except for a few thousand dollars, the South was left to make do with what resources both in money and speakers it had locally available.

The Northern Republicans also made little effort to aid their colleagues in the border states. Kentucky and Maryland seemed irretrievably lost to the Democrats, and National Committee chairman Claflin also pronounced Delaware beyond hope. Northern doubts about relying on border state support had been increased after the vote on President Johnson's impeachment; both senators from Tennessee and one senator each from Missouri and West Virginia had voted to keep him in office. Claflin was distrustful of all the border states; using West Virginia as an example, he declared he had "no confidence in these reconstructed states surrounded by rebel majorities." The Republicans had maintained control of West Virginia, Missouri, and Tennessee by means of extensive disfranchisement of former Confederates, and most Republicans in the North had never favored this means of maintaining party control. A number of border state Republicans were reaching the same conclusion; as early as September 12, 1867, a delegation of them had met in Washington to endorse universal manhood suffrage. They approved it not only as an act of justice but as a "measure of protection to the Border states," believing that blacks there would vote for the Republican party. The convention called upon Congress to approve a constitutional amendment establishing universal suffrage throughout the nation, but Republicans in Congress refused to act. Some, like Charles Sumner, supported the idea; he claimed that with such an amendment, "Maryland and Delaware will be saved—to say nothing of Kentucky." Most of Sumner's colleagues opposed action on the proposal, however. In 1868, when the Republicans had met in national convention, they had endorsed Negro suffrage in the reconstructed states but had admitted that in the border and North suffrage was still to be determined by state action. Once again, in their reluctance to antagonize Northern voters who opposed any extension of black rights, the Republicans had failed to respond to Southern pleas for help. As one Republican from Delaware protested, "A large majority of Northern men and newspapers hold the cause of Border State Republicans in indifference if not contempt."[61]

Ultimately, when the 1868 campaign was held, the Republicans sent $1,000 to West Virginia; the party failed to come up with money for any other border state, although Boston's reconstruction committee raised $1,000 for Delaware. In addition, Henry Wilson campaigned in the state, and a few other Northerners, such as Robert Schenck, ventured into border regions to speak after the October elections.[62] For the most part, however, the border states suffered even more than the former Confederate states from Republican party neglect. State Republicans made little effort to carry Delaware, Kentucky, or Maryland, and all three states went Democratic by large majorities in the fall. West Virginia voted for Grant but by a slim majority of two thousand, the smallest since the Republican party had emerged in the state. In Missouri, on the other hand, by relying on extensive disfranchisement, Republicans carried the entire state ticket and electoral vote by a twenty-thousand-vote margin. Tennessee again went Republican, but the party benefited here also from registration laws that reduced the white vote. The effects of Ku Klux Klan ravages were evident in Tennessee; where the Klan had been active the black vote dropped disastrously. In Middle Tennessee, Grant's vote was half that won the previous year by Governor Brownlow.[63]

In the rest of the former Confederate states, results were also discouraging for the Republicans. In Louisiana and Georgia, white violence succeeded in handing both states to the Democrats. In Louisiana, where Republicans had gained 58 percent of the vote in the spring state elections, the Democrats won in the fall by a majority of 71 percent. The low Republican vote reflected the state party leadership's decision not to contest the election actively in the face of white terrorism. In Georgia, a state where Republicans hoped for considerable white support, results were even more disappointing. The party had carried the Georgia spring elections by seven thousand votes, but in the fall the Democrats won the state for Horatio Seymour by a majority of forty-five thousand. Republicans won in Florida because the state legislature cast its electoral vote; in Arkansas Republicans kept power only because they controlled the voting mechanisms and disfranchised many former Confederates. Results in Alabama were slow to come in, and for a time Republicans thought they had lost the state; the final count showed they had carried it by a slight majority. Only North and South Carolina went Republican by significant margins, and in the latter state this was attributable almost entirely to black support.[64]

In their bid for white Southern support the Republicans continued to enjoy their greatest success in North Carolina; here about twenty-five thousand whites voted with seventy thousand blacks to carry the state. Returns from white counties in Arkansas and Tennessee also showed that the party could hope for biracial support there, but in both cases Republican ascendancy also depended heavily on disfranchisement. In the Lower South there was little evidence of significant white support for the Republicans, and the party's future remained in black hands. The results in Louisiana and Georgia, however, indicated how vulnerable the black vote was to white intimidation.[65]

Although the Republican party had failed to carry the South in 1868, Grant carried all the Northern states except Oregon, New Jersey, and New York, and with them he secured the election. His Southern electoral votes added to his majority but were not necessary to his success. The calculations of national party leaders about the necessity of carrying the same states that had elected Lincoln in 1864 proved correct. Grant's proportion of the total Northern vote was almost the same as Lincoln's, 55 percent. Scarcely any Northern state changed its vote by more than 1 or 2 percent between the two national elections, and only 7 percent of Northern counties switched from one party to another from 1864 to 1868. Grant carried the same states in the North that Lincoln did, with the exception of Oregon and New York. In New York, however, the Democratic margin was barely over 1 percent of the total vote.[66]

The continued sectional base of the Republican party indicated that the issues of slavery and civil war had solidified political attitudes among the whites in both the North and South. During the 1868 campaign Republicans in the North capitalized on the anti-Southern attitudes they had cultivated since the party was born in the 1850s. They warned their constituents that if the Southerners regained power through a Democratic victory, the results of the Civil War would be overturned. They reminded voters that Southerners had conducted a rebellion against the government that had cost hundreds of thousands of Northern lives and pointed to continued violence in the South as evidence of the unwillingness of former Confederates to accept defeat.[67] Although Republican waving of the "bloody shirt" proved an extremely effective political device in solidifying Northern support, it could not be expected to win any new votes from the South. Despite their efforts to recruit Southern support, when national elections came around, Republicans forsook that section to protect their Northern base.

RECONSTRUCTION WINDS DOWN:

THE GRANT YEARS, 1869–1877

Despite the evidence from the election of 1868 that the Southern Republican party was weak, lacked significant white support, and was receiving little Northern assistance, some Northern Republicans continued to harbor optimism about their Southern prospects. With Grant in the White House they would no longer have to contend with an obstructionist president; both executive and legislative branches of the federal government were firmly in their hands. Northern Republicans also hoped that with their victory in 1868 Southern Democrats and Conservatives would cease their violent opposition to Reconstruction measures, recognizing that the Republicans would hold power in Washington for at least four more years. Thus peace and order would return to the South, and many hoped that in an atmosphere of stability the party would have a chance to build on its base there. Perhaps Southern whites who had resisted the Republicans up to this point might reconsider their position and join the party.[1]

In the wake of optimism following Grant's election, many Northern Republicans believed their work in the South was done. Confident that Grant's presidency would restore order in the South, Benjamin Butler proclaimed early in 1869 that "we will want no army [there] after the 4th of March next." Butler had already been telling Southern Republicans that after the Reconstruction Acts had been implemented, they should expect no more help from the North: "Now you must help yourselves." Horace Greeley agreed, informing the Southern Republicans that it was time they ceased "hanging around the neck of the North." In Massachusetts, Edward Atkinson and other members of the Massachusetts Reconstruction Association, arguing that "the election of Grant settles the Southern question," disbanded the group, and in Washington, the Republican Congressional Committee was no longer as active as it had been in overseeing Southern affairs.[2]

Unfortunately for the Republicans, this optimism concerning the future of the South proved misplaced. The problems the party faced there before the election did not go away, but instead grew worse. Although the Republicans reelected Grant in 1872, by the end of his second term the party had lost control of every state in the South. The overthrow of the Republican party in the South was largely the result of Southern conditions, but it also came about because the Northern Republicans, for the most part, continued to be inattentive to the Southern party's needs. They saw the South as an unlikely region in which to build a permanent party able to contest with the Democrats for control.

President Grant and his fellow Northern Republicans were not blind to their party's needs in the South. The executive branch under Grant was more active than it had been under Lincoln or Johnson in promoting Republican fortunes below the Mason-Dixon line. For its part, Congress amended the Constitution again to ensure the permanence of Negro suffrage and then in 1870 and 1871 passed legislation to enforce the amendment. Nonetheless the policies the Northern Republicans followed in the South after 1868 were inconsistent and plagued by frustrations and disappointments. They continued to wrestle with problems that had appeared during and after the implementation of the Reconstruction Acts: whether to give amnesty to Southerners still under political disqualifications, whether to bolster the party's appeal among blacks, especially by appointing more to office and enacting new civil rights laws, and whether to use the federal government to protect black voters from white terrorism. Northern Republicans also continued to ignore or slight Southern Republican needs by not providing them with enough patronage, campaign funds, or federal economic assistance to help promote the party there. Instead, the national party continued to follow the pattern it had already set of giving top priority to maintaining its base among Northern voters, even if this meant sacrificing the interests of party colleagues in the South.

The party's emphasis on its Northern priorities was revealed in its support of the Fifteenth Amendment. After winning the election of 1868, the Republicans decided to amend the Constitution to establish black suffrage throughout the nation. Although Republicans hoped by this step to guarantee the continued existence of black voting in the South, it was already a fact there. In most Northern states, and throughout the border, however, black men were ineligible to vote. Congressional Republicans hoped, through national enfranchisement of blacks, to gain their votes for the party in closely contested Northern states. They also believed that through the black vote the party might be able to survive in border states where former Confederates were rapidly gaining the franchise.[3]

Early in 1869, as Congress debated the wording of the proposed amendment, Southern Republicans favored a stronger version than that ultimately enacted. They wanted to guarantee the right of blacks not only to vote but also to hold office, and they wanted the amendment to bar states from applying literacy or property tests to voters. The Northern Republicans opposed the officeholding guarantee, claiming it would unnecessarily extend the coverage of the amendment and risk its defeat in state ratification votes; they also proved unwilling to ban state literacy and property tests, in part because Northern and Western states might use them to reduce immigrant voting. Hence, despite complaints from Southern Republican congressmen, Northern interests in the amendment prevailed.[4]

After enacting the Fifteenth Amendment and sending it out to the states for ratification, the only work remaining for Congress to consider in winding up the Reconstruction of the South was to readmit the three Southern states still unrestored to the Union: Virginia, Mississippi, and Texas. Elections planned in each of these states, as well as in Tennessee for 1869, tested anew the viability of the Southern wing of the party and raised questions again about its relationship with the national Republican organization. Most Northern Republicans focused their attention on Virginia, which for more than two years they had been hoping to control.

Early in 1869 some leading Conservatives in the Old Dominion, hoping to eliminate the political disqualifications in the constitution drawn up the previous year, indicated to Congress and the president that they were willing to accept Negro suffrage if they could also obtain amnesty for whites. Horace Greeley, who had long championed such a policy, endorsed it, as did Republican senators such as Henry Wilson and John Sherman. Most important, Grant liked it and ordered an election on the constitution with separate votes on the disqualifying clauses. At the same time preparations were made for electing state officials, and the Virginia Republicans split over their party's nominations. Radicals who supported disfranchisement endorsed Governor Wells for another term; more conservative Republicans nominated another Northerner living in the state, Gilbert Walker, on a ticket recommending amnesty. Many Conservatives sought to take advantage of the Republican split by backing Walker instead of nominating their own candidate. The resulting coalition of Conservatives and moderate Republicans won easily when the election was held in July.[5]

Northern Republicans were divided in their assessment of the Virginia election. Greeley, who wanted to court the support of Conservatives in the South, eagerly supported the Walker movement. Senators Wilson and Sherman saw in Walker's success a sign that the "natural leaders" of the South were ready to accept the enfranchisement of blacks and to cooperate with the Republicans. Several members of Grant's cabinet also looked to Walker's victory with approval, hoping that the result would lead to sectional harmony and a greater opportunity for a permanent Republican organization in the South.[6]

Other Northern Republicans, however, particularly those sympathetic to the Radical wing of the Virginia organization, were skeptical about claiming Walker's victory as a party success. Rather, they feared that Conservatives had used the Walker candidacy only to gain influence in the government and ultimately to gain control of the state. Events were to prove these views correct. After 1869 the state legislature was controlled by the Conservatives, and within a year the Republicans had read Walker out of their party. The state over which Northern Republicans had labored so long had been lost to them. According to the *Boston Daily Advertiser*, the Conservatives of Virginia had "not only deceived the Republicans of Virginia, but the Republicans of Washington and of the whole country."[7]

Tennessee held its state elections in 1869 a few weeks later than Virginia's, and with similar results. The Republicans split over amnesty in this state, too, and Conservatives supported the moderate Republican gubernatorial candidate, DeWitt Senter, against the Radical Republican, William Stokes, who insisted that the test oaths had to remain. Because Senter, who in February had inherited the governorship upon William Brownlow's election to the U.S. Senate, controlled the registrars, a great many whites previously barred from voting were able to cast ballots. The result was an overwhelming victory for Senter and the Conservatives.[8]

Although some Republicans interpreted Virginia's elections in 1869 as a party victory, few saw the same results in Tennessee. The Volunteer State had been a stronghold of Unionist sentiment during and after the war, and Republican defeat there was, to the *Boston Commonwealth*, an indication that nowhere in the South was there "a loyal constituency strong enough to hinder the advance to power of the old secessionist leaders." William Fessenden, who had always been dubious about Republican party prospects in the South, observed that the Tennessee election was "but an indication of what we must expect in most of the rebel states at the next Presidential election." The *New York Independent* told its Republican readers to abandon all hope for Tennessee: "It will be Democratic."[9]

Because of Conservative successes in Virginia and Tennessee, worried Republicans prevailed upon Grant to postpone elections on the constitutions of Texas and Mississippi until after the fall state elections in the North. Grant also ordered that the Mississippi election, like that in Virginia, allow a separate vote on the disfranchising provisions of its proposed constitution. This step was not necessary in Texas, where moderates had been able to eliminate disfranchising clauses. The Republican party in both states was divided into conservative and Radical wings, and although for a time Grant tried to remain neutral in the intraparty disputes, under Radical pressure in Washington, especially following the election in Virginia, he agreed to throw government patronage and army influence behind the Radicals.[10]

Republican tickets in both states won victories; but other than President Grant's support, the party organizations got little outside help. Southern Republicans, particularly in Mississippi, again sought aid from their Northern colleagues in preparing for the elections, but little was forthcoming. The Congressional Committee sent Mississippi $1,000, and eventually William E. Chandler sent another $1,000 from the Republican National Committee; Chandler expressed doubt, however, that the state ticket would be elected. He admitted he felt guilty that the national party had done so little for the Southern Republicans. Not only was money not forthcoming from the North; even more important, according to Chandler, "the *attitude* of the Republicans of the North did not sustain, as it might, our Radical friends in Mississippi and Texas." He gave the Southern Republicans entire credit for their victories.[11]

Republican congressmen had hoped to complete Reconstruction by admitting Virginia, Texas, and Mississippi to the Union following their elections; but events in Georgia forced them to intervene again in that state. Because of the violence in Georgia in the fall of 1868 and the action of the state legislature in expelling its black members, Congress had refused to count the state's electoral vote or to seat its Conservative delegation. Northern Republicans, however, disagreed about what to do next. After nine months of hesitation and debate, the Congress returned Georgia to military supervision so that her legislature could be revamped and the state could be required to ratify the Fifteenth Amendment. Northern Republicans were worried that the amendment might fail and hence required not only Georgia but also Mississippi, Virginia, and Texas to ratify it before they were allowed to assume their seats in Congress.

Military intervention in Georgia gave control of the state to the Republicans, who then ratified the amendment, but Congress refused requests to delay new legislative elections and thereby prolong the regime of Governor Rufus Bullock. Having secured their national goal of approval of the amendment, Republicans in Congress were not about to court Northern dissatisfaction by continuing to interfere in Georgia politics, especially with midterm elections coming up. Consequently, in July 1870, Congress ordered that elections for the Georgia legislature be held the following December. Senator Simon Cameron, who was in Georgia to investigate the chances of Republican success, concluded that they were slight because enough blacks could be kept from the polls to ensure a Conservative victory. The state Republicans got only halfhearted support from the Union Leagues and none from the national Republican committees. When the election was held, Conservatives captured the legislature and sent two of their party to the United States Senate.[12]

The developments in Georgia revealed considerable tension between Northern and Southern Republicans. Many Republicans in Georgia believed that the party had sacrificed their interests to protect its Northern base. One Georgia Republican observed that Republican congressmen seemed indifferent to the fate of the party in the state and concluded that "on account of the peculiar composition of the Republican party of the South," it was "not entitled to as much weight as that of the party in the Northern states." Many Northern Republicans, for their part, were becoming increasingly exasperated and disenchanted with the quality of Southern Republican leadership. They were critical of men such as Brownlow of Tennessee and Bullock of Georgia and tended to blame them for Republican failures in those states.[13]

William Holden of North Carolina was another Southern Republican governor who soon fell into disfavor in the eyes of many Northerners. Northern Republicans, who failed to send aid to the Georgia party in 1870, were more optimistic about their party's future in North Carolina, where a considerable number of white voters had backed their state ticket. The Old North State held state and congressional elections in August, and the Union Republican Congressional Committee, chaired now by Henry Wilson, sent the state Republican committee in North Carolina $1,000 and another $2,000 to four Republican congressional candidates. The North Carolina governor, however, needed more than financial aid from the North. The Ku Klux Klan was terrorizing Republican voters, and Holden lacked adequate constitutional and legislative authority to deal with its challenge. He asked Grant and the Congress for federal aid, but none was forthcoming. He then proceeded to organize a state militia drawn in part from East Tennessee, and in the summer of 1870 it rounded up about one hundred men accused of fomenting Klan terrorism. When Holden, who lacked authority to suspend the writ, nevertheless ignored a federal court order to release the prisoners, Washington authorities supported the federal judge, and Holden had to back down. By the time the men were released, the August elections had been held, and the Conservatives had won control of the state legislature. Several Northern Republican papers blamed Holden for the party's defeat in the state, and newspaper opinion in general claimed that the governor had done more harm than good for the Republican cause. The Democratic legislature proceeded to impeach Holden for violating the state constitution, and he was expelled from office in March 1871.[14]

The continuation of Klan violence in the South after the election of 1868 posed a major problem for Republican hopes in that section. Because the Klan's terrorism was directed at Republican voters, its success could doom the party in the South. Unless Congress enacted legislation empowering Grant to use military force against the Klan, the Republican regimes in the South, like Holden's, could rely only on their militia forces, which were usually weak and inadequately armed. In 1869 Congress had allowed the restored states of the South to reconstitute their militias but did not provide them with arms. Several Republican governors, finding their own legislatures unwilling to raise state funds to arm the militias, appealed to Northern states for loans of weapons and ammunition. Powell Clayton of Arkansas and Henry Clay Warmoth of Louisiana sent representatives to the governor of Illinois, and Warmoth also approached the governor of Missouri for assistance. Governor Harrison Reed of Florida personally called on the governors of Massachusetts and New York. Their appeals all fell on deaf ears. Holden of North Carolina, however, was able to secure one thousand rifles from Vermont. Eventually, in 1873, Congress authorized the distribution of federal arms to the Southern states, but by then the crisis with the Klan had passed, and even with the arms, Southern state militias proved ineffective in dealing with continued white terrorism.[15]

As the level of Klan violence increased, the outcry in the North against it forced Congress to act. On May 31, 1870, it passed an Enforcement Act, so called because it was designed to enforce the Fourteenth and Fifteenth amendments. The law made it a crime for two or more people to conspire to deprive a citizen of any right of citizenship, but it was aimed primarily at deterring intimidation of voters. Its provisions were enforceable in federal courts. In 1870, federal authorities made little use of the new legislation, possibly hoping that the threat of federal intervention would be enough to discourage further Klan activity. In state elections held that summer and fall in North Carolina, Georgia, and Alabama, however, the threat of Klan violence reduced the Republican party's vote and helped Conservatives to win.[16]

Northern Republicans realized that if they did not authorize stronger federal action against the Klan, other Southern states would be lost as well. The *Boston Advertiser* noted that action was needed to give the Republican party "some hope of a fair election" in the South. Senator Edwin Morgan, long a leading figure on the party's national committees, declared that "it is of much importance to us politically" that Congress pass a stronger Ku Klux measure. He told several senators that new measures "were of great importance to the party and to all who want justice at the ballot box." The *Boston Com-*

monwealth also reflected the double motives of protecting both Southern Republican lives and votes when it commented that the Klan had to be broken, "if permanent peace is to come and the Republican party make any show of contesting the next election."[17]

On February 28, 1871, Congress enacted a second Enforcement Act, which allowed the federal government even more control over elections. It did not deal directly with the Ku Klux Klan, however, and many Republicans prevailed upon Grant to call the new Congress, the Forty-second, into session in March to enact new legislation. Benjamin Butler then drew up a strong anti-Klan bill, which a North Carolina correspondent praised as a "scheme for manipulating the South politically." Butler's proposal, which included provisions authorizing the president to suspend the writ and declare martial law in areas of excessive violence, produced some significant divisions within Republican congressional ranks, particularly in the House, which at first refused to approve the measure. Several important Republicans, including Carl Schurz and Lyman Trumbull in the Senate and James A. Garfield, Henry Dawes, and James G. Blaine in the House, questioned its constitutionality. They feared it would concentrate too much authority in Washington at the expense of the states and would subvert individual liberties. Trumbull also denounced the partisan intent behind the proposal. President Grant himself proved unwilling to endorse the bill until pressured to do so by prominent Republicans on Capitol Hill. With Grant's support, plus the continued news of Klan excesses in the South, the Congress enacted a new law, called the Ku Klux Act, by strict party votes. Republican leadership in the House, enforcing party discipline, obtained its passage there.[18]

Although the new measure was aimed at suppressing the Klan in the South, some Republicans believed that the public attention directed at the Klan during the congressional debates would be most effective in mobilizing anti-Southern feelings in the North behind the Republican party. Even while Congress was enacting the Klan bill, it created a committee to investigate terrorism in the South, which gathered twelve volumes of testimony condemning the Klan. Congress had already passed the desired legislation, however, and the evidence collected by the committee was not needed to make a case for the law, although it dramatized Klan violence for Northern voters. Attorney General Amos Akerman believed that one of the chief benefits of the congressional investigation would be to "horrify the North" and thus "hold the majority of northern voters to the Republican cause."[19]

The pattern of enforcement of the new legislation also revealed that the Republicans continued to worry as much or more about their Northern base as about protecting their Southern colleagues. In 1870 Edwards Pierrepont, a U.S. attorney general in New York, had told the president that congressional legislation to enforce the Fifteenth Amendment was needed to "save this state" from Democrats who were counting fraudulent votes. The first two Enforcement Acts granted effective power over election procedures only to supervisors in cities with populations of twenty thousand or more, thereby exempting many Southern polls. It was possible, however, for federal supervisors to intercede in Northern elections, where most of these cities were located, to root out Democratic frauds. The number of marshals and the amount of money spent for enforcement were greater in the North than in the South.[20]

In August 1871, federal enforcement of the anti-Klan law in North Carolina brought some immediate results, when Republicans in that state voted down a Conservative proposal to hold a convention to revise the state constitution. Attorney General Akerman congratulated Butler on the success of his anti-Klan measure, stating that its fruits appeared "in a fair election in that State with a most wholesome result."[21] Nonetheless, within a year after Grant began implementing the new laws, some Northern Republicans increased their criticism of the measures. They feared that the laws extended federal power too arbitrarily and would soon bring the Republican party into disrepute in the North. Many who had supported the acts because of outrages against blacks in the South feared that military intervention alone would not bring peace and stability to that section. Horace Greeley, who was one of the Republicans who had reluctantly accepted the need for the Enforcement Acts, believed that such forcible intervention in the South could succeed only temporarily and continued to argue, as he had since the end of the war, that a policy of moderation and amnesty toward Southern whites was the only way to win their acceptance of the Reconstruction settlement. Other Republicans echoed Greeley's views and worried lest the Enforcement Acts forever alienate the Southern white leaders whose support the Republicans might otherwise gain with more lenient measures.

James A. Garfield felt this way, and so did Jacob D. Cox, who served as Grant's secretary of the interior until resigning in 1870. Samuel Bowles of the *Springfield Republican* also wanted to appeal to the "best people" of the South for their support. Carl Schurz, now a senator from Missouri, lent the weight of his oratory to the cause of leniency, not harshness, in dealing with the South.[22]

Many of these men believed that Klan violence was, at least in part, caused by Southern anger and resentment at the political prohibitions still in place under the Fourteenth Amendment and the test oath for federal officeholders. Hence they argued that if Congress were to enact the Enforcement Acts, it should also give amnesty to Southern whites still facing political disqualification. William S. Robinson, the political correspondent of the *Springfield Republican*, noted with pleasure that when the House passed the Ku Klux bill, it was also considering an amnesty bill. Robinson said that many House Republicans believed that its passage, along with the Ku Klux bill, "cannot fail to give the Republican party strength in the South, and promote peace and good order in that ill-fated section."[23]

Once again, then, as it had repeatedly since 1866, the question of amnesty entered Republican debates over Southern policy. Republicans had been embarrassed by the implementation of political disqualifications since such measures had been enacted. Southern Republicans had long complained that such disqualifications discouraged the recruitment of potential white allies who could not take the required loyalty oaths. Although in several states Southern Republicans had written constitutions imposing some sort of test oath disfranchising classes of former Confederates, by the end of 1870 only Arkansas among the reconstructed states still imposed such tests. Because the granting of suffrage to all whites in Texas, Mississippi, Alabama, and Louisiana had not resulted in immediate defeat of the Republican party, advocates of amnesty argued that it was politically safe, and even desirable, to remove remaining political disqualifications.[24]

The foes of amnesty referred to the border states, as well as Tennessee, for evidence to sustain their views. They noted that as Kentucky, Maryland, and Tennessee eased their voting restrictions, the whites who had been barred from the ballot box voted Conservative, helping to keep the Republican party from controlling those states. On the other hand, advocates of political amnesty argued that prohibitions, whether on officeholding or voting, hopelessly alienated the vast majority of the white population of those states from the Republican party that maintained these laws. Rather than maintaining political disqualifications, the advocates of amnesty, or Liberal Republicans as they became known, pushed for their elimination while the Republican party could still take credit for such a generous action. They noted that the proscription helped unite Republican opponents in the border, and abandoning that policy would remove the issue from party debate. Horace Greeley warned the Republicans of West Virginia that a policy of conciliation of former Confederates was their only hope for survival: "Now you can amnesty the rebels—soon the question will be, shall they amnesty you?" Greeley warned the West Virginians that they would go the path of Kentucky and Maryland if they did not act. Jacob Cox, secretary of the interior, agreed with Greeley, telling him that universal amnesty would have saved Tennessee. "We must either accord amnesty voluntarily," he argued, "or have it taken from us against our will."[25]

Border state opponents of test oaths for voters were most effectively organized in Missouri. In September 1870, Liberal Republicans in that state bolted from their party and nominated B. Gratz Brown on a platform including amnesty. The Liberals in Missouri, led by Senator Carl Schurz, received national attention, and U. S. Grant used federal patronage against them, but without success. Benefiting from temporary Democratic aid, the Liberals won the election, gained control of the state, and repealed the state's test oath. The same process developed in West Virginia, where again restrictive voting registration laws were liberalized. Ultimately, however, these actions paved the way for Democratic or Conservative control of both states.[26]

By 1870 the chief political disqualification still under the control of Congress was the Fourteenth Amendment prohibition on officeholding for certain classes of former Confederates. In 1868 the Fortieth Congress had granted relief for this disability to 1,431 Southern whites, most of whom were Republicans elected to office that summer and fall. This policy of granting amnesty to individuals was continued into the Forty-first Congress, where it became increasingly cumbersome. In the second session of that Congress, which met in 1870, the Senate faced more than 30 disability bills and the House more than 160. Ultimately the Forty-second Congress amnestied another 3,185 Southerners. Because of the difficulty of examining so many individuals to see if they were loyal and the time expended on such names, support for a general amnesty began to build in Congress. Southern Republicans in particular pressed for a general act relieving most of the former Confederates still under the officeholding ban. David P. Lewis of Alabama, when asked by Northern Republicans what he would recommend to build up their party in the South, condemned the disqualification provisions and called for dealing with Southerners in a "liberal and magnanimous spirit." Republican conventions in Virginia, North Carolina, and Mississippi also called for a general amnesty. These Republicans believed that the wounds between the sections would never heal until amnesty was provided. They also continued to believe that Republicans courted disaster in the South by alienating white voters through their continued application of political disabilities.[27]

The Northern Republicans, unlike most of their Southern colleagues, were divided over the wisdom of granting amnesty, believing that it was not yet time to forgive those under the ban of the Fourteenth Amendment. President Grant planned to recommend a general amnesty in a message to Congress early in 1870, but his cabinet talked him out of it; later he told an interviewer that Northern public opinion would not sustain amnesty until the white South indicated its acceptance of the Fourteenth and Fifteenth amendments. Senator Zachariah Chandler of Michigan attacked the amnesty proposals, stating that the Ku Klux atrocities in the South proved white Southerners were unrepentant and undeserving of forgiveness. Attorney General Akerman agreed, claiming that "nothing is more idle than to attempt to conciliate by kindness that portion of the southern people who are still malcontent." In his opinion, the Republicans would "gain nothing by concession to the Democracy."[28]

The *New York Times*, speaking of the talk of adopting a magnanimous course toward the white South, warned that it was too late for such proposals. For such a policy to work, said the moderate Republican paper, lenience toward the South had to be "prompt and hearty —just the opposite of the captious and haggling and dilatory methods" of Congress. Nonetheless, the second session of the Forty-second Congress, which met in December following the Missouri election, again dissipated much time haggling over lists of individual names recommended for amnesty and fell further and further behind in its consideration of the petitions. Pressure was building, however, for a general amnesty. The Missouri Liberal Republican movement was threatening to spread across the nation as Republicans discontented with the Grant administration focused on the failure to provide amnesty. Also, the 1870 elections had cost the Republicans their two-thirds majority in the House, and hence they could no longer dispense relief to individuals on a partisan basis. In December 1871, Grant bowed to the pressure and came out for a general amnesty. In the House, where congressmen were facing consideration of a bill to grant relief to seventeen thousand individuals, and in the Senate, where members were prepared to add three thousand more names to the list, the alternative of a general amnesty bill proved impossible to reject.[29]

In May 1872, Benjamin Butler steered a general amnesty measure through the House, which had previously approved such a bill only to see it defeated in the Senate. This time, however, with the national Liberal Republican bolt from Grant a fact, the Senate approved the measure 38–2, hoping thereby to eliminate the amnesty question from the coming presidential election. The law did exempt some former Confederates from its provisions, but they numbered only in the hundreds. Six years after the passage of the Fourteenth Amendment, most Southerners were freed of its political disqualifications. The effort had come too late, however, to be of any assistance to those Republicans who hoped through such generosity to attract significant Southern white support.[30]

Although in 1872 Congress eliminated the ban on officeholding for most white Southerners necessitated by the Fourteenth Amendment, the ironclad oath of past loyalty required of federal officeholders still remained to embarrass the Republicans. Congress altered the oath to seat Republicans elected from the South but refused to give Democrats the same benefit. Northerners ignored pleas from Southern Republican congressmen to repeal the oath, but in 1868 they did approve a modified oath for Southern congressmen-elect who had been freed of their disabilities under the Fourteenth Amendment. In 1870 Congress also had to sanction a special oath for census-takers in the South who could not take the oath. Ignoring the embarrassment and difficulty caused by specifying not one but a variety of oaths and then administering them on a partisan basis, Congress refused to repeal them. From 1868 to 1871, eighteen bills to repeal or modify the oaths died in Congress. Despite the Liberal Republican movement, Congress did not change or repeal the oaths in 1872. By that time, very few Southerners were still affected by them, but not until 1884 were all test oaths repealed. By then the oath had long since lost its utility as a partisan method of controlling federal offices, and its arbitrary enforcement could only have alienated the Southern whites whose support the Republican party claimed to want.[31]

By 1872 Liberal Republicans' discontent with their party's Reconstruction policies was reaching major proportions. Greeley, Cox, Schurz, Samuel Bowles of the *Springfield Republican*, and others condemned the party for failing to repeal the ironclad oath and offer the South universal amnesty. They were also opposed to continued federal regulation of Southern elections through the Enforcement Acts and wanted an end to military intervention there. The Liberals were horrified at scandals that surfaced implicating some of Grant's subordinates and were eager for civil service reform that they hoped would bring honesty and efficiency to government bureaucracy. In addition, many Liberals were opposed to the protective tariff policies of the Republican administration. When the Republican party renominated Grant for president in 1872, the dissidents broke with their fellows and chose Horace Greeley to run as an independent on a Liberal Republican platform. The Democrats, despite their enormous distaste for Greeley, a lifelong Republican who had denounced their party for years, decided to support him instead of running a candidate of their own. Because the Democrats were most interested in home rule for the South and Greeley had little interest in civil service reform and was opposed to tariff reduction, the campaign centered on amnesty and self-government for the South.[32]

Even though the main issues in the campaign were related to Southern conditions, the Republicans believed, as they had in past years, that they would win or lose the election in the North, and they devoted most of their attention to that section. The institutions that were at hand for the party in 1868 to use in the campaign in the South were now missing. The Freedmen's Bureau had been largely withdrawn from the South after the election of 1868. The Union League, which the Republicans had used extensively in the South in 1867 and 1868 to organize voters, was now defunct in the North and virtually destroyed by Klan violence in the South. The Congressional Committee, which had closely supervised Southern developments while the Southern states were undergoing the Reconstruction process in 1867–69, no longer continued this responsibility and no longer maintained speakers and agents to send into the South. Once the Republicans had organized in each of the Southern states, the state parties were expected to be self-sufficient.[33]

Northern Republicans once again made North Carolina the major exception to their policy of stressing Northern priorities over Southern needs. The state's August elections were the first to be held in the presidential year, and many considered them to be an early indicator of voter loyalties for the fall. Hence Republican leaders recognized the importance of winning the state. When the Republican national convention met that summer, Judge Thomas Settle, one of North Carolina's most prominent white Republicans, was chosen chairman of the gathering. During the summer the Department of Justice redoubled its efforts to indict suspected Klan members in the state. Most significantly, the Northern Republicans made a major concession to the state in their allocation of campaign funds and speakers. The Republican National Committee agreed to send $10,000 to the state to help it carry the election. The committee also sent Northern speakers into the state, including cabinet secretaries George Boutwell and Columbus Delano and Senator Henry Wilson.[34]

Republicans both North and South were heartened when the Republican gubernatorial candidate in North Carolina won a narrow victory. But Republican success in that state did not encourage the national committee to send any more money southward. Instead, it resumed its customary policy of emphasizing campaigns in the Northern states. As Southern politics proved volatile and unpredictable, Republican hopes continued to rest on the states that had formed the party in 1855 and had elected Lincoln and Grant in the last three presidential canvasses. John Murray Forbes, an important fund-raiser for the now defunct Massachusetts Reconstruction Association, declared that the only way to protect black Republicans in the South was "by a united Republican North," and most party leaders agreed with him.[35]

As in previous elections, the national committee paid particular attention to the crucial Northern states that held state elections in October. The national committee spent at least as much in Maine as it had in North Carolina and sent $75,000 into Pennsylvania; the party leaders especially believed if they could carry that state, "the

fight is over." By September, the committee's members were struggling to raise the funds needed to pursue a vigorous campaign in the
"closely contested states," but they ultimately raised enough funds
to send $40,000 to Indiana and at least $10,000 to Ohio.[36]

In the meantime, party committees in the South sent urgent pleas
to the North for campaign funds. Edwin Morgan, chairman of the
national committee, told the Southern petitioners that they could expect no money until the October states in the North were secured for
the party. He also indicated that states like Tennessee, Georgia, and
Virginia, which were in Conservative hands, could expect almost no
help. Most Republican leaders in the South were understanding, realizing that, as before, they stood little chance of holding their states
if Northern voters deserted the Republican party. Nonetheless, they
urged Morgan and William E. Chandler to supply them with whatever aid they could.[37]

In late September, feeling more confident about the upcoming
elections in the North, Morgan agreed to send $2,000 to Alabama
and an equal amount to Florida, with promises of more aid if it
could be raised. After the Republicans swept the October states,
and thereby apparently sealed Grant's victory in November, Morgan
found it almost impossible to raise further funds.[38] Southern party
chairmen, realizing that Grant did not need their states' electoral
votes, still asked for aid, justifying it as necessary to keep the party
alive until the next presidential election. One Georgia Republican
importuned Chandler, asking for as little as $100 or "even a letter of
sympathy."[39] Senator James Harlan, a member of the Congressional
Committee, told Chandler that he believed that Grant would win in
November without the South. Nonetheless, he still professed "deep
solicitude" for the party's "feeble friends" there and hoped that the
national committee could send them a little help, arguing that "the
moral effect would be very great."[40]

Morgan admitted that because of demands for funds in the North,
the committee had "done but little for the Southern states." Later
in October, because some pledged money was still coming to his
committee, Morgan managed to send another $1,000 to Alabama; he
also distributed small amounts to Virginia, Arkansas, and Mississippi. Altogether, however, the Southern states, with the exception
of North Carolina, had received less aid than that given to the single
Northern state of Maine. Although the party did send more North-

ern speakers into the South than it had in 1868, the Republicans still kept their best orators before Northern audiences, at least until the October elections were over. In addition, the party brought some of its Southern speakers North to convince Northern voters of the existence of continued lawlessness in the South that could be quelled only by Grant's reelection.[41]

Once again, the Republican party in a national election had revealed that its Southern concerns were secondary to maintaining its Northern base. Southern Republicans were once again disappointed with the encouragement and assistance they received from the national party. The Northern strategy did pay off for the Republicans, as it had in 1860, 1864, and 1868; this time Grant swept the North, and with it the election. In 1872 he also carried all the former Confederate states except Georgia, Texas, and Tennessee, and in the border he won Delaware and West Virginia. In large part Grant was successful in the nation and in the South because of Greeley's weakness as a candidate; he won fewer electoral votes and a smaller percentage of the popular vote than the Democrats had won in 1868. In fact, his electoral vote and popular vote percentage totals were the lowest of any candidate between 1860 and 1892. Grant won six of his ten Southern states by narrow margins. There his success was owing not only to Democratic weakness but to the steadfast support of black voters, who were protected at the polls in many instances by the operation of the Enforcement Acts, which for the time being had stayed the hand of Southern vigilante groups like the Klan. Indeed, the election of 1872 was one of the most peaceful and democratic in Southern postbellum history.[42]

Although the 1872 election results in the South demonstrated the continued potential of the black vote for the Republican party, after Grant was reelected the Northern public and the Republican administration showed less and less interest in enforcing civil and political rights in the South. During Grant's second term, he authorized federal intervention in Arkansas and Louisiana but could not prevent the Conservatives from taking control of the former state. In Texas, Alabama, and Mississippi, he abstained from involvement in behalf of the Republican governments, and by the end of 1875 all of them were lost to the party. Communications between Northern and Southern Republicans, which had already begun to decline rapidly after Grant was elected in 1868, picked up momentarily in 1872 but fell off after the presidential election and never resumed the level matched during the period when the Republican party was organizing in the South. Financial aid from the party continued to dwindle, and few Northerners visited the South.[43]

This lack of support for Southern Republicans was reflected in Congress's continued failure to recognize their requests for federal patronage and economic assistance. The Northern Republicans had already set this pattern in the years 1867–68, when the Reconstruction program of Congress was being implemented in the South. Congress proved willing then to put troops in the South, enfranchise blacks, and create an environment in which the Republican party could emerge, but did nothing to provide economic assistance that might have increased the party's appeal to both races. Because blacks already were committed to the party through its advocacy of the Fourteenth and Fifteenth amendments, Republicans in the North saw the need to bid for white support in the South, but they were indicating as early as 1867 that they were not willing to provide whites with much incentive for voting Republican. This pattern was continued in both Grant administrations. Southern Republican petitions for patronage, for financial assistance in the way of railroad aid and levee improvement, or for currency redistribution or inflation were either ignored or barely recognized. Even though the Republicans advertised themselves to the South as the party of material progress and social improvement, they did little on the national level to give substance to those claims.

Even though Southern states were now fully represented in Congress, Southern Republicans did not get recognition in filling the important congressional committee posts. Nor did they get their fair share of federal patronage. During Grant's presidency no Southerners were appointed to the seven vacancies that appeared on the Supreme Court. Nor did any Southerner except Amos Akerman of Georgia serve in Grant's cabinet. After Akerman's appointment, the patronage of his office did not meet Southern expectations. A prominent Georgia Republican reprimanded Akerman for not giving "sufficient importance to the Federal patronage," reminding him that Southern Republicans "must be aided by the party." In 1872, Robert B. Elliott, a black congressman from South Carolina, complained to Grant himself about leaving the Republicans of his state to stand "self-sustained without any appreciable aid from official patronage."[44]

During Grant's administration Congress returned to many of the economic issues of concern to the South that had been raised in the Fortieth Congress, which had presided over the drafting and execution of the Reconstruction Acts. At that time Congress had turned a deaf ear to Southern pleas for federal aid for levee rebuilding, railroad construction, tax relief, and a redistribution of national bank currency that would provide badly needed circulating medium for the South. The four succeeding Congresses that sat while Grant was president did little more than their predecessor in answering these pleas.

From the time the South reentered Congress, Southern Republican congressmen sought federal aid for river and harbor improvements. As the South gained full representation, Congress did begin to appropriate such funds, particularly for harbor improvement, but Southerners still objected that the Great Lakes states of Michigan and Wisconsin got more funds for such purposes than the entire South. Southern representatives from states bordering on the Mississippi River were particularly concerned about getting federal aid for levee rebuilding; some virtually staked their political careers on acquiring it. James Lusk Alcorn, a white Mississippian who had helped organize the Republican party in his state and was its first Republican governor, was elected to the U.S. Senate in 1871 and worked mightily for federal funds for levee reconstruction. Not until 1881, however, did Congress agree to the expenditure, and by then the aid was too late to help the Republican party in the South.[45]

The Republican Congresses of the 1870s were of little more use to the Southerners when it came to appropriating funds or granting lands for railroad construction. Southern Republicans made a major issue of the importance of railroad building to the prosperity of the South and eagerly looked to Congress for federal aid. They knew that the North had benefited greatly from federal land grants to railroads during and after the war, especially for building transcontinental lines from the Mississippi to the Pacific; they thought it was now the South's turn for such largesse. They also argued that providing the South with such land grants would prove to white Southerners that the Republican party cared about their needs. Unfortunately for

Southern hopes, however, the Congress had decided to end the policy of railroad land grants. The South did win one victory in 1871, when the Forty-first Congress agreed to a land grant to aid in the building of the Texas and Pacific, the South's only transcontinental project. Even then the grant was smaller than that accorded previously to Northern lines, was not accompanied by any loan guarantees, and required that the road be built on the Northern gauge, which limited its usefulness to Southern cities that hoped to connect with it.[46]

Congress also turned a largely deaf ear to Southern pleas to adjust the revenue and currency structure of the nation to bear less heavily on the South. Southerners still resented the cotton taxes collected in the South from 1862 to 1868 and in 1873 sought to have the government refund $57 million in taxes collected in this manner. Southern representatives voted 60–3 for the proposal, but Northern Republicans voted 3–74 against it, and the proposal was easily defeated. The Congress was slightly more receptive to renewed pleas from the South that the country make more currency available to the South, which was sadly lacking in a circulating medium after the war. Southerners hoped to get a redistribution of existing currency, but Northerners defeated such proposals, fearing loss of bank notes from their own states. In 1870 the South did get some relief when Congress approved a law that would increase new bank note issues and allow a redistribution of $25 million worth of currency. Southerners continued, for the most part, to seek currency expansion, either through more bank notes or through more liberal use of greenbacks; in 1874 Congress agreed to expand greenback circulation, but Grant vetoed the measure. Southern Republicans were embarrassed by the president's action, but by then the party was on its last legs in the few Southern states where it remained.[47]

When Southern Republicans requested federal aid for education, this plea also fell on deaf ears in Washington. In 1870 and again in 1871 a number of petitions reached Congress asking for federal aid for schools; the requests all came from the South, primarily from North Carolina and Tennessee. The proposal for federal aid for Southern schools was not new. As early as 1867 Charles Sumner recommended it, and in the same year Greeley's *New York Tribune* endorsed the idea. As Negro suffrage in the South became a fact, and particularly after the Fifteenth Amendment was ratified, other

Northern Republicans, concerned about the advisability of enfranchising a largely uneducated race, began to consider federal aid to schools in the South more seriously. When President Grant sent a special message to Congress in 1870 applauding the ratification of the Fifteenth Amendment, he recommended legislation to promote education in the South. In that year Republican Congressman George F. Hoar of Massachusetts introduced a bill to promote schools in the South, stating that he preferred such a measure to enactment of further force acts. Hoar's proposal got nowhere, but in 1871 several Republicans, including Henry Wilson, introduced a bill to grant revenue from federal land sales to states needing support for their educational systems. In 1872 such a measure passed the House, but the Senate failed to act on the bill. Not until 1880 did the Republican party platform commit the party to the support of federal aid for schools, but legislation was never approved.[48]

In most cases, Northern Republicans did not vote down Southern proposals out of malice or vengeance toward the South. By the 1870s the general mood in the North was opposed to providing more federal aid for internal improvements no matter what section of the country was to be affected. Party and regional lines tended to blur when matters of currency and finance were raised in Congress, and the South could count on support from Western Republicans in working for currency inflation and banking reform. The proposal for federal aid to education brought opposition from the Democrats, who feared such legislation would allow the federal government to encroach on the domain traditionally assigned to the states, and many Republicans agreed. There was a precedent, however, for federal aid in the form of the Morrill Land Grant Act of 1862, which appropriated revenues from public land sales to help finance agricultural and mechanical colleges in the states; when the South rejoined the Union it was given funds under this program. In 1873, when Henry Wilson tried to amend a bill providing for the further support of land-grant colleges so as to extend federal aid to the common schools of the South, the Senate rejected his proposal.[49]

Although some of the unwillingness of Northern Republicans to aid their Southern brethren was based on considerations of public economy or state rights, another reason was Northern distrust of all things Southern. Northern Republicans had never felt comfortable with their Southern allies, black or white, as they made clear particularly in their attitude toward Southern Unionists. During and after the war the Southern whites who were most active in organizing the Republican party claimed to have opposed the Confederacy and supported the Union. Some Northern Republicans took these claims literally and hoped to build their party in the South on such support, but they soon developed misgivings about the numbers and convictions of such Unionists. The history of the Southern Claims Commission provides an excellent illustration of the power of this Northern suspicion of the South. After the war Southern Unionists asked the government to recognize their claims for the loss of property used by the federal armies during the conflict. Congress dragged its feet on the matter; Republican leaders frequently indicated that they feared if they did establish a commission to consider such claims, it would invite a raid on the U.S. Treasury. Southern Republicans pushed for the commission, claiming that the Unionists loyal to the federal government during the war deserved justice and also that the Republican party could gain political dividends among white voters by approving such a measure.[50]

In 1871 the Forty-first Congress, in addition to passing the Texas and Pacific railroad bill, recognized Southern concerns by creating the Southern Claims Commission. Under its terms Southerners filed a total of 22,298 claims against the U.S. government, totaling more than $60 million. The Congress was so suspicious of Southern Unionism, however, that it required exceedingly stringent tests for claimants to establish their loyalty. The process of making and supporting a claim became arduous and costly. One Southerner complained to Benjamin Butler that "persons of limited means cannot afford to prosecute claims, consequently the Commission is of no benefit to us, *politically.*" The commission fell far behind in its processing of the claims; as late as 1877, 11,282 cases, or 50 percent of those filed, were still unconcluded. When all accounts were finally closed, in 1880, the commission reported that it had approved a total payment of $4,636,920, or less than 10 percent of the amount claimed.[51]

By 1875 James G. Blaine, Republican Speaker of the House, was vehement in his denunciations of alleged Southern Unionists and their claims against the government. After the war was over, he recalled, Washington became "the resort of those suffering patriots from the South who through all Rebel persecutions had been true to the Union and the number was so great that the wonder often was where the Richmond Government found soldiers enough to fill its armies." Unless one were in the capital, he stated, it was impossible to appreciate "the beggars, the swindlers, and the scalawags wherewith the average Congressman is evermore afflicted."[52] Blaine's contempt for Southern white Republicans is reflected in his willingness to use the word "scalawag" for them, a term of opprobrium invented by the Conservatives. By then Northern Republicans had also begun to appropriate the Conservative epithet for Northern Republicans in the South, whom they called carpetbaggers. Northern Republican use of such terms was a measure of the lack of esteem in which they held their Southern colleagues. But at no time had they been hearty advocates of Southern Republicans.[53]

Much of the Northern Republicans' distaste for their Southern white allies continued to stem from their ignorance of Southern conditions. Benjamin Butler, a leading Northern Republican who did give a good deal of attention to the South, confessed to an Alabama correspondent that he could not understand the state's politics. Rarely did Northerners meet with their Southern colleagues except in Congress, and almost never did Republican politicians venture into the South to assess conditions there for themselves. And when they did they often returned with even less commitment to their Southern allies.[54]

By the early 1870s some of the Republican governments in the South deserved condemnation in the North because they ran up state debts and entered railroad deals that were often corrupt. The state of South Carolina acquired a particularly unsavory reputation for corruption. William Sprague, Republican senator from Rhode Island, claimed that his financial agent in South Carolina could buy himself a Senate seat from that state for $75,000 and that consequently he "distrusted the whole batch of carpetbag senators." One of the white Republicans of South Carolina insisted that his state had saddled the national party with a heavier burden than all the other Southern states combined. Another Republican from South Carolina complained that the state "has received nought but abuse from the party generally" and asked the Northern Republicans to give his party "able counsel and gallant leading, instead of upbraiding us so continually." Even Henry Wilson, a staunch defender of Southern Republicans, admitted by 1874 that affairs in the Southern states had hurt the party nationally. Indeed, a growing concern in the party about the political liabilities of continuing to intervene in the South to protect Republican regimes that were perceived in the North as corrupt was a major reason Grant stopped such interventions.[55]

Northern Republicans, for the most part, were no more enthusiastic about their black allies in the South than they were about their white supporters. The party had only reluctantly endorsed Negro suffrage in the South, and from the beginning of Reconstruction many Republicans had expressed doubts about the reliability of black voters who were uneducated, politically inexperienced, and subject to white domination. Many who became Liberal Republicans in 1872 felt this way. In 1868 Horace Greeley asked the editor of the Republican newspaper the *Independent* to prepare a stirring address to the "colored rabble of the South" explaining why they should vote Republican. Greeley believed that "many of the blacks are quite ignorant and credulous. They like to vote with those they have been accustomed to regard as gentlemen whenever they deem it safe to do so." Carl Schurz, who had supported universal suffrage, was contending by 1871 that the blacks "tend to blindly follow demagogues" and added that the carpetbag governments they helped elect "have often been scandalous." Liberal Republican criticism of black voters reached its epitome in the vitriolic pen of James Shepherd Pike, a Northern Republican journalist who stated that "the nigger is a porcupine who fills with quills everybody who undertakes to hug him." Pike visited South Carolina and returned to publish an article in the *New York Tribune* in which he condemned the Republican government of the state for holding its white population "under the heel of 400,000 pauper blacks, fresh from a state of slavery and ignorance the most dense."[56]

Pike, Greeley, and Schurz were all Liberals who broke with Grant and the Republicans; but even regular party members grew more vocal in expressing their doubts about black voters. In 1869 the editors of the *New York Independent*, the same paper that Greeley had asked to exhort black voters to vote Republican, wondered if the party could trust the "ignorant loyalty" of the freedmen. William E. Chandler, who was largely responsible in 1868 and 1872 for directing the Republican national campaigns, told Ben Butler in 1869 that he feared the Democrats would soon control every Southern state: with "the negroes deceived, coaxed or bullied" and the former Confederates voting solidly with the Democrats, "there can be but one result." William T. Sherman warned his brother John, senator from Ohio, that "negroes were generally quiescent and could not be relied on," and John Murray Forbes told Charles Sumner that "you cannot really understand what children most of them are." Such views spread even to ardent advocates of black rights. The editor of the *Boston Commonwealth*, a newspaper that long had supported Reconstruction, endorsed James S. Pike's condemnation of South Carolina's black legislators; by 1876 the paper was arguing that blacks, not habituated to arms or political agitation, were too docile and inoffensive in the face of white violence. This view was echoed by Benjamin Butler, who said in late 1875 that blacks would have to defend themselves against white terrorists: "So long as they will submit to be killed by every marauding white man who will do so, so long there will be no help . . . from the United States."[57]

Despite continued doubts about the reliability of black voters, the fact remained that they were the mainstay of the Republican party in the South; as the Republicans lost control of Virginia, Tennessee, Georgia, North Carolina, and the border states, they relied even more heavily on the large numbers of black votes in the Deep South. It was largely because of pressure from black voters, who had begun to doubt the Republican party's commitment to equal rights, that the Senate agreed in 1874 to pass a new civil rights bill. The measure was sweeping, requiring that blacks be given equal access to public accommodations, schools, institutions, colleges, and cemeteries, as well as the right to serve on juries. The bill had originally been drafted and introduced in the Senate by Charles Sumner on several occasions from 1870 through 1872. At those times he sought to add it as an amendment to amnesty bills, arguing that if whites were to be forgiven, blacks should be guaranteed racial justice. Sumner's proposal put his Republican colleagues in a bind. If they rejected his bill, they would risk alienating black voters in all sections of the country, and particularly in the Deep South, where they provided almost all of the party's votes. But if they passed it, whites would be offended, not only in the South but in the North as well. It provided a classic illustration of the problems the Republicans faced in trying to organize a biracial party.[58]

Although some Northern Republicans in the Senate either abstained or absented themselves from votes on the bill, it did pass that body twice, in 1872 and again in 1873, but was killed in the House. Several Senate Republicans voted for the measure, apparently in the hope that it would not pass the House. In the spring of 1874, in the wake of Sumner's death in March, the Senate again took up his proposal and passed it, and again the House failed to consider the bill. Nonetheless, by acting favorably on the measure, the Senate had projected the issue of civil rights into the fall congressional campaigns, and many Republicans feared that the party would suffer the consequences. The danger of white backlash against civil rights was especially great in the South. A number of Southern congressmen either abstained or voted against it. When Southern Republicans held a convention in Chattanooga, Tennessee, before the November elections, they were concerned about the adverse effects of the bill. A Mississippi Republican, writing to the president of the convention, warned that "it would be a bad exchange to secure success in a few southern states, on the agitation of the Civil Rights bill, at the sacrifice of Republicanism everywhere." The convention delegates agreed and did not discuss or endorse the Senate bill.[59]

When the totals from the election were counted, the Republicans had indeed suffered badly in the South: Democrats won control of thirty-seven of the fifty-four congressional seats available in the Southern states. Appalachian whites in the mountains of Virginia, North Carolina, Tennessee, and Kentucky deserted the Republican party in droves. Southern Republicans condemned their Northern allies for saddling them with the burden of the civil rights bill. A leading Republican judge in Kentucky accused the national party leaders of proposing a measure designed to keep the party from gaining a foothold among Southern whites. According to Albion Tourgée of North Carolina, the folly of the civil rights bill again proved that the Republican legislators in the North did not understand the South.[60]

The civil rights bill took its toll of Northern Republican votes as well. Civil rights did not furnish quite the issue in the North that it did in the South, but it was still a concern for voters in the Midwestern states. The backlash against civil rights, Northern dissatisfaction with the Grant administration's policy in dealing with the Panic of 1873, and a growing disillusionment with Reconstruction and Republican regimes in the South all led Northern voters to repudiate the Republicans. The party suffered its worst defeat in its two-decade history, losing a total of eighty-nine seats in Congress and consequently losing control of the House to the Democrats for the first time since the Civil War began.[61]

Ironically, in the wake of the 1874 election the lame-duck Republican House did take up and pass the civil rights bill, but only after weakening it by removing the provisions on integrating schools and cemeteries and by relaxing some of the Senate bill's enforcement clauses. Many Republicans voted for the bill on the assumption that the Senate would refuse to accept weakening it and it would never pass both houses. To their surprise, the Senate accepted the House changes, and Grant signed the measure on March 1, 1875. The law, which passed almost ten years after the end of the Civil War, at a time when there was almost no support left for using federal intervention for black rights, proved to be a dead letter, as most legislators expected it would. Thus, although the Republicans did enact a law aimed directly at the interests of Southern blacks, it was done at least in part from cynical motives and proved to be meaningless. Its only effect was to alienate Southern whites from the Republican party and threaten the party's base of support in the North.[62]

The same lame-duck session also considered a new enforcement act to renew some expired provisions of earlier laws authorizing the president to suspend the writ of habeas corpus and enacting vague, wide-ranging provisions to allow increased federal supervision of elections. Once again Republicans debated the wisdom of such legislation; its proponents argued that it was necessary to save the South for the party in 1876, and its critics claimed it would alienate Northern voters and cost the party support there. Speaker James G. Blaine believed that the bill could not save the South in any case and that it was better to "lose the South and save the North than to try through such legislation to save the South and thus lose both North and South." The House did pass the measure, but it failed to meet with approval in the Senate.[63]

Blaine's definition of his sectional priorities matched that of his party. Since its origins the Republicans had stressed building their Northern base rather than extending their party into the South, and whenever the Northern and Southern needs conflicted the latter always lost. In 1875 President Grant himself furnished an example of this regional priority, when he refused the pleas of Mississippi Governor Adelbert Ames to send troops to protect black voters during state elections there, arguing that if he did he would alienate Ohio voters who were about to go to the polls in that state. As a result, the Mississippi government was overthrown, leaving only Florida, South Carolina, and Louisiana still in Republican hands.[64]

By 1876 Republicans had virtually no hope of carrying any of the Southern states.[65] In the presidential campaign, the national party again followed its usual procedure of emphasizing the canvass in the Northern October states. Republicans also again waved the bloody shirt in an effort to rally their Northern supporters behind the party ticket.[66] This time, however, the October results were inconclusive, and for the first time since the Republican party entered the South, it seemed that Southern electoral votes might make the difference in the presidential campaign. In November, thanks to state returning boards that certified election results in the three states still in Republican hands, the party was able to claim all its electoral votes and contest what appeared to be a certain Democratic victory. As a result of the dispute over the election of 1876, compromises were arranged for counting the electoral vote and declaring a winner. The votes of Florida, South Carolina, and Louisiana were added to the Republican column, making the party's candidate, Rutherford B. Hayes, president by a single vote.

Thus at the very time the Republican party was about to disappear in the South, Southern votes helped make a Republican president.[67] In return for those votes, however, Hayes withdrew federal troops from the South, and the last three Republican regimes quickly collapsed. The Southern Republicans had made their last sacrifice for the interests of the national Republican party. Republicans would not reappear in these states, or in any other Southern state, in significant strength for the next one hundred years.

CONCLUSION

The Republican party was unsuc-
cessful in penetrating the South in the years following the Civil War.
Republican ideology reflected the nature of the Northern, not Southern, society and economy. It was based on a series of assumptions
that were not widely held in the South: the superiority of free labor,
the desirability of a diversified economy, including a significant industrial component, an emphasis on technological innovation, a
commitment to public education, and a belief that government had a
role to play in promoting economic growth. The prewar South was
committed to slave labor, an agricultural economy, and a limited role
for government. The resulting clash in values, which was greatly
heightened by antebellum competition for control of the western territories, produced a breakdown of national political parties and the
emergence of strongly sectional political attitudes.

The massive sacrifices brought about by a four-year civil war, both
in the North and the South, greatly exacerbated sectional hostilities.
The Northern Republican party emerged from the war as the righ-
teous champion of national unity and freedom; the defeated South
just as steadfastly avowed its veneration of the Lost Cause of Confederate independence. Republicans, who before the war had developed a battery of criticisms of the South, continued to attack the
section, keeping wartime hostilities alive by condemning the Confederates, whose rebellion had led to the sacrifice of so many Northern
lives. The Republicans who waved the "bloody shirt" insisted that
the South should not be allowed to return to the Union until its
loyalty was demonstrated, or at least until safeguards were taken to
ensure that the fruits of victory secured by the war were not endan-
gered in the peace that followed.

Most Republicans did not want a Reconstruction program that interfered unduly with the internal organization of the Southern

states. The application of federal power in the South, either through court action or military power, remained limited. Nonetheless, Southern whites were outraged by congressional actions, particularly the measures that granted blacks legal and political equality with whites. They particularly resented these laws because black suffrage was accompanied by at least the temporary disfranchisement of some whites. As a result, most Southern whites resisted Reconstruction either passively, by not registering and voting, or actively, by organizing to defeat the Republicans in the South, often by violent means. The ensuing strife in the South, which did not end until the last of the Reconstruction governments were overthrown, continued to feed sectional hostilities. Northerners eventually decided that to restore harmony between the sections, Reconstruction of the South had to end and the white Southerners had to be given complete control over their own affairs. By that time, however, the South was politically virtually a one-party section, united behind the Democrats in favor of white supremacy and hostility to federal intervention in state affairs.

In light of inflamed sectional hostilities throughout the twenty years or so after the formation of the Republican party in the North, it is surprising that the party ever hoped to build support in the South. Indeed, every step the party took, from attempting to ban slavery from the territories before the war, to fighting a war to defeat the movement for Southern independence, to emancipating slaves and granting them civil and political equality, further alienated the masses of Southern whites. Nonetheless, at least some Northern Republicans continued to hope that, somehow, after sectional issues had been decided and questions of the permanence of the Union and the future of slavery were resolved, they could build their party south of the Mason-Dixon line. They were convinced that white Southerners would respond to their ideology of government-supported, diversified economic development.

Before the Civil War, the Republicans made almost no effort to penetrate the South; they were too preoccupied with building their Northern base. Although fledgling Republican organizations did appear in the border states, they got very little encouragement or assistance from the Northern Republicans. Some party leaders, like the Blairs, advocated a strategy of pursuing border state support before the 1860 election, but it was evident to most Republicans that policies and candidates likely to appeal to the border states would not be popular in the North, and hence the strategy was ignored. During the secession crisis, President Lincoln also refused to conciliate Unionist sentiment in the border and other Southern states by offering compromises on slavery expansion, fearing that such action would alienate his Northern supporters.

After the Civil War began, opportunities developed to build Republican organizations in the border, which gained control of these states, but this was made possible only through military intervention, disfranchisement, and the disorganization of the Republicans' opponents. Border state Republicanism was an exotic plant in an alien environment; by 1868 Maryland, Delaware, and Kentucky had become Democratic, and after 1870 Missouri and West Virginia as well. During the war, Republican parties also emerged in some of the Confederate states, particularly Tennessee and Louisiana. President Lincoln, however, whose control over federal patronage and the army gave him much political influence in Southern areas controlled by the Union, subordinated party-building to the goals of convincing Southerners to abandon the war and emancipate their slaves. In Tennessee the Republicans held power only by following the border policy of massive disfranchisement of Confederates and their sympathizers. In Louisiana, as well as in Virginia and Arkansas, where test oaths were not used, Unionist Republican parties were inundated by a wave of votes from former Confederates after the end of the war, indicating clearly what would happen in other Southern states if whites were allowed to vote freely.

After the end of the war, Republicans in Congress drafted the Fourteenth Amendment as an effort to resolve a number of Reconstruction problems. It by no means, however, constituted a program for building a viable Republican party in the South; rather, it was a platform for carrying the Northern elections in 1866. During this "critical year" Republicans undertook almost no efforts to encourage Southern Republicanism until agreeing to join the convention of Southern loyalists called for the late summer. At that convention the Northern delegates rejected the pleas of the white Southern Unionists to endorse Negro suffrage as the only way to reorganize Southern politics effectively and establish a Republican party there. Only after Southern white Conservatives had rejected the amendment, and thereby weakened the arguments of those Northern Republicans who thought white support could be courted, did Congress turn to enfranchise blacks.

Northern Republicans took this step reluctantly and only after waiting for almost two years after the end of the war. Whatever Southern strategy the party had developed since 1855 had been aimed at attracting white votes in the South; until 1867 few considered the possibility of enfranchising blacks. By the end of the war only a few Northern states allowed blacks to vote, and Northern whites resisted moves to enfranchise those who could not. Northern Republicans had almost no knowledge of Southern blacks and were dubious about enfranchising a mass of people whom they regarded, at best, as illiterate, uneducated, and politically inexperienced. Because of black vulnerability to economic and physical intimidation from their former masters, Republicans had little faith that the black vote could be sustained for long as an independent political influence in the South. Black enfranchisement was a gamble; it seemed to the Republicans to provide the best answer to protecting black rights without massive federal intervention in the South. If the Republican party reaped political benefits from the enfranchisement of blacks, so much the better; but few Republicans counted on any long-term success with the black voters of the South. Not only were they subject to intimidation and coercion by whites; in most states blacks were not even a majority anyway.

Hence Northern Republicans concerned about the South came back to their belief that any hope for building a permanent Republican party there had to rest on obtaining enough white support to control at least some of the Southern states when their votes were added to those of the blacks. The relative mildness of congressional Reconstruction was in part motivated by a Republican hope that moderate terms would be more likely to acquire some increased Southern white support. But Republican moderation was also dictated by the fear that more radical terms would alienate Northern white voters as well. Republicans were particularly eager to get the Southern states back into the Union before the 1868 election, lest their Northern support be weakened by the delay. Republican anxiety about alienating both Northern and Southern whites was also revealed in efforts to discourage black Republicans in the South from enacting equal accommodations laws or redistributing property. Northern Republicans discouraged blacks from running for office or holding positions of influence in the Southern state parties. They also proved unwilling, in the crucial summer of 1868, to provide their Southern allies with the military means to protect themselves from white violence. They feared that arming and using state militia, particularly black men, would only worsen race hostilities, and they feared that such action would not be popular with Northern voters.

The result of these Republican attempts to conciliate whites was to give almost no encouragement to the Southern blacks who were loyal to the party to remain so. Hence the Republicans risked disillusioning the only people upon whose votes they could rely; but in the 1870s events were to prove that the Northern Republicans would abandon their black supporters before the blacks gave up on them. Although the Republicans managed to maintain their hold on the Northern voters through the presidential election of 1868, and hence continued to control the national government, they failed to build any appreciable strength among Southern whites. By the end of that year it was clear that the Republicans' Southern strategy of building support among whites while maintaining their black votes was a failure.

Much of the Republicans' political failure in the South stemmed from their own sectional propaganda, which alienated Southern whites, and from their misunderstanding or lack of knowledge about Southern attitudes, values, and loyalties. Republicans who harbored dreams of gaining white support in the South initially believed that the masses of Southern whites had been deluded into following the slaveholders to the detriment of their own interests. They thought that these Southern whites were fundamentally loyal to the Union and that they could be convinced that slavery was a handicap to their own prosperity. Once the Union was preserved and slavery overthrown, Northern Republicans believed that the South would develop much like the North if Northern, or Republican, ideas were allowed to be debated and adopted there.

Events were to prove that these Northern Republicans overestimated the degree and nature of Southern Unionism. Their knowledge of the South and of the combination of sectional, racial, and class loyalties of Southern whites was limited and inaccurate. They did not realize that although the Southerners might admit their defeat in the war and accept their continued membership in the Union, they were not about to repudiate their Confederate leaders. Nor did Northerners anticipate that most Southern whites would resent, not appreciate, the Republican party program. In large part this resentment stemmed from Republican support for the War for the Union and the abolition of slavery, and especially the Republican espousal of equal rights for blacks.

Graphic illustration of the difficulties the Republicans faced in courting and maintaining Southern white support can be seen by examining the course followed by the few prominent Southern whites who had endorsed the Republican party before the Civil War. All of these men—Cassius Clay of Kentucky, the Blairs of Missouri and Maryland, Gratz Brown of Missouri, and Hedrick, Goodloe, and Helper of North Carolina—had deserted the Republican party by 1872. They became disaffected for various reasons, but they all believed that the party threatened their sectional and racial loyalties. In North Carolina, Goodloe and Hedrick opposed adopting the name "Republican" for the new party when it held its first state convention in 1867, arguing that the name was anathema to Southern whites. Clay, Brown, and Goodloe were ardent advocates of amnesty for former Confederates and condemned the Republican party for limiting white political rights. Clay also vehemently condemned the Republican Congress for subjecting Southern whites to military domination.[1]

The Blairs, who were among the first to join the Republican party, were also the first to leave it. They were especially offended by the party's advocacy of immediate emancipation and later of the use of federal power against the states to protect black rights. White supremacy was also a major concern of Cassius Clay, who accused the Republican party of attempting to put Southern whites under Negro rule. In North Carolina, neither Goodloe nor Hedrick was sympathetic to black rights, and their lack of commitment to the postwar Republican party was in part based upon its championing of black equality. Hinton Rowan Helper excelled over the others in his denunciation of the party for its racial policies and claimed that its advocacy of black rights was a blow at Southern white Republicans.[2]

All of these Southerners had initially been attracted to the Republican party because of their concern for the Southern white nonslaveholders. They believed that the party did offer to bring prosperity to the masses of whites. But Northern Republicans ultimately failed to appeal to the interests of enough Southern whites to pry them loose from the racial and regional loyalties that separated them from the party. In large part the reason for this failure was Republican inability to agree upon where specific white support in the former Confederacy could be located. Sometimes Northern Republicans talked of appealing to economic interest groups, but these groups were always ill-defined. Republicans vaguely identified them as the middle class, or the working class, or as small farmers. But for the most part, Northerners, possibly because the Republican free labor ideology downplayed class antagonisms and emphasized a harmony of interest between economic groups, were not eager to exploit potential class divisions in the South. Class lines there were not well identified in any case. Instead, Northern Republicans, like many of the leaders of the Southern Republican party, followed an elitist approach, trying to convert to their cause influential Southerners who might bring with them into the party a sizable white following. Instead of raising issues of mass interest, Republicans appealed to pre–Civil War political affiliations in the South. They hoped especially to gain the support of former Whigs, who were considered more sympathetic than Democrats to the Union and to government-assisted economic development. Some Republicans, however, also courted the support of "Douglas Democrats" who had resisted the secession movement.[3]

Because of their inability to identify or agree upon what specific groups of whites in the South to court, Republicans ended up without the support of any. They ultimately failed to give the Southern whites any concrete or practical reasons for supporting them. In particular, they failed to offer the Southerners many of the same benefits that the North gained in the war. Republicans were reluctant to redistribute national bank currency in such a way that the South got its fair share. They also refused, for the most part, to grant the South lands for railroad development, and they repeatedly ignored Southern pleas, from members of their own party, for federal land for levee reconstruction. Southern Unconditional Unionists had to wait until 1870 for the federal government to agree to repay them for property lost as a result of Union army actions during the war, and when this was done, the money was doled out in such a way as further to anger those who had sought redress since the end of the war. When Congress voted in 1868 to remove the cotton tax, it was only removing an economic discrimination against the South, not providing it with any positive assistance. Even the 1866 Homestead Act, which was initially drawn up with Southern conditions in mind, failed to be of any assistance to the poor whites and blacks for whom it was supposedly intended.

Although Republicans were not eager to add to federal deficits after a terribly costly war, they were also reluctant to aid the South because of the hostilities engendered by that war. The cotton tax was one evidence of animosity toward the South; so also was the refusal to aid the South with further land grants. Congress was reluctant to allow Unionists to file claims against the government for losses incurred during the war, for fear that many of the claims would be fraudulent. This continued hostility toward, or suspicion of, Southern whites, even Unionists, certainly worked to thwart any major effort to build white support there.

Again and again the conflicting motives and purposes of Reconstruction legislation, especially as they reflected sectional hostilities, interfered with seeking white votes in the South. The best example of this situation, perhaps, is the Republican dilemma over allowing former Confederates to exercise political rights. Republicans who thought the best way to deal with the problem of suffrage in the South was to give the vote to blacks without denying it to whites were unable to have their way. Instead, the party, through Congress, embarked upon a halting, stumbling, and ultimately ineffective policy of temporarily denying certain classes of whites the right either to vote or to hold office. Republicans did this in large part because the passions unleashed by the war in the North would not allow whites in the South to resume their full political rights immediately. Yet the result was to alienate Southern whites without eliminating them, or their leaders, from political influence. Ultimately, the refusal to grant amnesty to former Confederates stands as one of the Republicans' major political mistakes, for they drove away some whites who might otherwise have cooperated with them.

The Northern Republicans' resolution of the amnesty issue reflected their concern over keeping their Northern political base intact, even at the expense of building a viable party in the South. Again and again their disposition of Reconstruction issues reflected their regional political priorities. The Fourteenth Amendment of 1866 was designed to win approval in the North, not to build a party in the South. When Republicans endorsed Negro suffrage in the South in 1867, they did not require it in the North, fearing they would lose the presidential election the following year if they did. In 1868 the Republican Congress hastened the Southern states back into the Union, even though their party's hold on those states was weak, fearing that if they did not Northern voters would have sufficient reason to reject their party's presidential candidate. Only after the election did the Republicans endorse the Fifteenth Amendment, making Negro suffrage national rather than sectional, and they took this step more to gain Northern black votes than to safeguard Southern black votes. Furthermore, when the Enforcement Acts were passed in the 1870s to enforce the Fifteenth Amendment, they were at least in part designed to protect Republican interests in the North against improper votes cast by immigrants for the Democratic party, as well as to protect Southern Republicans.

The continued preoccupation of the national Republican party with protecting its Northern base is clearly seen in the election campaign of 1868. Repeatedly, in elections going back to 1856, the party had made sure that its financial and oratorical resources were devoted to Northern audiences. In 1868, however, eight of the eleven former Confederate states were back in the Union and voting in the presidential election of that year. For the first time, Republicans had a chance to win the electoral votes of many of the Southern states. Nonetheless, the party again directed almost all of its resources into the Northern states that were considered crucial to the outcome of the campaign. Just as in 1856, 1860, and 1864, the party leaders recognized that by carrying the North they could carry the election, and again they proceeded to do just that. Northern speakers repeatedly waved the bloody shirt before their audiences, a tactic that promised to get Northern votes but could hardly prove attractive to Southern whites. Fledgling Republican parties in the South, which lacked funds and faced remorseless opposition, got only token financial support from the North, and almost no Northern public speakers made tours of the South. By their actions, as well as by their private observations, Republican leaders made it clear that they considered the South a secondary theater of action. This pattern was followed again in the presidential elections of 1872 and 1876. Ironically, it was not until three Southern states appeared to hold the key to the elections in the latter year that the Republicans made a major effort to save those states' electoral votes, and when they did gain them, it was at the cost of surrendering their governments to the Democrats. Thus the Republicans wrote the final chapter in their history of elevating Northern interests above Southern needs.[4]

It is not surprising that the Republicans followed this course of emphasizing the North. The South remained to them unfamiliar and unknown territory. Only two men of importance, Wilson and Kelley, even bothered to take extended tours of the South to learn more about it. Despite their hopes for Southern white support, most Northern Republicans remained suspicious of their Southern white colleagues. Southern Republicans were usually political unknowns, with little status or standing in their own communities. They had little in common with Northern Republicans, who represented the most educated, informed, and propertied classes of the North. Northern leaders did not respect the Southern white Republicans and remained skeptical of their commitment to the Republican party. Nor did Northern Republicans trust their black allies to remain constant in their affiliation.

Judging by this evidence, it is difficult to conclude that the Republicans ever counted heavily on building a party in the South or that their Reconstruction policy was influenced significantly by that anticipation. Historians have debated the motives for congressional Reconstruction ever since the Reconstruction Acts were passed. Some have charged the Republicans with vindictiveness toward the white South; others have claimed they wanted to protect their economic program from Southern interference. Republicans have been accused of launching Reconstruction and enfranchising blacks to gain political advantages, especially by building a Republican party in the South; and they have been praised for enacting measures to guarantee freedom, equality, and civil rights to the former slaves.

Although there is evidence of some congressional vindictiveness toward the South, the Reconstruction measures could have been much harsher than they were. Clearly the Republicans were more concerned about the future of their economic programs and about the political implications of the return of the South. They were also concerned about the future security of the freedmen. Republican anxieties about these matters, however, proved to be more easily assuaged by continuing to work to hold their Northern political base, rather than by extending their party into the South. If Republicans hoped to maintain their political hegemony and their economic program by continuing to control the North, rather than by building a party in the South, then anxiety about the status of blacks in the South must have been a primary motive for Congress's Reconstruction policies.

Unfortunately, as many historians have noted, Congress did little either to provide the economic resources or the institutional means whereby black rights in the South could have been protected. Congress chose not to make land available to blacks, refused to strengthen or extend the Freedmen's Bureau, and failed to maintain a significant federal troop presence in the South. Instead Congress hoped that enfranchisement would enable the blacks to protect their rights without any further intervention from the federal government. Unfortunately, the only way that blacks could have used their votes effectively would have been in a two-party situation, with at least one of the parties, the Republican party in this case, actively seeking black support and thereby offering blacks government assistance and protection in return. Here again, however, Northern Republicans failed, in this case by not working harder to encourage the development of the Republican party in the South as an instrument through which black rights and interests could have been promoted.

It is no doubt unrealistic to expect that Congress would have provided land or any other significant economic assistance to blacks, or that it would have been more willing to enlarge the federal government's role in Southern affairs. Nor can the Northern Republicans, who controlled Congress, be solely to blame for the failure of their party to succeed in the South. Their party there was poorly led, divided into factions based on race and sectional origin, and drew its support from an electorate that was poor, largely uneducated, and politically inexperienced. Its Conservative opponents controlled most of the wealth, educational attainment, and political talent in the South, and they unleashed an attack on the Republicans that ranged the spectrum from social ostracism to organized violence. Nonetheless, the Southern Republicans' limited chances would have been improved if their Northern colleagues had made more of an effort to encourage and support them. The failure of the party leadership to believe wholeheartedly in the possibilities of Southern Republicanism helped ensure that it would not develop. Southern Republicans did exist, and they needed every bit of sustenance their Northern colleagues could provide; they got very little. Hence the opportunity presented in the wake of the Civil War to nationalize the Republican party was lost.

Although the Republican party in the South continued to control some states until 1877, its demise was predictable, based upon the course Republicans pursued during the critical years from the end of the Civil War through the election of 1868. At that time Republicans formulated the policies they would pursue in the South and endeavored to create party machinery in the Southern states. Although the attempt was made, the effort was so limited, and the commitment so weak, that the future of Southern Republicanism was dim indeed. After 1868 events in the South drove Northern and Southern Republicans ever further apart, eroded the small white Republican vote that did exist, and ultimately neutralized the effect of the black vote. As in the border states, so also in the Lower South, the Republican party proved to be a fragile and exotic plant sown in alien and barren soil. The Republican Southern strategy turned out to be virtually no strategy at all.

NOTES

PREFACE

1. See, for example, Murphy and Gulliver, *Southern Strategy*.
2. This information is derived from Barone and Ujifusa, *Almanac of American Politics, 1982*.
3. For summaries of these studies, see two works by George B. Tindall: "Southern Strategy" and *Disruption of the Solid South*. For a recent addition to the literature on the Republican party and the South, see Sherman, *The Republican Party and Black America*.
4. Gillette, *Retreat from Reconstruction*.
5. See, for example, DeSantis, *Republicans Face the Southern Question*, 22–23; Franklin, *Reconstruction after the Civil War*, 59, 81; Stampp, *Era of Reconstruction*, 93–94; Benedict, *Fruits of Victory*, 16–17, 46; Perman, *Reunion without Compromise*, 270.
6. Woodward, "Political Legacy of Reconstruction," 95–97, and "Seeds of Failure in Radical Race Policy," 172–73; Trelease, *White Terror*, xxv; Gillette, *Retreat from Reconstruction*, xiii; Sherman, *Republican Party and Black America*, vii; Craven, *Reconstruction*, 261; Johnson, *Division and Reunion*, 200, 225.
7. Dunning, *Essays on the Civil War and Reconstruction*, 353–54.

CHAPTER 1

1. For recent studies of the reorganization of the party system in the 1850s, see Holt, *Political Crisis of the 1850s*, and Potter, *Impending Crisis*.
2. Foner, *Free Soil*, 11–39.
3. Ibid., 40–72.
4. Holt, *Political Crisis of the 1850s*, 180–81, 185, 191.
5. Craven, *Growth of Southern Nationalism*, 243–44; Barney, *Road to Secession*, 133–34, 136, 138–39, 160–61.
6. Holt, *Political Crisis of the 1850s*, 187.
7. Foner, *Free Soil*, 64–65; Van Deusen, *William Henry Seward*, 103, 119, 149, 185, 217.
8. Isely, *Horace Greeley and the Republican Party*, 57, 60, 153, 187, 193, 255–57, 263, 300. In this book references to the border states are meant to include

Missouri, Kentucky, Maryland, and Delaware. I shall also include Virginia in this category until the formation of West Virginia during the Civil War; West Virginia will then be considered a border state. The Upper South includes Virginia (after the Civil War began), North Carolina, Tennessee, and Arkansas. The remaining slave states that seceded in the winter of 1860–61 will be referred to as the Lower or Deep South.

9. Foner, *Free Soil*, 53–54.

10. McPherson, *Ordeal by Fire*, 23–46.

11. On Clay, see Smiley, *Lion of White Hall*, 22–30, 47, 53–56; on Breckinridge, see Degler, *Other South*, 20, 81, 93, and Eaton, *The Freedom-of-Thought Struggle in the Old South*, 74, 286, 295–96.

12. Bassett, *Antislavery Leaders in North Carolina*, 7–9, 11, 52.

13. Cox, "Freedom during the Fremont Campaign."

14. On Helper, see Bailey, *Hinton Rowan Helper*.

15. Hickin, "John C. Underwood."

16. Ibid., 156–59; Degler, *Other South*, 95; Smiley, *Lion of White Hall*, 35, 53, 150.

17. Smith, *The Francis Preston Blair Family in Politics*, 1:262–63, 291; Foner, *Free Soil*, 59–63, 150, 178–79.

18. Peterson, *Freedom and Franchise*, 12, 56–59, 72–74, 82; see also Bancroft, ed., *Speeches, Correspondence, and Political Papers of Carl Schurz*, 1:42–43, 160.

19. Smith, *The Francis Preston Blair Family in Politics*, 1:291, 300, 329–30; Isely, *Horace Greeley and the Republican Party*, 154, 159.

20. Johnson, comp., *Proceedings of the First Three Republican National Conventions*, 42; Smiley, *Lion of White Hall*, 158; Lowe, "Republican Party in Antebellum Virginia"; Malberg, "Republican Party in Kentucky," 10.

21. Johnson, comp., *Proceedings of the First Three Republican National Conventions*, 81; Rawley, *Edwin D. Morgan*, 104.

22. Holt, *Political Crisis of the 1850s*, 198–201; Potter, *Impending Crisis*, 264–65.

23. Smith, *The Francis Preston Blair Family in Politics*, 1:373–74, 429, 527.

24. Hickin, "John C. Underwood," 158–59, 160–61; E. D. Morgan to Underwood, June 7, 1859, William Seward to Underwood, Nov. 20, 1858, in Underwood Papers, LC; Underwood to Seward, Jan. 26, Nov. 12, 1858, copies in Underwood Papers, UV.

25. *New York Tribune*, Oct. 14, 1856, and *New York Times*, Oct. 14, 1856, both quoted in Hamilton, *Benjamin Sherwood Hedrick*, 24–25.

26. Isely, *Horace Greeley and the Republican Party*, 259–62; Bailey, *Hinton Rowan Helper*, 41, 46–47, 50–51.

27. Bailey, *Hinton Rowan Helper*, 54, 57; Cox, "Freedom during the Fremont Campaign," 317; Hickin, "John C. Underwood," 161.

28. Bailey, *Hinton Rowan Helper*, 53; Smiley, *Lion of White Hall*, 163; Isely, *Horace Greeley and the Republican Party*, 123; Holt, *Political Crisis of the 1850s*, 214.

29. Holt, *Political Crisis of the 1850s*, 191, 199–201.

30. Foner, *Free Soil*, 269–72; Peterson, *Freedom and Franchise*, 91–93; Smith, *The Francis Preston Blair Family in Politics*, 1:445–46, 464–77; Cain, *Lincoln's Attorney General*, 92–97; Luthin, *First Lincoln Campaign*, 51–64.

31. Johnson, comp., *Proceedings of the First Three Republican National Conventions*, 111–25; Hesseltine, ed., *Three against Lincoln*, 150–52; Fite, *Presidential Campaign of 1860*, 123.

32. Johnson, comp., *Proceedings of the First Three Republican National Conventions*, 126–29.

33. Mayer, *Republican Party*, 63–65; Isely, *Horace Greeley and the Republican Party*, 249–68; Potter, *Impending Crisis*, 424–28.

34. Smith, *The Francis Preston Blair Family in Politics*, 1:498, 500; Smiley, *Lion of White Hall*, 169.

35. Crenshaw, *The Slave States in the Presidential Election of 1860*, 174–75, 197; Smith, *The Francis Preston Blair Family in Politics*, 1:119, 506; Luthin, *First Lincoln Campaign*, 65–67; Baker, *Politics of Continuity*, 33–38, 44; Henig, *Henry Winter Davis*, 134–39.

36. Crenshaw, *The Slave States in the Presidential Election of 1860*, 124–25, 150; Luthin, *First Lincoln Campaign*, 67; Malberg, "Republican Party in Kentucky," 31; Hancock, "Political History of Delaware during the Civil War, Part I," 121–39.

37. McPherson, *Ordeal by Fire*, 137–38; for Republican faith in Southern Unionism, see Potter, *Lincoln and His Party in the Secession Crisis*.

38. Crofts, "The Union Party of 1861 and the Secession Crisis"; see also Webb, "Kentucky," 111.

39. Gilmer quoted in Crofts, "Reluctant Unionist," 244.

40. Crofts, "The Union Party of 1861 and the Secession Crisis," 358–61, and "Reluctant Unionist," 225–27.

41. Potter, *Lincoln and His Party in the Secession Crisis*, 37–38; Stampp, *And the War Came*, 141–58, 186–87.

42. Crofts, "The Union Party of 1861 and the Secession Crisis," 370.

43. Ibid., 370–71n.

CHAPTER 2

1. Baker, *Politics of Continuity*, 65–66, 68; Coulter, *Civil War and Readjustment in Kentucky*, 36.

2. Carman and Luthin, *Lincoln and the Patronage*, 186–92, 213–14.

3. On military involvement in border state politics, see Hesseltine, *Lincoln's Plan of Reconstruction*. In Maryland, the army had less political influence than it did elsewhere in the border. See Baker, *Politics of Continuity*, 71–72. On West Virginia, see Curry, *House Divided*, 68, 127–28; on Kentucky, see Coulter, *Civil War and Readjustment in Kentucky*, 148–49, 151–53, 155.

4. Avillo, "Ballots for the Faithful," 166–72; Balk and Hoogenboom, "Origins of Border State Liberal Republicanism," 226–27.

5. Kleppner, *Third Electoral System*, 107–17; Hancock, "Reconstruction in Delaware," 194; Hancock, "Political History of Delaware during the Civil War: Part II," 268–69.

6. Avillo, "Ballots for the Faithful," 164–65; Baker, *Politics of Continuity*, 63–65; Webb, "Kentucky," 111; Coulter, *Civil War and Readjustment in Kentucky*, 35; Smith, *The Francis Preston Blair Family in Politics*, 2:23–24.

7. Carman and Luthin, *Lincoln and the Patronage*, 193–212; Parrish, *Turbulent Partnership*, 95–122; Webb, "Kentucky," 109–10.

8. Balk and Hoogenboom, "Origins of Border State Liberal Republicanism," 224–25.

9. Parrish, *Turbulent Partnership*, 61–72; Peterson, *Freedom and Franchise*, 111–13.

10. Wagandt, *Mighty Revolution*, 77–78; Webb, "Kentucky," 109, 111; Coulter, *Civil War and Readjustment in Kentucky*, 156–60; Munroe, *History of Delaware*, 141.

11. Peterson, *Freedom and Franchise*, 121; Parrish, *Turbulent Partnership*, 123–36.

12. Henig, *Henry Winter Davis*, 173–77.

13. Peterson, *Freedom and Franchise*, 109–12; Baker, *Politics of Continuity*, 85–86; Kleppner, *Third Electoral System*, 117.

14. Baker, *Politics of Continuity*, 83–87; Parrish, *Turbulent Partnership*, 170–77.

15. Hood, "For the Union"; Munroe, *History of Delaware*, 141; Avillo, "Ballots for the Faithful," 165; Curry, "Crisis Politics in West Virginia," 91–92.

16. Silvestro, "None but Patriots," 14–19, 69–70, 75–76, 112, 118, 164–66; Malberg, "Republican Party in Kentucky," 73, 76; Baker, *Politics of Continuity*, 83–84; Parrish, *Turbulent Partnership*, 173.

17. Parrish, *Turbulent Partnership*, 149–70; Henig, *Henry Winter Davis*, 196–98.

18. Baker, *Politics of Continuity*, 92–96.

19. Ibid., 102; Peterson, *Freedom and Franchise*, 134–37.

20. Parrish, *Turbulent Partnership*, 169–77; Henig, *Henry Winter Davis*, 182–85, 198–99; Wagandt, *Mighty Revolution*, 140–41; Silvestro, "None but Patriots," 185.

21. Carman and Luthin, *Lincoln and the Patronage*, 323–24; Henig, *Henry Winter Davis*, 198, 230, 238; Wagandt, *Mighty Revolution*, 232–35; Baker, *Politics of Continuity*, 95; Peterson, *Freedom and Franchise*, 136–38; Parrish, "Reconstruction Politics in Missouri," 4–5.

22. Coulter, *Civil War and Readjustment in Kentucky*, 180–83.

23. Webb, "Kentucky," 114–16; Curry, "Crisis Politics in West Virginia," 92; Hancock, "Reconstruction in Delaware," 194; Wagandt, "Redemption or Reaction?" 165.

24. Mayer, *Republican Party*, 98–99; McKitrick, *Andrew Johnson and Reconstruction*, 4n., 43–44; Zornow, *Lincoln and the Party Divided*, 46–47, 92.

25. Zornow, *Lincoln and the Party Divided*, 93.

26. Hesseltine, *Lincoln's Plan of Reconstruction*, 28–30; Belz, *Reconstructing the Union*, 15–16, 43–44.

27. Hesseltine, *Lincoln's Plan of Reconstruction*, 48–65; Hamilton, *Reconstruction in North Carolina*, 81–95; Davis, *Civil War and Reconstruction in Florida*, 250–54.

28. Belz, *Reconstructing the Union*, 155–65.

29. Staples, *Reconstruction in Arkansas*, 9–43.

30. Patton, *Unionism and Reconstruction in Tennessee*, 30–44; Hesseltine, *Lincoln's Plan of Reconstruction*, 49–64.

31. Maslowski, *Treason Must Be Made Odious*, 74–75, 78–82; Patton, *Unionism and Reconstruction in Tennessee*, 44–50.

32. The following discussion of Lincoln's wartime Reconstruction efforts in Louisiana is drawn largely from McCrary, *Abraham Lincoln and Reconstruction*.

33. Ibid., 100–107.

34. Ibid., 159–60.

35. Ibid., 124–30.

36. Ibid., 161–69.

37. Ibid., 349.

38. Lawanda Cox contends that Banks and Hahn did not intend to base the Republican party in the South on the planter class but rather sought middle-class support from the type of men who were delegates to the constitutional convention (*Lincoln and Black Freedom*, 134).

39. McCrary, *Abraham Lincoln and Reconstruction*, 272–73.

40. Patton, *Unionism and Reconstruction in Tennessee*, 45–46; Davis, *Civil War and Reconstruction in Florida*, 295; Rose, *Rehearsal for Reconstruction*, 316–17; Carman and Luthin, *Lincoln and the Patronage*, 257–60.

41. Belz, *Reconstructing the Union*, 192–99, 215.

42. Johnson, comp., *Proceedings of the First Three Republican National Conventions*, 187–99.

43. Ibid., 203–22; McCrary, *Abraham Lincoln and Reconstruction*, 273; Zornow, *Lincoln and the Party Divided*, 93–94.

44. Johnson, comp., *Proceedings of the First Three Republican National Conventions*, 232, 240; Brown, *Raymond of the Times*, 253.

45. Belz, *Reconstructing the Union*, 198–243.

46. Zornow, *Lincoln and the Party Divided*, 215–16; Baker, *Politics of Continuity*, 104–10, 131; Curry, *House Divided*, 11.

47. Munroe, *History of Delaware*, 142; Coulter, *Civil War and Readjustment in Kentucky*, 187.

48. Avillo, "Ballots for the Faithful," 165, 174; Baker, *Politics of Continuity*, 131–36; Parrish, *Turbulent Partnership*, 190–200; Henig, *Henry Winter Davis*, 242–43; Peterson, *Freedom and Franchise*, 143; Curry, *House Divided*, 132–34.

49. Parrish, *Turbulent Partnership*, 206.

50. Balk and Hoogenboom, "Origins of Border State Liberal Republicanism," 232–33.

51. Patton, *Unionism and Reconstruction in Tennessee*, 48–50.

52. Cox, *Lincoln and Black Freedom*, 77–79, 80, 134.
53. Belz, *Reconstructing the Union*, 270–71.

CHAPTER 3

1. Curry, ed., *Radicalism, Racism, and Party Realignment*, xvi; Wagandt, "Redemption or Reaction?" 151; Donald, *Politics of Reconstruction*, 18; *Great Republic*, Oct. 18, 1866.

2. Detroit Post and Tribune, *Zachariah Chandler*, 281; Carl Schurz to Agathe Schurz, Nov. 9, 1863, in Schafer, ed., *Intimate Letters of Carl Schurz*, 292, and Schurz to Mrs. Schurz, Aug. 27, 1865, in Bancroft, ed., *Speeches, Correspondence, and Political Papers of Carl Schurz*, 1:268. On other opinions on the strength of Southern white Unionism, see Andrew, "Address of His Excellency John Andrew," 5; *Washington Morning Chronicle*, May 19, 1866; Brock, *American Crisis*, 16–17; West, *Lincoln's Scapegoat General*, 321; Warden, *Private Life and Public Services of Salmon Portland Chase*, 622; Richardson, *William E. Chandler*, 79.

3. Brock, "Reconstruction and the American Party System," 86–88; Van Deusen, *Horace Greeley*, 316–26, 343–44; Van Deusen, *William Henry Seward*, 378–79, 424–26, 428; McKitrick, *Andrew Johnson and Reconstruction*, 214–30.

4. Harrington, *Fighting Politician*, 97–98, 116, 172–73; West, *Lincoln's Scapegoat General*, 144, 155, 172; Sefton, ed., "Chief Justice Chase," 250–55; W. T. Sherman to John Sherman, Feb. 23, 1866, in Thorndike, ed., *Sherman Letters*, 263.

5. On Lincoln's faith in Southern Unionism, see Potter, *Lincoln and His Party*, 245–47; for his concern for the former Whig vote, see Stampp, *Era of Reconstruction*, 48–49; Hesseltine, *Lincoln's Plan of Reconstruction*, 19–20; Donald, "Devils Facing Zionwards," 87.

6. Hesseltine, *Lincoln's Plan of Reconstruction*, 53; Maslowski, *Treason Must Be Made Odious*, 146–47; McCrary, *Abraham Lincoln and Reconstruction*, 344; Brock, *American Crisis*, 17.

7. Cox, *Lincoln and Black Freedom*, 40–41; Donald, *Politics of Reconstruction*, 17–18; Benedict, *Fruits of Victory*, 3.

8. For a thorough discussion of Johnson's political aims in reconstructing the South, see Cox and Cox, *Politics, Principle, and Prejudice*. See also Donald, "Devils Facing Zionwards," 87–88.

9. Brown, *Raymond of the Times*, 295–97.

10. On Johnson and the Blairs, see Cox and Cox, *Politics, Principle, and Prejudice*, esp. 50–68.

11. Brock, "Reconstruction and the American Party System," 86–88; Donald, "Republican Party," 1291–92; Benedict, *Fruits of Victory*, 16–18; Kincaid, "Legislative Origins of the Military Reconstruction Act," 66–67.

12. Maddex, *Virginia Conservatives*, 35–44; McCrary, *Abraham Lincoln and Reconstruction*, 308–18; Staples, *Reconstruction in Arkansas*, 77, 83.

13. See Alexander, "Persistent Whiggery in the Confederate South."

14. Benedict, *Compromise of Principle*, 126–33.

15. Trefousse, *Radical Republicans*, 323–55; Stampp, *Era of Reconstruction*, 71–82; Brock, *American Crisis*, 183–84.

16. See McKitrick, *Andrew Johnson and Reconstruction*, 274–324, for a discussion of the president's breach with Congress during the spring of 1866.

17. Schurz to Charles Sumner, May 9, June 5, 1865, in Bancroft, ed., *Speeches, Correspondence, and Political Papers of Carl Schurz*, 1:254, 259; W. T. Sherman to John Sherman, August 1865, in Thorndike, ed., *Sherman Letters*, 254; *New York Times*, May 11, 1865; *Boston Commonwealth*, Feb. 18, June 17, 1865; *Washington Morning Chronicle*, Mar. 14, 1866.

18. Peskin, *Garfield*, 254–55; Charles Sumner to Francis Lieber, Aug. 14, 1865, Sumner Papers; Brodie, *Thaddeus Stevens*, 210–11, 271–72; McCrary, *Abraham Lincoln and Reconstruction*, 272; Riddleberger, *George Washington Julian*, 237–38; Julian, *Political Recollections*, 305–6; Brock, *American Crisis*, 131.

19. Brock, "Reconstruction and the American Party System," 85; Donald, "Republican Party," 1291–92.

20. Avillo, "Ballots for the Faithful," 168–70; *Great Republic*, Nov. 29, 1866; Kincaid, "Legislative Origins of the Military Reconstruction Act," 138–41.

21. Lyman Trumbull to Mrs. Gary, June 27, 1866, in Trumbull Papers; Blaine, *Twenty Years of Congress*, 2:310–11; Brock, *American Crisis*, 143–44.

22. Hyman, *Era of the Oath*, 54–84; W. W. Watson to Richard Yates, Apr. 30, 1866, and T. P. Robb to Yates, May 19, 1866, Yates Papers; Benedict, *Compromise of Principle*, 248.

23. W. T. Sherman to John Sherman, Feb. 23, 1866, in Thorndike, ed., *Sherman Letters*, 263–64; Alexander, *Political Reconstruction in Tennessee*, 136; Lewis Hanes to Benjamin S. Hedrick, Sept. 22, 1866, Hedrick Papers; A. H. H. Stuart to Horace Greeley, Dec. 27, 1866, Stuart Papers; Fleming, *Civil War and Reconstruction in Alabama*, 371–72.

24. McKitrick, *Andrew Johnson and Reconstruction*, 214–30; Van Deusen, *Horace Greeley*, 350, 360–61; Stewart, *Reminiscences*, 215.

25. Chase to Stanley Matthews, Apr. 14, 1865, in Nunns, ed., "Some Letters of Salmon P. Chase," 555; Trefousse, *Radical Republicans*, 333; McCrary, *Abraham Lincoln and Reconstruction*, 291, 316; *New York Times*, May 11, 1865; *Washington Morning Chronicle*, Mar. 24, 1866.

26. Butler, *Autobiography and Personal Reminiscences*, 960–61; Julian, *Political Recollections*, 305–6; Brock, *American Crisis*, 131; Foulke, *Life of Oliver P. Morton*, 1:448–51; W. T Sherman to John Sherman, Aug. 1865, in Thorndike, ed., *Sherman Letters*, 254; McKitrick, *Andrew Johnson and Reconstruction*, 58–59.

27. Riddleberger, *1866*, 107; Perman, *Reunion without Compromise*, 255; Brodie, *Thaddeus Stevens*, 300.

28. Brock, *American Crisis*, 105, 128, 142–44, 151; Hoar, *Autobiography*, 1:255–56; Perman, *Reunion without Compromise*, 119; Blaine, *Twenty Years of Congress*, 2:310–11.

29. Trefousse, *Radical Republicans*, 347; *Boston Commonwealth*, Apr. 7, 1866; Benedict, *Fruits of Victory*, 24–26.

30. Donald, "Republican Party," 1293; Benedict, *Fruits of Victory*, 19–21;

Kincaid, "Legislative Origins of the Military Reconstruction Act," 67–69, 101; Trefousse, *Benjamin Franklin Wade*, 271–72; Abbott, *Cobbler in Congress*, 175–78.

31. Patton, *Unionism and Reconstruction in Tennessee*, 124–32, 209–20; Alexander, *Political Reconstruction in Tennessee*, 113–19.

32. Benedict, *Compromise of Principle*, 196–97; Brock, *American Crisis*, 98, 132–33; George Boutwell to Charles Sumner, June 19, 1866, Sumner Papers; *Washington Morning Chronicle*, Feb. 15, Mar. 1, 1866.

33. Schuyler Colfax to Dr. Eddy, Jan. 25, 1866, in Hollister, *Life of Schuyler Colfax*, 283; *New York Independent* quoted in Benedict, *Compromise of Principle*, 197; *Congressional Globe*, 39th Cong., 2d sess., 191–92; 40th Cong., 1st sess., 145; *Washington Morning Chronicle*, Aug. 9, 1866.

34. Alexander, *Political Reconstruction in Tennessee*, 120; *Washington Morning Chronicle*, July 28, 1866.

35. Perman, *Reunion without Compromise*, 251–63.

36. *Philadelphia Press*, Aug. 3, 1867.

37. Alexander, *Political Reconstruction in Tennessee*, 142–46; *Washington Morning Chronicle*, July 27, 1866; Silvestro, "None but Patriots," 209, 234–35; Kolchin, *First Freedom*, 155; Shadgett, *Republican Party in Georgia*, 4; Staples, *Reconstruction in Arkansas*, 108.

38. Belz, *Reconstructing the Union*, 21, 32; *Washington Morning Chronicle*, Mar. 31, July 6, 1866; Carl Schurz to wife, Apr. 14, 1865, in Schafer, ed., *Intimate Letters of Carl Schurz*, 333; John Murray Forbes to G. V. Fox, July 6, 1865, and to Hugh McCulloch, July 7, 1865, in Hughes, ed., *Letters of John Murray Forbes*, 3:32–33, 33–35.

39. Olsen, *Carpetbagger's Crusade*, 39–46; Hamilton, *Reconstruction in North Carolina*, 133–42; Perman, *Reunion without Compromise*, 65; *Boston Commonwealth*, June 8, Aug. 5, 1865; *Washington Morning Chronicle*, July 16, 1866.

40. Moneyhon, *Republicanism in Reconstruction Texas*, 24–51.

41. Staples, *Reconstruction in Arkansas*, 101–9; Scroggs, "Carpetbagger Influence," 21–26; Alexander, "Political Reconstruction in Tennessee," 56.

42. *Washington Morning Chronicle*, Jan. 30, May 4, 1866; Moneyhon, *Republicanism in Reconstruction Texas*, 42; Fleming, *Civil War and Reconstruction in Alabama*, 398–99.

43. Cimprich, "Beginning of the Black Suffrage Movement in Tennessee," 185–96; Taylor, *Negro in Tennessee*, 20–21; Olsen, *Carpetbagger's Crusade*, 34–37; Hoffman, "Republican Party in North Carolina," 13–14; Litwack, *Been in the Storm So Long*, 502–9, 531–35.

44. Bentley, *History of the Freedmen's Bureau*, 187; Silvestro, "None but Patriots," 236.

45. McDaniel, "Georgia Carpetbagger," 106–13; *Washington Morning Chronicle*, Apr. 9, 10, July 31, 1866; Henry M. Turner to John Bryant, Apr. 6, 12, 13, 1866, John E. Bryant Papers.

46. McDaniel, "Georgia Carpetbagger," 117.

47. Cimprich, "Beginning of the Black Suffrage Movement in Tennessee," 191; Wiggins, *Scalawag in Alabama Politics*, 20–21; Fleming, *Political Reconstruction in Alabama*, 364, 388–89.

48. Silvestro, "None but Patriots," 235; Holt, *Black over White*, 11–12.

49. Richardson, *Negro in the Reconstruction of Florida*, 141–48; Chase to Andrew Johnson, May 21, 1865, in Sefton, ed., "Chief Justice Chase," 260; Shofner, *Nor Is It Over Yet*, 165–69.

50. Maddex, *Virginia Conservatives*, 39–43; Lowe, "Republicans, Rebellion, and Reconstruction," 161–228; J. R. S. Van Fleet to Benjamin Butler, Aug. 1, 1865, quoted in Alderson, "Influence of Military Rule and the Freedmen's Bureau on Reconstruction in Virginia," 75.

51. Alfred H. Terry to John Underwood, Sept. 30, Oct. 7, 1865, Underwood Papers, LC.

52. McCrary, *Abraham Lincoln and Reconstruction*, 317–33; White, *Freedmen's Bureau in Louisiana*, 17–19, 25; Taylor, *Louisiana Reconstructed*, 73–77.

53. Taylor, *Louisiana Reconstructed*, 76–79; Brodie, *Thaddeus Stevens*, 274–75; Nathans, *Losing the Peace*, 18; R. H. Shannon to Richard Yates, Mar. 19, 1866, and Thomas J. Durant to Yates, Mar. 1866, Yates Papers.

54. Reynolds, "The New Orleans Riot of 1866, Reconsidered," 17–20; Riddleberger, *1866*, 188, 200–201; Brodie, *Thaddeus Stevens*, 275–82.

55. Taylor, *Louisiana Reconstructed*, 111–13.

56. Wagstaff, "The Arm-in-Arm Convention," 101–19.

57. *Washington Morning Chronicle*, May 18, 19, June 29, July 9, 10, 12, 17, 20, 21, 1866; McPherson, *Political History of the United States*, 124; Moneyhon, *Republicanism in Reconstruction Texas*, 52–53.

58. Blaine, *Twenty Years of Congress*, 2:224–28; *New York Times*, Aug. 31, Sept. 3, 1866; *Washington Morning Chronicle*, Aug. 4, 1866; Olsen, *Carpetbagger's Crusade*, 51; *Great Republic*, Sept. 13, 1866.

59. *New York Times*, Sept. 4, 6, 1866; *Washington Morning Chronicle*, Aug. 22, 1866; John Underwood to W. D. Kelley, Aug. 27, 1866, in Underwood scrapbook, p. 119, Underwood Papers, LC; "Proceedings of the Southern Loyalist Convention," in *Reporter*, no. 34 (Sept. 24, 1866): 4–6.

60. George, *Zachariah Chandler*, 142–44; Ross, *Empty Sleeve*, 82; Richard Oglesby to Lyman Trumbull, Aug. 27, 1866, Trumbull Papers; A. G. Curtin to Thaddeus Stevens, Aug. 22, 1866, Stevens Papers; J. W. Forney to Zachariah Chandler, Aug. 14, 24, 1866, Zachariah Chandler Papers; *New York Times*, Sept. 6, 7, 1866; *Boston Commonwealth*, Aug. 25, Sept. 1, 1866.

61. *Boston Commonwealth*, Sept. 8, 1866; *New York Times*, Sept. 6, 1866; Joshua Hill to Horace Greeley, Sept. 22, 1866, Greeley Papers.

62. *New York Times*, Sept. 6, 7, 1866; *Washington Morning Chronicle*, Sept. 5, 1866.

63. "Proceedings of the Southern Loyalist Convention," *Reporter*, no. 35 (Oct. 1, 1866): 4; *New York Times*, Sept. 4, 8, 1866; *New York Herald*, Sept. 5, 1866; Foner, ed., *Life and Writings of Frederick Douglass*, 4:195–97; Bancroft, ed., *Speeches, Correspondence, and Political Papers of Carl Schurz*, 1:403.

64. *New York Times*, Sept. 4, 7, 8, 1866; *Boston Commonwealth*, Sept. 15, 1866; Moneyhon, *Republicanism in Reconstruction Texas*, 53–56.

65. McPherson, *Political History of the United States*, 241–42.

66. Thaddeus Stevens to W. D. Kelley, Sept. 6, 1866, Stevens Papers; *New York Times*, Sept. 6, 7, 8, 1866; Foner, ed., *Life and Writings of Frederick Doug-*

lass, 4:26; Julian, *Political Recollections,* 303; "Proceedings of the Southern Loyalist Convention," *Reporter,* no. 34 (Sept. 24, 1866): 10.

67. *New York Times,* Sept. 10, 1866; "Proceedings of the Southern Loyalist Convention," *Reporter,* no. 39 (Oct. 29, 1866): 9–10; *Great Republic,* Oct. 26, 1866; *Boston Commonwealth,* Dec. 8, 1866.

68. John Lightner to Lyman Trumbull, Oct. 12, 1866, Trumbull Papers; to Thaddeus Stevens, Oct. 12, 1866, Stevens Papers; and to John Andrew, Oct. 12, 1866, Andrew Papers; Parrish, *Missouri under Radical Rule,* 98.

69. Avillo, "Ballots for the Faithful," 169–73; Baker, *Politics of Continuity,* 158–65; Parrish, "Reconstruction Politics in Missouri," 19; Webb, "Kentucky," 117–20; Curry, "Crisis Politics in West Virginia," 93; Hancock, "Reconstruction in Delaware," 195–98.

70. *Washington Morning Chronicle,* Nov. 7, 8, 10, 21, 1866; Patton, *Unionism and Reconstruction in Tennessee,* 132; Coulter, *William G. Brownlow,* 328–29; *Boston Commonwealth,* May 19, Aug. 18, 1866; Wagandt, "Redemption or Reaction?" 176; Alexander, "Political Reconstruction in Tennessee," 56–57; Parrish, "Reconstruction Politics in Missouri," 19–20.

71. *Washington Morning Chronicle,* Dec. 18, 1866; Alexander, "Political Reconstruction in Tennessee," 56; Blaine, *Twenty Years of Congress,* 2:240–41.

72. *Washington Morning Chronicle,* Dec. 22, 31, 1866; H. B. Allis to Richard Yates, Dec. 23, 1866, Yates Papers.

73. *Washington Morning Chronicle,* Dec. 24, 25, 28, 1866; Trefousse, *Radical Republicans,* 351–52, 360.

74. Kincaid, "Legislative Origins of the Military Reconstruction Act," 115–16, 135–37.

CHAPTER 4

1. Benedict, *Compromise of Principle,* 210–13; Brock, *American Crisis,* 182–83.

2. *Washington Morning Chronicle,* Feb. 7, Mar. 2, 1867; *Great Republic,* Jan. 3, 1867.

3. Benedict, *Compromise of Principle,* 214–15, 231.

4. Kincaid, "Legislative Origins of the Military Reconstruction Act," 198–99; Benedict, *Compromise of Principle,* 215–16; Brock, *American Crisis,* 171–72.

5. *Congressional Globe,* 39th Cong., 1st sess., 74, 259; 39th Cong., 2d sess., 103–5; *Harper's Weekly,* June 15, 1867, pp. 370–71; *Boston Commonwealth,* June 8, 1867; *Atlantic Monthly* quoted in Foner, ed., *Life and Writings of Frederick Douglass,* 4:30; Horace Greeley to James Lawrence, Dec. 16, 1866, Greeley Papers; Trefousse, *Radical Republicans,* 341n.; Thaddeus Stevens to F. A. Conkling, Jan. 6, 1868, Stevens Papers.

6. *Congressional Globe,* 39th Cong., 2d sess., 1209–10, 1316, 1323; Kincaid, "Legislative Origins of the Military Reconstruction Act," 235–37.

7. *New York Times* quoted in *National Anti-Slavery Standard,* Mar. 30, 1867; Jellison, *Fessenden of Maine,* 217–18; *Nation,* Mar. 14, 1867, p. 212; *New York Commercial Advertiser* quoted in *National Anti-Slavery Standard,* Apr. 13, 1867.

8. *Congressional Globe*, 39th Cong., 1st sess., 303; 40th Cong., 1st sess., 144, 146; J. C. Emerson to D. Richards, Jan. 11, 1867, Norman Brownson to Richards, Jan. 12, 1867, R. J. Hubard to William P. Fessenden, Jan. 12, 1867, all in Fessenden Papers; John O'Neill to Benjamin Butler, Mar. 11, 28, 1867, C. L. Robinson to Butler, Mar. 17, 1867, Butler Papers; Christopher Happoldt to Marcus Ward, May 26, 1867, Ward Papers; *Washington Morning Chronicle*, Jan. 11, 1867; *Boston Commonwealth*, Mar. 9, Apr. 13, 1867; *New York Tribune*, June 7, Aug. 23, 1867; *Harper's Weekly*, Mar. 16, 1867, p. 163; Williamson, *After Slavery*, 336.

9. Horace Smith to Benjamin Butler, July 25, 1867, Butler Papers; Brigham, *James Harlan*, 229–30; *Nation*, Mar. 14, 1867, p. 212, Mar. 21, 1867, p. 235, Mar. 28, 1867, pp. 247, 255; *Congressional Globe*, 39th Cong., 2d sess., 1181; 40th Cong., 1st sess., 60, 168; Foulke, *Life of Oliver P. Morton*, 1:466–68, 485–87; Lorenzo Sherwood to George Julian, Apr. 18, 1867, Julian Papers; Schurz, *Reminiscences*, 3:205, 255.

10. Kincaid, "Legislative Origins of the Military Reconstruction Act," 238–39; Brock, *American Crisis*, 176; *Congressional Globe*, 39th Cong., 2d sess., 1334, 1563; 40th Cong., 1st sess., 148–49; Hoar, *Autobiography*, 1:255–56.

11. Kincaid, "Legislative Origins of the Military Reconstruction Act," 246–48; Donald, *Charles Sumner*, 298; Brock, *American Crisis*, 181–95; *Congressional Globe*, 39th Cong., 2d sess., 1211, 1563–64, 1626; *Nation*, Feb. 21, 1867, p. 150, Mar. 26, 1867, p. 245; *Great Republic*, Nov. 29, 1866.

12. Greeley to James Lawrence, Dec. 16, 1866, Greeley Papers; Merriam, *Life and Times of Samuel Bowles*, 2:30, 31; Samuel Hooper to Horatio Woodman, Dec. 14, 1866, Woodman Papers; *Congressional Globe*, 39th Cong., 2d sess., 43, 63.

13. Benedict, *Compromise of Principle*, 214–15.

14. Ibid., 220–40; *Congressional Globe*, 39th Cong., 2d sess., 1123, 1203, 1337–38, 1369, 1563.

15. *Boston Commonwealth*, Feb. 16, 1867; Bedford Brown and J. M. Leach to Jonathan Worth, Jan. 13, 1867, and Benjamin S. Hedrick to Worth, Feb. 22, 1867, Worth Papers; Kincaid, "Legislative Origins of the Military Reconstruction Act," 217–18; Brock, *American Crisis*, 205–6.

16. Benedict, *Compromise of Principle*, 242–44; Kincaid, "Legislative Origins of the Military Reconstruction Act," 258–60; Brock, *American Crisis*, 202–3.

17. Brock, *American Crisis*, 204–6.

18. Abbott, *Cobbler in Congress*, 182–86; *Congressional Globe*, 40th Cong., 1st sess., 102–3, 183–84.

19. Benedict, *Compromise of Principle*, 241; Abbott, *Cobbler in Congress*, 185; *Congressional Globe*, 40th Cong., 1st sess., 102, 116, 147.

20. *Congressional Globe*, 40th Cong., 1st sess., 114, 144; Henry Wilson to Angelina Grimke Weld, Apr. 12, 1867, Weld Papers.

21. *Boston Daily Advertiser*, Mar. 27, 1867; *Indianapolis Daily Journal*, Mar. 27, 1867, quoted in Smith, *Schuyler Colfax*, 250; *Washington Morning Chronicle*, Apr. 16, 1867; *New York Tribune*, Apr. 20, May 13, 1867; *Boston Commonwealth*, Apr. 13, 1867; *Nation*, Apr. 25, 1867, p. 325.

22. G. Gordon Adam to Charles Sumner, Apr. 19, 1867, Sumner Papers;

Philadelphia Press, June 12, 28, 1867; *Washington Morning Chronicle,* Aug. 24, 1867.

23. John Minor Botts to Richard Yates, Mar. 7, 1867, Yates Papers; Gillett F. Watson to Benjamin Butler, Mar. 23, 1867, Butler Papers; John Underwood scrapbook, p. 209, Underwood Papers, LC; F. R. Cape to John Covode, Aug. 28, 1867, Covode Papers; E. S. Plumb to Charles Sumner, Mar. 20, 1867; J. J. Noah to Sumner, Mar. 25, 1867, Sumner Papers; *Washington Morning Chronicle,* Apr. 30, May 4, 17, 1867.

24. *Washington Morning Chronicle,* Jan. 19, 1867; O. H. Howard to Marcus Ward, May 3, 20, 1867, D. H. Clary to Ward, May 24, 1867, William Claflin to Ward, June 8, 1867, Ward Papers.

25. *Washington Morning Chronicle,* May 18, 1867; Marcus Ward to Joseph Hawley, May 10, 1867, and Ward to [?], May 30, 1867, Ward Papers.

26. Kleeberg, *Formation of the Republican Party,* 224–27, 231; Detroit Post and Tribune, *Zachariah Chandler,* 312–17; *Washington Morning Chronicle,* Dec. 13, 18, 1866, Mar. 26, 27, Apr. 1, 1867; Thomas Tullock to Lyman Trumbull, Apr. 18, 1867, Trumbull Papers; Tullock to Charles Sumner, Apr. 18, 1867, Sumner Papers.

27. *Washington Morning Chronicle,* Apr. 11, 15, 1867; *Boston Commonwealth,* June 15, 1867; George W. Jones to Columbus Delano, June 27, 1867, Delano Family Papers.

28. See report of Union Congressional Republican Committee executive committee, July 20, 1867, in Schenck Papers; *Washington Morning Chronicle,* May 13, July 16, 1867.

29. Joseph Bradley to John Sherman, May 24, 1867, William Bassford to Sherman, May 31, 1867, Sherman Papers; Jonathan Odom to Horace Greeley, May 18, 1867, Greeley Papers; W. W. Holden to Charles Sumner, June 12, 1867, Sumner Papers; W. W. Holden to Benjamin Butler, June 12, 1867, Butler Papers.

30. *Washington Morning Chronicle,* June 8, 1867; J. M. Parker to Benjamin Butler, May 4, 1867, Butler Papers; *Great Republic,* May 23, 1867.

31. Col. T. P. Robb to Richard Yates, June 7, 1867, Yates Papers; *New York Tribune,* May 23, 27, 1867.

32. *Boston Commonwealth,* May 11, 18, 1867; C. C. Bowen to Benjamin Butler, May 30, 1867, Butler Papers; George C. McKee to Richard Yates, June 9, 1867, Yates Papers; C. Gordon Adam to Charles Sumner, Apr. 19, 1867, Sumner Papers.

33. An undated roster of committee agents can be found in the Schenck Papers. Judging by other materials found with the roster, it was drawn up early in 1868. By that time the committee listed 118 agents, of whom 79 were designated as black on the roll. Of the blacks who can be identified, at least 31 were ministers. See also the committee's report in *New York Tribune,* July 22, 1867.

34. Silvestro, "None but Patriots," 249–53, 258; *Great Republic,* Jan. 31, Mar. 21, May 23, June 13, 1867.

35. J. M. Edmunds to Marcus Ward, June 5, 1867, Union League of

America circular, with notation from Edmunds to Ward, May 23, 1867, Ward Papers; Edmunds to William Claflin, Apr. 29, 1867, Claflin Papers.

36. Silvestro, "None but Patriots," 348–49; J. M. Edmunds to William Sprague, July 11, Aug. 7, 1867, Sprague Papers.

37. *Washington Morning Chronicle*, July 17, 18, 1867; *Great Republic*, May 16, 1867; Silvestro, "None but Patriots," 280–98.

38. A copy of the law, dated March 14, 1867, can be found in the McPherson Papers; see also *Washington Morning Chronicle*, Mar. 28, 1867.

39. Charles Whittlesey to Edward McPherson, Mar. 4, 1867, McPherson Papers; *Great Republic*, Jan. 10, 1867; *Washington Morning Chronicle*, Mar. 20, Apr. 12, June 19, Oct. 23, 1867.

40. The McPherson Papers are full of correspondence, especially in 1867 and 1868, bearing on this point. See also *New York Tribune*, July 9, 1867.

41. For an overview of Reconstruction legislation relating to the army, see Sefton, *United States Army and Reconstruction*; see also Mantell, *Johnson, Grant, and the Politics of Reconstruction*.

42. Thomas and Hyman, *Stanton*, 530–31.

43. Sefton, *United States Army and Reconstruction*, 128–35; Thomas and Hyman, *Stanton*, 533–40.

44. Tod R. Caldwell to J. W. Broomall, July 8, 1867, Hayes Library, Fremont, Ohio; Thomas and Hyman, *Stanton*, 539; W. W. Holden to William McPherson, July 6, 1867, McPherson Papers; *Congressional Globe*, 40th Cong., 1st sess., 527–33; Benedict, *Compromise of Principle*, 252–55.

45. *Congressional Globe*, 40th Cong., 1st sess., 554; Benjamin S. Hedrick to Jonathan Worth, July 12, 1867, Worth Papers.

46. Foulke, *Life of Oliver P. Morton*, 2:35; Russ, "Registration and Disfranchisement under Radical Reconstruction," 176–79. James M. McPherson estimates that 10 to 15 percent of the potential white electorate was disfranchised under the Reconstruction Acts; see McPherson, *Ordeal by Fire*, 535. Wood, in his "On Revising Reconstruction History," argues that at the most disfranchisement could not have exceeded one hundred thousand whites and was not responsible for creating a black majority in any state.

47. R. W. Flournoy to Benjamin Butler, Apr. 8, 1867, Butler Papers; Isaac Murphy to General John Logan, Dec. 2, 1867, in House Select Committee on Reconstruction, Arkansas, 40th Cong.; Robert Dick to J. D. Cox, July 6, 1867, Sherman Papers; Perman, *Reunion without Compromise*, 306; *Great Republic*, Feb. 7, 1867.

48. J. M. Caleb Wiley to William P. Fessenden, Mar. 4, July 14, 1867, Fessenden Papers; L. P. Gudger to Benjamin Wade, July 8, 1867, Wade Papers; J. D. Bell to Benjamin Butler, Mar. 20, 1867, C. H. Woodman to Butler, July 22, 1867, and Butler's reply, Aug. 5, 1867, Butler Papers; W. J. Loftin to Charles Sumner, Feb. 25, 1867, F. L. Claiborne to Sumner, Mar. 10, 1867, Sumner Papers; W. D. Bloxham to Lyman Trumbull, July 26, 1867, Trumbull Papers; Warden, *Private Life and Public Services of Salmon Portland Chase*, 668. See also the large number of letters in the John Sherman Papers in March and April 1867 seeking clarification of the disfranchising clauses.

49. Pope's letter quoted in Cash, "Alabama Republicans during Reconstruction," 84; Swayne's letter quoted in Wiggins, *Scalawag in Alabama Politics*, 29; Sickles's letter quoted in *Harper's Weekly*, July 27, 1867, p. 467; Nelson Miles to Charles Sumner, July 13, 1867, Sumner Papers.

50. Sefton, *United States Army and Reconstruction*, 118, 130–31, 137; Charles W. Clarke to John Covode, Aug. 31, 1867, Covode Papers; William Leahy to Benjamin Butler, July 9, 1867, and Butler's response, July 15, Butler Papers.

51. Sefton, *United States Army and Reconstruction*, 130–44, 156–57; Moneyhon, *Republicanism in Reconstruction Texas*, 67–72; Taylor, *Louisiana Reconstructed*, 139–41; Richter, " 'We Must Rubb Outt and Begin Anew,' " 334–41; Dawson, "General Phil Sheridan and Military Reconstruction in Louisiana."

52. Sefton, *United States Army and Reconstruction*, 137–39, 148–49; John Pope to Robert Schenck, May 20, 1867, Schenck Papers.

53. Sefton, *United States Army and Reconstruction*, 118–19, 174; R. W. Flournoy to General Ord, May 7, 1867, and Flournoy to Benjamin Butler, May 23, 1867, W. B. Padgett to Benjamin Butler, Mar. 9, 1867, all in Butler Papers; Charles W. Clarke to John Covode, Aug. 31, 1867, Covode Papers; James A. Butler to Richard Yates, July 5, 1867, Yates Papers; E. O. C. Ord to Zachariah Chandler, Sept. 16, 1867, Zachariah Chandler Papers; Harris, *Day of the Carpetbagger*, 106–7.

54. McDonough, "John Schofield," 246–47; Cox, "Military Reconstruction in Florida," 226–27.

55. Cox and Cox, "General O. O. Howard and the 'Misrepresented Bureau,' " 442–43.

56. There is now a large body of literature on the Freedmen's Bureau, some of which discusses its political activities. Generally, Cox and Cox, in "General O. O. Howard and the 'Misrepresented Bureau,' " and Carpenter, *Sword and Olive Branch*, defend the bureau from charges that it was heavily engaged in partisan politics, whereas George Bentley's *History of the Freedmen's Bureau* presents evidence of its commitment to the Republican party.

57. Bentley, *History of the Freedmen's Bureau*, 187–94; Langston, *From the Virginia Plantation to the National Capitol*, 263–92; O. O. Howard to officers and agents of the Freedmen's Bureau, Apr. 12, 1867, Thomas Tullock to Howard, May 15, 1867, and Howard to E. B. Ward, Oct. 7, 1868, all in Howard Papers; O. O. Howard to Thomas Tullock, June 6, 1867, in Records of the Bureau of Refugees, Freedmen, and Abandoned Land, Letters Sent, 3:261.

58. Thomas W. Conway to General Howard, Apr. 26, May 14, 1867, and Howard to Conway, May 11, 1867, in Howard Papers; White, "Wager Swayne," 93–100; Hume, "The Freedmen's Bureau and the Freedmen's Vote in the Reconstruction of Southern Alabama"; Willard Warner to John Sherman, Dec. 19, 1867, and Wager Swayne to Sherman, Dec. 28, 1867, Sherman Papers; Bethel, "Freedmen's Bureau in Alabama," 74–75, 82; Perman, *Reunion without Compromise*, 304; Kolchin, *First Freedom*, 156, 161, 174.

59. Bentley, *History of the Freedmen's Bureau*, 190–94; Muggleston, ed., "Freedmen's Bureau and Reconstruction in Virginia," 46–48, 64–65, 79, 81; *Great Republic*, July 16, 1867; Taylor, *Negro in Tennessee*, 54; Patton, *Unionism*

and Reconstruction in Tennessee, 127; Alexander, *Political Reconstruction in Tennessee,* 146; Phillips, "History of the Freedmen's Bureau in Tennessee," 60–62, 85, 296–97.

60. Bentley, *History of the Freedmen's Bureau,* 192, 198; Abbott, *Freedmen's Bureau in South Carolina,* 31–35; Nathans, *Losing the Peace,* 19–20.

61. White, *Freedmen's Bureau in Louisiana,* 25, 27–28; Bentley, *History of the Freedmen's Bureau,* 195; J. A. Mower to O. O. Howard, May 30, 1867, and Howard to Mower, June 6, 1867, Howard Papers.

62. Bentley, *History of the Freedmen's Bureau,* 192, 198–99; Alvord to Pease, Nov. 2, 1867, Records of the Educational Division, Bureau of Refugees, Freedmen, and Abandoned Land; Eliphalet Whittlesey to General Gillem, Aug. 7, 1867, Records of the Bureau of Refugees, Freedmen, and Abandoned Land, Letters Sent, 3:427; O. O. Howard to General Gillem, Aug. 8, 1867, ibid., 3:431.

63. On the limits of the Freedmen's Bureau as a political machine for the Republican party, see Abbott, *Freedmen's Bureau in South Carolina,* 31–35; Cash, "Alabama Republicans during Reconstruction," 90; Shofner, *Nor Is It Over Yet,* 79; Patton, *Unionism and Reconstruction in Tennessee,* 160–61; May, "Freedmen's Bureau at the Local Level," 10; Carpenter, *Sword and Olive Branch,* 144–45.

64. Dawson, "Army Generals and Reconstruction," 261–69; Richter, " 'We Must Rubb Outt and Begin Anew,' " 334–41; Sefton, *United States Army and Reconstruction,* 163, 175–77; Thomas Conway to Thomas L. Tullock, Dec. 10, 1867, Benjamin Butler Papers.

65. Heyman, "The 'Great Reconstructor,' " 52–80; Mantell, *Johnson, Grant, and the Politics of Reconstruction,* 76; Sefton, *United States Army and Reconstruction,* 170–72, 183–84; George G. Meade to Henry Wilson, Jan. 9, 1868, Wilson Papers; W. H. Watson to Richard Yates, Dec. 30, 1867, Yates Papers.

66. Dawson, "Army Generals and Reconstruction," 261–64; Bentley, *History of the Freedmen's Bureau,* 197–98; Sefton, *United States Army and Reconstruction,* 163.

67. *Cincinnati Gazette,* July 3, 1867, quoted in Russ, "Congressional Disfranchisement," 270.

68. Coulter, *William G. Brownlow,* 333–34; *Washington Morning Chronicle,* Feb. 4, 1867; W. G. Brownlow to Amos Lawrence, May 5, 1867, Lawrence Papers; Richard Yates to H. H. Thomas, May 16, 1867, Yates Papers; *Boston Traveller,* June 14, 1867.

69. Alexander, *Political Reconstruction in Tennessee,* 142–45; *Washington Morning Chronicle,* Jan. 22, Feb. 4, 1867; Owens, "Union League of America," 46–47; Coulter, *William G. Brownlow,* 331; *Boston Traveller,* Aug. 6, 1867.

70. *Washington Morning Chronicle,* Aug. 3, 1867; *Boston Traveller,* Aug. 3, 1867; *Boston Commonwealth,* Aug. 10, 24, Sept. 14, 1867; Marcus Ward to Elihu B. Washburne, Aug. 7, 1867, Washburne Papers; see also *New York Tribune,* Aug. 3, 1867, and *Harper's Weekly,* Aug. 17, 1867, p. 514.

71. *Nation,* Aug. 15, 1867, quoted in Russ, "Congressional Disfranchisement," 269; R. W. Flournoy to Benjamin Butler, June 25, 1867, Butler Papers;

Washington Morning Chronicle, June 20, 24, 26, 29, July 1, Oct. 9, 1867; Rawley, *Edwin D. Morgan*, 227; A. T. Stone to Richard Yates, July 25, 1867, Yates Papers; Daniel R. Goodloe to Charles Sumner, May 4, 1867, Sumner Papers.

72. *Great Republic*, Aug. 6, 1867; Rawley, *Edwin D. Morgan*, 225; Circular of Union Congressional Committee, Aug. 23, 1867, in Ward Papers; Robert Schenck to Zachariah Chandler, May 8, 1867, Zachariah Chandler Papers; Thomas Tullock to Dear Sir, Sept. 13, 1867, and Union League circular, dated Sept. 23, 1867, both in Morgan Papers; Henry S. Vanderbilt to General Schenck, Aug. 19, 23, 1867, Thomas Tullock to T. W. Conway, Sept. 11, 1867, Tullock to George F. Edmunds, Sept. 19, 1867, Tullock to Robert Schenck, [Sept.], Oct. 16, 1867, and circular of Sept. 12, 1867, signed by Tullock, all in Schenck Papers; Edward Atkinson to Thomas Tullock, Aug. 9, 1867, Atkinson Papers; J. M. Edmunds to General Howard, Oct. 12, 1867, Howard Papers.

73. Benedict, "Rout of Radicalism," 334–44; Current, *Old Thad Stevens*, 304.

74. McPherson, *Ordeal by Fire*, 535; *Washington Morning Chronicle*, Oct. 29, 1867; *Boston Traveller*, Oct. 11, 1867; James A. Butler to Richard Yates, Nov. 17, Dec. 8, 1867, Yates Papers.

75. *Boston Traveller*, Dec. 5, 1867; *Washington Morning Chronicle*, Dec. 6, 1867; Thomas Tullock to E. D. Morgan, Nov. 30, 1867, Morgan Papers.

76. *Washington Morning Chronicle*, Oct. 28, Nov. 15, 25, 1867; *New York Tribune*, Dec. 5, 1867. On the work of the Union League in registering black voters in 1867 for the Republican party, see Silvestro, "None but Patriots," 326–30, 334–45.

CHAPTER 5

1. Silvestro, "None but Patriots," 303–5, 330–38.

2. *Great Republic*, May 23, 1867; *Washington Morning Chronicle*, Apr. 24, 1867.

3. *Boston Daily Advertiser*, July 18, 1867; *Great Republic*, May 2, 1867.

4. *Congressional Globe*, 39th Cong., 2d sess., 1178, 1644; *Great Republic*, Jan. 24, 1867; *New York Tribune*, Nov. 21, 1867; *Washington Morning Chronicle*, Dec. 12, 1866.

5. Owens, "Union League of America," 88–89, 91–92; Raper, "William Woods Holden," 192–200; Staples, *Reconstruction in Arkansas*, 109–10, 115, 119–20.

6. Hoffman, "Republican Party in North Carolina," 25–30; Olsen, *Carpetbagger's Crusade*, 70; Hamilton, *Reconstruction in North Carolina*, 240–43; McPherson, *Political History of the United States*, 251–52.

7. *Boston Commonwealth*, Apr. 6, 1867; *Nation*, Apr. 4, 1867.

8. Staples, *Reconstruction in Arkansas*, 166–71.

9. See Maddex, *Virginia Conservatives*, esp. pp. 49–50.

10. John Minor Botts to My Dear Sir, Mar. 8, 1867, Sumner Papers; *Boston Daily Advertiser*, Apr. 9, 1867.

11. E. L. Van Lew to John Andrew, Apr. 1, 1867, Andrew Papers; Ambler, *Francis H. Pierpont*, 288–89; Eckenrode, *Political History of Virginia during the Reconstruction*, 68–70.

12. *New York Times*, Apr. 7, 1867; *Richmond Times*, Apr. 6, 1867; *Washington Morning Chronicle*, Mar. 28, 1867.

13. *Great Republic*, May 2, 1867; Maddex, *Virginia Conservatives*, 50; Lowe, "Republicans, Rebellion, and Reconstruction," 254–55.

14. *Boston Daily Advertiser*, Apr. 23, 1867; *Boston Traveller*, Apr. 19, 23, 24, 30, 1867.

15. Lowe, "Republicans, Rebellion, and Reconstruction," 256–60; *New York Tribune*, Apr. 12, May 20, 1867.

16. *New York Tribune* quoted in *Richmond Enquirer*, Apr. 15, 1867; see also *Richmond Enquirer*, Apr. 17, 23, 25, 1867; *Washington Morning Chronicle*, Apr. 23, 1867.

17. *Richmond Enquirer*, Apr. 20, 1867; *Washington Morning Chronicle*, Apr. 24, 1867; *New York Times*, Apr. 22, 24, 1867.

18. On Wilson's tour, see Abbott, *Cobbler in Congress*, 186–91.

19. *Augusta Daily Press*, May 9, 1867; *Charleston Daily News*, May 4, 1867; *Richmond Enquirer*, May 23, 1867.

20. *Charleston Daily News*, May 4, 1867; *Charleston Courier*, May 3, 1867; *New Orleans Republican*, May 17, 1867; *New York Tribune*, Apr. 25, 1867.

21. *Charleston Mercury*, Apr. 22, 1867; *Raleigh Tri-Weekly Standard*, May 4, 1867; *Richmond Enquirer*, May 8, 10, 1867; *National Anti-Slavery Standard*, June 15, 1867.

22. *New Orleans Republican*, May 17, 1867; *Charleston Daily News*, May 4, 1867.

23. Fleming, *Civil War and Reconstruction in Alabama*, 508–9; *Boston Commonwealth*, May 11, June 15, 1867; Edwin Morgan to Zachariah Chandler, May 24, 1867, Morgan Papers.

24. *New Orleans Crescent* quoted in *Richmond Enquirer*, May 23, 1867; *Charleston Daily News*, May 6, 1867; *Raleigh Tri-Weekly Standard*, Apr. 30, 1867; B. S. Hedrick to Dear Wife, May 9, 1867, Hedrick Papers.

25. *New York Tribune*, Apr. 30, 1867; J. A. Brisbin to Benjamin Wade, Apr. 30, 1867, with notation from Wade to Zachariah Chandler, Zachariah Chandler Papers; *Boston Commonwealth*, May 25, 1867; *Cincinnati Gazette*, July 3, 1867, quoted in Russ, "Congressional Disfranchisement," 270.

26. *New York Tribune*, Apr. 12, 1867; *Boston Evening Journal* quoted in Benedict, *Compromise of Principle*, 259; *Harper's Weekly*, May 4, 1867, p. 274; J. H. Brisbin to Benjamin Wade, Apr. 30, 1867, Zachariah Chandler Papers.

27. W. D. Kelley to Rutherford B. Hayes, Dec. 17, 1876, quoted in De-Santis, *Republicans Face the Southern Question*, 28; *Washington Morning Chronicle*, May 22, 1867; *Boston Daily Advertiser*, Apr. 26, 1867; *New York Tribune*, May 21, 27, June 10, 1867; Kemp Battle to B. S. Hedrick, May 13, July 5, 1867, Hedrick Papers.

28. *New York Tribune*, May 23, 1867; *Boston Daily Advertiser*, May 25, 1867; *Nation*, May 30, 1867, p. 425; *Boston Commonwealth*, May 25, 1867.

29. Henry Wilson to J. M. Edmunds, May 4, 1867, Rare Book Room, Bos-

ton Public Library, Boston, Massachusetts; *New York Tribune*, May 4, 1867; *Washington Morning Chronicle*, May 4, 8, June 12, 1867; Lowe, "Republicans, Rebellion, and Reconstruction," 263–64.

30. Charles Weyman to John Andrew, May 3, 1867, Andrew Papers; Edward Atkinson to Henry Wilson, July 9, 1866, and Atkinson to Hugh McCulloch, Aug. 7, 1867, Atkinson Papers; *Boston Commonwealth*, June 15, 1867; *Boston Daily Advertiser*, Apr. 9, July 9, 1867; Benedict, *Compromise of Principle*, 263–64.

31. John Andrew to John Binney, Sept. 10, 1867, Andrew Papers; John Murray Forbes to George H. Boker, June 8, 1867, in Hughes, ed., *Letters of John Murray Forbes*, 3:93–94.

32. Union League Club of New York, *Report of Proceedings of Conference in Richmond*, 3–13; Lowe, "Republicans, Rebellion, and Reconstruction," 264–65.

33. *Nation*, July 18, 1867, pp. 42, 50; *Washington Morning Chronicle*, May 25, July 31, 1867; *National Anti-Slavery Standard*, May 4, 1867.

34. *Boston Commonwealth*, May 4, 1867; *Philadelphia Press*, June 14, 1867; Foner, ed., *Life and Writings of Frederick Douglass*, 4:78, 191.

35. *National Anti-Slavery Standard*, Apr. 6, May 11, 1867.

36. *Washington Morning Chronicle*, May 24, Oct. 23, 1867; *Great Republic*, June 20, July 26, 1867; *Boston Traveller*, Aug. 6, 1867.

37. *New York Tribune*, June 12, 1867. In his perceptive analysis of Southern Reconstruction politics, Michael Perman has argued that Southern Republicans had two options in recruiting a constituency: they could follow a "centrist" approach, seeking to conciliate whites, particularly the wealthy and influential ones, through a policy of economic moderation, or a "radical" approach geared to the needs of the masses of poor blacks and any poor whites who might be brought into the party. The Republicans, he notes, chose not to make a class appeal to poor whites. They did not believe that economic or class appeals to interest groups would work and did not attempt them. Instead, they adopted the centrist approach, which was based on an elitist conception of politics that argued that if leading whites could be enticed into the Republican ranks, the masses of whites would follow. See Perman, *Road to Redemption*, 25–26, 104–7.

Perman's insight, derived from his study of Southern Republicans, seems to me perfectly applicable to the Northern Republicans who hoped to organize white support in the South. With few exceptions, they too eschewed a class approach to the South and instead courted the support of significant Southern white leaders in the belief that they would bring a substantial white following with them into the Republican party. Hence, as Perman says, they neglected grass-roots mobilization of voters in favor of courting an elite.

Eric Foner has also discussed these options facing the Republicans in the South. He distinguishes between the "modernizers," who hoped to mold the South along Northern lines by bringing in railroads, industry, and a diversified economy, and "redistributionists," who wanted to use the state governments to promote land redistribution or in other ways to help the poor of both races. He notes that the state parties in the South generally followed the lead of the modernizers and also points out that Northern Republicans were not in sympathy with the plans of the redistributionists. Foner does, however, see some evidence of the "first stirring of class politics within the white community," which later manifested itself in the Populist party revolt of the 1890s. See Foner, *Politics and Ideology,* 113–25. See also Summers, *Railroads, Reconstruction, and the Gospel of Prosperity,* for a thorough study of the philosophy and program of the modernizers.

Elizabeth Nathans, in her study of Georgia Republicans, argues that the party failed in that state because it did choose to appeal to small white farmers rather than bidding for support from more business-oriented elements in the state. See Nathans, *Losing the Peace.* Otto Olsen, however, has argued that the Republicans failed in the South because they did not undertake a more radical program of appealing to poorer whites and attempting more vigorously to protect their black voters from Ku Klux Klan violence. See Olsen, "Reconsidering the Scalawags," 317–18, and his review of Nathans's book in *Civil War History* 15 (June 1969): 184–86.

38. Thomas Tullock to Robert Schenck, Aug. 4, 1867, Schenck Papers; *National Anti-Slavery Standard,* Aug. 24, 1867; *Richmond Whig* quoted in Smith, "Virginia during Reconstruction," 58; *Washington Morning Chronicle,* Aug. 2, 3, 1867; Lowe, "Republicans, Rebellion, and Reconstruction," 270–76.

39. Wiggins, *Scalawag in Alabama Politics,* 19–20; *Washington Morning Chronicle,* Mar. 15, 1867; *Philadelphia Press* quoted in *Chronicle,* Apr. 18, 1867.

40. Wiggins, *Scalawag in Alabama Politics,* 22–23; Schweninger, "Alabama Blacks and the Congressional Reconstruction Acts of 1867," 183–97.

41. Taylor, *Louisiana Reconstructed,* 145–47; J. R. G. Pitkin to Benjamin Butler, July 6, 1867, Butler Papers; L. S. Allard to Richard Yates, July 1, 1867, Yates Papers; *Boston Commonwealth,* Dec. 28, 1867.

42. Taylor, *Louisiana Reconstructed,* 147–48; *Great Republic,* May 23, 1867.

43. *Washington Morning Chronicle,* June 13, 1867; *Boston Commonwealth,* June 15, 1867; *New York Tribune,* June 11, 1867; Sanger and Hay, *James Longstreet,* 332–33, 636.

44. Parks, *Joseph E. Brown of Georgia,* 365–66, 388–89; Nathans, *Losing the Peace,* 40–44.

45. Parks, *Joseph E. Brown of Georgia,* 375–76; *Cincinnati Commercial* quoted in Roberts, *Joseph E. Brown and the Politics of Reconstruction,* 47.

46. Shofner, *Nor Is It Over Yet,* 165–67; Richardson, *Negro in the Reconstruction of Florida,* 141–48; C. D. Lincoln to William Pitt Fessenden, Sept. 20, 1867, Fessenden Papers; Thomas Tullock to Robert Schenck, Sept. 20, 1867, Schenck Papers.

47. *Boston Daily Advertiser,* May 13, 1867; Scroggs, "Carpetbagger Influence," 72; Holt, *Black over White,* 18, 26–27; *Charleston Daily Courier,* July 26, 30, 1867; *Washington Morning Chronicle,* May 31, July 25, 26, 27, Aug. 16, 1867; Williamson, *After Slavery,* 340.

48. Harris, *Day of the Carpetbagger,* 104–6; *Great Republic,* June 13, 1867; on Lynch, see Harris, "James Lynch," 40–61.

49. *New York Tribune,* Sept. 9, 1867; Scroggs, "Carpetbagger Influence," 94,

94n.; J. M. Edmunds to J. Henry Harris, Mar. 26, 1867, Harris Papers.

50. Moneyhon, *Republicanism in Reconstruction Texas*, 62–66.

51. Lowe, "Republicans, Rebellion, and Reconstruction," 281–82; Alderson, "Influence of Military Rule and the Freedmen's Bureau on Reconstruction in Virginia," 131–32, 149, 185, 194–95; Bentley, *History of the Freedmen's Bureau*, 189; C. H. Lewis to Henry Wilson, Nov. 19, 1867, Wilson Papers; Orlando Brown to O. O. Howard, June 13, 1867, Howard Papers.

52. Harris, *Day of the Carpetbagger*, 2–7, 67–72; John Pope to Robert Schenck, May 20, 1867, Schenck Papers; Scroggs, "Carpetbagger Influence," 72; *Great Republic*, Aug. 2, 1867; Shofner, *Nor Is It Over Yet*, 169; Bentley, "Political Activity of the Freedmen's Bureau in Florida," 32–34.

53. Nathans, *Losing the Peace*, 24–25; McDaniel, "Georgia Carpetbagger," 112–13; John Forney to Edward McPherson, Mar. 13, 1867, R. B. Bullock to McPherson, Mar. 19, 1867, E. H. Pughe to McPherson, Mar. 20, Apr. 6, 1867, William L. Scruggs to McPherson, Apr. 3, 1867, Foster Blodgett to McPherson, Nov. 30, 1867, McPherson Papers; T. P. Robb to John D. Strong, May 20, Oct. 2, 1867, Strong Papers.

54. A. G. Murray to Edward McPherson, Mar. 2, 1867, J. E. Bryant to McPherson, Aug. 1, 1867, William L. Scruggs to McPherson, Jan. 14, 1868, McPherson Papers.

55. Parks, *Joseph E. Brown of Georgia*, 371, 388–89; Samuel Bard to Richard Yates, Nov. 24, Dec. 9, 1867, Yates Papers; Yates to Edward McPherson, Aug. 31, 1867, C. L. Culbert to McPherson, Oct. 19, 1868, John Pope to Richard Yates, Nov. 30, 1867, all in McPherson Papers; John Pope to Robert Schenck, May 20, 1867, Schenck Papers; Joseph Brown to John Sherman, Mar. 22, Apr. 6, 1867, Sherman Papers; *Washington Morning Chronicle*, Nov. 30, 1867.

56. Harris, *Day of the Carpetbagger*, 142, 142n., 185, 187; Oliver P. Morton to Edward McPherson, Mar. 22, 1867, W. H. Christy to McPherson, Mar. 22, 1867, Harrison Reed to McPherson, Oct. 14, 1867, J. R. Smith to McPherson, Feb. 26, 1869, McPherson Papers; Shofner, *Nor Is It Over Yet*, 173; Olsen, *Carpetbagger's Crusade*, 72–74; Albion Tourgée to Benjamin Wade, Mar. 29, 1867, Wade Papers.

57. James W. Hunnicutt to Charles Sumner, [July 1867], McPherson Papers; Alderson, "Influence of Military Rule and the Freedmen's Bureau on Reconstruction in Virginia," 170n., 235; Taylor, *Louisiana Reconstructed*, 149–51, 156–57; Warmoth, *War, Politics, and Reconstruction*, 32.

58. *Washington Morning Chronicle*, Oct. 15, 1867; *Harper's Weekly*, Oct. 12, 1867, p. 643; *National Anti-Slavery Standard*, July 20, 1867; *Boston Daily Advertiser*, May 17, 1867; *New York Tribune*, June 25, Oct. 8, 1867; *Congressional Globe*, 40th Cong., 1st sess., 145.

59. *New York Tribune*, Sept. 4, 1867; see Schenck Papers for Tullock's calculations of registration and voting in each Southern state.

60. McPherson, *Ordeal by Fire*, 535.

61. Except for Virginia, the votes in the Southern elections were not recorded by race. Hence the white vote has been estimated, based on various contemporary sources. For such estimates, see Mantell, *Johnson, Grant, and*

the Politics of Reconstruction, 48–49; McPherson, Political History of the United States, 374; Rhodes, History of the United States, 6:196. In Arkansas neither the voting registration nor the vote was broken down by race; contemporary estimates put the white Republican vote at around nine thousand. See Ellenberg, "Reconstruction in Arkansas," 60. Approximately fifty-four thousand white Arkansans cast ballots in the 1860 election; allowing for failures to register and disfranchisement, the white Republican vote might have represented 20 to 25 percent of the white vote in 1867. On Texas, see Moneyhon, *Republicanism in Reconstruction Texas*, 80–81; on Georgia, see Nathans, *Losing the Peace*, 54–55.

62. Mantell, *Johnson, Grant, and the Politics of Reconstruction*, 48–49; New York Tribune, Oct. 26, 31, Nov. 21, 25, 1867; Harper's Weekly, Nov. 9, 1867, p. 706.

63. Washington Morning Chronicle, Nov. 15, 1867; Boston Traveller, Oct. 11, 1867; Albany Evening Journal and New York Times, both quoted in National Anti-Slavery Standard, Nov. 23, 1867.

64. Benedict, Fruits of Victory, 39; Horace Binney to William Pitt Fessenden, Nov. 2, 1867, Fessenden Papers.

65. Washington Morning Chronicle, Nov. 25, 29, 1867; Nation, Nov. 21, 1867, p. 405, and Nov. 28, 1867, p. 427.

66. Mantell, *Johnson, Grant, and the Politics of Reconstruction*, 73–74; New York Times, quoted in National Anti-Slavery Standard, Nov. 23, 1867; John Binney to William Pitt Fessenden, Nov. 15, Dec. 19, 1867, Fessenden Papers; New York Tribune, Nov. 20, 1867; Harper's Weekly, Nov. 23, 1867, p. 738.

67. Nation, Oct. 31, 1867, p. 354; Boston Traveller, Dec. 5, 1867.

68. Mantell, *Johnson, Grant, and the Politics of Reconstruction*, 76–77; Boston Advertiser quoted in Washington Morning Chronicle, Dec. 16, 1867; Nation, Dec. 19, 1867, p. 495, Mar. 26, 1868, p. 242; New York Times, Nov. 18, 1867; Boston Traveller, Nov. 16, Dec. 6, 1867; Fleming, Civil War and Reconstruction in Alabama, 520–27.

69. Wiggins, Scalawag in Alabama Politics, 27; Washington Morning Chronicle, Nov. 11, 15, 20, 22, 1867; New York Times, Nov. 15, 1867.

70. Joseph Medill to E. B. Washburne, Jan. 10, 1868, Washburne Papers; Wiggins, Scalawag in Alabama Politics, 36–37; Huntsville Advocate quoted in Washington Morning Chronicle, Dec. 28, 1867; Wilson letters in Farish, "An Overlooked Personality in Southern Life," 341–53.

71. Washington Morning Chronicle, Nov. 25, Dec. 11, 1867; New York Tribune, Dec. 7, 14, 1867; Harper's Weekly, Dec. 28, 1867, p. 818; John Murray Forbes to Charles Nordhoff, Jan. 20, 1868, in Hughes, ed., Letters of John Murray Forbes, 3:107.

72. Philadelphia Press quoted in Washington Morning Chronicle, Nov. 28, 1867; ibid., Dec. 16, 1867; Nation, Mar. 26, 1868, p. 242; New York Times, Feb. 8, 1869; W. B. Rodman to David M. Carter, Jan. 23, Mar. 10, 1868, Carter Papers.

73. Washington Morning Chronicle, Nov. 15, 1867, Jan. 29, 31, 1868.

74. Ibid., July 13, 1868; New York Times, Nov. 16, 1867; Nation, Mar. 26,

1868, p. 242; Lamson, *Glorious Failure,* 55; Thomas Conway to O. O. Howard, Jan. 5, 1868, Howard Papers; Conway to Thomas Tullock, Dec. 10, 1867, Butler Papers; Taylor, *Louisiana Reconstructed,* 147–55.

75. Mantell, *Johnson, Grant, and the Politics of Reconstruction,* 74; Harris, *Day of the Carpetbagger,* 74; Harris, "Mississippi," 79–80; W. H. Gibbs to E. B. Washburne, Sept. 30, Nov. 26, 1867, Washburne Papers; *Washington Morning Chronicle,* July 13, 1867.

76. Nathans, *Losing the Peace,* 65–68, 104; *Washington Morning Chronicle,* June 5, 1868; B. M. Long and J. W. Steward to Thaddeus Stevens, W. E. Kelley, and others, May 15, 1868; E. H. L. Deister to Stevens, May 18, 1868, and Jonathan McGunn to Stevens, May 26, 1868, all in Stevens Papers.

77. Shofner, *Nor Is It Over Yet,* 172–78; Daniel Richards to E. B. Washburne, Nov. 11, 19, 1867, Washburne Papers; Bentley, "Political Activity of the Freedmen's Bureau in Florida," 34–35.

78. Shofner, *Nor Is It Over Yet,* 179–83.

79. Ibid., 182–87; Shofner, "Florida," 41; Edward M. Cheney to Thomas Tullock, May 26, 1868, Records of House Select Committee on Reconstruction, Florida, 40th Cong.

80. Shofner, *Nor Is It Over Yet,* 186–88; Daniel Richards to E. B. Washburne, Jan. 27, Feb. 2, 11, Apr. 2, 8, 21, 29, May 28, 1868, Washburne Papers; Daniel Richards to Thaddeus Stevens, May 25, 1868, S. L. Robinson to Stevens, May 29, 1868, Stevens Papers; *Washington Morning Chronicle,* Mar. 20, 1868.

81. *Nation,* Oct. 31, 1867, p. 354; *Boston Daily Advertiser* quoted in *Washington Morning Chronicle,* Nov. 11, 1867; *Boston Commonwealth,* Nov. 2, 1867; *New York Tribune,* Nov. 9, 1867; John C. Underwood to Horace Greeley, Nov. 27, 1867, Greeley Papers.

82. E. B. Washburne to John Underwood, Dec. 7, 1867, Jan. 6, 1868, and Schuyler Colfax to Underwood, Jan. 7, 1867, Underwood Papers, LC; Underwood to E. B. Washburne, Dec. 9, 16, 1867, Jan. 4, 1868, Washburne Papers.

83. E. B. Washburne to John Underwood, Dec. 7, 1867, Underwood Papers, LC; Lowe, "Republicans, Rebellion, and Reconstruction," 295–96.

84. *Boston Traveller,* Dec. 20, 1867; *New York Times,* Dec. 19, 1867, Jan. 3, 1868; *Washington Morning Chronicle,* Dec. 12, 1867, Jan. 15, 17, 1868; *New York Tribune,* Dec. 10, 1867; *Nation,* Jan. 16, 1868, p. 42.

85. "Winegar" in *National Anti-Slavery Standard,* Jan. 4, 1868; Alderson, "Influence of Military Rule and the Freedmen's Bureau on the Reconstruction of Virginia," 202–4.

86. Scroggs, "Carpetbagger Influence," 186; McPherson, *Ordeal by Fire,* 536–37.

87. E. M. McPherson quoted in Trefousse, *Impeachment of a President,* 113; *New York Tribune,* Jan. 20, 1868; *Harper's Weekly,* Apr. 25, 1868, p. 258; *Nation,* May 21, 1868, pp. 405–6; John Murray Forbes to Charles Nordhoff, Jan. 20, 1868, in Hughes, ed., *Letters of John Murray Forbes,* 3:107.

CHAPTER 6

1. Trefousse, *Impeachment of a President*, 118–19, 140–42, 159–60.
2. Benedict, *Compromise of Principle*, 246–56, 279–87.
3. Ibid., 289–90; Foster Blodgett to William Pitt Fessenden, Dec. 30, 1867, Fessenden Papers; B. W. Norris to Dear Sir, Jan. 4, 1868, Records of House Select Committee on Reconstruction, Alabama, 40th Cong.; Bentley, *History of the Freedmen's Bureau*, 196–97; Milton J. Saffold to Thaddeus Stevens, Mar. 2, 1868, Stevens Papers; W. J. Morgan to Benjamin Wade, Mar. 10, 1868, Wade Papers; J. Tarbell to Benjamin Butler, Mar. 15, 1868, Butler Papers.
4. James Butler to Richard Yates, Jan. 1, 1868, Yates Papers; M. D. Brainard to Benjamin Butler, Mar. 23, 1868, Butler Papers; W. H. Gibbs to E. B. Washburne, Jan. 29, Feb. 3, 1868, Washburne Papers; E. J. Castello to Robert Schenck, Dec. 17, 1867, Records of House Select Committee on Reconstruction, Mississippi, 40th Cong.; Thomas Conway to Robert Schenck, Dec. 9, 1867, Records of House Select Committee on Reconstruction, Louisiana, 40th Cong.; Scroggs, "Carpetbagger Influence," 116–17.
5. George Ely to E. B. Washburne, Feb. 9, 1868, C. W. Buckley to Washburne, May 1, 1868, Washburne Papers; Ely to Richard Yates, Feb. 12, 1868, Yates Papers; John Bornier to W. P. Fessenden, May 12, 1868, Fessenden Papers; Wiggins, *Scalawag in Alabama Politics*, 21; *Washington Morning Chronicle*, Feb. 19, 21, 1868.
6. Fleming, *Civil War and Reconstruction in Alabama*, 493–96; Sefton, *United States Army and Reconstruction*, 185; Cash, "Alabama Republicans during Reconstruction," 103–4; *Harper's Weekly*, Apr. 11, 1868, p. 226; Daniel Sickles to Lyman Trumbull, July 5, 1867, quoted in *New York Tribune*, July 10, 1867.
7. Benedict, *Compromise of Principle*, 290–93; John Binney to William Pitt Fessenden, Dec. 30, 1867, Fessenden Papers.
8. Thomas Conway to Thomas Tullock, Feb. 13, 1868, quoted in *Washington Morning Chronicle*, Feb. 15, 1868; ibid., Feb. 13, 1868; E. J. Castello to Tullock, Jan. 17, 1868, Records of House Select Committee on Reconstruction, Mississippi, 40th Cong.
9. Trefousse, *Impeachment of a President*, 120–25, 140–42; Mantell, *Johnson, Grant, and the Politics of Reconstruction*, 87.
10. Mantell, *Johnson, Grant, and the Politics of Reconstruction*, 96–97.
11. John Pope to Robert Schenck, May 20, 1867, Schenck Papers.
12. John Binney to John Andrew, Sept. 13, 1867, Andrew Papers; Binney to William Pitt Fessenden, Nov. 15, 1867, Fessenden Papers; *Washington Morning Chronicle*, Oct. 18, 1867, Apr. 9, 1868.
13. *National Anti-Slavery Standard*, July 18, 1868; *Springfield Republican* quoted in ibid., July 20, 1867; *Nation*, Oct. 8, 1868, p. 281; Lamson, *Glorious Failure*, 69n.; *Congressional Globe*, 39th Cong., 1st sess., 74; A. J. Ransier to Benjamin Butler, Feb. 11, 1868, with response by Butler, Mar. 10, 1868, Butler Papers; Edward M. Cheney to Thomas Tullock, May 26, 1868, Records of House Select Committee on Reconstruction, Florida, 40th Cong.; *New York Tribune*, Mar. 31, 1868; Wood, "On Revising Reconstruction History," 112–13.

14. *Washington Chronicle*, Apr. 24, 28, 1868.

15. Ibid., Jan. 23, Mar. 25, 1868; *Philadelphia Press*, Aug. 3, 1867; *New York Tribune*, June 15, Aug. 6, 1867, Nov. 10, 1868; *Boston Commonwealth*, Aug. 10, 1867; Coulter, *William G. Brownlow*, 340; John Binney to William Pitt Fessenden, Nov. 2, 1867, Fessenden Papers; *Great Republic*, Aug. 6, 1867; *New York Times*, July 26, Aug. 3, 1867; *Nation*, Oct. 31, 1867, p. 346, Mar. 26, 1868, p. 245; *Harper's Weekly*, July 6, 1867, p. 418.

16. Brown to W. D. Kelley, Mar. 18, 1868, Brown Papers; *Washington Morning Chronicle*, Apr. 15, Dec. 14, 1867; Frank Fuller to Benjamin S. Hedrick, May 8, 1868, Hedrick Papers; Raper, "William Woods Holden," 228.

17. Fleming, *Civil War and Reconstruction in Alabama*, 494; John Bornier to William P. Fessenden, May 12, 1868, John Binney to Fessenden, Feb. 5, 1868, Fessenden Papers.

18. J. Tarbell to Benjamin Butler, July 15, 1868, Butler Papers; Thomas Tullock to Edward Atkinson, Apr. 10, 1868, Atkinson Papers; *Washington Morning Chronicle*, Apr. 24, 1868.

19. Fleming, *Civil War and Reconstruction in Alabama*, 539–52; *Washington Morning Chronicle*, Aug. 15, 1868; *Harper's Weekly*, Apr. 25, 1868, p. 258; *Nation*, Feb. 20, 1868, p. 144; *New York Independent* quoted in *National Anti-Slavery Standard*, Feb. 29, 1868.

20. *Washington Morning Chronicle*, Apr. 28, 1868; *New York Tribune*, Apr. 6, 1868; *National Anti-Slavery Standard*, Apr. 25, 1868.

21. Thompson, *Reconstruction in Georgia*, 180, 199–202; Nathans, *Losing the Peace*, 95–100; McPherson, *Ordeal by Fire*, 538; Shofner, *Nor Is It Over Yet*, 191–95; Taylor, *Louisiana Reconstructed*, 151–61; Simkins and Woody, *South Carolina during Reconstruction*, 106–10; Hamilton, *Reconstruction in North Carolina*, 280–90; *Nation*, May 14, 1868, p. 382; Bentley, *History of the Freedmen's Bureau*, 199.

22. *Washington Morning Chronicle*, Feb. 29, Apr. 22, 1868; Sefton, *United States Army in Reconstruction*, 185–86; Nathans, *Losing the Peace*, 70–72.

23. Harris, *Day of the Carpetbagger*, 51–52, 136–39, 190–95, 199–204; A. C. Fisk to William E. Chandler, July 4, 24, Aug. 24, 1868, and A. C. Fisk to John O. Johnson, Aug. 29, 1868, all in William E. Chandler Papers; J. L. Alcorn to E. B. Washburne, June 29, 1868, W. H. Gibbs to Washburne, June 20, 1868, Washburne Papers; Benjamin Leas to Richard Yates, July 2, 1868, Yates Papers; Leas to Benjamin Butler, July 4, 1868, and J. Tarbell to Butler, July 15, 1868, Butler Papers.

24. Benedict, *Compromise of Principle*, 313–17; *Congressional Globe*, 40th Cong., 2d sess., 2690–91.

25. George Spencer to E. B. Washburne, May 23, 1868, Washburne Papers; Benedict, *Compromise of Principle*, 317–21.

26. Lowe, "Republicans, Rebellion, and Reconstruction," 302–6; McDonough, "John Schofield," 252–55; Alderson, "Influence of Military Rule and the Freedmen's Bureau on Reconstruction in Virginia," 216–20.

27. Orlando Brown to O. O. Howard, Mar. 20, Apr. 3, 24, May 28, 1868, and Howard to Brown, Apr. 7, 23, 1868, Howard Papers.

28. Lowe, "Republicans, Rebellion, and Reconstruction," 307–24; Maddex, *Virginia Conservatives*, 62.

29. Moneyhon, *Republicanism in Reconstruction Texas*, 83–95.

30. Mantell, *Johnson, Grant, and the Politics of Reconstruction*, 103; Bentley, *History of the Freedmen's Bureau*, 199–202.

31. John Binney to William Pitt Fessenden, Nov. 2, 1867, Fessenden Papers; *New York Tribune*, Nov. 20, 23, 1867, Apr. 14, 1868; *Cincinnati Commercial* quoted in ibid., Jan. 30, 1868; *Great Republic*, July 16, 1867; *Congressional Globe*, 40th Cong., 1st sess., 115, 144.

32. Parks, *Joseph E. Brown of Georgia*, 381; Russ, "Congressional Disfranchisement," 140–49.

33. *Washington Morning Chronicle*, Dec. 10, 1867; Dorris, *Pardon and Amnesty under Lincoln and Johnson*, 365; Wiggins, *Scalawag in Alabama Politics*, 29–32, 48, 50; Woolfolk, "Amnesty and Pardon and Republicanism in Alabama"; Cash, "Alabama Republicans during Reconstruction," 76–78, 149; Milton J. Saffold to Thaddeus Stevens, Mar. 2, 1868, Stevens Papers; Russ, "Congressional Disfranchisement," 151–52.

34. Thomas Tullock to Thaddeus Stevens, Feb. 12, 1868, Records of House Select Committee on Reconstruction, Alabama, 40th Cong.; A. W. Tourgée to James A. Garfield, Dec. 23, 1867, and W. W. Holden to Thomas Tullock, Feb. 13, 1868, copied in letter from Tullock to Thaddeus Stevens, Feb. 17, 1868, Records of House Select Committee on Reconstruction, North Carolina, 40th Cong.; Samuel Linsley to Thaddeus Stevens, Mar. 15, 1868, Stevens Papers; Joseph Brown to W. D. Kelley, Mar. 18, 1868, Brown Papers; B. F. Chapman to Benjamin Butler, Dec. 12, 1868, and Butler notation, Dec. 19, 1868, Butler Papers.

35. *Congressional Globe*, 40th Cong., 2d sess., 1929, 2414, 3180, 3366–67; Thomas Tullock to Committee on Reconstruction, Dec. 9, 1868, and W. W. Holden to George Boutwell, Jan. 28, 1869, in Records of House Select Committee on Reconstruction, North Carolina, 41st Cong.; Nathaniel Boyden to James G. Ramsay, July 26, 1868, Ramsay Papers; Parks, *Joseph E. Brown of Georgia*, 403–4.

36. W. B. Rodman to D. M. Carter, Feb. 11, 1868, Carter Papers; Peterson, *Freedom and Franchise*, 169; B. S. Hedrick to Jonathan Worth, Apr. 3, 1868, Worth Papers; *Washington Morning Chronicle*, Apr. 8, 1868; Park, *Joseph E. Brown of Georgia*, 403–4; *Congressional Globe*, 40th Cong., 2d sess., 3179–80.

37. Russ, "Congressional Disfranchisement," 162n., 167–73; *New York Tribune*, Jan. 3, Apr. 10, 1868; Merriam, *Life and Times of Samuel Bowles*, 2:33–34.

38. *Congressional Globe*, 40th Cong., 2d sess., 766, 777, 1933, 3307.

39. Ibid., 1933, 3301–2.

40. Ibid., 3307, 3367; *Washington Morning Chronicle*, June 22, 1868; Russ, "Congressional Disfranchisement," 162–63; Hyman, *Era of the Oath*, 132–34.

41. Russ, "Congressional Disfranchisement," 166.

42. Coleman, *Election of 1868*, 73–76; Benedict, *Compromise of Principle*, 280–82; Mantell, *Johnson, Grant, and the Politics of Reconstruction*, 79; Silvestro, "None but Patriots," 364–67; Daniel Richards to E. B. Washburne, Nov. 11,

13, 19, 1867, May 6, June 15, 1868, Washburne Papers; Ben Perley Poore to W. W. Clapp, Jan. 31, 1868, Clapp Papers.

43. Trefousse, *Impeachment of a President*, 94–95, 120–21, 184; F. W. Kellogg to E. B. Washburne, Dec. 16, 1867, Washburne Papers.

44. Mantell, *Johnson, Grant, and the Politics of Reconstruction*, 79; Schuyler Colfax to Theodore Tilton, Jan. 4, 1868, Colfax Papers.

45. Coleman, *Election of 1868*, 75–76; Schuyler Colfax to Theodore Tilton, Jan. 4, 1868, Colfax Papers; *Nation*, Jan. 9, 1868, p. 24.

46. Johnson, comp., *Official Proceedings of the Republican National Conventions*, 6, 13–17, 30–34, 66–67, 70–72; Coleman, *Election of 1868*, 89–92.

47. Johnson, comp., *Official Proceedings of the Republican National Conventions*, 80–82, 92, 97–103.

CHAPTER 7

1. Johnson, comp., *Official Proceedings of the National Republican Conventions*, 55; *Washington Morning Chronicle*, Apr. 3, June 20, 28, 1866; *Congressional Globe*, 40th Cong., 1st sess., 654; 40th Cong., 2d sess., 245–47.

2. Abbott, *Cobbler in Congress*, 186–93.

3. *Washington Morning Chronicle*, June 23, 27, July 28, 1866, Mar. 23, 1867, July 15, 1868; Pereyra, *James Lusk Alcorn*, 74–75; Harris, *Day of the Carpetbagger*, 43–44, 47; *Boston Commonwealth*, June 8, 1867; *New York Tribune*, June 10, 1867, July 6, 1868.

4. *Washington Morning Chronicle*, Mar. 26, June 20, 24, 1868.

5. Sanborn, *Congressional Grants of Land*, 68–70; Thompson, *Arkansas and Reconstruction*, 197, 202; Donaldson, *Public Domain*, 269–72, 274, 281, 285; *Washington Morning Chronicle*, Oct. 16, 1868.

6. Mantell, *Johnson, Grant, and the Politics of Reconstruction*, 111–12; *Congressional Globe*, 40th Cong., 2d sess., 3187; Sharkey, *Money, Class, and Party*, 235–38.

7. Klingberg, *Southern Claims Commission*, 24, 37, 201; Thomas and Hyman, *Stanton*, 529, 615–16; *Congressional Globe*, 39th Cong., 2d sess., 1001; *Washington Morning Chronicle*, Dec. 15, 1866; Howe, *Portrait of an Independent*, 55; Olsen, *Carpetbagger's Crusade*, 47; Fessenden, *Life and Public Services of William Pitt Fessenden*, 2:311.

8. *New York Tribune*, Feb. 3, July 6, 1868; Sanborn, *Congressional Grants of Land*, 69–70; Alexander, *Political Reconstruction in Tennessee*, 131–35.

9. *Congressional Globe*, 40th Cong., 1st sess., 83, 91.

10. Ibid., 40th Cong., 1st sess., 84–91, 235, 259.

11. *Washington Morning Chronicle*, Mar. 11, 1867; *New York Tribune*, Feb. 3, 1868.

12. McPherson, "Federal Taxes on Cotton," iv, 72–77, 135, 148; *New York Tribune*, Nov. 2, 1867.

13. McPherson, "Federal Taxes on Cotton," 77–78, 120–32; *New York Times*,

Sept. 5, Nov. 16, 1867; *Washington Morning Chronicle*, Oct. 18, 29, Nov. 22, 23, 1867; Willard Warner to Ben Wade, Dec. 9, 1867, and H. H. Armstrong to John Sherman, Dec. 28, 1867, both in Sherman Papers.

14. Riddleberger, *George Washington Julian*, 243–46; *Great Republic*, Sept. 13, 1866.

15. *Congressional Globe*, 40th Cong., 2d sess., 810, 839–41, 843, 870–71, 985, 3146.

16. Hoffnagle, "Southern Homestead Act," 612–30.

17. *Washington Morning Chronicle*, Aug. 5, Sept. 17, 1868; *Harper's Weekly*, June 6, 1868, p. 355.

18. Information for the preceding two paragraphs is drawn from the following campaign publications published by the Union Republican Congressional Committee: *Nationality vs. Sectionalism: An Appeal to the Laboring Men of the South* [Washington, D.C., 1867–69]; *The Position of the Republican and Democratic Parties: A Dialogue between a White Republican and a Colored Citizen* [Washington, D.C., 1868]; *Homes for the Homeless: What the Republican Party Has Done for the Poor Man* [Washington, D.C., 1868]; *Shall Capital Own Labor?* [Washington, D.C., 1868]; *The Policy of Congress in Reference to the Restoration of the Union* [Washington, D.C., 1867].

19. J. H. Caldwell to W. E. Chandler, July 4, 1868, Volney Spaulding to Chandler, Aug. 14, 1868, W. E. Chandler Papers; Conway, *Reconstruction of Georgia*, 161; Nathans, *Losing the Peace*, 102–4.

20. Conway, *Reconstruction of Georgia*, 165–67; Nathans, *Losing the Peace*, 109–10, 130–34.

21. J. H. Caldwell to William Claflin, Sept. 1, 1868, Foster Blodgett to Dear Sir, Sept. 16, 1868, both in W. E. Chandler Papers; Foster Blodgett to My Dear Sir, Sept. 18, 1868, Morgan Papers; J. H. Caldwell to Robert Schenck, Aug. 28, 1868, Jacob R. Davis to Schenck, Sept. 5, 1868, Schenck Papers; L. P. Gudger to William Claflin, Sept. 7, 1868, Claflin Papers.

22. Thomas Conway to Edwin Morgan, June 26, 1868, Morgan Papers; Taylor, *Louisiana Reconstructed*, 138, 159–60.

23. S. A. Stockdale to W. E. Chandler, Sept. 24, 1868, Thomas Tullock to Chandler, Sept. 25, 1868, M. A. Southworth to Chandler, Oct. 9, 21, 1868, W. E. Chandler Papers; J. R. G. Pitkin to Benjamin Butler, Oct. 31, 1868, Butler Papers; Taylor, *Louisiana Reconstructed*, 179; Ficklin, *History of Reconstruction in Louisiana*, 207–8; *Nation*, Aug. 20, 1868, p. 141.

24. Shofner, *Nor Is It Over Yet*, 201–3; *Nation*, Sept. 10, 1868, p. 200, and Oct. 1, 1868, p. 261; Holt, *Black over White*, 143–44.

25. *New York Times* quoted in *National Anti-Slavery Standard*, Sept. 5, 1868.

26. Trelease, *White Terror*, 28–64.

27. Ibid., 65–174.

28. Ibid., 119–20; J. H. Caldwell to W. E. Chandler, Aug. 7, 1868, M. A. Southworth to Chandler, Oct. 6, 1868, W. E. Chandler Papers; Fleming, *Civil War and Reconstruction in Alabama*, 741–42; *Washington Morning Chronicle*, Oct. 10, 13, 1868.

29. *Harper's Weekly*, Aug. 29, 1868, pp. 546–47; *Nation*, Aug. 13, 1868, p. 121, and Aug. 27, 1868, pp. 164–65; *New York Tribune*, July 29, Aug. 12, 1868; *National Anti-Slavery Standard*, Aug. 1, 1868.

30. Trelease, *White Terror*, 95–103, 116–24, 127–36, 149–74.

31. Singletary, *Negro Militia and Reconstruction*, 4–7; *Congressional Globe*, 40th Cong., 2d sess., 4238–39, 4467; *New York Tribune*, July 23, 24, 1868; *National Anti-Slavery Standard*, Aug. 1, 1868.

32. J. H. Caldwell to W. E. Chandler, July 4, 1868, S. B. Conover to Chandler, Sept. 3, 1868, R. K. Scott to Chandler, Oct. 20, 1868, and M. A. Southworth to Chandler, Oct. 31, 1868, W. E. Chandler Papers; C. C. Bliss to Robert Schenck, Sept. 4, 1868, Schenck Papers.

33. *National Anti-Slavery Standard*, Sept. 5, 12, 1868; *New York Times* quoted in ibid., Aug. 29, 1868, and *New York Tribune* quoted in ibid., Sept. 12, 1868; *Harper's Weekly*, Sept. 5, 1868, p. 563.

34. *New York Tribune*, Sept. 8, 12, 1868; *National Anti-Slavery Standard*, Aug. 8, 1868; *Harper's Weekly*, Sept. 12, 1868, p. 578; John Coburn to Robert Schenck, Sept. 14, 1868, Schenck Papers; Mantell, *Johnson, Grant, and the Politics of Reconstruction*, 135–36; Coleman, *Election of 1868*, 308–9; Taylor, *Louisiana Reconstructed*, 170–71.

35. Hamilton, *Reconstruction in North Carolina*, 346–47; T. W. Osborn to Benjamin Butler, Aug. 21, 1868, Butler Papers; Trelease, *White Terror*, 119–20, 155–57.

36. Sefton, *United States Army and Reconstruction*, 213–15; Trelease, *White Terror*, 125–26, 158; Taylor, *Louisiana Reconstructed*, 171; M. A. Southworth to W. E. Chandler, Oct. 21, 28, 1868, W. E. Chandler Papers; Dawson, "General Lovell H. Rousseau," 381–89.

37. Taylor, *Louisiana Reconstructed*, 171–72; Foster Blodgett to W. E. Chandler, Sept. 16, 1868, M. A. Southworth to Chandler, Oct. 31, 1868, W. E. Chandler Papers.

38. John Sherman to W. T. Sherman, Aug. 9, 1867, in Thorndike, ed., *Sherman Letters*, 293; Zachariah Chandler to Horace Greeley, Aug. 19, 1867, Greeley Papers; *New York Herald* quoted in Benedict, *Compromise of Principle*, 269; *Boston Daily Advertiser*, Oct. 29, 1867.

39. *Washington Morning Chronicle*, Dec. 14, 1867, Nov. 10, 1868; Thaddeus Stevens to Edward McPherson, Aug. 16, 27, 1867, quoted in Current, *Old Thad Stevens*, 288; Fessenden, *Life and Public Services of William Pitt Fessenden*, 2:306–7; *New York Tribune*, Nov. 21, 1867; *Nation*, Oct. 17, 1867, p. 317, Nov. 14, 1867, pp. 395–96, Sept. 3, 1868, p. 180, Sept. 10, 1868, p. 200.

40. M. A. Southworth to W. E. Chandler, Oct. 27, 1868, Volney Spaulding to Chandler, Sept. 1, 1868, John W. Morris to William Claflin, Sept. 14, 1868, and Joseph Brown to Chandler, Oct. 8, 1868, all in W. E. Chandler Papers; Daniel Richards to E. B. Washburne, July 2, 1868, Washburne Papers; John Bornier to W. P. Fessenden, May 12, 1868, Fessenden Papers; Thomas Smith to Benjamin Wade, Mar. 26, 1868, Wade Papers; L. P. Gudger to William Claflin, Nov. 1868, Claflin Papers.

41. George Boutwell to Robert Schenck, Sept. 2, 1868, Schenck Papers;

Springfield Republican, Aug. 10, 1868, quoted in Merriam, *Life and Times of Samuel Bowles*, 2:125; *New York Times*, Feb. 21, 1868, quoted in Russ, "Congressional Disfranchisement," 270; Salmon P. Chase to August Belmont, May 30, 1868, quoted in Schuckers, *Life and Public Services of Salmon P. Chase*, 585; *Boston Commonwealth*, Jan. 11, 1868; *Harper's Weekly*, Sept. 12, 1868, p. 578.

42. *Boston Traveller*, June 11, 1867; *Boston Commonwealth*, July 18, 1868; *Philadelphia Press* quoted in *Washington Morning Chronicle*, May 30, 1868; W. Rid to Benjamin Butler, July 26, 1868, with notation by Butler dated July 31, Butler Papers; *Washington Morning Chronicle*, Nov. 6, 1867, June 12, 1868; Bancroft, ed., *Speeches, Correspondence, and Political Papers of Carl Schurz*, 1:449; *New York Tribune*, July 8, 1867.

43. Richardson, *William E. Chandler*, 90–91, 101.

44. Ibid., 93–96; minutes of meeting of National Republican Committee, July 9, 1868, F. W. Kellogg to W. E. Chandler, Aug. 1, 1868, Thomas Tullock to William Claflin, Sept. 4, 1868, all in W. E. Chandler Papers.

45. Schuyler Colfax to Horace Greeley, July 15, 1868, Greeley Papers; E. D. Morgan to William P. Fessenden, Sept. 8, 1868, Fessenden Papers; Carl Schurz to Mrs. Schurz, Aug. 2, 1868, in Schafer, ed., *Intimate Letters of Carl Schurz*, 440; Schurz to William Claflin, Aug. 2, 1868, Claflin Papers; Claflin to W. E. Chandler, July 1868, W. E. Chandler Papers; Claflin to Marcus Ward, Sept. 28, 1868, Ward Papers.

46. Richardson, *William E. Chandler*, 96; W. E. Chandler to My Dear Sir, Aug. 7, 1868, Schenck Papers; George H. Boker to E. D. Morgan, Feb. 10, 1868, Morgan Papers; David Atwood to W. E. Chandler, July 24, 1868, W. E. Chandler Papers; J. G. Blaine to E. B. Washburne, Aug. 27, 1868, Washburne Papers.

47. William Claflin to Godlove Orth, Oct. 10, 1868, W. E. Chandler Papers; W. E. Chandler to E. B. Washburne, Oct. 19, 1868, J. G. Blaine to Washburne, Oct. 24, 1868, Washburne Papers; Richardson, *William E. Chandler*, 110–13; Coleman, *Election of 1868*, 332–42.

48. Coleman, *Election of 1868*, 301, 340–41; *Washington Morning Chronicle*, Oct. 14, 16, 19, 1868; *Nation*, Sept. 24, 1868, p. 244, Oct. 8, 1868, p. 281; Thomas Tullock to W. E. Chandler, Sept. 25, 1868, W. E. Chandler Papers; *New York Tribune*, Oct. 6, 31, 1868.

49. Richardson, *William E. Chandler*, 115; W. E. Chandler to Robert Schenck, Oct. 1, 3, 1868, Schenck Papers; W. E. Chandler to William Sprague, Oct. 16, 1868, Sprague Papers; Henry Wilson to W. E. Chandler, Oct. 17, 1868, W. E. Chandler Papers.

50. Thomas Tullock to W. E. Chandler, Oct. 26, 1868, W. E. Chandler Papers; Tullock to Edward Atkinson, Sept. 15, 1868, and Atkinson to John Murray Forbes, Sept. 18, 1868, Atkinson Papers.

51. Edward Atkinson to Thomas Tullock, Aug. 9, 1867, Apr. 14, 1868, Atkinson to Nourse, June 15, 1867, Atkinson to Dear Sir, Aug. 7, 1867, Mar. 19, 1868; see also statement dated Mar. 14, 1868, all in Atkinson Papers; Shapiro, "Aristocracy, Mud, and Vituperation," 345, 355–56.

52. E. D. Morgan to Thomas Tullock, Aug. 7, 1868, Morgan Papers; C. W.

Arnold to Horace Greeley, Sept. 19, 1868, Thomas Tullock to Chandler, Sept. 18, Oct. 13, 27, 1868, Foster Blodgett to Chandler, Sept. 16, 1868, Charles Miller to Thomas Tullock, Oct. 13, 1868, John E. Stanton to William Claflin, W. E. Chandler Papers.

53. J. M. Edmunds to W. E. Chandler, June 13, 22, 1868, F. W. Kellogg to Chandler, Aug. 1, 1868, Thomas Tullock to William Claflin, Sept. 4, 1868, Tullock to W. E. Chandler, Sept. 12, 18, 25, Oct. 7, 13, 1868, W. E. Chandler Papers.

54. Thomas Tullock to W. E. Chandler, Sept. 24, Oct. 12, 1868, Thomas Glasscock to Chandler, Oct. 3, 1868, B. F. Rice to Chandler, Oct. 3, 1868, Barbour Lewis to Chandler, Nov. 5, 1868, W. E. Chandler Papers.

55. Richardson, *William E. Chandler*, 99–100; John Runnels to W. E. Chandler, July 25, 1868, Thomas Tullock to Chandler, Sept. 17, 1868, W. E. Chandler Papers; W. E. Chandler to My Dear Sir, Aug. 7, 1868, Schenck Papers.

56. Thomas Tullock to W. E. Chandler, Aug. 8, 21, Sept. 4, 18, 25, Oct. 7, 13, 20, 1868, W. E. Chandler Papers.

57. *New York Tribune*, Aug. 27, 1867; J. H. Caldwell to Thomas Tullock, Aug. 19, 1868, Claflin Papers; William Claflin to W. E. Chandler, July 20, 22, 1868, Thomas Tullock to Chandler, Sept. 18, 1868, T. A. Sawyer to Chandler, Oct. 22, 1868, W. E. Chandler Papers; Holt, *Black over White*, 115–16.

58. Thomas Tullock to W. E. Chandler, Oct. 26, 27, 1868, W. E. Chandler Papers; *Washington Morning Chronicle*, Sept. 26, 30, 1868.

59. Rufus Barringer to Thomas Tullock, Oct. 3, 1868, B. F. Randolph to William Claflin, Oct. 9, 1868, Isaac Seeley to W. E. Chandler, Oct. 13, 1868, J. C. Harris to Chandler, Oct. 1868, W. E. Chandler Papers; E. C. Camp to Columbus Delano, Sept. 19, 1868, Delano Family Papers.

60. *Washington Morning Chronicle*, Sept. 30, 1868; James H. Clements to W. E. Chandler, Aug. 12, 1868, Jonathan Morris to Dear Sir, Sept. 12, 1868, Niles Parker and others to Chandler, Sept. 12, 1868, Paul Strobach to Chandler, Oct. 2, 1868, Thomas Tullock to Chandler, Oct. 9, 1868, Henry Wilson to Chandler, Oct. 17, 1868, W. E. Chandler Papers; Parks, *Joseph E. Brown of Georgia*, 425.

61. William Claflin to Marcus Ward, Sept. 28, 1868, Ward Papers; Claflin to W. E. Chandler, Oct. 23, 1868, W. E. Chandler Papers; *Washington Morning Chronicle*, Sept. 13, 1867, June 25, 1868; Donald, *Charles Sumner*, 299; *Boston Commonwealth*, Nov. 9, 1867.

62. John Carlile to William Claflin, Sept. 19, 1868, Anthony Higgins to Marcus Ward, Oct. 17, 1868, to William Claflin, Oct. 22, 1868, and to W. E. Chandler, Oct. 24, 1868, Robert Schenck to W. E. Chandler, Oct. 19, 1868, William Claflin to Chandler, Oct. 19, 1868, all in W. E. Chandler Papers.

63. Curry, ed., *Radicalism, Racism, and Party Realignment*, 24–25, 71, 124–25, 179–80, 201–2; Curry, *House Divided*, 135.

64. Brock, "Reconstruction and the American Party System," 95–97; McPherson, *Ordeal by Fire*, 544; early returns for 1868 elections found in U. S. Grant Papers, CHS; Benedict, *Compromise of Principle*, 327–28.

65. Mantell, *Johnson, Grant, and the Politics of Reconstruction*, 147; *Washington Morning Chronicle*, Nov. 2, 1868; Brock, "Reconstruction and the American Party System," 97–99.

66. McPherson, *Ordeal by Fire*, 544–45; Mantell, *Johnson, Grant, and the Politics of Reconstruction*, 148.

67. Coleman, *Election of 1868*, 287, 290–91, 306–7, 310; Gillette, *Retreat from Reconstruction*, 3–9.

CHAPTER 8

1. Sefton, *United States Army and Reconstruction*, 208; Degler, *Other South*, 223–24; Hesseltine, "Economic Factors in the Abandonment of Reconstruction," 196; Van Deusen, *Horace Greeley*, 374; *Harper's Weekly*, May 30, 1868, p. 339; Bancroft, ed., *Speeches, Correspondence, and Political Papers of Carl Schurz*, 1:455–57.

2. Sefton, *United States Army and Reconstruction*, 208; notations by Butler on letters from A. Vallas to Butler, Feb. 18, 1867, and B. Wardwell to Butler, Mar. 6, 1867, Butler Papers; Edward Atkinson to Hugh McCulloch, Nov. 6, 1868, Atkinson Papers; *New York Tribune*, May 24, 1869, quoted in Seip, *The South Returns to Congress*, 271n.

3. Gillette, *Right to Vote*. Gillette's conclusion that the Fifteenth Amendment was concerned primarily with securing the vote for Northern blacks to help Republicans swing elections in narrowly contested states has been challenged by Lawanda Cox and John H. Cox, "Negro Suffrage and Republican Politics." The Coxes claim that Gillette has downplayed the idealistic motives of Republicans who sponsored the amendment, and in light of the subsequent election history in the North and border, they question its political utility for the Republicans. Gillette dealt with their arguments in a revised edition of his work, cited above, pp. 166–90. Although Gillette emphasizes the pragmatic political aims of Republicans in sponsoring the amendment, he is not blind to their idealistic goals.

My own research leads me to conclude that Gillette has the better of the argument. Northerners were clearly interested in applying the amendment to their own states as well as to the border; the history of the Enforcement Acts passed in 1870 and 1871 supports this theory. Because almost every step the Republicans took during Reconstruction was taken with the North in mind, as much or as more than the South, it seems to me unlikely that the Fifteenth Amendment would be an exception to their regional priorities.

4. Gillette, *Right to Vote*, 50, 56, 71; Benedict, *Compromise of Principle*, 333–35.

5. Maddex, *Virginia Conservatives*, 67–86; Eckenrode, *Political History of Virginia during the Reconstruction*, 112.

6. Gillette, *Retreat from Reconstruction*, 82–83; *New York Independent*, July 22, 1869; Nevins, *Hamilton Fish*, 292.

7. Nevins, *Hamilton Fish*, 290–91; *Boston Commonwealth*, July 17, 1869; Trefousse, *Radical Republicans*, 428–29; Gillette, *Retreat from Reconstruction*, 84–85; *Boston Daily Advertiser*, Aug. 4, 1871.

8. Alexander, "Political Reconstruction in Tennessee," 70–75.

9. Alexander, *Political Reconstruction in Tennessee*, 202–3; *Boston Commonwealth*, Aug. 14, 1869, Mar. 12, 1870; *New York Independent*, Sept. 9, 1869; Fessenden, *Life and Public Services of William Pitt Fessenden*, 2:328.

10. Gillette, *Retreat from Reconstruction*, 99; Harris, *Day of the Carpetbagger*, 218–25; Moneyhon, *Republicanism in Reconstruction Texas*, 97–117.

11. J. I. Fisher to Thomas Tullock, July 13, 1869, W. E. Chandler Papers; John R. Lynch to William Claflin, Aug. 10, 1869, W. E. Chandler to Claflin, Oct. 19, 1869, Jan. 18, 1870, R. C. Powers to Claflin, Oct. 25, 1869, Adelbert Ames to Claflin, Jan. 7, 1870, Claflin Papers.

12. Nathans, *Losing the Peace*, 148–96; Scroggs, "Carpetbagger Influence," 296n.

13. John E. Bryant to George F. Edmunds, Jan. 1869, and Bryant to Amos Akerman, Oct. 7, 1871, Bryant Papers; Gillette, *Retreat from Reconstruction*, 86–90.

14. Gillette, *Retreat from Reconstruction*, 91–94; Hamilton, *Reconstruction in North Carolina*, 520–21n.; J. H. Clendening to William Holden, July 18, 1870, Holden Papers, SDAH.

15. Singletary, *Negro Militia and Reconstruction*, 27–29.

16. Trelease, *White Terror*, 223, 240–41, 270–73, 385.

17. *Boston Daily Advertiser*, Aug. 25, 1871; Edwin Morgan to Lyman Trumbull, Feb. 21, 1871, and to Zachariah Chandler, Feb. 21, 1871, Morgan Papers; *Boston Commonwealth*, Mar. 25, 1871.

18. Thomas Keogh to Benjamin Butler, Nov. 25, 1871, Butler Papers; Krug, *Lyman Trumbull*, 276, 285, 297–98; Peskin, *Garfield*, 332; Merriam, *Life and Times of Samuel Bowles*, 2:273; Bancroft, ed., *Speeches, Correspondence, and Political Papers of Carl Schurz*, 1:484, 500; Samuel Shellabarger to George F. Hoar, Sept. 11, 1871, Hoar Papers; Hoar, *Autobiography*, 1:204–5.

19. Gillette, *Retreat from Reconstruction*, 46–47; Amos Akerman to Foster Blodgett, Nov. 8, 1871, to Major Lewis Merrill, Nov. 9, 1871, to H. P. Farrow, Nov. 26, 1871, Akerman Papers.

20. Edwards Pierrepont to U. S. Grant, May 19, 1870, Grant Papers, RBH; Gillette, *Retreat from Reconstruction*, 48–51.

21. Amos Akerman to Benjamin Butler, Aug. 9, 1871, Butler Papers; *Boston Commonwealth*, Aug. 12, 1871.

22. Gillette, *Retreat from Reconstruction*, 52–54; Van Deusen, *Horace Greeley*, 380–82; Peskin, *Garfield*, 332–34; Hesseltine, "Economic Factors in the Abandonment of Reconstruction," 202; Bancroft, ed., *Speeches, Correspondence, and Political Papers of Carl Schurz*, 2:3–8; Merriam, *Life and Times of Samuel Bowles*, 2:127–28.

23. Horace Greeley to W. E. Chandler, Jan. 15, 1872, in Richardson, *William E. Chandler*, 135; Robinson quoted in *Boston Commonwealth*, Apr. 15, 1871.

24. J. D. Cox to Horace Greeley, July 17, 1869, Greeley Papers; Seip, *The South Returns to Congress*, 131–32; Van Deusen, *Horace Greeley*, 401; Wiggins, *Scalawag in Alabama Politics*, 61.

25. Balk and Hoogenboom, "Origins of Border State Liberal Republicanism," 229–40; Curry, *House Divided*, 135; Donald, *Charles Sumner*, 518; J. D. Cox to Horace Greeley, July 17, 1869, Greeley Papers.

26. Balk and Hoogenboom, "Origins of Border State Liberal Republicanism," 240–42.

27. Rhodes, *History of the United States*, 6:435, 435n.; Russ, "Congressional Disfranchisement," 173–79; Balk and Hoogenboom, "Origins of Border State Liberal Republicanism," 243; McKinney, *Southern Mountain Republicans*, 42–43, 48; David P. Lewis to My Dear Sirs, Nov. 26, 1870, House Select Committee, 41st Cong., Alabama.

28. *Boston Commonwealth*, Dec. 24, 1870; Nevins, *Hamilton Fish*, 293; George, *Zachariah Chandler*, 191; Amos Akerman to Foster Blodgett, July 1871, and to E. P. Jacobson, Aug. 18, 1871, Akerman Papers.

29. *New York Times*, Jan. 17, 1870, quoted in Gillette, *Retreat from Reconstruction*, 84; Russ, "Congressional Disfranchisement," 180–202; Rhodes, *History of the United States*, 6:436–37; Blaine, *Twenty Years of Congress*, 2:512–13.

30. Rhodes, *History of the United States*, 6:439–40; Russ, "Congressional Disfranchisement," 216–17.

31. Hyman, *Era of the Oath*, 129–50.

32. McPherson, *Ordeal by Fire*, 567–71; Gillette, *Retreat from Reconstruction*, 56–57.

33. On the Union League, see Silvestro, "None but Patriots," 396–416.

34. Hamilton, *Reconstruction in North Carolina*, 586–89; Edwin Morgan to William Claflin, June 18, 1872, and to J. S. C. Abbott, July 8, 1872, Morgan Papers.

35. John Murray Forbes to Charles Sumner, Aug. 10, 1872, in Hughes, ed., *Letters of John Murray Forbes*, 2:178–83.

36. Richardson, *William E. Chandler*, 155–58; E. D. Morgan to George Boutwell, Sept. 15, 1872, Morgan to William Claflin, Sept. 2, 25, 27, 1872, Morgan Papers; O. E. Babcock to Simon Cameron, Aug. 16, 1872, Cameron Papers; Morgan and W. E. Chandler to William H. Howard, Sept. 13, 1872, O. E. Babcock to W. E. Chandler, Sept. 26, 1872, W. E. Chandler Papers.

37. H. P. Farrow to W. E. Chandler, Sept. 5, 17, 1872, J. H. Harris to Chandler, Sept. 5, 1872, D. C. Whiting to Chandler, Sept. 16, 1872, A. Warner to Chandler, Sept. 10, 1872, John Woltz to J. M. Taliaferro, Oct. 1, 1872, F. W. DeKlyne to Chandler, Sept. 18, 1872, W. E. Chandler Papers; M. H. Hale to John Bryant, Oct. 8, 1872, Bryant Papers; Richardson, *William E. Chandler*, 158.

38. E. D. Morgan to William Claflin, Sept. 23, 1872, Claflin Papers; Morgan to Horace Maynard, Oct. 22, 1872, Morgan Papers; William Claflin to W. E. Chandler, Sept. 23, 1872, W. E. Chandler Papers; Rawley, *Edwin D. Morgan*, 244.

39. H. M. Cooper to W. E. Chandler, Oct. 9, 1872, E. H. Smith to editor,

New York Times, Oct. 10, 1872, J. S. Fanning to E. D. Morgan, Oct. 10, 1872, H. M. Cooper to W. E. Chandler, Oct. 9, 1872, James Atkins to Chandler, Oct. 12, 1872, Allen White to Chandler, Oct. 13, 1872, W. E. Chandler Papers.

40. James Harlan to W. E. Chandler, Oct. 11, 1872, W. E. Chandler Papers.

41. Edwin Morgan to O. C. Moore, Oct. 22, 1872, Morgan Papers; Richardson, *William E. Chandler*, 159; Wiggins, *Scalawag in Alabama Politics*, 82; O. C. French to W. E. Chandler, Nov. 8, 1872, James Blener to Chandler, Nov. 13, 1872, W. E. Chandler Papers.

42. Gillette, *Retreat from Reconstruction*, 71; McPherson, *Ordeal by Fire*, 567, 571.

43. Gillette, *Retreat from Reconstruction*, 98–103, 157–60; Seip, *The South Returns to Congress*, 87–88, 94–99; Scroggs, "Carpetbagger Influence," 312, 330.

44. Seip, *The South Returns to Congress*, 115–25; John E. Bryant to Amos Akerman, May 15, 1871, Bryant Papers; Nevins, *Hamilton Fish*, 304–5; Lamson, *Glorious Failure*, 151–52.

45. Seip, *The South Returns to Congress*, 169, 221, 232; Pereyra, *James Lusk Alcorn*, 77, 113, 116–17, 167.

46. Summers, *Railroads, Reconstruction, and the Gospel of Prosperity*, 163–68; Seip, *The South Returns to Congress*, 244–47.

47. Seip, *The South Returns to Congress*, 155, 159–61, 172–201.

48. Lee, *Struggle for Federal Aid*, 39–61, 83; McPherson, *Ordeal by Fire*, 612; *New York Tribune*, Oct. 18, 1867; *New York Independent*, June 17, 1869; *Boston Commonwealth*, Apr. 2, 1870; Hoar, *Autobiography*, 1:256–57.

49. *Congressional Globe*, 42d Cong., 3d sess., 563, 1710.

50. Seip, *The South Returns to Congress*, 7–8; Klingberg, *Southern Claims Commission*, passim; E. M. Dodge to Columbus Delano, Mar. 5, 1871, Delano Family Papers; David P. Lewis to My Dear Sirs, Nov. 26, 1870, House Select Committee, 41st Cong., Alabama.

51. Klingberg, *Southern Claims Commission*, 17–18, 68–72; Thomas Keogh to Benjamin Butler, Nov. 25, 1871, Butler Papers.

52. James G. Blaine to Samuel Langhorne Clemens, Oct. 9, 1875, quoted in Klingberg, *Southern Claims Commission*, 177; see also W. T. Sherman to John Sherman, Feb. 3, 1875, in Thorndike, ed., *Sherman Letters*, 344.

53. Gillette, *Retreat from Reconstruction*, 95–96, 180–82; Seip, *The South Returns to Congress*, 179; William Holden to My Dear Son, Aug. 16, 1871, Holden Papers, DU.

54. Seip, *The South Returns to Congress*, 8; T. Pearson to Benjamin Butler, Sept. 2, 1871, Butler Papers; Pearce, *Benjamin H. Hill*, 231–32.

55. Durden, *James Shepherd Pike*, 188; Lamson, *Glorious Failure*, 160; *New York Tribune*, Nov. 10, 1874; *Boston Commonwealth*, Aug. 1, 29, Dec. 5, 1874.

56. Horace Greeley to O. Johnson, July 23, 1868, Greeley Papers; *New York Tribune*, Sept. 5, 1868; Schurz, *Reminiscences*, 3:205, 255; Bancroft, ed., *Speeches, Correspondence, and Political Papers of Carl Schurz*, 2:283; Durden, *James Shepherd Pike*, 186–87.

57. *New York Independent*, June 17, 1869; W. E. Chandler to Benjamin Butler,

Aug. 10, 1869, quoted in Gillette, *Right to Vote*, 163; W. T. Sherman to John Sherman, July 8, 1861, in Thorndike, ed., *Sherman Letters*, 331; J. M. Forbes to Charles Sumner, Aug. 10, 1862, in Hughes, ed., *Letters of John Murray Forbes*, 2:178–83; *Boston Commonwealth*, Dec. 27, 1873, Aug. 19, 1876; Benjamin Butler to H. Adams, Nov. 28, 1875, quoted in West, *Lincoln's Scapegoat General*, 363; see also Stewart, *Reminiscences*, 232; W. C. Morrill to Simon Cameron, Nov. 9, 1872, Cameron Papers.

58. Donald, *Charles Sumner*, 530–50; Gillette, *Retreat from Reconstruction*, 202–3.

59. Gillette, *Retreat from Reconstruction*, 205–8, 228; Wiggins, *Scalawag in Alabama Politics*, 95; A. Burnell to President of Convention, Oct. 10, 1874, Grant Papers, RBH.

60. Gillette, *Retreat from Reconstruction*, 217–24, 247; McKinney, *Southern Mountain Republicans*, 39, 49–50, 54–57; Webb, *Kentucky in the Reconstruction Era*, 84; Olsen, *Carpetbagger's Crusade*, 193.

61. Gillette, *Retreat from Reconstruction*, 246–58.

62. Ibid., 257–79.

63. Ibid., 280–93; Lynch, *Reminiscences*, 161.

64. Gillette, *Retreat from Reconstruction*, 158–59.

65. Edwards Pierrepont to Rutherford B. Hayes, Aug. 31, 1876, W. A. Wheeler to Hayes, Oct. 16, 1876, Edwin Morgan to Dear Sirs, Oct. 24, 1876, Marshall Jewell to Benjamin Bristow, Oct. 16, 1876, all in Hayes Papers.

66. Polakoff, *Politics of Inertia*, 100, 115, 140–50.

67. Gillette, *Retreat from Reconstruction*, 324.

CHAPTER 9

1. Smiley, *Lion of White Hall*, 215–17, 224, 226; Peterson, *Freedom and Franchise*, 159–62, 180–86; Hamilton, *Reconstruction in North Carolina*, 238, 242, 245, 280–81, 582.

2. Smith, *The Francis Preston Blair Family in Politics*, 2:340–85; Smiley, *Lion of White Hall*, 222; Degler, *Other South*, 259; Bailey, *Hinton Rowan Helper*, 143–45.

3. See Foner, *Politics and Ideology in the Age of the Civil War*, 98, 125, and Perman, *Road to Redemption*, 106–7.

4. William Gillette, in his study of Reconstruction during the Grant administration, has emphasized that the Republicans during these years repeatedly sacrificed the interests of Southern Republicans to protect their Northern base. He concludes that the party never had great hopes for the South after 1868. See Gillette, *Retreat from Reconstruction*, esp. 370–74. My own findings parallel those of Gillette; I have attempted in my own work to push the evidence of this regional priority back to the beginnings of Reconstruction and even to the formation of the party itself. By the time of Grant's election, I believe that Republican political attitudes toward the South were already established.

BIBLIOGRAPHY

MANUSCRIPT COLLECTIONS

Albany, New York
  New York State Library
    Edwin D. Morgan Papers
Athens, Georgia
  University of Georgia, Manuscript Collection
    Joseph E. Brown Papers
Boston, Massachusetts
  Massachusetts Historical Society
    John A. Andrew Papers
    Edward Atkinson Papers
    Amos Lawrence Papers
    Horatio Woodman Papers
Brunswick, Maine
  Bowdoin College Library, Manuscript Collection
    O. O. Howard Papers
Cambridge, Massachusetts
  Harvard University, Houghton Library Manuscript Collection
    Charles Sumner Papers
Chapel Hill, North Carolina
  University of North Carolina, Southern Historical Collection
    David Miller Carter Papers
    James McGready Ramsey Papers
Charlottesville, Virginia
  University of Virginia, Alderman Library, Manuscript Collection (UV)
    Amos Akerman Papers
    A. H. H. Stuart Papers
    John Underwood Papers
Chicago, Illinois
  Chicago Historical Society (CHS)
    Ulysses S. Grant Papers
Durham, North Carolina
  Duke University, Manuscript Collection (DU)
    John E. Bryant Papers

Benjamin S. Hedrick Papers
William W. Holden Papers
Fremont, Ohio
Rutherford B. Hayes Library (RBH)
William Claflin Papers
Ulysses S. Grant Papers
Robert S. Schenck Papers (microfilm)
Indianapolis, Indiana
Indiana State Library, Indiana Division
George Julian Papers
Newark, New Jersey
New Jersey Historical Society, Collections
Marcus Ward Papers
New York, New York
Columbia University, Manuscript Collection
William Sprague Papers
New York Public Library
Schuyler Colfax Papers
Horace Greeley Papers
Raleigh, North Carolina
State Department of Archives and History (SDAH)
James H. Harris Papers
William W. Holden Papers
Jonathan Worth Papers
Springfield, Illinois
Illinois State Historical Society
John D. Strong Papers
Richard Yates Papers
Washington, D.C.
Library of Congress (LC)
Benjamin Butler Papers
Simon Cameron Papers
William E. Chandler Papers
Zachariah Chandler Papers
W. W. Clapp Papers
John Covode Papers
Delano Family Papers
William Pitt Fessenden Papers
Edward McPherson Papers
John Sherman Papers
Thaddeus Stevens Papers
Lyman Trumbull Papers
John Underwood Papers
Benjamin Wade Papers
Elihu B. Washburne Papers
Theodore Dwight Weld Papers
Henry Wilson Papers

UNPUBLISHED U. S. GOVERNMENT MANUSCRIPTS

Washington, D.C.
    National Archives.
        United States Congress. Papers of the United States House of Representatives. Select Committee on Reconstruction, 40th and 41st Congresses.
        United States War Department. Records of the Bureau of Refugees, Freedmen and Abandoned Land.

U. S. GOVERNMENT PUBLICATIONS

United States Congress. *Congressional Globe.*

NEWSPAPERS AND MAGAZINES

Augusta Daily Press. (Georgia). 1867.
Boston Commonwealth. 1865–76.
Boston Daily Advertiser. 1867, 1871.
Boston Traveller. 1867.
Charleston Daily Courier. (South Carolina). 1867.
Charleston Daily News. (South Carolina). 1867.
Great Republic. (Washington, D.C.). 1866–67.
Harper's Weekly. 1867–68.
Nation. (New York). 1867–68.
National Anti-Slavery Standard. (New York). 1867–68.
New York Herald. 1866.
New York Independent. 1869.
New York Times. 1865–69.
New York Tribune. 1867–68, 1874.
Philadelphia Press. 1867.
Raleigh Tri-Weekly Standard. (North Carolina). 1867.
Richmond Enquirer. (Virginia). 1867.
Richmond Times. (Virginia). 1867.
Washington Morning Chronicle. 1866–68.

THESES AND DISSERTATIONS

Alderson, William T. "The Influence of Military Rule and the Freedmen's Bureau on Reconstruction in Virginia, 1865–1870." Ph.D. dissertation. Vanderbilt University, 1952.
Cash, William McKinley. "Alabama Republicans during Reconstruction, 1867–1880." Ph.D. dissertation. University of Alabama, 1973.

Ellenburg, Martha A. "Reconstruction in Arkansas." Ph.D. dissertation. University of Missouri, 1967.

Hoffman, Richard L. "The Republican Party in North Carolina, 1867–1872." M.A. thesis. University of North Carolina, 1960.

Kincaid, Larry. "The Legislative Origins of the Military Reconstruction Act, 1865–1867." Ph.D. dissertation. Johns Hopkins University, 1968.

Lowe, Richard G. "Republicans, Rebellion, and Reconstruction: The Republican Party in Virginia, 1856–1870." Ph.D. dissertation. University of Virginia, 1968.

Malberg, Edward I. "The Republican Party in Kentucky, 1856–1867." M.A. thesis. University of Kentucky, 1967.

McDaniel, Ruth Currie. "Georgia Carpetbagger: John Emory Bryant and the Ambiguity of Reform during Reconstruction." Ph.D. dissertation. Duke University, 1973.

McPherson, Milton M. "Federal Taxes on Cotton, 1862–1868." Ph.D. dissertation. University of Alabama, 1970.

Owens, Susie L. "The Union League of America: Political Activities in Tennessee, the Carolinas, and Virginia, 1865–1870." Ph.D. dissertation. New York University, 1943.

Phillips, Paul David. "A History of the Freedmen's Bureau in Tennessee." Ph.D. dissertation. Vanderbilt University, 1964.

Raper, Horace W. "William Woods Holden: A Political Biography." Ph.D. dissertation. University of North Carolina, 1951.

Russ, William A. "Congressional Disfranchisement, 1866–1898." Ph.D. dissertation. University of Chicago, 1933.

Scroggs, Jack Benton. "Carpetbagger Influence in the Political Reconstruction of the South Atlantic States, 1865–1876." Ph.D. dissertation. University of North Carolina, 1951.

Silvestro, Clement M. "None but Patriots: The Union Leagues in Civil War and Reconstruction." Ph.D. dissertation. University of Wisconsin, 1959.

Smith, James D. "Virginia during Reconstruction, 1865–1870: A Political, Economic, and Social Study." Ph.D. dissertation. University of Virginia, 1960.

PUBLISHED PRIMARY SOURCES

Abbott, Martin, ed. "Reconstruction in Louisiana: Three Letters." *Louisiana History* 1 (Spring 1960): 153–57.

Andrew, John. *Address of His Excellency John Andrew to the Two Branches of the Legislature of Massachusetts.* Boston, 1861.

Bancroft, Frederick, ed. *Speeches, Correspondence, and Political Papers of Carl Schurz.* 6 vols. New York, 1913.

Blaine, James G. *Twenty Years of Congress.* 2 vols. Norwich, Conn., 1893.

Butler, Benjamin F. *Autobiography and Personal Reminiscences.* Boston, 1892.

Foner, Philip S., ed. *The Life and Writings of Frederick Douglass*. 4 vols. New York, 1950–55.

Hoar, George F. *Autobiography of Seventy Years*. 2 vols. New York, 1903.

Hughes, Sarah Forbes, ed. *Letters of John Murray Forbes*. Supp. Ed., 3 vols. Boston, 1905.

Hume, Richard L. "The Freedmen's Bureau and the Freedmen's Vote in the Reconstruction of Southern Alabama: An Account by Agent Samuel S. Gardner." *Alabama Historical Quarterly* 38 (Fall 1975): 217–24.

Johnson, Charles, comp. *Official Proceedings of the National Republican Conventions of 1868, 1872, 1876, and 1880*. Minneapolis, 1903.

————. *Proceedings of the First Three Republican National Conventions of 1856, 1860, and 1864*. Minneapolis, 1893.

Julian, George W. *Political Recollections, 1840 to 1872*. Chicago, 1884.

Langston, John Mercer. *From the Virginia Plantation to the National Capitol*. Hartford, Conn., 1894.

Lynch, John Roy. *Reminiscences of an Active Life: The Autobiography of John Roy Lynch*. Edited with an Introduction by John Hope Franklin. Chicago, 1970.

Muggleston, William F., ed. "The Freedmen's Bureau and Reconstruction in Virginia: The Diary of Marcus Sterling Hopkins, a Union Officer." *Virginia Magazine of History and Biography* 86 (1978): 45–102.

Nunns, Annie A., ed. "Some Letters of Salmon P. Chase, 1848–1865." *American Historical Review* 34 (April 1929): 536–55.

Schafer, Joseph, ed. *Intimate Letters of Carl Schurz, 1841–1869*. Madison, Wis., 1928.

Schurz, Carl. *The Reminiscences of Carl Schurz*. 3 vols. New York, 1907–8.

Stewart, William M. *Reminiscences of Senator William M. Stewart*. New York, 1908.

Thorndike, Rachel Sherman, ed. *The Sherman Letters: Correspondence between General Sherman and Senator Sherman from 1837 to 1891*. New York, 1894.

Union League Club of New York. *Report of Proceedings of Conference in Richmond, June 11–12, 1867*. New York, 1867.

Warmoth, Henry Clay. *War, Politics, and Reconstruction: Stormy Days in Louisiana*. New York, 1930.

SECONDARY SOURCES

Abbott, Martin. *The Freedmen's Bureau in South Carolina, 1865–1872*. Chapel Hill, 1967.

Abbott, Richard H. *Cobbler in Congress: Life of Henry Wilson, 1812–1875*. Lexington, Ky., 1972.

Alexander, Thomas B. "Persistent Whiggery in the Confederate South, 1860–1877." *Journal of Southern History* 27 (1961): 305–29.

————. *Political Reconstruction in Tennessee*. Nashville, 1950.

_____. "Political Reconstruction in Tennessee." In *Radicalism, Racism, and Party Realignment: The Border States during Reconstruction*, edited by Richard O. Curry, pp. 37–80. Baltimore, 1969.

Ambler, Charles H. *Francis H. Pierpont: Union War Governor of Virginia and Father of West Virginia*. Chapel Hill, 1937.

Avillo, Philip J., Jr. "Ballots for the Faithful: The Oath and the Emergence of Slave State Republican Congressmen, 1861–1867." *Civil War History* 22 (June 1976): 164–74.

Bailey, Hugh C. *Hinton Rowan Helper: Abolitionist-Racist*. Montgomery, Ala., 1965.

Baker, Jean H. *The Politics of Continuity: Maryland Political Parties from 1858 to 1870*. Baltimore, 1973.

Balk, Jacqueline, and Ari Hoogenboom. "The Origins of Border State Liberal Republicanism." In *Radicalism, Racism, and Party Realignment: The Border States during Reconstruction*, edited by Richard O. Curry, pp. 220–45. Baltimore, 1969.

Barney, William L. *The Road to Secession*. New York, 1972.

Barone, Michael, and Grant Ujifusa. *The Almanac of American Politics, 1982*. Washington, 1981.

Bassett, John Spencer. *Antislavery Leaders in North Carolina*. Baltimore, 1898.

Belz, Herman. *Reconstructing the Union: Theory and Policy during the Civil War*. Ithaca, N.Y., 1969.

Benedict, Michael Les. *A Compromise of Principle: Congressional Republicans and Reconstruction, 1863–1869*. New York, 1974.

_____. *The Fruits of Victory: Alternatives in Restoring the Union, 1865–1877*. Philadelphia, 1975.

_____. "The Rout of Radicalism: Republicans and the Election of 1867." *Civil War History* 18 (December 1972): 334–45.

Bentley, George R. *A History of the Freedmen's Bureau*. Philadelphia, 1955.

_____. "The Political Activity of the Freedmen's Bureau in Florida." *Florida Historical Quarterly* 28 (1949–50): 28–37.

Bethel, Elizabeth. "The Freedmen's Bureau in Alabama." *Journal of Southern History* 14 (1948): 49–92.

Brigham, Johnson. *James Harlan*. Iowa City, 1913.

Brock, William E. *An American Crisis: Congress and Reconstruction, 1865–1867*. New York, 1966.

_____. "Reconstruction and the American Party System." In *A Nation Divided: Problems and Issues of the Civil War and Reconstruction*, edited by George M. Frederickson, pp. 81–113. Minneapolis, 1975.

Brodie, Fawn M. *Thaddeus Stevens: Scourge of the South*. New York, 1959.

Brown, Francis. *Raymond of the Times*. New York, 1951.

Cain, Marvin. *Lincoln's Attorney General: Edward Bates of Missouri*. Columbia, Mo., 1965.

Carman, Harry J., and Reinhard H. Luthin. *Lincoln and the Patronage*. New York, 1942.

Carpenter, John A. *Sword and Olive Branch: Oliver Otis Howard*. Pittsburgh, 1964.

Cimprich, John. "The Beginning of the Black Suffrage Movement in Tennessee, 1864–1865." *Journal of Negro History* 65 (Summer 1980): 185–96.

Coleman, Charles H. *The Election of 1868: The Democratic Effort to Regain Control*. New York, 1933.

Conway, Alan. *The Reconstruction of Georgia*. Minneapolis, 1966.

Coulter, E. Merton. *The Civil War and Readjustment in Kentucky*. Chapel Hill, 1926.

———. *William G. Brownlow: Fighting Parson of the Southern Highlands*. Chapel Hill, 1937.

Cox, Lawanda. *Lincoln and Black Freedom*. Columbia, S.C., 1981.

Cox, Lawanda, and John Cox. "General O. O. Howard and the 'Misrepresented Bureau.'" *Journal of Southern History* 19 (1953): 427–56.

———. "Negro Suffrage and Republican Politics: The Problem of Motivation in Reconstruction Historiography." *Journal of Southern History* 33 (1967): 303–30.

———. *Politics, Principle, and Prejudice, 1865–1866: Dilemma of Reconstruction America*. Glencoe, Ill., 1963.

Cox, Merlin G. "Military Reconstruction in Florida." *Florida Historical Quarterly* 46 (January 1968): 219–33.

Cox, Monty Woodall. "Freedom during the Fremont Campaign: The Fate of One North Carolina Republican in 1856." *North Carolina Historical Review* 45 (Autumn 1968): 357–83.

Craven, Avery. *The Growth of Southern Nationalism, 1848–1861*. Baton Rouge, 1953.

———. *Reconstruction: The Ending of the Civil War*. New York, 1969.

Crenshaw, Ollinger. *The Slave States in the Presidential Election of 1860*. Baltimore, 1945.

Crofts, Daniel W. "A Reluctant Unionist: John A. Gilmer and Lincoln's Cabinet." *Civil War History* 24 (September 1978): 225–50.

———. "The Union Party of 1861 and the Secession Crisis." *Perspectives in American History* 11 (1977–78): 327–76.

Current, Richard N. *Old Thad Stevens: A Story of Ambition*. Madison, Wis., 1942.

Curry, Richard O. "Crisis Politics in West Virginia, 1861–1870." In *Radicalism, Racism, and Party Realignment: The Border States during Reconstruction*, edited by Richard O. Curry, pp. 80–105. Baltimore, 1969.

———. *A House Divided: A Study of Statehood Politics and the Copperhead Movement in West Virginia*. Pittsburgh, 1964.

———, ed. *Radicalism, Racism, and Party Realignment: The Border States during Reconstruction*. Baltimore, 1969.

Davis, William W. *The Civil War and Reconstruction in Florida*. New York, 1913.

Dawson, Joseph. "Army Generals and Reconstruction: Mower and Hancock as Case Studies." *Southern Studies* 17 (Fall 1978): 255–73.

―――. "General Lovell H. Rousseau and Louisiana Reconstruction." *Louisiana History* 20 (Fall 1979): 381–89.

―――. "General Phil Sheridan and Military Reconstruction in Louisiana." *Civil War History* 24 (June 1978): 133–52.

Degler, Carl N. *The Other South: Southern Dissenters in the Nineteenth Century.* New York, 1974.

DeSantis, Vincent P. *Republicans Face the Southern Question: The New Departure Years, 1877–1897.* Baltimore, 1959.

Detroit Post and Tribune. *Zachariah Chandler: An Outline Sketch of His Life and Public Services.* Detroit, 1880.

Donald, David. *Charles Sumner and the Rights of Man.* New York, 1970.

―――. "Devils Facing Zionwards." In *Grant, Lee, Lincoln and the Radicals,* edited by Grady McWhiney, pp. 72–92. Evanston, Ill., 1964.

―――. *The Politics of Reconstruction, 1863–1867.* Baton Rouge, 1965.

―――. "The Republican Party, 1864–1876." In *History of U.S. Political Parties,* Vol. II, edited by Arthur M. Schlesinger, Jr., pp. 1281–1407. New York, 1973.

Donaldson, Thomas. *The Public Domain: Its History with Statistics.* 1884. Reprint. New York, 1970.

Dorris, Jonathan T. *Pardon and Amnesty under Lincoln and Johnson.* Chapel Hill, 1953.

Dunning, William A. *Essays on the Civil War and Reconstruction.* New York, 1897.

Durden, Robert F. *James Shepherd Pike: Republicanism and the American Negro, 1850–1882.* Durham, N.C., 1957.

Eaton, Clement. *The Freedom-of-Thought Struggle in the Old South.* Rev. ed. New York, 1964.

Eckenrode, Hamilton James. *The Political History of Virginia during the Reconstruction.* Baltimore, 1904.

Farish, Hunter Dickinson. "An Overlooked Personality in Southern Life." *North Carolina Historical Review* 12 (1935): 341–53.

Fessenden, Francis. *Life and Public Services of William Pitt Fessenden.* 2 vols. Boston, 1907.

Ficklin, John R. *History of Reconstruction in Louisiana through 1868.* Baltimore, 1910.

Fite, Emerson D. *The Presidential Campaign of 1860.* New York, 1911.

Fleming, Walter Lynwood. *Civil War and Reconstruction in Alabama.* New York, 1905.

Foner, Eric. *Free Soil, Free Labor, Free Men: The Ideology of the Republican Party before the Civil War.* New York, 1970.

―――. *Politics and Ideology in the Age of the Civil War.* New York, 1980.

Foulke, William D. *Life of Oliver P. Morton.* 2 vols. Indianapolis, 1899.

Franklin, John Hope. *Reconstruction after the Civil War.* Chicago, 1961.

George, Sister Mary Karl. *Zachariah Chandler: A Political Biography.* East Lansing, Mich., 1969.

Gillette, William. *Retreat from Reconstruction, 1869–1879.* Baton Rouge, 1979.
————. *The Right to Vote: Politics and the Passage of the Fifteenth Amendment.* Rev. ed. Baltimore, 1969.
Hamilton, J. G. deR. *Benjamin Sherwood Hedrick.* Chapel Hill, 1910.
————. *Reconstruction in North Carolina.* New York, 1914.
Hancock, Harold Bell. "The Political History of Delaware during the Civil War, Part I: The Campaign and Election of 1860." *Delaware History* 7 (September 1956): 105–42.
————. "The Political History of Delaware during the Civil War, Part II: The Coming of the War." *Delaware History* 7 (March 1957): 217–62.
————. "Reconstruction in Delaware." In *Radicalism, Racism, and Party Realignment: The Border States during Reconstruction,* edited by Richard O. Curry, pp. 188–220. Baltimore, 1969.
Harrington, Fred Harvey. *Fighting Politician: Major General N. P. Banks.* Philadelphia, 1948.
Harris, William C. *The Day of the Carpetbagger: Republican Reconstruction in Mississippi.* Baton Rouge, 1979.
————. "James Lynch: Black Leader in Southern Reconstruction." *Historian* 34 (1971): 40–61.
————. "Mississippi: Republican Factionalism and Mismanagement." In *Reconstruction and Redemption in the South,* edited by Otto Olsen, pp. 78–113. Baton Rouge, 1980.
Henig, Gerald S. *Henry Winter Davis: Antebellum and Civil War Congressman from Maryland.* New York, 1974.
Hesseltine, William B. "Economic Factors in the Abandonment of Reconstruction." *Mississippi Valley Historical Review* 22 (1935): 191–210.
————. *Lincoln's Plan of Reconstruction.* Tuscaloosa, Ala., 1960.
————, ed. *Three against Lincoln: Murat Halstead Reports the Caucuses of 1860.* Baton Rouge, 1960.
Heyman, Max L. "The 'Great Reconstructor': General E. R. S. Canby and the Second Military District." *North Carolina Historical Review* 31 (January 1955): 52–81.
Hickin, Patricia. "John C. Underwood and the Antislavery Movement in Virginia, 1847–1860." *Virginia Magazine of History and Biography* 73 (April 1965): 156–68.
Hoffnagle, Warren. "The Southern Homestead Act: Its Origins and Operations." *Historian* 32 (August 1970): 612–30.
Hollister, O. J. *Life of Schuyler Colfax.* New York, 1886.
Holt, Michael. *The Political Crisis of the 1850s.* New York, 1978.
Holt, Thomas. *Black over White: Negro Political Leadership in South Carolina during Reconstruction.* Urbana, Ill., 1977.
Hood, James Larry. "For the Union: Kentucky's Unconditional Unionist Congressmen and the Development of the Republican Party in Kentucky, 1863–1865." *Kentucky Historical Society Register* 76 (July 1978): 197–216.
Howe, M. A. DeWolfe. *Portrait of an Independent: Moorfield Storey, 1845–1929.*

Cambridge, Mass., 1932.

Hyman, Harold M. *Era of the Oath: Northern Loyalty Tests during the Civil War and Reconstruction.* Philadelphia, 1954.

Isely, Jeter Allen. *Horace Greeley and the Republican Party, 1853–1861.* Princeton, 1947.

Jellison, Charles A. *Fessenden of Maine: Civil War Senator.* Syracuse, N.Y., 1962.

Johnson, Ludwell. *Division and Reunion: America, 1848–1877.* New York, 1978.

Kleeberg, Gordon S. P. *The Formation of the Republican Party as a National Political Organization.* New York, 1911.

Kleppner, Paul. *The Third Electoral System, 1853–1892.* Chapel Hill, 1979.

Klingberg, Frank W. *The Southern Claims Commission.* Berkeley, 1955.

Kolchin, Peter. *First Freedom: The Responses of Alabama's Blacks to Emancipation and Reconstruction.* Westport, Conn., 1972.

Krug, Mark M. *Lyman Trumbull, Conservative Radical.* New York, 1965.

Lamson, Peggy. *The Glorious Failure: Black Congressman Robert Brown Elliott and Reconstruction in South Carolina.* New York, 1973.

Lee, Gordon. *The Struggle for Federal Aid: First Phase.* New York, 1949.

Litwack, Leon. *Been in the Storm So Long: The Aftermath of Slavery.* New York, 1979.

Lowe, Richard G. "The Republican Party in Antebellum Virginia, 1856–1860." *Virginia Magazine of History and Biography* 81 (July 1973): 259–79.

Luthin, Reinhard H. *The First Lincoln Campaign.* Cambridge, Mass., 1944.

Maddex, Jack P., Jr. *The Virginia Conservatives, 1867–1879: A Study in Reconstruction Politics.* Chapel Hill, 1970.

Mantell, Marvin E. *Johnson, Grant, and the Politics of Reconstruction.* New York, 1973.

Maslowski, Peter. *Treason Must Be Made Odious: Military Occupation and Wartime Reconstruction in Nashville, Tennessee, 1862–1865.* Millwood, N.Y., 1978.

May, J. Thomas. "The Freedmen's Bureau at the Local Level: A Study of a Louisiana Agent." *Louisiana History* 9 (Winter 1968): 5–19.

Mayer, George H. *The Republican Party, 1854–1964.* New York, 1967.

McCrary, Peyton. *Abraham Lincoln and Reconstruction: The Louisiana Experiment.* Princeton, 1978.

McDonough, James L. "John Schofield as Military Director of Reconstruction in Virginia." *Civil War History* 15 (1969): 237–56.

McKinney, Gordon. *Southern Mountain Republicans, 1865–1900: Politics and the Appalachian Community.* Chapel Hill, 1978.

McKitrick, Eric L. *Andrew Johnson and Reconstruction.* Chicago, 1960.

McPherson, Edward. *The Political History of the United States of America during the Period of Reconstruction.* New York, 1875.

McPherson, James M. *Ordeal by Fire: The Civil War and Reconstruction.* New York, 1982.

McWhiney, Grady, ed. *Grant, Lee, Lincoln and the Radicals*. Evanston, Ill., 1964.

Merriam, George S. *The Life and Times of Samuel Bowles*. 2 vols. New York, 1885.

Moneyhon, Carl H. *Republicanism in Reconstruction Texas*. Austin, 1979.

Munroe, John A. *A History of Delaware*. Cranbury, N.J., 1979.

Murphy, Reg, and Hal Gulliver. *The Southern Strategy*. New York, 1971.

Nathans, Elizabeth Studley. *Losing the Peace: Georgia Republicans and Reconstruction, 1865–1871*. Baton Rouge, 1968.

Nevins, Allan. *Hamilton Fish*. New York, 1957.

Olsen, Otto. *Carpetbagger's Crusade: The Life of Albion Winegar Tourgée*. Baltimore, 1965.

————. "Reconsidering the Scalawags." *Civil War History* 12 (December 1966): 304–20.

————, ed. *Reconstruction and Redemption in the South*. Baton Rouge, 1980.

Parks, Joseph. *Joseph E. Brown of Georgia*. Baton Rouge, 1977.

Parrish, William. *Missouri under Radical Rule, 1865–1870*. Columbia, Mo., 1965.

————. "Reconstruction Politics in Missouri, 1865–1870." In *Radicalism, Racism, and Party Realignment: The Border States during Reconstruction*, edited by Richard O. Curry, pp. 1–37. Baltimore, 1969.

————. *Turbulent Partnership: Missouri and the Union, 1861–1865*. Columbia, Mo., 1963.

Patton, James W. *Unionism and Reconstruction in Tennessee, 1860–1869*. Chapel Hill, 1934.

Pearce, Haywood J., Jr. *Benjamin H. Hill*. Chicago, 1928.

Pereyra, Lillian A. *James Lusk Alcorn, Persistent Whig*. Baton Rouge, 1966.

Perman, Michael. *Reunion without Compromise: The South and Reconstruction, 1865–1868*. Cambridge, England, 1973.

————. *The Road to Redemption: Southern Politics, 1869–1879*. Chapel Hill, 1984.

Peskin, Allan. *Garfield*. Kent, Ohio, 1978.

Peterson, Norma L. *Freedom and Franchise: The Political Career of B. Gratz Brown*. Columbia, Mo., 1965.

Polakoff, Keith Ian. *The Politics of Inertia: The Election of 1876 and the End of Reconstruction*. Baton Rouge, 1973.

Potter, David. *The Impending Crisis, 1848–1861*. New York, 1976.

————. *Lincoln and His Party in the Secession Crisis*. New Haven, 1942.

Rawley, James A. *Edwin D. Morgan, 1811–1893*. New York, 1955.

Reynolds, Donald E. "The New Orleans Riot of 1866, Reconsidered." *Louisiana History* 5 (Winter 1964): 5–27.

Rhodes, James Ford. *History of the United States*. 8 vols. New York, 1920.

Richardson, Joe M. *The Negro in the Reconstruction of Florida, 1865–1877*. Tallahassee, 1965.

Richardson, Leon B. *William E. Chandler, Republican*. New York, 1940.

Richter, William L. " 'We Must Rubb Outt and Begin Anew': The Army and the Republican Party in Texas Reconstruction, 1867–1870." *Civil War History* 19 (1973): 334–52.

Riddleberger, Patrick W. *1866: The Critical Year Revisited.* Carbondale, Ill., 1979.

———. *George Washington Julian, Radical Republican.* Indianapolis, 1966.

Roberts, Derrell C. *Joseph E. Brown and the Politics of Reconstruction.* University, Ala., 1973.

Rose, Willie Lee. *Rehearsal for Reconstruction: The Port Royal Experiment.* Indianapolis, 1964.

Ross, Sam. *The Empty Sleeve: A Biography of Lucius Fairchild.* Madison, Wis., 1964.

Russ, William A., Jr. "Registration and Disfranchisement under Radical Reconstruction." *Mississippi Valley Historical Review* 21 (September 1934): 163–79.

Sanborn, John Bell. *Congressional Grants of Land in Aid of Railways.* Madison, Wis., 1899.

Sanger, Donald Bridgeman, and Thomas R. Hay. *James Longstreet.* Baton Rouge, 1952.

Schuckers, J. W. *Life and Public Services of Salmon P. Chase.* New York, 1874.

Schweninger, Loren. "Alabama Blacks and the Congressional Reconstruction Acts of 1867." *Alabama Review* 31 (July 1978): 182–98.

Scroggs, Jack P. "Southern Reconstruction: A Radical View." *Journal of Southern History* 24 (1958): 407–39.

Sefton, James E., ed. "Chief Justice Chase as an Advisor on Presidential Reconstruction." *Civil War History* 13 (September 1967): 242–64.

———. *The United States Army and Reconstruction, 1865–1877.* Baton Rouge, 1967.

Seip, Terry. *The South Returns to Congress: Men, Economic Measures, and Intersectional Relationships, 1868–1879.* Baton Rouge, 1983.

Shadgett, Olive Hall. *The Republican Party in Georgia, from Reconstruction to 1900.* Athens, Ga., 1964.

Shapiro, Samuel. "Aristocracy, Mud, and Vituperation: The Butler-Dana Campaign in Essex County in 1868." *New England Quarterly* 31 (September 1958): 340–60.

Sharkey, Robert P. *Money, Class, and Party: An Economic Study of Civil War and Reconstruction.* Baltimore, 1959.

Sherman, Richard. *The Republican Party and Black America: From McKinley to Hoover, 1896–1933.* Charlottesville, Va., 1973.

Shofner, Jerrell H. "Florida: A Failure of Moderate Republicanism." In *Reconstruction and Redemption in the South,* edited by Otto Olsen, pp. 13–48. Baton Rouge, 1980.

———. *Nor Is It Over Yet: Florida in the Era of Reconstruction, 1863–1877.* Gainesville, 1974.

Simkins, Franklin Butler, and Robert H. Woody. *South Carolina during Reconstruction.* Chapel Hill, 1932.

Singletary, Otis A. *Negro Militia and Reconstruction.* Austin, 1957.

Smiley, David L. *Lion of White Hall: The Life of Cassius M. Clay.* Madison, Wis., 1962.

Smith, Willard H. *Schuyler Colfax: The Changing Fortunes of a Political Idol.* Indianapolis, 1952.

Smith, William Ernest. *The Francis Preston Blair Family in Politics.* 2 vols. New York, 1933.

Stampp, Kenneth. *And the War Came: The North and the Secession Crisis, 1860–1861.* Baton Rouge, 1950.

————. *Era of Reconstruction, 1865–1877.* New York, 1965.

Staples, Thomas S. *Reconstruction in Arkansas, 1862–1874.* New York, 1923.

Summers, Mark W. *Railroads, Reconstruction, and the Gospel of Prosperity: Aid under the Radical Republicans, 1865–1877.* Princeton, 1984.

Taylor, Alrutheus Ambush. *The Negro in Tennessee, 1865–1880.* Washington, 1941.

Taylor, Joe Gray. *Louisiana Reconstructed, 1863–1877.* Baton Rouge, 1974.

Thomas, Benjamin P., and Harold M. Hyman. *Stanton: The Life and Times of Lincoln's Secretary of War.* New York, 1962.

Thompson, George H. *Arkansas and Reconstruction: The Influence of Geography, Economics, and Personality.* Port Washington, N.Y., 1976.

Thompson, Mildred C. *Reconstruction in Georgia: Economic, Social, Political, 1865–1872.* New York, 1915.

Tindall, George B. *The Disruption of the Solid South.* Athens, Ga., 1972.

————. "Southern Strategy: A Historical Perspective." *North Carolina Historical Review* 48 (April 1971): 126–41.

Trefousse, Hans L. *Benjamin Franklin Wade: Radical Republican from Ohio.* New York, 1963.

————. *Impeachment of a President: Andrew Johnson, the Blacks, and Reconstruction.* Knoxville, 1975.

————. *The Radical Republicans: Lincoln's Vanguard for Racial Justice.* New York, 1969.

Trelease, Allen W. *White Terror: The Ku Klux Klan Conspiracy and Southern Reconstruction.* New York, 1971.

Van Deusen, Glyndon G. *Horace Greeley: Nineteenth-Century Crusader.* New York, 1953.

————. *William Henry Seward.* New York, 1967.

Wagandt, Charles L. *The Mighty Revolution: Negro Emancipation in Maryland, 1862–1864.* Baltimore, 1964.

————. "Redemption or Reaction? Maryland in the Post–Civil War Years." In *Radicalism, Racism, and Party Realignment: The Border States during Reconstruction,* edited by Richard O. Curry, pp. 146–88. Baltimore, 1969.

Wagstaff, Thomas. "The Arm-in-Arm Convention." *Civil War History* 14 (1968): 101–19.

Warden, Robert. *Private Life and Public Services of Salmon Portland Chase.* Cincinnati, 1874.

Webb, Ross A. *Kentucky in the Reconstruction Era.* Lexington, 1979.

———. "Kentucky: Pariah among the Elect." In *Radicalism, Racism, and Party Realignment: The Border States during Reconstruction*, edited by Richard O. Curry, pp. 105–46. Baltimore, 1969.

West, Richard S., Jr. *Lincoln's Scapegoat General: A Life of Benjamin F. Butler, 1818–1893*. Cambridge, Mass., 1965.

White, Howard A. *The Freedmen's Bureau in Louisiana*. Baton Rouge, 1970.

White, Kenneth B. "Wager Swayne: Racist or Realist?" *Alabama Review* 31 (April 1978): 92–109.

Wiggins, Sarah Woolfolk. *The Scalawag in Alabama Politics, 1865–1881*. University, Ala., 1977.

Williamson, Joel. *After Slavery: The Negro in South Carolina during Reconstruction, 1861–1877*. Chapel Hill, 1965.

Wood, Forrest G. "On Revising Reconstruction History: Negro Suffrage, White Disfranchisement, and Common Sense." *Journal of Negro History* 51 (April 1966): 98–113.

Woodward, C. Vann. "The Political Legacy of Reconstruction." In *The Burden of Southern History*, pp. 89–109. Baton Rouge, 1960.

———. "Seeds of Failure in Radical Race Policy." In *American Counterpoint: Slavery and Racism in the North-South Dialogue*, pp. 163–84. Boston, 1964.

Woolfolk, Sarah Van V. "Amnesty and Pardon and Republicanism in Alabama." *Alabama Historical Quarterly* 26 (Summer 1964): 240–48.

Zornow, William F. *Lincoln and the Party Divided*. Norman, Okla., 1954.

INDEX

Akerman, Amos, 212–13, 216, 222
Alabama Republicans, 100–101, 140–41, 159; organize, 127–28; and restoration, 152–62 passim; and 1868 election, 201–2
Alcorn, James Lusk, 223
Alden, George, 144
Allison, David, 78
Alvord, John W., 102
American party, 4, 11, 14
Ames, Adelbert, 231–32
Amnesty, 30, 47, 49; and Republican party, 53–54, 79–80, 166–71, 240; and 1872 amnesty act, 214–17. See also Disfranchisement
Andrew, John, 44, 53, 114–15, 123, 126
Arkansas Republicans, 60, 73, 112; and 1864 Republican convention, 29, 35–36; and Reconstruction, 30–31, 37; and 1868 elections, 159–60, 201–2
Armstrong, William J., 130–31
Arnell, Samuel, 81
Atkinson, Edward, 123, 126, 197, 204

Baird, Absalom, 65
Baird, Simeon, 62
Baker, Jehu, 142
Banks, Nathaniel, 32–34, 40, 44–45, 65
Bard, Samuel, 134–35
Bates, Edward, 14, 15–16, 19
Beecher, Henry Ward, 105

Bell, John, 32
Berry, Lawrence, 127
Billings, Liberty, 144–45
Bingham, Daniel H., 67
Bingham, John, 79, 82, 167–70
Binney, John, 138, 156, 158, 165
Black Codes, 49
Black enfranchisement: border states, 39; Republicans debate, 53, 106–7, 228, 236; and Fourteenth Amendment, 55; sought by blacks, 61; and loyalist convention, 69–71; and Fifteenth Amendment, 200, 205–6
Blaine, James G., 96, 182, 212, 231; and 1868 election, 195–96; on Southern Unionists, 226–27
Blair, Austin, 181
Blair, Frank, 8–10
Blair, Frank, Jr., 10, 12; on slavery, 9, 23, 26; joins Republicans, 11, 22; and 1860 election, 14, 16; and Johnson, 47; leaves Republican party, 238
Blodgett, Foster, 151, 191
Border state Republicans, 43, 93; and 1860 election, 16–17; during Civil War, 20–29; and 1864 election, 38–39; and loyalist convention, 67–71; and amnesty, 168, 214–15; and 1868 election, 200–201; weakness of, 234–35. See also individual states
Boreman, Arthur, 70
Botts, John Minor: seeks Northern

aid, 64; and Virginia Republicans, 114–16, 123–26, 132
Boutwell, George, 77, 81, 82, 192, 219
Bowles, Samuel, 80, 169, 192, 214, 218
Bradley, Aaron A., 139
Breckinridge, Robert, 7–8, 24, 29
Bromwell, Henry, 169
Brown, B. Gratz, 24, 25, 43; on slavery, 9, 23; and black suffrage, 39; and Liberal Republicans, 215; leaves Republican party, 238
Brown, John, 13
Brown, Joseph: and Republican party, 129, 133–35, 158, 173; and amnesty, 166–67
Brown, Orlando, 133, 163
Brownlow, William G., 57, 207; disliked in North, 29, 157, 210; for black suffrage, 61, 72; and 1867 election, 105–6
Bryant, John, 62, 134
Buchanan, Robert, 104
Bullock, Rufus, 158, 184, 209, 210
Butler, Benjamin, 32, 64, 85, 89, 128, 190, 226, 228; and Southern Unionists, 44–45; and loyalist convention, 68; speaks in South, 72, 88–89; for black suffrage, 78; on disfranchisement, 78, 97, 146, 217; on Reconstruction Acts, 98; on Florida constitution, 145; on Southern blacks, 156–57, 229; on Southern Republicans, 179, 186, 204, 227; and Ku Klux Klan, 212

Caldwell, J, H., 184
Cameron, Simon, 209
Canby, E. R. S., 103
Cardozo, Francis, 63, 157
Carter, Jimmy, ix
Chandler, William E., 189–90, 208–9, 228; and 1868 election, 195–99; and 1872 election, 220

Chandler, Zachariah, 43, 68, 99, 120–21, 191, 216
Chase, Salmon P., 11, 32, 63, 85, 97; as presidential candidate, 26, 171; assesses South, 44–45; on black suffrage, 54, 192
Civil rights issue, 229–31
Claflin, William, 86, 110, 185, 195, 200
Clanton, James H., 120
Clark, Daniel, 176
Clay, Cassius, 11, 13, 17; on slavery, 7, 9, 12; joins Republicans, 8, 10; on 1860 election, 13, 16; leaves Republican party, 238
Clayton, Powell, 188–91, 211
Coburn, John, 169, 191
Colfax, Schuyler, 15, 146, 173, 194–95
Confiscation issue: in North Carolina, 113, 131; in Virginia, 114–17, 126–27; in South Carolina, 130, 142; in Mississippi, 131; in Louisiana, 142–43
Constitutional Union party, 17, 21, 22, 32
Conway, Thomas, 109, 144, 153, 171; and Southern blacks, 65, 112, 138; tours South, 91–92, 100, 102; and Louisiana, 104, 128, 136, 143, 151, 185; and Virginia, 115, 117
Cotton tax, 180–81
Covode, John, 54
Cox, Jacob D., 51, 214, 215, 218
Cox, John, 275 (n. 3)
Cox, Lawanda, 275 (n. 3)

Davis, Henry Winter, 22, 24, 25, 27, 43; and 1860 election, 16–17; for black suffrage, 39; condemns Louisiana government, 46
Dawes, Henry, 212
Delaney, Martin, 63
Delano, Columbus, 219
Delaware Republicans, 10, 14, 17,

38; during Civil War, 28–29

Democratic party: and South, 3, 8–9, 11, 14, 183; and border states, 22–23, 72; and 1864 election, 37–38; and Johnson, 46–48, 50; and Fourteenth Amendment, 58; and amnesty, 168; and Freedmen's Bureau, 180; and 1868 election, 187, 201–2; and 1872 election, 218, 221

Disfranchisement: in border states, 38–39, 52, 72, 200–201; in Tennessee, 40, 48, 57; in Arkansas, 48, 60; debated by Republicans, 51–52, 78–80, 165–71; and Fourteenth Amendment, 55; and Reconstruction Acts, 82–83, 96; in South, 96–97, 214–15, 257 (n. 46); in Alabama, 140–41; in Virginia, 146–48, 162–63. *See also* Amnesty; Ironclad oath

Donnelley, Ignatius, 77, 179, 181

Douglas, Stephen, 32

Douglass, Frederick, 71, 125

Dunning, William A., xi–xii

Durant, Thomas, 33–34, 65

Edmunds, James, 61, 111, 112, 181; and Union League, 90–91, 107, 110, 122

Elections: of 1856, 10–11; of 1860, 11–17; of 1864, 38–39; of 1866, 72; of 1867, 107–8, 136–38; of 1868, 193–203, 241; of 1872, 218–21; of 1874, 230–31; of 1876, 232

Elliott, Robert B., 222

Enforcement Acts, 211–14, 221, 241. *See also* Ku Klux Klan

Fairchild, Lucius, 68

Farnsworth, John, 169

Fee, John, 7, 10

Fessenden, William Pitt, 97, 110, 130, 158; on black suffrage, 54, 77, 192; on Tennessee, 208

Fifteenth Amendment: enacted, 205–6; ratified, 209, 224–25; enforced, 211; and Republican party, 241. *See also* Enforcement Acts; Ku Klux Act

Fisk, Clinton B., 62, 101

Florida Republicans: and 1864 Republican convention, 29, 35–36; and blacks, 63; organize, 129–30; and factionalism, 135, 144–45, 186; and state constitution, 143–44; and 1868 elections, 160, 201. *See also* Reed, Harrison

Foner, Eric, 262–63 (n. 37)

Forbes, John Murray, 115, 123, 197; on Southern constitutions, 141, 149; on Southern prospects, 219; on blacks, 229

Forney, John W.: on Southern Republicans, 59, 75, 92–93, 126–27, 134, 156; and loyalist convention, 68; assesses elections, 72, 85, 106, 160, 193; on Southern whites, 124–25, 138; on Southern constitutions, 141, 142, 160; on black officeholding, 157; on amnesty, 169; on economic aid to South, 176–77, 178, 180

Fourteenth Amendment, 69, 166, 167; drafted, 55–56; and Tennessee, 56–57; South rejects, 58; in 1866 election, 72–73; and First Reconstruction Act, 81–82; enforced, 211; and amnesty, 214–17; and Republican party, 235

Fowler, Joseph, 77

Freedmen's Bureau, 88, 133, 180, 182; created, 50; and Union League, 61–62; and black vote, 62–63, 86; aids Southern Republicans, 99–103; and Virginia Republicans, 133, 163; in Florida, 133, 144; expires, 162, 218; and 1868 election, 164–65. *See also* Howard, O. O.

Free Soil party, 9

Frémont, John C.: presidential candidate, 7, 10–11, 26, 27, 38; in Missouri, 23

Garfield, James A., 169, 212, 214
Georgia Republicans: organize, 129; party newspapers, 133–34; and state constitution, 143; and 1868 elections, 160, 201–2; weakness of, 184–85; and restoration, 209. *See also* Brown, Joseph
Gibbons, Charles, 122
Gibbs, Jonathan, 144
Gillem, Alvan, 102, 104, 160, 161
Gillette, William, 275 (n. 3), 279 (n. 4)
Gilmer, John, 18–19
Givens, John, 126
Godkin, E. L.: on black suffrage, 78; on Virginia Republicans, 124, 139, 146; on Southern constitutions, 149; on 1868 election, 192
Goodlow, Daniel R., 7, 8, 13, 238
Grant, Ulysses S., x, xi, xii, 97, 163; supports Congress, 94; as secretary of war, 103, 172; as presidential candidate, 171, 173–74, 196, 202; first term of, 204–21 passim; and Southern Republicans, 205–13, 221–23; and 1872 election, 205, 220–21; and Ku Klux Klan, 212–13; and Liberal Republicans, 215, 218; on amnesty, 215–18; second term of, 221–32 passim; and civil rights, 231; Northern priorities of, 231–32
Greeley, Horace, 7, 8, 10, 11, 122, 146; assesses South, 5–6, 12, 44–45, 126, 136, 137–38; and Blairs, 9; and Helper, 12; Northern priorities of, 13, 165; on Bates nomination, 15; advocates amnesty, 53, 79–80, 140–41, 169; on black suffrage, 76, 228; on Southern Republicans, 116–17, 122–23, 157, 204, 206–7; and Joseph Brown, 129; on Southern constitutions,

139, 148–49; on Arkansas election, 160; on aid to South, 180, 224; on 1868 election, 192, 193, 195; on Enforcement Acts, 213; as Liberal Republican, 218, 221
Griffin, Charles, 98, 102

Hahn, Michael, 34–35, 40, 65
Hamilton, Andrew J., 60, 67, 70, 71
Hancock, Winfield Scott, 98, 103, 151
Hanes, Lewis, 53
Harlan, James, 78, 220
Harris, James H., 131
Hart, Ossian, 129–30
Hassaurek, Frederick, 175
Hayden, Julius, 104, 152
Hayes, John E., 134
Hayes, Rutherford B., ix, xii, 232
Hedrick, Benjamin S., 12, 13, 120; antislavery views of, 7–8; on amnesty, 168; leaves Republican party, 238
Helper, Hinton Rowan, 7–8, 12, 13, 128
Hoar, E. R., 10
Hoar, George G., 225
Holden, William W., 95, 101, 112, 135; as governor, 60, 158, 190, 210–11; on black suffrage, 61; and amnesty, 167
Howard, Jacob, 83
Howard, O. O., 61, 143, 179; and Southern Republicans, 100–102, 163, 199
Hunnicutt, James, 129, 139; and Virginia Republicans, 114–17, 122–26, 132–33; and Virginia newspaper, 135–36; and Virginia constitution, 146–47

Iron-clad oath: enacted, 52; adverse effects of, 53; and Patterson, 58; and Reconstruction Acts, 95–96; and Alabama, 152–53; amended, 170; repealed, 217–18

Jackson, Andrew, 9
Johnson, Andrew, 57, 58, 60, 63, 87, 92, 191, 198; as governor, 31, 35; nominated for vice-president, 35, 37; becomes president, 41; and Reconstruction program, 47–48, 52–53; and Congress, 48–50; and 1866 election, 66, 72, 73; and Reconstruction Acts, 81, 94; removals by, 98, 103–4; impeachment of, 150–51, 154–56, 200
Julian, George: on Reconstruction, 51; and black suffrage, 54, 76, 78; on disfranchisement, 78; and homesteads, 181–82

Kansas-Nebraska Act, 3
Keffer, John, 62, 127
Kelley, William D., 111, 135, 158, 167; tours South, 27, 88–89, 110, 121, 128, 176, 242; on black suffrage, 54; and loyalist convention, 68; and Southern whites, 85, 126; and Georgia Republicans, 129, 135; on aid to South, 179, 180
Kentucky Republicans: organize, 10; at 1860 Republican convention, 14–15; and 1860 election, 17; during Civil War, 22, 24–25, 28–29; and 1864 election, 38
Know-Nothing party. *See* American party
Ku Klux Act, 212, 214
Ku Klux Klan: in 1868, 187–91, 201; and Congress, 210–14; in North Carolina, 210–11, 219; investigated, 212–13; and 1872 election, 221. *See also* Enforcement Acts

Laflin, Addison, 142
Lane, James H., 36
Langston, John Mercer, 100, 143
Lewis, David P., 216
Liberal Republicans, 215–18, 228
Lincoln, Abraham, 26, 85, 194, 202, 235; assesses South, 13, 45, 46; and 1860 election, 16–17; and secession, 18–19; and patronage, 20–22, 25–27; and slavery, 23–24, 37; and Reconstruction, 29–35, 37–38, 40–41, 45; assassinated, 41
Longstreet, James, 128, 167
Louisiana Republicans, 66, 136; and 1864 Republican convention, 29, 36; during Civil War, 32–35; post-war organization of, 64–66, 128; and civil rights, 185–86; and 1868 elections, 201–2
Lynch, James, 131, 143

McClellan, George B., 37, 38
McPherson, Edward, 92, 133–36, 144, 148
Maryland Republicans: organization of, 10; at 1860 Republican convention, 14–15; and 1860 election, 16–17; during Civil War, 21–29; and 1864 election, 38–39
Massachusetts Reconstruction Association, 141, 197; organized, 106; and Virginia Republicans, 123–24; disbanded, 204, 219
Meade, George G., 104, 141, 158, 184; and Florida constitution, 144–45, 160; and Alabama constitution, 152–53
Medill, Joseph, 141
Miles, Nelson, 97
Mississippi Republicans, 131, 135, 161, 208–9
Missouri Republicans, 11, 14, 16, 37, 201; during Civil War, 22–29; and 1864 election, 38–39; and Liberal Republicans, 215–17
Morgan, Edwin, 110, 185, 211; as Republican national chairman, 10; and Union Congressional Committee, 87; assesses black vote, 107; and 1868 election, 195; and 1872 election, 220
Morris, John W., 198, 199
Morton, Oliver P., 54, 70–71, 78, 96

Mower, Joseph, 101, 103, 104
Murphy, Isaac, 60

Nash, Beverly, 130
Nathans, Elizabeth, 263 (n. 37)
National Union convention, 66, 68
New Orleans riot, 66
Nixon, Richard, ix, xii
Nordhoff, Charles, 149
North Carolina Republicans, 60, 135; organize, 112–13, 131; and elections of 1868, 159, 202; and 1870 election, 210; and 1872 election, 219
Nye, James, 83, 84

Olsen, Otto, 263 (n. 37)
Ord, Edward O. C., 151, 177; and Reconstruction Acts, 94, 95, 98, 99, 102; resigns, 104; and Mississippi Republicans, 133, 143
Orr, James L., 142, 167
Osborne, Thomas, 63

Patterson, David, 58
Patton, Robert, 166
Pease, E. M., 98
Pease, Henry R., 102
People's party, 17
Perman, Michael, 262 (n. 37)
Pierpont, Francis H., 29, 48, 162; and Virginia Republicans, 63–64, 114–16; seeks Northern aid, 123
Pierrepont, Edwards, 213
Pike, James Shepherd, 228–29
Pomeroy, Samuel, 146
Pope, John: administers Reconstruction Acts, 94, 95, 98–99, 104; favors amnesty, 97, 140–41, 166; removed by Johnson, 104, 151; and Southern Republicans, 133, 134–35, 156
Printing contracts, 92–93, 133–36
Pughe, E. M., 134

Randolph, Benjamin, 130, 187–88, 198–99

Raymond, Henry J., 37, 46–48, 68, 87, 116
Reagan, Ronald, ix
Reconstruction Acts: First, x, 81–82, 94–104, 132–33; Second, 82–84, 94–95; Third, 96, 99; Fourth, 153, 155, 162
Redpath, James, 63
Reed, Harrison: and Florida Republicans, 63, 129–30, 144–45; as Florida governor, 186, 190, 211
Republican National Committee: discusses South, 86–87; short of funds, 107; and Southern organization, 126; and amnesty, 168; and Georgia, 191; and 1868 election, 194–201; and Mississippi, 208; and North Carolina, 219; and 1872 election, 219–20. *See also* Chandler, William E.; Claflin, William; Morgan, Edwin
Republican national conventions: of 1856, 9; of 1860, 14–16; of 1864, 27–29, 35–37; of 1868, 172–74
Republican party: enters South, ix, 10–11, 29–35, 59–65; assessments of South, xi, 4–6, 10, 42–47, 136–38, 191–93, 234–35; and Southern blacks, xii, 69–71, 72–74, 76–78, 84–85, 110–11, 156–57, 192, 205–6, 228–29; inception of, 3, 9–10; ideology of, 3–5, 233; and 1860 election, 11, 13–17; Northern priorities of, 13–16, 38, 58, 72, 85, 154–55, 161, 165, 173–74, 190, 193–94, 200, 202–3, 205–6, 213, 221, 231–32, 240–42; and Southern Unionists, 17–19, 43–46, 50, 58–59, 68–71, 79, 83, 225–27, 237–38; and 1864 election, 26–28; and Reconstruction programs, 51–53, 55–56; and amnesty, 78–80, 166–71, 214–17; and Conservative governments, 80–82; and aid to South, 88, 174–83, 222–27, 239–40; and Virginia Republicans, 113–17, 126–27, 205–6; and impeachment, 150–

51, 154–56; and Georgia Republicans, 185, 209–10; and Louisiana Republicans, 185–86; and Southern militias, 189–90; and 1868 election, 191–203; and Tennessee Republicans, 208; and 1872 election, 219–21; and civil rights, 229–31; and 1876 election, 232. *See also* Border state Republicans; Grant, Ulysses S.; Lincoln, Abraham; Southern Republicans; individual states

Reynolds, J. J., 98, 102, 164
Richards, Daniel, 130, 144–45
Rives, Alexander, 163
Robinson, William P., 192
Robinson, William S., 214
Rousseau, Lovell H., 191

Saunders, William, 130, 144–45
Saxton, Rufus, 63
Schenck, Robert, 110, 151, 156, 189; and Union Republican Committee, 87–89, 98, 107; and constitutional conventions, 109, 139–40; and Southern whites, 121; and Holden, 158; on amnesty, 168; on economic aid to South, 179, 180; and 1868 election, 196, 201
Schofield, John: and Reconstruction Acts, 94, 95, 98; and Virginia Republicans, 132, 148, 162–63
Schurz, Carl: and Southern Unionists, 43–44, 50; and amnesty, 173; and 1868 election, 193, 195; and Ku Klux Act, 212; on black voters, 228; as Liberal Republican, 215, 218
Scott, Robert K., 101, 133, 189–90
Senter, Dewitt, 207–8
Settle, Thomas, 219
Seward, William Henry, 7, 8, 16, 77, 92; assesses South, 5, 44–45; and Virginia Republicans, 11–12; on secession, 18–19; and Johnson, 47–48; encourages Southern Republicans, 85

Seymour, Horatio, 201
Shepley, George, 33
Sheridan, Philip, 94, 95, 98, 103, 151
Sherman, John, 45, 50, 110, 135, 181, 229; and Helper, 12; and amnesty, 79, 166; on Southern Republicans, 191; on Virginia, 206–7
Sherman, William T., 45, 50, 53, 134, 229
Sickles, Daniel, 94, 95, 97, 103, 133
Smith, John R., 135
Smith, William H., 188
Smithers, Nathaniel, 25
Smythe, Governor, 146
South Carolina Republicans: and 1864 Republican convention, 29, 35–36; organize, 63, 130–31; and 1868 election, 160; divisions among, 186
Southern Claims Commission, 226–27
Southern Conservatives: in border states, 23–28; emerge in South, 48–49; and blacks, 53; and 1866 elections, 58–60; in Virginia, 64, 206–8; and Reconstruction, 80–82, 95, 151, 155; and Republicans, 183, 187; in Tennessee, 207–8; in Georgia, 209
Southern Homestead Act, 181–82, 240
Southern loyalist convention, 67–71, 235
Southern militia, 188–89, 210–11
Southern Republican Association, 73, 75
Southern Republican Press Association, 92
Southern Republicans: at 1856 Republican convention, 10; factionalism of, 40, 198; and Reconstruction plans, 75–76; and Conservative governments, 80–81; seek Northern aid, 85–86, 88, 176–81; newspapers of, 92–93; and constitutional conventions, 108, 139–49; and impeachment,

150–51; and Chase, 171–73; and
1868 election, 197–202; and Fifteenth Amendment, 206; and 1872
election, 220–21; and civil rights,
230. *See also* Border state Republicans; individual states
Southern Unionists: Republican
faith in, 17–19, 43–44, 45–46; and
Civil War, 20–41 passim; weakness of, 39–40, 45–46, 50, 52, 54,
58, 63, 73, 81–82, 153; and Lincoln, 45, 46; attack Johnson, 49;
Reconstruction views of, 51; and
black suffrage, 61–65; and loyalist
convention, 66–71; and war
claims, 178, 226–27. *See also*
Southern Republicans; individual
states
Southworth, M. A., 186
Sprague, William, 227
Stanbery, Henry, 95–96
Stanton, Edwin M., 94, 96, 103, 151,
154
Stevens, Thaddeus, 71, 92, 119, 151–
52, 158; at 1864 Republican convention, 36; on disfranchisement,
51, 78, 82, 146; Reconstruction
views of, 51, 120, 122; on black
suffrage, 54, 76, 78, 156, 191–92;
on Tennessee, 57; on Fourteenth
Amendment, 73
Stewart, William, 79, 81, 166
Stokes, William, 207
Stuart, A. H. H., 53
Sumner, Charles, 89, 135, 136, 229;
on Louisiana, 40; on disfranchisement, 51, 146; on Conservative
governments, 81; on black officeholders, 156; and Fifteenth
Amendment, 200; and aid to education, 224; on civil rights, 229
Swayne, Wager: on black suffrage,
62; favors amnesty, 97, 140, 166;
and Southern Republicans, 100–
101; removed from office, 104,
151, 152; on Alabama Republicans, 188

Tennessee Republicans: and 1864
Republican convention, 29, 35–36;
and Fourteenth Amendment, 56–
57; enfranchise blacks, 72; and
1867 elections, 105–6; and 1868
election, 201–2; and 1869 election,
207–8
Terry, Alfred, 64
Texas Republicans: at 1860 Republican convention, 14–15; organize,
60, 98, 131–32; and constitutional
convention, 164
Thirteenth Amendment, 37, 38
Thompson, Holland, 127
Tillson, David, 62
Tilton, Theodore, 58, 71
Tomlinson, Reuben, 63
Tourgée, Albion, 112, 135, 167, 230
Trumbull, Lyman, 52, 97, 212, 214
Tullock, Thomas, 126, 136, 144, 164;
and Union Republican Committee, 87–88, 107, 138–39, 159; and
1867 elections, 136–37; and Chase,
172; and Louisiana Republicans,
185; and 1868 election, 196–99
Turner, Henry M. 62

Underwood, John: joins Republicans, 8, 10; and 1856 campaign,
11–12; and Brown raid, 13; and
Virginia constitution, 146
Union Claims Commission, 178,
226–27
Union League, 68, 89, 97, 104; organized, 25; in Tennessee, 31, 105–6;
enters lower South, 59–65; and
black suffrage, 61–62; and Union
Republican committee, 88, 90–91;
and Southern Republicans, 90–92;
112–14, 158; and Freedmen's Bureau, 100; short of funds, 107;
dominated by blacks, 111; in Arkansas, 112; in North Carolina,
112, in Virginia, 114–15, 122–23; in
Alabama, 127–28; in South Carolina, 130; in Florida, 130; in Texas,
132; and Chase candidacy, 171;

and Ku Klux Klan, 187; and 1868
election, 197; in Georgia, 209; defunct, 218. *See also* Conway,
Thomas; Edmunds, James
Union Republican Congressional
Committee, 98, 104–5; organized,
87–88; sends speakers South, 89–
90; and Union League, 90–91; and
Freedmen's Bureau, 100; and Tennessee, 105–6; short of funds,
107–8; and Southern whites, 121–
22, 125–26; and Virginia, 123–24;
and South Carolina, 130; and
Florida, 130, 144; and Mississippi,
131, 208–9; and North Carolina,
131, 210; and 1867 elections, 136–
37; and 1868 elections, 159, 194–
201; and amnesty, 167–68; and
Chase, 172; and aid to South, 180,
182; on Southern violence, 190;
grows inactive, 205, 218–19. *See
also* Morgan, Edwin; Schenck,
Robert; Tullock, Thomas; Ward,
Marcus
Union Republican Executive Committee. *See* Union Republican
Congressional Committee
United States Army: and Reconstruction, 93–104; promotes Republican party, 97–104; and Southern Republicans, 132–33; in 1868
election, 191

Vallandigham, Clement, 196
Virginia Republicans: organize, 10,
63–64, 113–16; at 1860 convention,
14–15; and 1860 election, 17; and
1864 Republican convention, 29,
35–36; divisions among, 114–17,
122–25, 135–36; and state constitu-

tion, 145–48; 162–63; and 1869
election, 207. *See also* Hunnicutt,
James

Wade, Benjamin, 73, 97, 107, 120–21,
135
Wade-Davis bill, 37, 46
Walker, Gilbert, 207
Wall, O. S. B., 63
Ward, Marcus, 63, 86, 106, 195, 207
Warmoth, Henry Clay, 128, 185–86,
188, 191, 211
Warner, Willard, 180–81
Washburne, Elihu B., 145, 146, 196
Weed, Thurlow, 77
Wells, Henry H., 163, 207
Wells, J. Madison, 40, 48, 65
West Virginia Republicans, 22, 25,
29, 38, 39, 201
Whittlesey, Charles, 92
Wilmot, David, 14–15
Wilson, Henry, 100, 110, 111, 210;
on Southern Unionists, 50, 83,
126, 178; for black suffrage, 54, 76;
for amnesty, 80, 96, 140–41, 146,
166; and Southern Republicans,
84, 227; speaks in South, 88–89,
117–21, 176, 242; and Reconstruc-
tion Acts, 95, 104; and Virginia
Republicans, 114–17, 122–23, 133,
206–7; in Louisiana, 128; on confiscation, 142; on restoration of
South, 161–62; as vice- presidential candidate, 173; on aid to
South, 176, 178, 180, 225; and
Southern militia, 189; and 1868
elections, 192, 196, 199, 201; in
North Carolina, 219

Yates, Richard, 52, 80, 89, 108, 135